THE FATHERS
OF THE CHURCH

A NEW TRANSLATION

VOLUME 110

THE FATHERS OF THE CHURCH

A NEW TRANSLATION

EDITORIAL BOARD

Thomas P. Halton
The Catholic University of America
Editorial Director

Elizabeth Clark
Duke University

Robert D. Sider
Dickinson College

Joseph T. Lienhard, S.J.
Fordham University

Michael Slusser
Duquesne University

David G. Hunter
Iowa State University

Cynthia White
The University of Arizona

Kathleen McVey
Princeton Theological Seminary

Rebecca Lyman
Church Divinity School of the Pacific

David J. McGonagle
Director
The Catholic University of America Press

FORMER EDITORIAL DIRECTORS

Ludwig Schopp, Roy J. Deferrari, Bernard M. Peebles,
Hermigild Dressler, O.F.M.

Carole C. Burnett
Staff Editor

ST. PETER CHRYSOLOGUS
SELECTED SERMONS
VOLUME 3

Translated by

WILLIAM B. PALARDY
*St. John's Seminary School of Theology
Brighton, Massachusetts*

THE CATHOLIC UNIVERSITY OF AMERICA PRESS
Washington, D.C.

Copyright © 2005
THE CATHOLIC UNIVERSITY OF AMERICA PRESS
All rights reserved
Printed in the United States of America

The paper used in this publication meets the minimum requirements of the American National Standards for Information Science—Permanence of Paper for Printed Library Materials, ANSI Z39.48 - 1984.

LIBRARY OF CONGRESS CATALOGING-IN-PUBLICATION DATA
Peter, Chrysologus, Saint, Archbishop of Ravenna, ca. 400–450.
　[Sermons. English. Selections]
　St. Peter Chrysologus : selected sermons / translated by William B. Palardy.
　　p. cm. — (The Fathers of the church, a new translation, v. 110)
　Vol. 1 published in 1953, by Fathers of the Church, New York, under title: Saint Peter Chrysologus : selected sermons; and Saint Valerian : homilies. Vol. 2 published in 2004, by The Catholic University of America Press, Washington, D.C., under title: Saint Peter Chrysologus : selected sermons; volume 2.
　Includes bibliographical references and index.
　ISBN 0-8132-0110-1 (alk. paper)
　ISBN 978-0-8132-2635-4 (pbk.)

　1. Sermons, Latin—Translations into English.　2. Sermons, Early Christian.　I. Title: Saint Peter Chrysologus.　II. Title.　III. Fathers of the church ; v. 110.　IV. Series.
BR60.F3P474 2004
252'.014—dc22
2004004195

In memory of my mother and father

CONTENTS

Preface		xi
Abbreviations		xiii
Select Bibliography		xv

SELECTED SERMONS, VOLUME 3

72A	A First on the Lord's Passion	1
72B	A Second on the Lord's Passion	6
73	On the Holy Day of Easter	12
75	A Second on the Lord's Resurrection	15
76	A Third on the Lord's Resurrection	20
77	A Fourth on the Lord's Resurrection	25
78	A Fifth on the Lord's Resurrection	31
79	A Sixth on the Lord's Resurrection	35
81	An Eighth on the Lord's Resurrection	39
82	A Ninth on the Lord's Resurrection	44
84	An Eleventh on the Lord's Resurrection	49
85	On the Middle of the Fifty Days	55
85A	[A Second] On the Middle of the Fifty Days	58
85B	On the Day of Pentecost	60
86	Sermon on Zechariah, After the Most Blessed Bishop Peter of Ravenna Was Silent	63
87	A Second <on Zechariah>	68
89	A Fourth <on Zechariah>	73
90	A Fifth <on Zechariah>	79

CONTENTS

91	A Sixth \<on Zechariah\>	85
92	A Seventh \<on Zechariah\>	91
94	A Second \<on the Meal of the Pharisee\>	95
97	A Second on the Tares	100
99	A Fourth on the Same \<or on the Parable about the Yeast\>	105
99A	Against the Pharisees; On the Gospel Text: A Certain Pharisee Asked Jesus to Dine with Him, and Jesus Cured the Man with Dropsy	110
100	On the Syrophoenician Woman	114
102	On the Centurion's Servant	117
103	When He Raised the Widow's Son from the Dead	123
104	On the Rich Man Whose Field Yielded a Fruitful Harvest	128
105	On the Infirmity the Woman Had for Eighteen Years	132
106	On the Fig Tree to Be Chopped Down	137
110	A Third \<on the Apostle\>	142
113	A Sixth \<on the Apostle\>	146
118	An Eleventh \<on the Apostle\>	150
121	On Lazarus and the Rich Man	155
123	A Third on the Same	161
124	A Fourth on the Same	169
125	On the Unjust Steward	175
126	A Second on the Same	181
127	On the Birth of St. John the Baptist	187
128	On the Birth of St. Apollinaris	192
130	On the Birth of a Bishop	195
130A	On the Ordination of a Bishop	198

CONTENTS

131	On the Gospel Where It Says: "If anyone keeps my word, he will not see death forever"	200
136	In Praise of the Holy Bishop Adelphius	206
137	When John Flees to the Desert	209
139	On the Gospel Where It Says: "If my brother sins against me"	216
140A	On the Nativity of the Lord	221
140B	\<A Second\> on the Birth of the Lord	225
142	\<A Second\> on the Annunciation of the Lord	229
143	\<A Third\> on the Annunciation of the Lord	236
144	\<A Fourth\> on the Annunciation of the Lord	242
148A	\<A Fourth on the Nativity of the Lord\>	248
150	On the Lord's Flight into Egypt	251
151	A Second on the Same	257
153	A Second on Herod and the Infants	261
155A	\<A Second\> on January First	264
157	A Second on Epiphany	267
158	A Third on Epiphany	272
160	A Fourth on Epiphany	277
161	On the Servant Who Came in from the Field	282
162	Where It Says: "Teacher, tell my brother to divide the inheritance with me"	288
163	Where It Says: "Do not be anxious about your life, about what you are to eat"	292
164	Where It Says: "I have come to light a fire on the earth"	297
167	A Second on Fasting	303
168	Where It Says: "Tax collectors and sinners drew near to the Lord to listen to him"	308
169	On the Woman Who Lost the Silver Coin	312

CONTENTS

171	Where It Is Said by the Pharisees that the Lord's Disciples Ate with Unwashed Hands	316
172	Where It Says: "Woe to you lawyers, you take away the key of knowledge, have not gained entrance yourselves, and have hindered others from entering"	320
173	On John the Baptist and Herod	324
174	A Second on the Same	330
175	When Marcellinus Was Made Bishop of Voghenza on the First of November	335
176	On the Man Born Blind	339
177	On the Anger of Brothers	344
178	On Loving One's Enemies	349
179	\<On St. John the Baptist\>	354

INDICES

General Index	361
Index of Holy Scripture	366

PREFACE

With the publication of this volume all of Chrysologus's authentic sermons are now available in English in the Fathers of the Church series. This translation is based upon the text edited by Dom Alejandro Olivar in CCL 24A and 24B. If a reading at variance with the CCL text is used, indication is given in a footnote. I have also used Olivar's extensive notes in the CCL edition for cross-referencing terms and similar ideas within Chrysologus's corpus, for pointing out parallels in classical and other patristic texts, and for signaling works of contemporary scholarship where appropriate. In addition but to a lesser extent I have benefitted from the recent Italian translation (which also includes the Latin of the CCL) by G. Banterle, who corrected the CCL text and provided some additional notes.

The citations from the Old Testament follow the Septuagint (and Vetus Latina) rendering and numeration. When the numeration differs from the New Revised Standard Version of the Bible, that of the NRSV is noted in parentheses. The translation of Scripture is based on Chrysologus's Latin text. Translations of other texts are mine unless otherwise indicated.

Any sermon of Chrysologus indicated in a footnote without reference to FOTC 17 or FOTC 109 (the previous two volumes of Chrysologus's sermons) is translated in this volume. Sermons 107, 119, and 159 are not translated because they are judged to be spurious. See FOTC 109.28, n. 144, regarding such textual issues. The fifteen recently attributed sermons are given the designation "a" and "b" in this volume as in FOTC 109, rather than the "bis" and "ter" of the CCL (e.g., *Sermon* 72bis is designated here as "72a," and 72ter as "72b"). Unless otherwise noted, "[ ]" indicate insertions I have made into the translation for the sake of clarity, and "< >" indicate additions that Olivar has made to the text or to the sermons' titles which themselves postdate Chrysologus. Scriptural texts upon which Chrysologus preaches in sequence are rendered in italics. In footnoting other patristic texts I cite the FOTC edition, if available; otherwise, in general, the best text available to me in the original Latin or Greek is referenced. For more information on Chrysologus, his times, and his preaching, please consult the Introduction to FOTC 109.1–32.

The individuals to whom I expressed gratitude in the Preface to FOTC 109 continue to merit my deep appreciation for their assistance in enabling me to complete this project. I owe additional and special thanks to Dr. Carole Burnett for her meticulous work in editing this volume and providing the indices for both this volume and FOTC 109.

ABBREVIATIONS

ACCR	*Atti dei convegni di Cesena e Ravenna I (1966–1967).* Cesena, 1969.
BSS	*Bibliotheca Sanctorum.* Ed. F. Caraffa. Rome, 1962–2000.
CCL	Corpus Christianorum, Series Latina. Turnhout, 1953–.
CSEL	Corpus scriptorum ecclesiasticorum Latinorum. Vienna, 1866–.
DACL	*Dictionnaire d'archéologie chrétienne et de liturgie.* Ed. F. Cabrol and H. Leclercq. Paris, 1907–1953.
DSp	*Dictionnaire de spiritualité ascétique et mystique.* Ed. M. Viller et al. Paris, 1933–1995.
FOTC	The Fathers of the Church. New York: Cima, 1947–49; New York: FOTC, Inc., 1949–60; Washington, D.C.: The Catholic University of America Press, 1960–.
GCS	Die griechischen christlichen Schriftsteller der ersten drei Jahrhunderte. Leipzig and Berlin, 1897–.
LXX	The Septuagint.
MGH.AA	Monumenta Germaniae historica: Auctores antiquissimi. Hannover and Berlin, 1877–1919.
NRSV	New Revised Standard Version.
NT	New Testament.
NTApo	*New Testament Apocrypha,* revised edition of collection of E. Hennecke. Ed. W. Schneemelcher and R. McL. Wilson. Cambridge: J. Clarke, 1991; Louisville, KY: Westminster/John Knox Press, 1991.
OECT	Oxford Early Christian Texts. Oxford, 1971–.
OT	Old Testament.
PG	Patrologiae Cursus Completus: Series Graeca. Ed. J.-P. Migne. Paris, 1857–66.

ABBREVIATIONS

PL	Patrologiae Cursus Completus: Series Latina. Ed. J.-P. Migne. Paris, 1841–94.
PLS	Patrologiae Latinae Supplementum. Ed. A. Hamman. Paris, 1958–74.
PRE	*Paulys Real-Enzyclopädie der classischen Altertumswissenschaft.* Ed. Pauly, Wissowa, and Kroll. Stuttgart, 1893–1978.
RAC	*Reallexikon für Antike und Christentum.* Stuttgart, 1950–.
RSCI	*Rivista di storia della chiesa in Italia.* Rome, 1947–.
SC	Sources chrétiennes. Paris, 1941–.
Vg	The Vulgate.
ZKTh	*Zeitschrift für katholische Theologie.* Vienna, 1876–.

SELECT BIBLIOGRAPHY

Other than the references below to the text of Migne and the translations of Böhmer and Held, the items found in the Bibliography in FOTC 17.24 will not be repeated here.

Texts

Agnellus. *Agnelli qui et Andreas Liber Pontificalis Ecclesiae Ravennatis.* Ed. O. Holder-Egger. In *Scriptores Rerum Langobardicarum et Italicarum,* ed. G. Waitz. Hannover: Impensis bibliopolii Hahniani, 1878.
Peter Chrysologus. *Epistula ad Eutychen.* In *Acta Conciliorum Oecumenicorum II,* ed. E. Schwartz, II, vol. 3, part 1, 6–7. Berlin and Leipzig: Walter de Gruyter, 1935.
_____. *Sermones.* CCL 24, 24A, and 24B. Ed. A. Olivar. 1975, 1981, and 1982.
_____. *Sancti Petri Chrysologi Archiepiscopi Ravennatis. Opera Omnia.* PL 52:183–666. 1894. Supplemented in PLS 3:153–83, 4:659–65, 5:397–98. 1963, 1967, 1974.

Translations

Agnellus. *Il Libro di Agnello Istorico.* Trans. Mario Pierpaoli. Ravenna: Diamond Byte, 1988.
_____. *The Book of Pontiffs of the Church of Ravenna.* Trans. Deborah Mauskopf Deliyannis. Washington, D.C.: The Catholic University of America Press, 2004.
Pedro Crisólogo. *Homilías Escogidas.* Intro. and notes by A. Olivar. Trans. J. Garitaonandia. Madrid: Editorial Ciudad Nueva, 1998.
San Pietro Crisologo. *Sermoni e Lettera a Eutiche.* 3 vols. Trans. G. Banterle et al. Intro. and notes by R. Benericetti, C. Truzzi, et al. Rome: Città Nuova Editrice, 1996–97.
Pier Crisologo. *Omelie per la vita quotidiana.* Trans. and intro. by Mario Spinelli. Rome: Città Nuova Editrice, 1978.
San Pier Crisologo. *I CLXXVII Sermoni.* 3 vols. Trans. A. Pasini. Siena: Cantagalli, 1953.
Saint Peter Chrysologus. *Selected Sermons and Letter to Eutyches.* Trans. G. Ganss. FOTC 17. 1953.
Saint Peter Chrysologus. *Selected Sermons. Volume 2.* Trans. William B. Palardy. FOTC 109. 2004.
Petrus Chrysologus. *Des hl. Petrus Chrysologus, Erzbischofs von Ravenna,*

ausgewählte Predigten. Trans. G. Böhmer. Bibliothek der Kirchenväter 43. Munich and Kempten: J. Kösel and F. Pustet, 1923.

———. *Ausgewählte Reden des hl. Petrus Chrysologus.* Trans. M. Held. Bibliothek der Kirchenväter 67. Kempten: J. Kösel, 1874.

Secondary Sources

Baldisserri, D. L. *San Pier Crisologo, Arcivescovo di Ravenna.* Imola: Stabilimento Tipografico Imolese, 1920.

Benelli, Augusto. "Note sulla vita e l'episcopato di Petro Crisologo." In *In Verbis Verum Amare,* ed. P. Serra Zanetti, 63–79. Florence: La Nuova Italia, 1980.

Benericetti, Ruggero. *Il Cristo nei Sermoni di S. Pier Crisologo.* Cesena: Centro studi e ricerche sulla antica provincia ecclesiastica Ravennate, 1995.

Bonner, Gerald. "Petrus Chrysologus." In *Theologische Realenzyclopädie* 26:290–91. Berlin: Walter de Gruyter, 1996.

Cortesi, Giuseppe. "Cinque note su San Pier Crisologo." *Felix Ravenna* 128 (1984): 117–32.

Del Ton, Josephus. "De Sancti Petri Chrysologi Eloquentia." *Latinitas* 6 (1958): 177–89.

De Margerie, Bertrand. "L'Exégèse de Saint Pierre Chrysologue, théologien biblique." Ch. 3 in *Introduction à l'histoire de l'exégèse: IV. L'Occident latin de Léon le Grand à Bernard de Clairvaux,* 75–108. Paris: Cerf, 1990.

Fitzgerald, Allan. *Conversion through Penance in the Italian Church of the Fourth and Fifth Centuries.* Lewiston, Queenston, and Lampeter: Edwin Mellen Press, 1988.

Jossua, J.-P. *Le Salut, Incarnation ou Mystère Pascal chez les Pères de l'Eglise de Saint Irénée à Saint Léon le Grand.* Paris: Cerf, 1968.

Koch, H. "Petrus Chrysologus." In *PRE* 38:1361–72 (1938).

Kochaniewicz, Boguslaw. *La Vergine Maria nei sermoni di San Pietro Crisologo.* Rome: Pontifical Theological Faculty "Marianum," 1998.

Ladino, Rolando. *La iniciación cristiana en San Pedro Crisólogo de Ravenna.* Rome: Pontifical Gregorian University, 1969.

Lanzoni, F. *Le diocesi d'Italia dalle origini al principio del Secolo VII (An. 604).* Studi e Testi 35. Faenza: Stabilimento Grafico F. Lega, 1927.

La Rosa, Virgilio. *Il commento al Pater Noster nei sermoni di S. Pier Crisologo.* Rome: Pontifical Lateran University, 1965.

Lemarié, Joseph. "La liturgie de Ravenne au temps de Pierre Chrysologue et l'ancienne liturgie d'Aquilée." In *Antichitá Altoadriatiche XIII: Aquileia e Ravenna,* 355–73. Udine: Arti Grafiche Friulane, 1978.

Lodi, E. "La preghiera in S. Pietro Crisologo." In *La preghiera nel tardo antico: Dalle origini ad Agostino: XXVII Incontro di studiosi dell'antichità cristiana,* 389–417. Rome: Institutum Patristicum Augustinianum, 1999.

SELECT BIBLIOGRAPHY

_____. "L'esegesi biblica nei testi rituali dei sermoni di s. Pier Crisologo." In *L'esegesi nei padri latini: Dalle origini a Gregorio magno: XXVIII Incontro di studiosi dell'antichità cristiana,* 2:617–53. Rome: Institutum Patristicum Augustinianum, 2000.

Lucchesi, G. "Stato attuale degli studi sui santi dell'antica provincia ravennate." In *ACCR,* 51–80.

McGlynn, Robert H. *The Incarnation in the Sermons of Saint Peter Chrysologus.* Mundelein, IL: Saint Mary of the Lake Seminary, 1956.

Old, Hughes Oliphant. "Peter Chrysologus." Ch. VI.II in *The Reading and Preaching of the Scriptures in the Worship of the Christian Church: Volume 2: The Patristic Age,* 416–24. Grand Rapids, MI: Eerdmans, 1998.

Olivar, A. "Els principis exegètics de sant Pere Crisòleg." In *Miscellanea biblica B. Ubach,* ed. Romualdo M. Díaz, 413–37. Montserrat: Abadía de Montserrat, 1953.

_____. "Clavis S. Petri Chrysologi." *Sacris Erudiri* 6 (1954): 327–42.

_____. *Los sermones de San Pedro Crisólogo: Estudio crítico.* Montserrat: Abadía de Montserrat, 1962.

_____. "La duración de la predicación antigua." *Liturgica* 3 (1966): 143–84.

_____. "La consagración del Obispo Marcelino de Voghenza." *RSCI* 22 (1968): 87–93.

_____. "Pietro Crisologo, arcivescovo di Ravenna, Dottore della Chiesa, santo." In *BSS* 10:685–91. 1968.

_____. "Preparación e improvisación en la predicación patristica." In *Kyriakon: Festschrift J. Quasten,* ed. P. Granfield and J. A. Jungmann, 2:736–67. Münster: Verlag Aschendorff, 1970.

_____. "Reseña de las publicaciones recientes referentes a San Pedro Crisólogo." *Didaskalia* 7 (1977): 131–51.

_____. "Die Textüberlieferung der Predigten des Petrus Chrysologus." In *Texte und Textkritik: eine Aufstatzsammlung.* Texte und Untersuchungen zur Geschichte der altchristlichen Literatur 133, ed. J. Dummer, 469–87. Berlin: Akademie-Verlag, 1987.

_____. *La predicación cristiana antigua.* Barcelona: Herder, 1991.

_____. "Les exordes des sermons de saint Pierre Chrysologue." *Revue bénédictine* 104 (1994): 88–105.

Olivar, A., and A. Argemi. "La Eucaristía en la predicación de San Pedro Crisólogo." *La Ciencia Tomista* 86 (1959): 605–28.

Paganotto, R. D. A. *L'apporto dei Sermoni di San Pier Crisologo alla storia della cura pastorale a Ravenna nel secolo V.* Rome: Pontifical Gregorian University, 1969.

Palardy, William. "The Church and the Synagogue in the Sermons of Saint Peter Chrysologus." Ph.D. dissertation, Catholic University of America, Washington, D.C., 1992.

_____. "Peter Chrysologus' Interpretation of the Raising of Lazarus." In *Studia Patristica* 25, ed. E. A. Livingstone, 129–33. Louvain: Peeters, 1993.

Schlitz, E. "Un trésor oublié: Saint Pierre Chrysologue comme théologien." *Nouvelle revue théologique* 55 (1928): 265–76.
Scimè, Giuseppe. *Giudei e cristiani nei Sermoni di San Pietro Crisologo.* Rome: Institutum patristicum Augustinianum, 2003.
Sottocornola, Franco. *L'anno liturgico nei sermoni di Pietro Crisologo.* Cesena: Centro studi e ricerche sulla antica provincia ecclesiastica Ravennate, 1973.
Speigl, Jakob. "Petrus Chrysologus über die Auferstehung der Toten." *Jahrbuch für Antike und Christentum* 9 (1982): 140–53.
Spinelli, Mario. "L'eco delle invasioni barbariche nelle omelie di Pier Crisologo." *Vetera Christianorum* 16 (1979): 87–93.
―――. "Il ruolo sociale del digiuno in Pier Crisologo." *Vetera Christianorum* 18 (1981): 143–56.
―――. "Sangue, martirio e redenzione in Pier Crisologo." In *Sangue e antropologia biblica nella patristica*, ed. Francesco Vattioni, 1:529–46. Rome: Pia Unione Preziosissimo Sangue, 1981.
―――. "La simbologia ecclesiologica di Pier Crisologo." In *Sangue e antropologia biblica nella patristica*, ed. Francesco Vattioni, 1:547–62. Rome: Pia Unione Preziosissimo Sangue, 1981.
Studer, Basil. "Peter Chrysologus." In *Patrology*, Vol. 4: *The Golden Age of Latin Patristic Literature From the Council of Nicea to the Council of Chalcedon*, ed. A. di Berardino, 575–77. Trans. P. Solari. Westminster, MD: Christian Classics, 1986.
Wilkins, M. *Word-Order in Selected Sermons of the Fifth and Sixth Centuries.* Washington, D.C.: Catholic University of America, 1940.
Zangara, Vincenza, "I silenzi nella predicazione di Pietro Crisologo." *Rivista di Storia e Letteratura Religiosa* 32 (1996): 225–68.
Zattoni, Girolamo. "Cronologia crisologhiana." In *Scritti Storici e Ravennati*, 309–18. Ravenna: Tonini, 1975.

SELECTED SERMONS

VOLUME 3

SERMON 72A

A First on the Lord's Passion[1]

AFTER THE HEAVENLY MIRACLE of the Virgin birth shone throughout the whole world, the joyful festivities marking the Lord's birth were completed, and the venerable feast of Epiphany also has been celebrated, the Lord foretells the sequence of the events surrounding his Passion to his disciples when he speaks as follows: *Behold, we are now going up to Jerusalem,* he says, *and the Son of Man will be handed over to the chief priests, and they will condemn him to death, and they will hand him over to the gentiles, and they will mock him and spit at him, and after three days he will rise* (Mt 20.18–19). He who was able to announce what would happen was also able to avoid it.

Adversities overtake the ignorant, not those who have knowledge. He willed to suffer since of his own accord he went up to the place where he would suffer. Death has sway over the unwilling, but is the servant of those who are willing. Therefore, since he is willing to die, it is not a mishap, but an act of power. "I have power," he says, "to lay down my own life, and I have

1. On the authenticity of this sermon, see A. Olivar, *Los sermones de San Pedro Crisólogo: Estudio crítico* (Montserrat: Abadía de Montserrat, 1962), 357–65. F. Sottocornola, *L'anno liturgico nei sermoni di Pietro Crisologo* (Cesena: Centro studi e ricerche sulla antica provincia ecclesiastica Ravennate, 1973), 132–36, is of the opinion that this and the following sermon were preached after the feasts of Christmas and Epiphany had ended, and prior to the beginning of Lent. He bases his contention on the first sentence of this sermon and on the fact that this *Sermon* 72a is not about Christ's Passion *per se* but about his *prediction* of the Passion. A. Olivar, by contrast, in *Los sermones*, 264, indicates that although Chrysologus was not in the habit of preaching at Passiontide, he did make an exception with *Sermons* 72a and 72b. The only bit of support for Olivar's contention of a late Lenten setting for this sermon is the collection of allusions to the Creed in section 4, and the Creed was the focus of much of Chrysologus's preaching during Lent (see *Sermons* 56–62a). However, Sottocornola's placement of this and the following sermon in the period between Epiphany and the beginning of Lent seems far more likely.

power," he says, "to take it up; no one takes it from me."[2] Where there is the power to lay down life and to take it up, dying in this case is not something inevitable, but something that is willed.[3] "No one," he says, "takes it from me." If no one, then certainly not even death.

Indeed, death was not able to take his life away, nor was the underworld able to hold onto it, since, as it trembled at his[4] bidding, it lost even those souls that it was holding in captivity: "And the tombs were split open," it says, "and many of the bodies of the saints rose up."[5] Just as, when Christ was being born, conception did not follow its usual order, birth did not proceed according to custom, nature did not observe its own laws,[6] so too at his death Tartarus lost those he was keeping under his sway, hell forfeited the prerogative of its age-old power, and death relinquished what had been guaranteed under the ancient law by decree of the new order.[7]

2. But let us return to what we have begun. *We are now going up to Jerusalem*, he says, *and the Son of Man will be handed over to the chief priests, and they will condemn him to death, and they will hand him over to the gentiles* (vv.18–19). But God, who knows all that is to be known, knew, because he had foreseen what was going to happen, that at the scandal of the cross, at the violence of the Passion, at the injustice done to the Creator, the earth would quake, the sky would tremble, light would flee, the sun would hide, hell would shudder, and all creation would be disturbed and thrown into confusion.[8] For the world, which could not endure divinity covered with our body, foresaw that it would be stripped of flesh, a thing it would not bear; and especially since it had recognized how great were the sacrileges committed against the Man, it supposed that they had actually inflicted injury on his divinity.

---

2. Jn 10.18.
3. See *Sermons* 23.1 (FOTC 109.97) and 40.3 (FOTC 17.87).
4. Literally, "at his life's bidding": *qua iubente*. The antecedent of *qua* is *anima*.
5. Mt 27.52.
6. See *Sermon* 153.1.
7. See *Sermon* 65.6 and 9 (FOTC 109.263–265, 266).
8. See Mt 27.50–52.

The Lord kept warning his disciples of these things time and time again, placing them before their eyes, and, as it were, setting up the arena[9] for his Passion and leading them into it. He was signifying that there would be as many kinds of abuse as there would be kinds of wild beasts; that there would be as many spectators as persecutors, who, in seeking not a victory from the conflict, but only an assent to the death of the Victor, would shout: "Crucify, crucify."[10] They would go so far as to lift up their savage eyes and their lethal voices to heaven, or rather against heaven, until in their cruel feeding frenzy[11] by contending with holy blood they would smear themselves and their posterity and wallow in that blood, as they yell: "His blood be upon us and upon our children."[12]

3. *The Son of Man*, he says, *will be handed over to the chief priests* (v.18). The Lord Jesus was depicting what his Passion would look like by very often mentioning it in this way, so that his disciples would expect what was to be expected and not be overcome by the weight of an unforeseen burden, nor be overwhelmed by a surprise assault. Things that are known prepare the spirit, things announced make it strong, things expected give people warning and render them stronger through it all.

Just as a soldier is endangered by the sudden arrival of the enemy, so too if he should have prior knowledge about the enemy, he wins the victory. A strong king, even if he is protected by a garrison of strong men, is not able to guard against the unknown; even a warrior who is all alone has no fear concerning troops whose movements he knows. And so the Lord wanted his disciples to know in advance the whole stormy course of his Passion, so that in the midst of that very tempest he would make them courageous and render them stronger.

Behold, we are now going up to Jerusalem (v.18). Just as one who by making one alteration props up a large house in the wake of damage resulting from structural defects, so after the weighty

---

9. Whereas better English would be "setting the stage," *harena* is translated literally since Chrysologus uses imagery from the "arena" in the rest of this section.
10. Lk 23.21; Jn 19.6.
11. Reading the variant *sagnitio* for the *segnitie* of Olivar's CCL text.
12. Mt 27.25.

and multiple burdens resulting from his Passion Christ likewise set in place one support, namely, his Resurrection, in order to prop up the faith of the apostles that was already beginning to be defective, and make it permanently firm.

4. *After three days he will rise* (v.19). The departure is not quite as sad, when the return is so speedy. *After three days:* this leaving and returning was such that it would be clear that he was not ever absent there. When God goes, he is here; since he is here, he is never absent. Christ went, but he never left the apostles; the Lord went to death, but he never departed from life; he descended into hell, but he was not absent from heaven,[13] as he himself attests when he says: "No one has ascended to heaven, except the One who has descended from heaven, the Son of Man who is in heaven."[14]

Not wishing to die is characteristic of human fear; dying and rising characterize God alone.[15] *And after three days* (v.19): why not after four days? Why not after five, but after three? So that in the Passion of the Son the assent of the whole Trinity[16] would be demonstrated. He says "three days" to symbolize the Trinity, because the Trinity, which had created the human being in the beginning through the work of Christ, Itself in the end restores the human being through the Passion of Christ.[17] "Let us make the human being,"[18] he says. "Go," he says, "and baptize all nations in the name of the Father, and of the Son, and of the Holy Spirit"[19] in remission of sins.[20] If in the remission of sins the

---

13. The belief that even while incarnate the Son was never absent from heaven is articulated by Chrysologus when expounding on the Creed, as in *Sermons* 58.8 and 62.11 (FOTC 109.223, 244).

14. Jn 3.13.

15. See *Sermon* 61.6 on the Creed (FOTC 17.113).

16. In *Sermon* 65.8 (FOTC 109.266) Chrysologus notes the consent of the whole Trinity to Christ's death and Resurrection so as to redeem and liberate the holy ones held in the bondage of Tartarus.

17. In his sermons on the Creed, Chrysologus finds in Christ's rising "on the third day" an allusion to the Trinity, to whom the credit belongs for Christ's victory over death. See *Sermons* 57.8 and 61.7 (FOTC 17.108, 114) and *Sermons* 58.7, 59.9, 60.9, 62.10, and 62a.6 (FOTC 109.223, 228, 235, 244, 247).

18. Gn 1.26.

19. Mt 28.19.

20. *In remissione peccatorum*, a likely reference to the tenet in the Creed that has the same terminology.

Trinity is united in showing mercy, how is the whole Trinity not one in will in the Passion of the Son? "Just as Jonah was in the belly of the whale for three days and three nights," he says, "so also will the Son of Man be in the heart of the earth."[21]

He said "in the heart of the earth"; he did not say "in the power of the earth," meaning that the earth would sense, recognize, and tremble at its Creator, but not hold him; it would receive him so as to pay homage to him, it would not afflict him with corruption; the earth would not suppose that the Lord's Body was its allotted portion, but would receive him as One who shares in heavenly majesty.

5. But it disturbs the mind as to why the Father willed or permitted that the Son undergo death in this fashion; why the Lord willed to restore the life of mortal beings by such a death, by so dishonorable a death. Why did the Holy Spirit agree to it that divinity descend to suffer such indignities in the flesh, that more would perish from the scandal than would be saved through believing? The human intellect does not grasp that God is born and dies. Brothers, if we want to comprehend this, let us put it off for today, so that a more extensive sermon may respond to this very important question with Christ himself assuring our satisfaction.[22]

21. Mt 12.40.
22. The promised "more extensive sermon" on this topic is *Sermon* 72b.

SERMON 72B

A Second on the Lord's Passion[1]

ECENTLY WHEN WE HEARD the many bitter[2] indignities comprising the Lord's Passion, we suddenly came to wonder why God, who has created by his command and has marked off by his decree everything that heaven has, that the earth bears, that the sea contains, and that Tartarus used to summon, has arranged the world in such beauty, yet in order to absolve the sentence of death shed that stream of sacred blood.[3]

Why did the Origin of the universe, the Author of nature, will to be born, except that he willed to die? Why did God assume flesh with all its weakness, except that[4] he chose to take on the indignities associated with the flesh? Why did the Lord of all creation enter the form of slavery except to endure all the indignities of slavery? The Judge chooses to be judged, the Advocate chooses to be put on trial, when he has endured being judged by reprobates. What need is there for him to suffer when he has both the capacity and the power to save? Or what is the reason then for him to die, when he has both the strength and the means to give life?

2. *Behold, we are now going up to Jerusalem, and the Son of Man will be handed over to*[5] *the chief priests, and they will condemn him to*

---

1. On this sermon's authenticity, see A. Olivar, *Los sermones*, 357–65. On when this sermon was preached, see *Sermon* 72a, n. 1. At any rate, it was the next sermon Chrysologus preached after *Sermon* 72a.

2. Emending Olivar's *acervas*, with *acerbas*, from PLS 4.662.

3. The question of why the Son of God suffered death was posed at the end of *Sermon* 72a, and a sermon on that topic was promised, namely, this *Sermon* 72b.

4. Emending Olivar's *qua* with *quia*, from PLS 4.662.

5. Emending Olivar's CCL text by omitting *a*, as in PLS 4.662, especially since that preposition is not found in *Sermon* 72a's citation of Mt 20.18–19.

death, and they will hand him over to the gentiles, and they will mock him and spit at him, and after three days he will rise (Mt 20.18–19). *We are going up to Jerusalem*, and on the day of Passover, so that the entirety of the Jewish city would gather at the display of the Passion, at the public spectacle of his death, and at the scandal of the cross. An ordinary kind of passion is not sufficient, nor a private death, nor a regular kind of death, nor a death like any other death;⁶ the uniqueness of the Passion had to match the uniqueness of the Sufferer.

It was done so that the Creator of the world would die with the world as his witness; and so that the Lord of the world would be recognized by the world through his pain before he would be through his glory. The Peace of heaven is betrayed by the kiss of deceit,⁷ the One who holds all is held fast, the Bond of all is bound, the One who draws all is led forth, Truth is accused by falsehood, and the One for whom all things stand at his service, is made to stand trial; the Jews hand him over to the gentiles, the gentiles return him to the Jews; Pilate sends him to Herod, Herod sends him back to Pilate, and piety becomes the business of impiety, and holiness is brought to the market of cruelty. Forgiveness is beaten, Pardon is condemned, Majesty is mocked, Virtue is ridiculed; the Bestower of rain is drenched with spittle, the One who has arrayed the heavens is restrained by nails of iron, the Giver of honey is fed with gall, the One who makes springs of water flow is given vinegar to drink; and when there is no longer any punishment left, death takes cover, death hesitates, because it does not notice anything there that is its own.

Newness is looked at with suspicion by antiquity; he was the first, he was the only man it saw innocent of sin, free of guilt, owing nothing to the laws of its domain. It is amazed to see on earth One who has no trace of earthliness in him. "The first man," Scripture says, "is earthly from earth, the second man is

---

6. Literally, "a death similar to death" *(mors morti similis)*.

7. Scriptural allusions in this paragraph are too numerous to mention, coming from the four Passion accounts in Mt 26–27, Mk 14–15, Lk 22–23, and Jn 18–19. A similar list of antitheses associated with Christ's Passion is found in Cyprian, *The Good of Patience* 7 (FOTC 36.269–70).

heavenly from heaven."[8] Nevertheless, death, united with Jewish fury, advances, and in its desperation it then seizes and assails the Author of life, willing to perish completely so long as it not lose so great a prize.

3. But now let us begin what has been promised: why did God the Father send his own Son to death, and to this kind of death? Why did he submit to so shameful a Passion? Why did the Holy Spirit permit Christ, reigning together with him and one in divinity with him, to undergo so great an indignity in his flesh? Pray, brothers, that by the gracious favor with which he suffered, he may reveal the mystery of his Passion, and enlighten[9] us all as to the reason for so sacred a death.[10]

4. First of all we must consider, when is a king more glorious? When he is decked out in his purple, adorned with the diadem, covered with gold, high on his throne, only when he is ready to go in solemn procession or seated in private? Or is he more glorious when wearing ordinary attire for the battlefield, last in honor, first in perils, laden with a sword, heavily equipped with arms, when for his country, for his citizens, for his children, and for the life of all the people he destroys the enemy, despises dangers, thinks little of wounds, and is willing to endure his own death for the safety of his people, so that he gains a greater victory and triumph by despising death than by defeating the enemy itself?

And so what is the problem if Christ came to our condition of slavery from the bosom of his Father, from the hidden realm of divinity, in order to restore us to his liberty; he endured our death in order that we might have life by his death; when by disdaining death he brought us mortals back as gods, and put us earthly beings on the same level as heavenly ones? Yet how is it that God summons Christ to such extreme indignity, but raises and exalts human beings to such great glory? But someone

---

8. 1 Cor 15.47.
9. Literally, "breathe into" or "inspire" *(inspiret)*.
10. For a detailed study of the reasons for and the effects of the suffering and death of Christ in Chrysologus's preaching, see R. Benericetti, *Il Cristo nei Sermoni di S. Pier Crisologo* (Cesena: Centro studi e ricerche sulla antica provincia ecclesiastica Ravennate, 1995), 270–84.

says: "This has to do with the constraints of being human, divine power has nothing to do with this." He speaks the truth: divine power has nothing to do with this, but the divine bond of kinship does, and accepts this.

"No one," he says, "has greater love, than to lay down his life for his friends."[11] Are you amazed if he, who did such great things for us and bestowed such blessings upon us, has laid down for us what he received from us? As resplendent as the excellence, power, and magnificence of the Creator were when one contemplated his works, all the same the love of God was concealed, and the charity of God kept hidden. To give to his subjects, to bestow things on servants is what usually characterizes a donor; to suffer for one's subjects, to die for one's servants, this is a sign of immense charity and evidence of a love that is unique.

"God shows his charity towards us," it says, "in that while we were mere sinners, Christ died for us."[12] And in another place: "God so loved this world, that he handed over his only-begotten Son."[13] Anyone can grant favors, anyone can bestow gifts, any prosperous benefactor can love those who are deferential to him; but will he be comparable to him who took the adversities of his own people onto himself; who puts himself forward to block dangers threatening his own; who hands himself over to punishments for his own, who confronts death face-to-face in order to remove them from destruction and preserve them for life? Love is proved by adversities, the weight of affection is determined by the dangers endured, benevolence is tested by punishments, perfect charity is confirmed by death.

This is why Christ exposes himself to fleshly indignity, why he undergoes the abuse that he suffered, why he perseveres through various forms of punishment, and why he endured a very bitter death, because he willed to be condemned since he had such love for what he had created. But God's will in this instance is nothing new; the first words of the ancient Law insisted on this: "You shall love the Lord your God," it says, "with all

---

11. Jn 15.13. 12. Rom 5.8.
13. Jn 3.16.

your heart and with all your soul";[14] because that dominion is true which commands by love, not by fear; which subjects both bodies and hearts to itself by means of affection; which by loving furnishes servants for itself who are not unwilling, but willing. So this is the first reason for the Lord's Passion, whereby he wanted it to be known how much God loved humanity, since he wanted to be loved rather than feared.[15]

5. The second reason is so that he would abrogate in an even more just manner the sentence of death, which he had imposed with justice. God wanted to fulfill his own statute by suffering, so that he would not enforce it by a command, as he himself says: "I have come not to abolish the Law, but to fulfill it."[16] God's promise of good things for good people is unreliable, if what has been established by God for the wicked comes to nothing. "Not a single letter," he says, "not a dot of the Law will pass away, until all these things occur."[17] Whoever is wise has knowledge of what is revealed here; let the one who perceives it understand.

If on account of his own sentence he did not spare his own Son,[18] whom can he forgive contrary to his sentence? He who is unable to lie is unable to forgive. So since the first man had on account of his guilt incurred death by the sentence rendered by God, and he passed death onto his race and transmitted it to his posterity, because one who is now mortal in body generates mortals, guilty, not free, not acquitted, but in bondage, there came from heaven a second Man, there came the only One not to know sin, there came the only One who was a stranger to our guilt, there came One who owed no debt to sin and death.

He came to become free among the dead, so that death would be condemned to death;[19] death, which had been or-

---

14. Dt 6.5.
15. For other references in Chrysologus's sermons to this formulation about God's love, see A. Olivar, *Los sermones*, 362. For references in other ancient authors (classical and Christian), see Karl Gross, "*Plus amari quam timeri:* Eine antike politische Maxime in der Benediktinerregel," *Vigiliae Christianae* 27 (1973): 218–29.
16. Mt 5.17.   17. Mt 5.18.
18. See Rom 8.32.
19. The idea that death dies at Christ's death recurs in Chrysologus's sermons. See, e.g., *Sermons* 40.4, 57.7, and 166.8 (FOTC 17.88, 108, 198).

dered to seize the guilty, presumed to capture the Author of innocence himself, so that just as the guilt of the human being resulted in death, so innocence would return to the human being. Consequently, having become a transgressor, death would be delivered over to Christ, death to which Adam previously had been delivered over as a result of his transgression. So then Christ would be the new origin, the life-giving origin, the Father of the living,[20] as the Apostle said: "Just as in Adam we all died, so let us all live and be brought to life in Christ."[21]

6. And because there are many reasons for the Lord's Passion, and because now our sermon must be brought to a close, let us put it off for today, so that a hasty discussion may not obscure what a more extensive treatment will be able to reveal.[22]

---

20. This Pauline notion of Christ's role as a new Adam reversing the calamities of the Fall finds similar expression in *Sermon* 110.4.
21. See 1 Cor 15.22.
22. The promised sermon is not extant.

SERMON 73

On the Holy Day of Easter[1]

ODAY'S FEAST, brothers, does not connect the old with the new, nor does it keep the flesh of the lamb for tomorrow,[2] but while it makes the past a partner with the present in solemn devotion, and joins our Passover[3] with the Passover that returns, it weans the infants newly regenerated, because as the Apostle says, "The old has passed away, [and] see all things have been made new."[4] The year of the Lord progresses through seasons, it does not grow old, since it repeats its cycle for as long as it takes to lead us to the day of recompense.[5] Today's solemnity of Easter now withdraws from milk those whom it bore earlier, so that they might be strengthened by eating more solid food and be made into the perfect man of Christ.[6]

2. That Abraham held a great banquet, and that he spread

---

1. The Latin is *Pascha*, which means "Pasch" and "Passover" as well as "Easter." F. Sottocornola, *L'anno liturgico*, 83–84 and 188–90, argues persuasively that this sermon was preached right before or shortly after the beginning of the Easter season on the one-year anniversary of Baptism for those initiated the previous Easter—called *Pascha annotinum* in later Roman liturgical practice (see ibid., 188, n. 21, for more on the Roman practice). That this sermon is not focused on Easter *per se* is evident in that there is no reference to Christ's Resurrection. Also, the complaint Chrysologus notes in section 3 about this particular celebration being alleged to be "of no benefit" *(otiosum)* and both a reversion to Jewish practice and a novelty to Christianity would not reasonably be directed against the celebration of Easter, but against this newly established celebration of the "weaning" of the year-old neophytes, marking their adulthood as Christians. In his *monitum* to the CCL edition of this sermon (24A.446), A. Olivar concurs with Sottocornola, and notes that the latter's conclusion about this sermon solves many of the otherwise inexplicable matters in the text, given solely an Easter context, and that this sermon is the most ancient witness to a *Pascha annotinum* celebration anywhere.

2. See Ex 12.10.
4. 2 Cor 5.17.
6. See Eph 4.13.

3. See 1 Cor 5.7.
5. See Lk 4.19.

joy throughout all his house when Isaac was weaned, we know from what divine history relates.⁷ And if the child born to aged parents,⁸ indeed and only child of a barren mother, prompted and moved the hearts of the whole family to rejoice with dancing choruses, lyre, timbrel, and the psaltery all playing in harmony, how much more today is it appropriate for us to exult in spiritual hymns or canticles, when the numerous offspring of a fertile virgin are weaned?

Anna, barren like Sarah, wet her dry body and nature with the tears of her prayers for as long as posterity had been denied her over the lengthy period of her life. Since she had received Samuel as a gift from God, she soon returned him weaned as a gift to God, and she added her own happiness to the sacrificial victims to make a plentiful libation;⁹ all the more is it right for us to offer a sacrifice of praise,¹⁰ to pay our vows, and to present sweet incense and offerings, as ample as any holocaust, to God the Father, since the Virgin Mother presents to the Father children from throughout the whole world who have been nourished and weaned and are as numerous as the stars of the sky, so that the words of the prophet might be fulfilled: "You will bless the crown of the year with your bounty, and your fields will be full of a fertile harvest."¹¹

3. So let no one believe that the saving mystery that we celebrate in this feast is of no benefit, nor think that we sew a new patch onto an old cloak,¹² where we join none of the old Jewish ways to the new Christian ones, knowing, as the Apostle teaches, that for us the whole of creation has emerged new in Christ,¹³ but we contribute to their growth in heavenly virtue and in the knowledge of God.

Consequently, while the recently born¹⁴ are trained in what they ought to do, and at the same time those who were born earlier¹⁵ are instructed in how much thanks they owe to God on

---

7. See Gn 21.8.
8. Literally, "of old age" *(senectutis)*.
9. 1 Sm 1.10–28.
10. See Ps 49 (50).14.
11. Ps 64.12 LXX; Ps 65.11.
12. See Mt 9.16.
13. See 2 Cor 5.17.
14. Most likely those who are this day celebrating their first anniversary of Baptism.
15. Those who have been Christians for some time.

account of their being perfected, those who have just been born[16] cleave to the neck and completely devote themselves to clinging to the breasts of their Mother the Church,[17] they swallow the food of innocence in their tender throats, give thought to extending their arms in holy work, and strive to make their trembling steps firm on the journey of faith. Are those who have been nourished now to be abandoned? Shouldn't they instead be governed by the care of the Father, by the hand of the Father, and by the will of the Father, and likewise be protected by the counsel of the Mother and by the faith of the Mother, such that they take and make off with not merely human things but even the saving divine wisdom?

4. Thus Jacob, very timid on his own, but quite daring when his mother provided her counsel, more symbolically than deceitfully came forward to make off with his father's blessing, for he did not lie when he said that he was the firstborn,[18] since he was the first that heavenly grace, not mortal nature, generated. When he was wearing goatskin,[19] he prefigured us who, in order to die to sin, at the encouragement of our Mother the Church put on the clothes of a mortified body and reek of the odor of the field with the continuous and abundant fruits of professing our faith, until we profit from deluding the Jews in their blindness and make off with the Father's blessing by the completely mysterious workings of faith, as the Apostle says: "Blindness has come upon part of Israel, until the full number of the gentiles come in."[20]

---

16. Those just baptized at Easter. This remark implies that the first Sunday of Easter on which these individuals were baptized was very recent, perhaps the previous Sunday, suggesting that at least when this sermon was preached, *Pascha annotinum* was observed on the Octave of Easter. See n. 1 above.

17. The Church as a fruitful and nurturing mother recurs in Chrysologus's preaching. See *Sermons* 68.11 (FOTC 109.279), 72.3 (FOTC 109.294), 117.4–5 (FOTC 17.201–2), and 130.1–2.

18. See Augustine, *Against Lying* 10.24 (FOTC 16.152–55), assessing what Jacob did, not as a lie but as signifying a deeper mystery.

19. See Gn 27.

20. Rom 11.25.

SERMON 75

A Second on the Lord's Resurrection[1]

S LONG A TIME as I was absent from you, that long has preaching been absent from my life; but pray, brothers, that just as God has brought me back to you, so he may deign to bring back and restore to me the means to preach.[2]

2. You heard the evangelist say: *On the evening of the Sabbath,* he says, *which was beginning to dawn on the first day of the week* (Mt 28.1). What does human intelligence comprehend here? What does worldly wisdom understand here? *On the evening which was beginning to dawn.* Evening ends, it does not start the day; it produces, not light, but darkness. But here the Author of the elements changes the course of the elements, so that in the Lord's Resurrection you will perceive something that is entirely divine, and not human at all.

And so when Christ rises, evening begins to dawn for believers, while day brings darkness on unbelievers; for the disciples night is changed into day, but for the Jews day is turned and changed into night. "From noon until three in the afternoon,"

---

1. *Sermons* 74–84 are on the theme of Christ's Resurrection as recorded in the four Gospels. *Sermons* 74, 80, and 83 are translated in FOTC 17.123–37. As F. Sottocornola, *L'anno liturgico,* 87, notes, *Sermon* 79.1 (see *Sermon* 82.1 also) indicates the order in which Chrysologus preached in the Easter season, as follows: on the Resurrection accounts in Matthew, then Mark, then Luke, and concluding presumably with John. It is likely that two sets of the extant sermons were preached sequentially: *Sermons* 75, 76, 82, 83, 79, followed by at least one sermon not extant, and 81; and *Sermons* 74 and 80. See F. Sottocornola, *L'anno liturgico,* 85–88 and 172–74; A. Olivar, *Los sermones,* 177–79 and 263–66; and FOTC 17.128, n. 1. This *Sermon* 75 was probably preached on Easter Sunday (see Sottocornola, 85).

2. In the previous sermon Chrysologus states that the arduousness of the vigils and fasting prevented him from preaching immediately prior to Easter. See *Sermon* 74.1 (FOTC 17.123).

it says, "it became dark,"³ so that the entire brightness of midday would be covered over, and what was written in Scripture would be fulfilled: "For them the sun sets at midday."⁴ It sets for them, that is, for the Jews; but for us "night will shine like the day,"⁵ because evening, which always declines into deep gloom, at that time inclined and rose unto the full light of Christ, and filled all the hearts of mortals with complete brightness when Christ arose from the underworld.

On the evening of the Sabbath, which was beginning to dawn on the first day of the week: because the Sabbath is being illumined by means of Christ, it is not destroyed. "For I have come not to abolish the Law, but to fulfill it."⁶ It is being illumined so that it might shed light onto the Lord's day, and so that what was made opaque in the synagogue by the obscurantist Jews might shine clearly in the Church.

3. *Mary Magdalene and the other Mary came to see the tomb* (v.1). Women, who in their sex come after men, who in rank come after the disciples, go ahead of the apostles for ministry. But in this they do not make the apostles lazier, since they are bringing not their images as women, but a type of the Churches⁷ to the Lord's tomb. Mary and Mary: thus the second as the first, the first as the second. Mary, the one name of the Mother of Christ, is doubled in two women, because here the Church, coming from two peoples, is prefigured as one from the two peoples, that is from the gentiles and the Jews,⁸ since "the first shall be last, and the last shall be first."⁹

Mary came to the tomb. She came to the womb of the Resurrection, she came to the birth of Life, so that Christ, who had been brought forth from the womb of flesh, would be born a

---

3. Mt 27.45.
4. Am 8.9.
5. Ps 138 (139).12.
6. Mt 5.17.
7. In *Sermon* 82.6 Chrysologus repeats the idea of one of the Marys as a type of the Church.
8. In *Sermon* 74.3 (FOTC 17.124–25) the two Marys have a different signification, representing Eve and the new Eve, the Virgin Mary. See also *Sermon* 64.2 (FOTC 109.255–57) on the name Mary signifying the Virgin. In *Sermon* 82.7 the two disciples described in Mk 16.12, like the two Marys as interpreted in this *Sermon* 75, are taken to represent the two peoples, gentiles and Jews, to whom the news of the Resurrection will be preached.
9. Mt 19.30.

second time from the tomb of faith; and so that the sealed tomb would render to eternal life him whom the sealed womb of the Virgin[10] had brought forth into the present life.[11] It is a characteristic of divinity to have left the Virgin intact after birth; it is a characteristic of divinity to have come out of the tomb with his body. Mary and Mary came to see the tomb. You see that they came, not to look at the Lord, but at the tomb: they were not searching among the dead for one who was now living,[12] since they believed that the Lord had now risen.

4. But an angel came down, and *rolled back the stone* (v.2). *He rolled back the stone*, not to provide a passageway for the Lord to go out, but to show the world that the Lord had already risen; to give his fellow servants confidence to believe, not to supply aid for the Lord to rise. *He rolled back the stone.* He rolled it back for faith, since it had been rolled forward to take faith away.[13] *He rolled back the stone*, in order that the same stone that had assumed custody over him while dead might be the announcement that he was alive.

Pray, brothers, that the angel may descend now and roll away all hardness from our heart, and remove the barriers to our understanding, and show that Christ has also risen out of our mental limitations,[14] since just as that heart is heaven in which Christ lives and reigns, so too that breast is a tomb in which Christ is still held to be dead and buried. Just as we believe that Christ's death occurred, so too must we believe that it

---

10. Literally, "sealed virginity" *(clausa virginitas)*.
11. Connecting the sealed womb of the Virgin Mary and the sealed tomb where Jesus' body reposed is common among early Christian preachers and teachers. See, for example, Jerome, *Adversus Iovinianum* 1.31 (PL 23.265); Augustine, *Faith and the Creed* 5.11 (FOTC 27.328); and Maximus of Turin, *Sermon* 78.2 (CCL 23.325). Chrysologus makes this connection in *Sermon* 83.2 also. For other references, see J. A. de Aldama, *Virgo Mater: estudios de teologia patristica* (Granada: Faculty of Theology, 1963), 249–74; and B. Kochaniewicz, *La Vergine Maria nei sermoni di San Pietro Crisologo* (Rome: Pontifical Theological Faculty "Marianum," 1998), 149, n. 143.
12. See Lk 24.5.
13. In his sermons on the raising of Lazarus, Chrysologus makes a similar point that, in addition to the raising of one from the dead, those dead in faithlessness would rise to a newfound faith. See, e.g., *Sermons* 63.2 and 65.1 (FOTC 109.250–52, 260).
14. Literally, "minds" *(mentibus)*.

is entirely a thing of the past. Christ as Man suffered, died, and was buried; he is, lives, reigns, continues, and remains forever as God. Listen to the Apostle as he says: "Even if we came to know Christ according to the flesh, now we no longer know him in this way."[15] "That he died to sin, he died once for all, but he lives for God,"[16] that is, he lives as God.

5. But the angel *rolled back the stone, and sat upon it* (v.2). He sat in order to teach the Resurrection, not to relieve his weariness. A heavenly nature knows no weariness, it knows no fatigue. But the stone became the location for the angel's instruction-session, the chair of heavenly teaching, and the school of life, which had been put in place by the Jews to be the door of death, at the service of ashes, and to maintain grim silence.

6. *His appearance*, it says, *was like lightning, but his garments were like snow* (v.3). The brightness of his countenance is distinguished from the dazzling whiteness of his clothing, in that the angel's face is compared with lightning, and his clothing is compared to snow, because lightning comes from heaven and snow from the earth. Listen to the prophet as he says: "Praise the Lord from the earth, you fire, hail, and snow."[17] So in the face of the angel the brightness of the celestial nature is preserved, in his clothing the grace of communion with humanity is represented, and the appearance of the angel who is speaking is tempered, in such a way that eyes of flesh may both bear the gentle brightness of the clothing, and from the lightning-like gleam of his countenance tremble before the messenger of their Creator and stand in awe of him.

7. *But out of fear of him the guards were terrified* (v.4). Why terrified? Because they were standing guard with the zeal that stems from cruelty, not with the obedience coming from reverence. He is ruined, he is forsaken, he is unable to stand, he whom his conscience forsakes, and his guilt urges on. This is why the angel struck the unholy with terror but addressed these words of comfort to the holy: *Do not be afraid* (v.5). That is, "Let them be afraid: not the ones who seek, but those who persecute." *Do not*

---

15. 2 Cor 5.16.
16. Rom 6.10.
17. Ps 148.7–8.

be afraid; I know that you are seeking Jesus the Crucified. He is not here (vv.5–6). That is, "I have come to instruct you, not to remove him, because he it is who has both created us and raised himself up."

Do not be afraid, he is not here, he has risen as he said (vv.5–6). You see that the angel came so that as a servant he might verify with deeds what the Lord had predicted with words, and show that he had the power to die and to live, since before his own death he had predicted his Resurrection. For, to be sure, the One who was able to know was also able to avoid it; but because he was able to conquer he refused to evade it, because the glory of rising buried the dishonor of dying.

8. We shall treat what follows, brothers, in the following sermon,[18] because our weariness from so recent a journey[19] prevents us from prolonging and extending this sermon.

---

18. *Sermon* 76, where he begins with Mt 28.5–6, the last verses treated in this sermon, and he continues his discussion of the two Marys.

19. Chrysologus means the rigor of the final days of Lent. See n. 2 above.

SERMON 76

A Third on the Lord's Resurrection

N THE PREVIOUS SERMON we said that Mary and the other Mary prefigured the Church coming from two peoples.[1] We desire to confirm this today from what follows, provided that you give us a favorable hearing. *The angel, it says, said in response: "Do not be afraid, for I know that you are seeking Jesus who was crucified. He is not here, he has risen; come and see the place where the Lord had been laid"* (Mt 28.5–6). The angel first mentions the name, tells of the cross, speaks of the Passion, acknowledges the death, but next professes the Resurrection, and then professes the Lord. And thus the angel identifies him as his Lord after such great tortures and after the tomb, he speaks of his condition of servitude, and he realizes that all the dishonor of the Passion has been transformed into all the glory of the Resurrection.

Why then does the human being judge that God has been diminished[2] in the flesh, or think that his power became deficient in the Passion, or believe that his sovereignty was wasted away by his condition as a servant? Rightly does he say that he was crucified, rightly does he show the place where the Lord had been laid, lest it be believed that it was someone else and not he himself, one and the same, who rose from the dead.

---

1. See *Sermon* 75.3. In *Sermon* 75.8 Chrysologus promises this *Sermon* 76 as a sequel; see also n. 18 on that passage. *Sermon* 76, in turn, was immediately followed by *Sermon* 82. See *Sermon* 75, n. 1. It is unclear whether Chrysologus preached every day during the Octave of Easter. If he did, then this *Sermon* 76 was preached on Easter Monday; if not, then whenever he preached next after Easter Sunday. See F. Sottocornola, *L'anno liturgico*, 172–73.

2. Chrysologus issues similar warnings against interpreting the Incarnation or Christ's suffering and death as a dishonor to or diminishment of God. See *Sermon* 58.5 and n. 15 (FOTC 109.223), *Sermon* 59.4 (FOTC 109.226), and *Sermon* 84.6.

SERMON 76

And if the Lord returns with the same flesh, brings back his wounds, still bears the very holes from the nails, and makes these pieces of evidence, which had been the indignities inflicted on his body in the Passion, into proofs of his Resurrection, why does the human being think that he will return in someone else's flesh rather than in his own? Or is it perhaps that the servant disdains his own flesh, when the Lord did not change ours? Be content, O man, that you will be yourself in your own flesh, lest you not be yourself, if you rise in flesh that is not yours.[3]

2. The angel added: *Go and tell his disciples that he has risen and will go ahead of you to Galilee, and there you will see him* (v.7). The angel here is not sending women, but sending the one Church in the two women;[4] he sends her, in order by sending her to spread her far and wide. The angel here is sending the bride to the Bridegroom. And so the Lord *met them* as they were going and greeted them: *Hello!* (v.9) *He met them*, and did not terrify them with his power, but came before them with burning charity; he did not disturb them with his might, but he greeted them; he subjects them to the law of betrothal and not to his sovereign majesty, but he honors them with a spouse's love.[5]

He greets them: *Hello!* He had said to his disciples: "Greet no one along the way";[6] and why is it that he comes upon them and greets them here so hastily along the way? He does not wait to be identified, he does not seek to be recognized, he does not permit any questions, but he comes forward solely to greet them, he comes forward impetuously, and he himself abolishes his own mandate by his greeting. He did it, yes, he did it, because the power of love conquers and surpasses all. As soon as Christ greets himself in his Church, he has made it thus become his flesh, he has thus taken it to be his Body, as the Apostle says: "And he is the head of the Body, the Church."[7]

---

3. A similar affirmation about one's personal identity surviving in eternal life is made in *Sermon* 60.16 (FOTC 109.236). In addition, in *Sermon* 88.6 (FOTC 17.142), Chrysologus explicitly refutes any notion of transmigration of souls.

4. See *Sermon* 75.3 and nn. 7 and 8.

5. Love has precedence over fear also in *Sermon* 80.6 (FOTC 17.130–31), treating the same biblical text.

6. Lk 10.4.   7. Col 1.18.

In fact the very reality shows clearly that in these women the Church is perfectly prefigured, since Christ convinces his disciples in their hesitancy about the Resurrection, he strengthens them in their anxiety by showing them his side and the nail marks, and by his consumption of food he calls them back to faith, but only with difficulty. For this reason it was appropriate for him to call the ones deficient in faith "children," when he said: "Children, do you have anything to eat?"[8]

And elsewhere he calls Mary, who was herself weeping as if for a dead man, "Woman," and does not give her permission to touch him;[9] but he finds them so perfected, so full of trust, so lacking in anxiety for women, but hastening to the mystery, seeking their Lord with such complete and ardent faith, that he lets himself be held by them, and he greets them with: *Hello,* that is, "Have me for yourselves."[10] The angel had said, *that you are seeking Jesus the Crucified* (v.5), and Christ responded to them in their search, *Hello.* However, elsewhere Mary was not allowed to touch him;[11] here it was permitted to them not only to touch but even to embrace him completely.

3. *But they came up,* it says, *and held his feet* (v.9). They hold Christ's feet whose haste makes them a type, and deservedly so, of the preaching of the Gospel in the Church, and by their faith they touch the footsteps of their Savior,[12] to such an extent that they attain to the glory and reach the honor of the whole Deity. But it is right that she hears: "Do not touch me,"[13] since she weeps on earth for the Lord, and looks for his corpse in the tomb, to such an extent that she does not know that he is reigning in heaven with the Father. "Do not touch me," that is, "Do not pay homage with the touch of your flesh to the one whom

---

8. Jn 21.5. See also *Sermon* 78.4 for the "littleness" or deficiency in faith of some of the disciples.

9. See Jn 20.15 and 17.

10. Chrysologus engages in wordplay with the two verbs: *avete* and *habetote.* The same wordplay is found in *Sermon* 80.6, although this sentence is omitted from the translation in FOTC 17.131.

11. See Jn 20.17.

12. See Is 52.7. On the women being a type of the Church, see section 2 and n. 4 above.

13. Jn 20.17.

you ought to have touched with the touch of faith, and do not presume to touch him on earth as if he were only a man, since you do not yet have the wisdom to adore him as God in heaven.

"Let the woman's concern cease, let feminine solicitude desist, let manly belief come into your mind, let the breadth of your heart grasp my Ascension, so that you may enjoy completely the blessedness of touching me eternally in heaven, according to the words of the prophet: 'Blessed is the man whose help is from you,' Lord; 'in his heart is the ascent to you.'"[14] The one on earth who does not ascend by faith to Christ in heaven does not touch Christ with his hand.

And so one and the same Mary is at one moment established on the summit of faith, raised aloft on the pinnacle of the Church, and touches and holds Christ with complete and holy affection; at another moment she is brought low and is wavering on account of the weakness of the flesh and feminine feebleness and is not worthy to touch her Creator. This causes no difficulty, since she is the former as a symbol, she is the latter from her sex; the former comes from divine glory, the latter from human nature, because likewise for us when we know divine things, it is a gift from God; when we are humanly wise, we are blinded from our own devices. Thus is Peter blessed while he recognizes Christ as the Son of God by the revelation of the Father,[15] but when he denies Christ he experiences and suffers the blindness of the flesh.[16]

4. Meanwhile, the Jews either wickedly buy their crimes, or, even worse, they sell someone else's, while setting a price on sins, paying out money in compensation for offenses, and pouring out in wicked deeds what they gathered with all wickedness. So they procure Judas as the betrayer of their Lord, and they settle on a price for the blood of the Redeemer of the world;[17] so with a purse they seal off faith in the opened tomb, so as to purchase with cash acquired by sins the sin of denying the Resurrection.

They gave the soldiers, it says, *a large sum of money and said: "Say*

---

14. Ps 83.6 LXX; Ps 84.5.
15. See Mt 16.16–17.
16. See Mt 26.69–75.
17. See Mt 26.15.

that his disciples came at night, and stole him while we were asleep. And if the governor hears about it, we shall persuade him and keep you safe." And they took the money and did as they had been taught, and that is the story that has spread among the Jews to this very day (vv.12–15). *Among the Jews:* but not among the Christians? Jew, what you were trying to conceal in Judea with gold, has shone and radiated throughout the whole world by faith. The disciples received Christ, they did not steal him; you have procured unbelief, but you have not stolen the truth. O Jew, Christ has risen, and you have lost your money. "His blood be on us and on our children."[18] O Jew, Christ is alive, but you have killed yourself and your descendants.[19]

18. Mt 27.25.
19. See *Sermon* 80.8 (FOTC 17.131–32) for similar remarks.

SERMON 77

A Fourth on the Lord's Resurrection[1]

T IS AN UNMISTAKABLE indication of complete and perfect devotion that at the time of the Passion all creation suffers together with its Creator. When the earth trembled, what flesh did not tremble, what mind did not become paralyzed, what innate talent has not been found wanting, when the sun set ahead of time, and when light dissipated? And so, brothers, our body also slumped over at that time, our capacity to understand died with him, our speech has been buried with its Creator, so as to be raised up to give him all the glory. This was the reason for my silence, this was why I was delayed in paying what I owed you, as I promised.[2]

And it is no wonder, brothers, if with all due respect and affection my preaching providentially followed its Provider even to the underworld, because without him I had nothing to give back to you, such great and good creditors as you are. But if there is anyone who is eager and zealous to exact his due and complains about the tardiness of the payment, let him not cease from raising objections about time, because my rich Lord increases the interest rate and pays back far greater interest on

---

1. This sermon was preached on Easter Sunday morning, when the Resurrection account from the Gospel of Matthew was read. As indicated below in n. 2, *Sermons* 74 (FOTC 17.128–32), 75, and 77 all refer to Chrysologus's lack of preaching at the end of Lent, making it very likely that it was his custom not to preach during Passiontide (see *Sermon* 72a, n. 2). I agree with the assessment of F. Sottocornola, *L'anno liturgico*, 86–87 and 170–73. By contrast, V. Zangara, "I silenzi nella predicazione di Pietro Crisologo," *Rivista di Storia e Letteratura Religiosa* 32 (1996): 228–30, claims that the references to the preacher's silence in *Sermons* 74, 75, and 77 are exceptions to Chrysologus's usual practice of preaching during Passiontide, but Zangara fails to provide convincing evidence for this assertion.

2. See *Sermons* 74.1 (FOTC 17.123) and 75.1 for other examples of Chrysologus's not preaching in the period immediately preceding Easter.

this very loan. So let the bountiful kindness of the Gospel reading now absolve us whom the obligations of our office have led and put into such great debt.

2. *On the evening of the Sabbath,* it says, *which was beginning to dawn on the first day of the week* (Mt 28.1). In the rising of the Lord not only is the law of human nature altered, but even the very order of creation is changed in a remarkable way. It is *the evening that was beginning to dawn.* Notice that when the Lord rises, evening does not bring darkness, but it begins to dawn, and what had been accustomed to be the start of night becomes the beginning of light.³ *The evening that was beginning to dawn on the first day of the week.*

Just as mortality is being transformed into immortality, corruption into incorruption, flesh into God, so darkness is being transformed into light, such that night itself rejoices that it did not perish in this circumstance, but has merely been changed; it has surrendered its hold on gloom rather than on time; it was more than happy to lose the periodic cycles of its enslavement, so as to flow freely and burst forth into the liberty of unending light, as the prophet says: "And night is my illumination for my delights."⁴

3. *In the evening, which was dawning on the first day of the week.* The Sabbath is happy that it has become second; the Sabbath, which by the command of the Law was groggy with leisure, now on account of the primacy of the Lord's day is wondrously roused for works of divine power. The inactivity based on Jewish observance was making it a stranger to beneficial works of power, as the Lord says: "Is it unlawful on the Sabbath to grant a cure to the sick, aid to the afflicted, sight to the blind, and life to the dead?"⁵ And by interpreting it in this fashion they had

---

3. This alteration of the order of nature as a result of Jesus' Resurrection is also indicated in *Sermons* 74.2 (FOTC 17.124) and 75.2. F. Sottocornola, *L'anno liturgico,* 171, notes that such statements of night becoming light are christological and not liturgical; that is, Chrysologus is not speaking about the liturgical setting being night. Hence this is not an allusion to an Easter Vigil service. All three of these sermons on the Resurrection according to Matthew were most likely preached on Easter Sunday morning.
4. Ps 138.11 LXX.
5. See Mk 3.4.

wretchedly consigned a day intended by God for the study of the sacred Law merely to enslavement to their bellies.

4. *In the evening, which was dawning on the first day of the week, Mary Magdalene and the other Mary came* (v.1). *Mary:* she came in name only one, she who the reading now says is "the other," in terms of being a different person. *Mary and the other Mary came,* whereby both the unity of name would represent one in two, and the difference of persons would reveal that the woman had been changed. For *she came,* not "they came";[6] and when it says *the other,* it designates with mystic language that the same person is in both, in order to show that one came before faith and another would return after faith. The woman came, but Mary returns; there came the one who brought death, there returns the one who gave birth to life;[7] there came the one who led Adam down to the underworld, there returns the one who received Christ from the underworld.

5. *Mary and the other Mary came.* Why? *To see the tomb* (v.1), and not to look for Christ.[8] Merely to see the tomb, the proof of her guilt, the grim evidence of her wicked deed, of her presumptuous collaboration with the devil, the fatal business she transacted, so that she might recover her faith from the very place from which she was enduring the unending shame of her transgression.

6. *And suddenly a great earthquake occurred* (v.2). If the earth shook so much when the Lord rises to pardon his people, how much will it quake when he will come to punish the guilty? As the prophet says: "The earth trembled when God arose in judgment."[9] And that which could not endure the presence of fellow servants, that is, angels, how will it ever endure the awesome presence of the Lord?

7. *An angel of the Lord,* it says, *came down from heaven, and rolled*

---

6. Chrysologus emphasizes that the verb is singular: *venit* rather than the plural *venerunt.*
7. This contrast between Eve and Mary the new Eve is also found in *Sermon* 74.3 (FOTC 17.124–25); in *Sermon* 79.2 the contrast is between Eve as bearer of death and now a woman as bearer of the news of life, but without explicit reference to the Virgin Mary.
8. See *Sermon* 75.3.
9. Ps 75.9–10 LXX; Ps 76.8–9.

back the stone, and sat upon it (v.2). Truly, as the Apostle says, "Who has known the mind of the Lord?"[10] See how human salvation is recovered along the same lines by which it had been lost.[11] The woman, first in faithlessness, is the first to be brought to faith; she is the first to run to the destroyer of death, she who had been the first to run to the author of death. She was the first to run, and she was the first to hear from an angel, she who had been the first to converse with the devil.

An angel came down from heaven and sat down on the stone, not to bring about the Resurrection by such an action, but to reveal it,[12] as the Lord says: "I have the power to lay down my life, and I have the power to take it up."[13] He opens up what had remained shut to us, he discloses what had been hidden from us, and he does not lead out into daylight his Creator, who was no longer in the tomb, but he brings his fellow servants, who had been stuck in the darkness of doubt, to faith in the Resurrection, as he himself attests when he says: *He is not here, he has risen* (v.6).

8. *He rolled back the stone, and sat upon it.* Why is it that he did not roll it, but *rolled it back?* So that the stone which, according to the prophet, the unbelief of the Pharisees rolled forward as a stumbling block and scandal, the angel would roll back for faith and salvation, as the prophet says: "See, I am placing in Zion a stone of stumbling and a rock of scandal."[14] So the stone is rolled back, so that what had locked life up when it was rolled forward, would roll death away, as Scripture says: "You will see your life hanging on wood."[15]

And he sat upon it, not to revive himself from weariness, but

---

10. Rom 11.34; 1 Cor 2.16.
11. In two of his sermons on the Annunciation and Birth of Christ (*Sermons* 142.1 and 148.5 [FOTC 17.251]) Chrysologus says something very similar, namely, that salvation in Christ reverses the events of the Fall, in that it retraces the same steps that had led to humanity's downfall so as now to occasion a renewal, a restoration, and new life. On the ways in which the Latin patristic tradition took up Irenaeus's theme of "recapitulation," see J.-P. Jossua, *Le Salut, Incarnation ou Mystère Pascal chez les Pères de l'Église de saint Irénée à saint Léon le Grand* (Paris: Cerf, 1968), esp. 227–37 on Chrysologus.
12. See *Sermons* 75.4 and 80.3 (FOTC 17.129).
13. Jn 10.18. 14. Is 28.16.
15. Dt 28.66.

to show in this way that he was the guardian of the sacred and life-giving tomb,[16] and in carrying out a ministry from heaven he was declaring by this kind of gesture, namely, taking his seat, that death was destroyed, and that he who had suffered was God, God who had been received in the narrow confines of our body, God to whom the speaker clothed in heavenly attire and sitting in this manner was bearing witness. And why need I say more, brothers? He is seated, because from so venerable a tomb as that the angel never departs.

9. *But for fear of him the guards were terrified, and became like dead men* (v.4). Death returns to the accomplices whom terror overwhelms in their guilt. Thus, thus when the innocent will rise up, terror and death will gain possession of the unjust and the unholy. *And his appearance was like lightning, and his garments like snow* (v.3). What is the point of clothing when there is no nakedness? What is the reason for apparel when there is no need for covering? But the angel, brothers, prefigures in this way our condition, our form, our likeness at the resurrection, when the human being is clothed in the very brilliance coming from his own body,[17] as the Lord says: "Then the just will gleam like the sun in my Father's kingdom."[18]

10. *But the angel said in response to the women: "Do not be afraid, for I know that you are looking for Jesus who was crucified"* (v.5). They were looking for one who was still crucified and dead, they whose faith the brutal violence of the Passion had thrown into turmoil, and the burden of this trial had bent them over so far that they were still looking for the Lord of heaven in the grim tomb. *He is not here*, in the way he was in that place, but he is here to the extent that he is everywhere, and is not limited by a location's size.

Come and see the place where the Lord had been laid (v.6). The angel calls the woman to see, so that the place of his sacred Body

---

16. In *Sermons* 74.6 (FOTC 17.126–27) and 75.5 Chrysologus likewise states that the angel did not sit because of any weariness, but those other two sermons, unlike this one, attribute the angel's being seated to his purpose of instructing about the Resurrection.

17. See *Sermons* 74.6 (FOTC 17.127) and 82.5, regarding the similarity of the angel's appearance to that of the risen human body in the future.

18. Mt 13.43.

would cleanse her eyes, which the sight of the forbidden apple on the tree[19] had defiled and the devil had shut. They enter the tomb, so that having been buried with the Lord they may rise up to have a fully saving faith.[20] "If we have been joined together with him in a death like his, so too shall we be in a resurrection like his."[21]

11. *Go and tell his disciples* (v.7). Go back to man now as a healed woman, and urge him to believe, you who urged him not to believe; bring back to man evidence of the Resurrection, to whom you earlier brought forward your advice of temptation and ruin.

19. See Gn 3.6.
20. This idea of a resurrection in faith is mentioned in two of the sermons on the raising of Lazarus (*Sermons* 63.2 and 65.1 [FOTC 109.252, 260]) and in two other sermons on Jesus' Resurrection (*Sermons* 75.4 and 80.5 [FOTC 17.130]).
21. Rom 6.5.

SERMON 78

A Fifth on the Lord's Resurrection[1]

FTER THAT TEMPEST OF the Lord's Passion, which had never before been experienced on earth, which filled the heavens with dread, which was unheard of at any time, and unbearable to the underworld, the Lord came to the sea and found his disciples adrift in the darkness of night. For after the sun fled, what relief from the night could come from the light of the moon or from the stars? For a somber and disorienting gloom was all there was which kept in darkness not only bodily vision, but even the mind's own capacity to see, and it kept preventing the sailors from seeking or trying to reach again the shore of faith and the port of safety.[2]

2. *As soon as morning had broken,* the evangelist says, *Jesus stood on the shore, but the disciples did not recognize that it was Jesus* (Jn 21.4). All creation had fled the indignity done to the Creator, the world strove to keep away from the murder of its Lord, realizing that vengeance extends to the whole house in which the master was killed by the criminal behavior of the servants.

This is why the earth shook with its foundations coming apart beneath it, the sun fled so as not to see it, the light of day departed so as not to be an accessory; rocks, since they were unable to leave on account of their nature, were rent in two by means of a novel kind of blow, accusing such a terrible deed by their noise, since they could not with words;[3] when hell saw the Judge himself penetrating it, it wailed in its defeat as it lost those whom it was holding. Consequently, it happened that the souls restored to their bodies announced to the living that the

---

1. This sermon was preached during the Easter season, perhaps during the Octave. See F. Sottocornola, *L'anno liturgico,* 86.
2. Or the "harbor of salvation" *(portum salutis).*
3. For a similar description of the chaos at Christ's death, see *Sermon* 72a.2.

dead, who the world had thought had utterly perished, would rise again.[4]

3. So, when in this fashion all the underpinnings of the world were askew in confusion and disorder, and believed that they were tumbling down to the primordial darkness and the ancient chaos[5] because of the death of its Creator, all of a sudden the Lord restored daylight by the light of his Resurrection, and refashioned the whole world into its original form, so that the world, which he saw had suffered with him to such an extent, he would raise up with him to his own glory.

And so the evangelist says: *As soon as morning had broken*, that is, "after the night of the Lord's Passion had passed," *Jesus stood on the shore*, so that he might call the universe back within its old boundaries, make strong what was wavering, rein in what had exceeded its bounds, compose what had been disturbed, and by his standing there stabilize the very foundations of the world, which had been so shaken, so that the world returned at once to the service of its Creator, the same world that had dispersed at the indignity done to its Creator.

4. *But when morning had broken Jesus stood on the shore*, so that the Church above all, in which the disciples were then being tossed about by the waves of the sea, he might lead back to firmness of faith in him. And so because he had found them destitute of any power of faith and thoroughly lacking any manly strength, he scolded them, such as they were, by calling them "children," when he addressed these words to them: *Children, do you have anything to eat?* (v.5) For there they were: Peter, who had denied;[6] Thomas, who had doubted;[7] and John, who had fled.[8]

4. See Mt 27.45, 51–53.
5. See Gn 1.2.
6. See Mt 26.69–75, and parallels.
7. See Jn 20.24–29.
8. See Mk 14.51–52 and *Sermon* 84.5. Chrysologus often couples the denial of Peter and the flight of John, while omitting the doubts of Thomas. See *Sermons* 81.3, 150.4, 161.7, and 170.5 (FOTC 17.280). On the identification of the young man in Mk 14 with John, see Ambrose, *Expositio Psalmorum XII* 36.53 (CSEL 64.111–12); here, however, John is not criticized for fleeing but commended for leaving behind all his possessions to follow Jesus! See also Gregory the Great, *Moralia in Iob* 14.49.57 (CCL 143A.732), where the fleeing John musters enough courage to return and be present at the cross with Jesus' mother (Jn 19.25–27).

Therefore, he addresses them not as the bravest of soldiers, but as timid children; and since he finds them not yet fit for battle, he invites them as fragile youths to the table, when he says: *Children, do you have anything to eat?* He does this so that kindness may call them back to grace, bread to confidence, and food to faith. For they would not believe that his Body had risen unless they saw him eating in a completely human fashion. The reason why the One who completely fills the universe asks for food, why the Bread himself eats, is not because he hungers for food, but because he always hungers for the love of his own people.

5. *"Children, do you have anything to eat?" They answered: "No"* (v.5). And what did they have who did not have Christ, who was located so close to them? What did they have who did not yet see with their own eyes the Lord standing in front of them? *But the disciples*, it says, *did not recognize that it was Jesus* (v.4). *He said to them: "Cast your net over the right side of the boat, and you will find something"* (v.6). He calls back to the right side those whom the storm of the Passion had driven and reduced to the left.[9] *They cast it*, it says, *and they were not able to haul it in because of the great number of fish* (v.6). They had cast to the right, they had cast to the manly part, but as children they were not yet able to haul it in. Nevertheless, they realized from how heavy it was, they realized that the fish had come at the command of the One who gave the order, and that they had not been captured by human skill.

6. *That disciple who was loved by Jesus said: "It is the Lord!"* (v.7) The one who is loved is the first one to see, because the eye of love always gazes more intently, and the one who is loved always perceives things more keenly. *When Peter heard this* (v.7). What had slowed down Peter's mind so much that he who had been accustomed to bring news to the rest now heard from another that it was the Lord? Where is that singular testimony of his: "You are the Christ, the Son of the living God"?[10] Where is it? He lost it in the house of Caiaphas the leader of the Jews. He

---

9. The Latin *sinister* connotes not only location on the "left" but weakness, evil, and sin, as in Mt 25.33 and 41. See also *Sermon* 58.9 (FOTC 109.224).

10. Mt 16.16.

was more tardy in seeing the Lord, after having found it easy to hear the voice of a murmuring servant-girl.[11]

When he heard it, it says, *he put on his tunic, for he was naked* (v.7). It is a wonder, brothers! When the Lord was arrested, John took off his linen cloth,[12] and Peter was found naked, since John's escape covered him up, while Peter's denial thus left him naked. And it is a wonder, brothers, truly a wonder, that the one who was naked in the boat, put on some clothes before jumping into the sea, because innocence is never naked, and guilt always hastens to take cover. And so, just like Adam,[13] now Peter also attempts to cover his nakedness after his sin, both of whom had at any rate before their sin been clothed in holy nakedness.

7. *He put on his tunic, and plunged into the sea* (v.7) so that the sea might wash what his denial had made so dirty. He *plunged into the sea,* so that the one who had received the primacy[14] of rank might be the first to return. And *he put on his tunic,* he who was to be girt with the suffering of martyrdom, as the Lord said: *Another will gird you, and lead you where you do not want to go* (v.18).

The others arrive by boat, and haul along their catch of fish, in order to bring with them to the Lord the results of their faithful labor, namely, the Church tossed about by the storms of this world and those whom they catch with the net of the Gospel and raise out of the deep to the light from above. *They were not far from the land,* it says (v.8). They were not far from "the land of the living,"[15] since the end of the present order had already made them very close to the future. *But only about two hundred cubits* (v.8). From the Jews and the gentiles he doubles the number one hundred, he who by being the Lord of the two peoples joins together the life and salvation of them both for glory.

8. We shall discuss the remaining part of the reading in our next sermon with the Lord's help.[16]

---

11. See Mt 26.57–58 and 69–75.   12. See Mk 14.51–52.
13. See Gn 2.25; 3.7 and 11.
14. The primacy or "headship" *(principatus)* of Peter is also mentioned in *Sermons* 8.6 (FOTC 109.45) and 154.3 (FOTC 17.260–61).
15. Ps 26 (27).13.
16. This subsequent sermon is not extant.

SERMON 79

A Sixth on the Lord's Resurrection

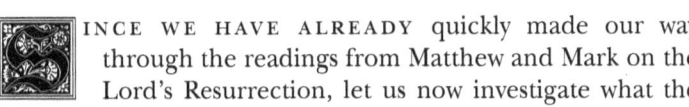INCE WE HAVE ALREADY quickly made our way through the readings from Matthew and Mark on the Lord's Resurrection, let us now investigate what the most blessed Luke has proclaimed about it.[1] *On the first day of the week*, he says, women *came to the tomb bringing the spices that they had prepared* (Lk 24.1). We have often said that the events surrounding the Lord's Resurrection form the pattern for our resurrection.[2] This is why the Evangelists relate the sequence of Christ's deeds in language that is more mystical than it is new. *On the first day of the week*, he says. It is appropriate that he said *first*,[3] because the day of the Resurrection knows no other; the mother of eternal light[4] has no knowledge of nighttime; a day without end shines on those whose life is without end; the light of those who rise is unable to die; the light that conquers the night cannot be extinguished.

2. *They came to the tomb*, it says, *bringing the spices that they had prepared, and when they came they found the stone rolled back, and upon entering* the tomb *they did not find Jesus' body* (vv.1–3). Why is it that earlier they had run away from the tomb, but now they boldly return to the grave, return unafraid to the terrible burial place, confidently rush into the sadness of the grave, and when

---

1. This sermon was preached most likely after *Sermon* 83, on the conclusion of Mk 16, and perhaps on the Thursday of the Easter Octave (see *Sermon* 75, n. 1; F. Sottocornola, *L'anno liturgico*, 173–74; and A. Olivar, *Los sermones*, 265).

2. See, e.g., *Sermons* 60.16 (FOTC 109.236), 74.6 (FOTC 17.127), 76.1, and 77.9.

3. The Latin word translated here as "first" is *una*, which also means "one alone," "unique," and "solitary"; Chrysologus is making use of all these meanings here.

4. In contrast to the dawn of Resurrection as "the mother of eternal light," in *Sermon* 74.2 Chrysologus refers to evening as "the mother of night" (FOTC 17.124).

they do not find the Lord, they persistently search, they more persistently linger, and they do not tremble at the fact that, in addition to everything else, it is night which, by generating darkness, increases the fear engulfing the tomb?

Brothers, woman is the source of evil,[5] the author of sin, the way of death, the reason for the grave, hell's entryway, and the whole explanation of the need for lamentation. For this reason they are born with tears, they are delivered with sadness, they are brought forth with groans, and they are as strong in lamentation as they are found to be weak in strength; and they are as unequipped for labors as they are equipped for tears. Thus it is that they conquer arms with tears, they fell kingdoms with their weeping, and they break all the strength of men with their lamentation.

And so it is no wonder if the women here seem more ardent than the apostles for tears, the burial place, the grave, and for paying reverence to the Lord's body,[6] when a woman is the first to proceed to tears, since she was the first to fall into guilt; she leads the way to the grave, since she led the way to death; she becomes the messenger of the Resurrection, since she was the agent of death; and she who had brought the man the message of such destruction, herself brings men the announcement of great salvation, in order to compensate with her message of faith for what she took away by her faithless announcement.[7]

3. The order here is not reversed, but mystical; the apostles are not ranked behind the women, but they are kept for greater things.[8] The women take up reverent service to Christ, the apostles take up the sufferings of Christ; the former bear

---

5. See Sir 25.23 (24).

6. Reading the variant *ad obsequium dominici corporis feminae ardentiores apostolis hic videntur* (see PL 52.423) instead of *ab obsequium dominici corpus feminae ardentiores apostoli sic videntur* from Olivar's CCL text.

7. Chrysologus often plays up the antithesis between woman as the means whereby death entered the world and woman as new Eve, bearer of life as Mary, and messenger of life and resurrection. See, for example, *Sermons* 63.3 and n. 11 (FOTC 109.252–53), 64.2 and n. 7 (FOTC 109.255–57), 65.4 (FOTC 109.261–62), 74.3 (FOTC 17.124–25), 77.4–5, 80.3–4 (FOTC 17.129–30), 99.5, and 142.9. On this topic, see Ambrose, *Expositio Evangelii secundum Lucam* 10.156 (CCL 14.390): "Through the mouth of a woman death had formerly begun its course; through the mouth of a woman life is restored."

8. On this same point, see *Sermons* 75.3 and 80.4 (FOTC 17.130).

spices, the latter stripes; the former enter the tomb, the latter the prison; the women hasten in reverent service, the apostles hurry to their chains; the women pour oil, the apostles shed their blood; the former are astounded at death, the latter accept death.

And why need I say more? The women remain at home, the apostles head for the battle line, and as dedicated soldiers they manifest their faith in the midst of adversities, their strength in labors, their patience in suffering indignities, their death in facing perils, their endurance in wounds, their allegiance in tortures, and their constancy in the mangling of their flesh. So the women bring their tears for Christ, and the apostles bring back[9] to Christ both victory and triumph when the devil is overcome and their enemies are conquered.

4. But as to the fact that the apostles either did not believe that the Lord had risen when the women relayed the message, or were said to have judged it nonsense, let no one blame them severely.[10] He doubts deeply who believes more deeply. The one who is not inclined to listen is unable to be deceived. He is very foolish if after a previous example he is not found to be on his guard. It is an inexperienced soldier who when he rushes to the battle line does not know the cause of the war, and is unaware of the power of the opponent. It is experience, it is not sluggishness, when a veteran soldier proceeds tentatively.

So the novice Adam fell quickly, while he was quick to believe; and while he readily gives his ears to listen to the woman, he has consigned himself and his posterity to the worst enemy.[11] But Peter as a man of experience does not readily listen to a woman, he is slow to believe what the women have to say, and he deliberates as one who has experience, in order not to make a childish mistake.

And so when two of the disciples, who after the Resurrection were counted worthy of having Christ as a companion on their journey, returned with the news that they had seen the Lord,

---

9. The Latin verb *referunt* also means "refer" or "ascribe." Chrysologus may be intending both the notion that the apostles dedicate their victory to Christ and the idea that they credit Christ and his grace with their achievement of such a victory.

10. See Lk 24.11.   11. See Gn 3.

the apostles do not consider what they hear to be nonsense, but worthy of men;[12] they give their ears, they direct their gaze, they open their eyes, they unseal their hearts, they commit what is said to their minds to such an extent that after having vacillated in reluctance they are eager to drink up what they have heard in faith from the river that the tongue of their companions was pouring out.

5. Just as cold drinks quench a burning thirst, so does happier news refresh[13] people's minds after sorrow. Brothers, who is able to grasp the reasons for the Lord's birth? Who is able to assess the significance of the Lord's Resurrection? Who is worthy of appraising the matter of Christ's Resurrection? No one will be able to consider, grasp, evaluate, and understand these matters unless he receives the power from God Himself.

That the Creator of the universe is born of a woman, that the Lord of the world[14] is seen in the servile condition of a human, that the Shepherd of all needs to eat, that the Judge of heaven is examined by guilty judges, that he is condemned who forgives everyone, that the Life of the world is punished, that he who raises the dead dies, that the One who encompasses all things is encompassed in a tomb, and that the God of the celestial realm is found within the underworld:[15] the one who can grasp these matters is not surprised when he examines on a deep level the apostles' periods of hesitation, alarm, fear, flight, and hiding.

So, brothers, that the apostles doubt, that they are slow to accept these things on faith, let us not be surprised, since we do not even believe this much, but let us pray, brothers, that we may be considered worthy of understanding as much from these things as he has given, he who grants the human being an understanding of divine realities.

6. In the next sermon we shall investigate, with God's help, what follows and is left to be considered in the reading.[16]

12. See Lk 24.13–35.
13. Reading the variant *refrigerat* rather than the *refrigerant* of Olivar's CCL text.
14. For a similar pairing of titles for Christ, see *Sermon* 50.3 (FOTC 109.194–95).
15. For a similar list of antitheses, see *Sermon* 72b.2 and n. 7.
16. This subsequent sermon is not extant.

SERMON 81

An Eighth on the Lord's Resurrection[1]

WHILE REBELLIOUS JUDEA STRIVES to vanquish its Creator and raise unholy hands for the murder of its Author, it has removed peace from the earth, it has dissolved the harmony of the universe, and it has so ruptured what joined the elements together, that it was drawing the whole world back to its ancient chaos. And so it puts day to flight with night, it attacks light with darkness, it removes heaven from the universe, it makes the earth quake, it mingles the dead with the living, it jumbles together those who dwell in the lower and the upper worlds, and with the whole order among creatures disrupted it leaves absolutely nothing that is peaceful or harmonious. That is why when Christ returned from the underworld, so that he might restore peace to the universe,[2] he exclaims: *Peace be with you!* (Lk 24.36)

2. *While* the disciples *were speaking*, it says, Jesus *stood in their midst and said to them: "Peace be with you!"* (v.36) It was well that he added *with you*, because the earth had already stood firm, day had returned, the sun had come back, and the physical structure of the world already had its order restored. But war was still raging for the disciples, and the conflict between faith and faithlessness was brutally crushing them. The turbulence of the Passion had not shaken the earth as severely as

---

1. This sermon was likely preached toward the end of the Easter Octave some time after *Sermon* 79, and preceded by at least one sermon on the intervening verses of Luke (24.4–35) that is not extant. See *Sermon* 75, n. 1; F. Sottocornola, *L'anno liturgico*, 172–74; and A. Olivar, *Los sermones*, 265–66.

2. The sympathy of creation toward the death of its Creator is a theme in many of Chrysologus's sermons on Christ's death and Resurrection. See *Sermons* 72a.2, 74.4 (FOTC 17.125), 77.1, 78.1–3, 82.2, and 83.1 (FOTC 17.134).

39

the disciples' hearts,[3] and so the battle between belief and unbelief, tenacious in its struggle, was devastating to their spirits.

A vast host of thoughts was weighing heavily on their minds, and their bodies, although strong, were being broken by attacks of despair and hope. The ideas and deliberations of the disciples were being borne to and fro between Christ's many miraculous signs and the wide variety of his sufferings, between the manifestations of his divinity and the weaknesses of his flesh, and between what he lost in death and what he gave in life.

At one moment their spirit was being raised up to heaven, the next moment their soul came crashing down to earth, and with such a storm seething deep within them they were unable to find any calm harbor, any peaceful port. When Christ the Scrutinizer of hearts sees this, he who gives orders to the winds, who has command over storms, and merely at his nod changes tempests into tranquillity, right away he strengthens them with his peace, as he says:

3. *Peace be with you! It is I. Do not fear* (v.36). "It is I, the One who was crucified, dead, and buried. It is I, in and of myself God, but for your sake a man. *It is I*, not a spirit[4] in the form of flesh, but Truth itself in the flesh. *It is I*. Back from the dead, I am alive; back from the underworld, I am from heaven. It is I whom death has fled, at whom hell has trembled, whom Tartarus, shuddering, has confessed as God.

"*Do not fear:* Peter, on account of your denial;[5] John, on account of having fled;[6] all of you, on account of having deserted me,[7] of forming judgments about me with every one of your thoughts devoid of faith, and of still not believing even though you see me. *Do not fear, it is I*, who have called you by means of grace, have chosen and pardoned you, have sustained you by my steadfast kindness, have supported you with my love, and

---

3. The same point with similar terminology is made by Leo the Great, *Sermon* 73.1.2 (FOTC 93.322).

4. Or "ghost" *(spiritus)*.

5. See Mt 26.69–75 and parallels.

6. See Mk 14.51–52. For other references that identify the fleeing young man in Mk 14 with John, see *Sermon* 78.4 and n. 8.

7. See Mt 26.56 and parallels.

out of goodness alone I now take you back, because when a father receives his son, and when affection recovers its own, neither one is able to see any faults."

4. *In their confusion*, it says, *they thought that they were seeing a spirit* (v.37).[8] Why? Because the Lord had entered though the doors were locked.[9] So the disciples, overwhelmed and drowsy from their mourning, were attributing to Christ not what divine power can do, but what human nature perceives. *They thought that they were seeing a spirit.* For certainly it is true that a spirit of a human being passes into what is enclosed in the womb, in that it penetrates its walls, in order to enter the body enclosed within a confined body; thus when the soul grants to life its end, when it leaves the sweet dwelling of the body, it is not constrained by the confines of its home nor by any worldly barriers.

A heavenly substance cannot be enclosed within earthly prisons, according to the passage: "You do not know from where the Spirit comes or where it is going."[10] So after the Resurrection, when the Lord entered through locked doors, the disciples did not believe that he had a real[11] body, but had the idea that his soul had returned in the mere image of the flesh, like the corporeal images that are accustomed to appear to people when they are asleep. *They thought*, it says, *that they were seeing a spirit.*

Therefore, as we have said, within the disciples the wars of their thoughts were not subsiding: they were not subsiding, but the wars of their thoughts were growing greater and greater, the agitation in their minds was being augmented even by the very thing they saw, and every anxious doubt was originating from the very source where faith in the Resurrection was being affirmed. That he had come was the reality: that he had entered though the doors were locked was not a matter of faith; it was not a matter of faith but a matter of power; it was not a human event, but he was a man, such that there was a true body under the power of God, not an empty semblance of flesh in an

---

8. As in n. 4 above, *spiritus* can also be rendered "ghost."
9. See Jn 20.19 and 26.
10. Jn 3.8.
11. Literally, "firmness of body" *(soliditatem corporis).*

affront to the Resurrection. So in order to curb the conflicting thoughts originating from this, Christ responded:

5. *Why are you troubled, and why do these thoughts climb up into your hearts?* (v.38) It was well that he said *climb up* and not "climb down," because human thoughts, weighed down by the burden of the flesh, try to *climb up* to the lofty mystery of God, and in their very attempts they are crushed, thrown down, and plunge to the earth, if he who allows the human being to think divine thoughts does not help. *Why are you troubled, and why do these thoughts climb up into your hearts? Look at my hands and my feet* (vv.38–39).

Look at, that is to say: "Wake up." Why? "Because it is not a dream that you are looking at. *Look at my hands and my feet*, because you are not yet able to gaze upon my head on account of your heavy eyes. Look at the wounds to my flesh, since you are not looking at the works of God. Pay heed to the marks made by my enemies, because you have not yet paid heed to the signs of God.

"*Touch* (v.39), so that at least your hand may produce faith, since when your eye looks it is so blind. The eye does not see, so let your touch do the seeing: let your fingers explore the nail-marks, let your hands examine the deep wounds. Penetrate the holes in my hands, dig into my side, reopen my wounds,[12] because I cannot refuse my disciples for their faith what I did not refuse my cruel enemies for my punishment. Touch, touch, and in your diligent quest reach all the way to my bones, so that the bones at least may verify the true nature of my flesh, and the continuing existence of my wounds, at least, may attest to the fact that it is really I.

6. "I ask you, why do you not believe that I have risen, I who have raised up innumerable[13] dead people before your very eyes? Unless perhaps my power, which benefitted others, failed in my own regard, just as it was said to insult me as I hung on the cross: 'Hah, so the One who saved others cannot save him-

---

12. Similar expressions with the same emphasis on the physicality of Christ's risen body are found in *Sermons* 35.4 (FOTC 109.151), 83.3 (FOTC 17.135) and 84.8.

13. Chrysologus's rhetoric is a bit overblown here!

self. Let him come down from the cross, and we shall believe.'[14] And what is greater, to come down from the cross by dislodging the nails, or to come up from the underworld after trampling upon death?

"See, I have indeed saved myself, I have come up to the heights by smashing the chains of hell,[15] and, nevertheless, I have not found in you any faith in my divinity. Or is it perhaps that a three-day death takes away the credibility from faith? Didn't my voice call forth Lazarus, who was four-days dead and already emitting a stench, from the underworld before your eyes, and didn't my command call him back to life?[16] And if the servant rises after four days, why won't his Lord rise after three days?"[17]

7. *But still they did not believe on account of pure joy* (v.41). When longed-for joys have been given, it is hard to believe; when hopes have been fulfilled, one is dumbfounded. The reason that the apostles are astonished at Christ's Resurrection is that it happened more quickly than they had expected, and that they are so slow to believe is due not to their unbelief but to their love. For by examining their faith to such an extent they do not reject it, but they investigate it thoroughly, and while they pursue it more deeply, they greatly desire that what they see be true and not false.

Brothers, it was not the terror of unbelief, but the magnitude of the matter that made the apostles slow when confronted with these things and astonished in the face of such great events. It is not lack of faith but the uniqueness of the miracle that causes them not to see what is visible, not to know what is knowable, and not to believe what is believable. Brothers, before these wondrous deeds our nature is very much an infant, which unless it grows through God's involvement is unable to grasp mature matters and cannot perceive what is perfect. So what we cannot accomplish on our own, may God himself grant that we grasp and perceive through his aid.

---

14. Mt 27.42.
15. For the same expression with reference to the raising of Lazarus, see *Sermon* 65.9 (FOTC 109.266).
16. See Jn 11.38–44.
17. See *Sermon* 63.1 (FOTC 109.249–50) for a similar formulation.

SERMON 82

A Ninth on the Lord's Resurrection[1]

INCE SAINT MATTHEW HAS already pointed out in the interest of our salvation what he knew about the Lord's Resurrection, today let us also hear what blessed Mark has to say.[2] *And when the Sabbath had passed,* he says, *Mary Magdalene, Mary the mother of James, and Salome bought spices in order to come and anoint him* (Mk 16.1). In this text the women hasten with feminine devotion; they bring to the tomb not faith in One who is alive, but ointments for one who is dead; and they prepare for the duties of mourning for one who is buried instead of preparing for the joys of divine triumphs for One who is risen.

Woman, Christ accepted death so that death would die.[3] Christ, by being killed, killed what was killing everyone. Christ entered the tomb in order to open up hell. So, having abolished the authority of Tartarus, having destroyed the prison of hell, and having annihilated the very power of death, Christ

---

1. This sermon was the next one preached after the two sermons on Matthew's account of the Resurrection (*Sermons* 75–76), perhaps on Tuesday of the Octave of Easter (see F. Sottocornola, *L'anno liturgico,* 172–73, n. 13). In particular, in section 7 of this *Sermon* 82, Chrysologus makes reference to the women at the tomb representing the one Church from the two peoples, "as we have said." At the beginning of *Sermon* 76 he also made reference to the same interpretation, found in *Sermon* 75.3. See F. Sottocornola, *L'anno liturgico,* 88. A. Olivar, *Los sermones,* 265–66 and 277, in accord with Sottocornola, considers it more probable that this *Sermon* 82 followed *Sermon* 76, although he leaves open the possibility that it could instead have followed *Sermon* 80, which, like *Sermon* 76, was on the latter part of Mt 28.

2. See *Sermon* 75, n. 1, regarding the sequencing of the Gospel texts during Easter in Ravenna.

3. Chrysologus frequently makes this or a similar formulation. See *Sermons* 40.4 and 57.7 (FOTC 17.88, 108), and *Sermons* 58.15, 59.8, and 60.8 (FOTC 109.224, 227–28, 235).

now should not be anointed as a dead man, but should be adored as Victor.

2. The women stay up all night, keep vigil, do without sleep, they enter the darkness as dawn begins to burst forth, whereby it seems that they find the light to be dim in their heart no less than for their body. *And very early in the morning*, it says, *they came to the tomb, as soon as the sun had risen* (v.2). If *very early in the morning*, then how is it that the sun had just risen? Does the evangelist thus not know what he is saying? The evangelist knows what he is saying, but he does not know what the one who has not learned hears. This narrative is not erroneous but true, and it does not suffer from a lapse in human speech, but reveals the truth of heavenly accomplishments.

He had said: "From noon until three in the afternoon it became dark."[4] Therefore, the sun, which had departed at the hour when the Lord began to suffer the Passion, came to meet him ahead of the time when he rose; in order to die with its Creator, it had put to death its own midday brightness, and, in order to rise with its Creator, it vanquished the darkness and burst forth before dawn. *Very early in the morning*, because the sun then came out in order to make it morning, and the same sun that had fled before nightfall, now came ahead of time to put the night to flight, so that the night would restore to light the hours which it had usurped in the terror of the Lord's Passion.[5]

3. *They were saying to one another*, it says, *"Who will roll back the stone for us from the entrance of the tomb?"* (v.3) From the entrance of the tomb or of your heart? From the tomb or from your eyes? Women, your heart has been bolted, your eyes have been shut, and so you do not see the glory of the opened tomb. If you wish to see, pour the oil not now on the Lord's body, but to illumine your heart, so that there may be made visible by the light of faith what is concealed in the darkness of unbelief.

4. *And when they looked up*, it says, *they saw that the stone had been rolled back; it was very large indeed* (v.4). Certainly large, and

---

4. Mk 15.33.
5. See likewise *Sermons* 75.2 and 77.2.

very large, and larger now in merit than in size, since it was big enough to conceal and to reveal the Body of the Creator of the world. *And when they entered the tomb they saw a young man sitting on the right, clothed in a white garment* (v.5). They entered the tomb, so that having been buried together with Christ they might rise from the tomb with Christ,[6] and fulfill the words of the Apostle: you have been "buried with him, and in him you have risen."[7]

They see *a young man*, in order to discern the age of our resurrection. They see *a young man*, because the resurrection does not know old age, and eternal perfection is ageless.[8] O man, since it is unable to be born, it is unable to die; and whereas it is unable to be born and to die, therefore it experiences no losses through the years, nor does it need to grow. They see *a young man sitting on the right*, because the resurrection does not tolerate anything on the left.[9] "The Lord knows the paths that are on the right."[10] And: "Then he will put" the righteous "on his right."[11]

Pray, brothers, that we also may die to the vices and be buried to temporal vanities, so that we may rise to eternity in Christ, and be found worthy of being placed on his right and hearing: "Come, blessed of my Father, receive the kingdom which has been prepared for you from the beginning of the world."[12]

5. *Clothed in a white garment.* This garment is not from the fleece of sheep destined to die, but from living power; glowing with heavenly light, not with any earthen colors; and made bright by the favor of the Creator, not by the skill of a fuller, as the prophet says: "Wrapped in light as with a robe."[13] And concerning the righteous: "Then the righteous will shine like the sun."[14] The earthly are covered with earthly clothes, and so just as they glisten when they are new, so they become dirty when

---

6. Regarding the idea that their faith needed to rise from the dead, see *Sermon* 77.10 and n. 20.

7. Col 2.12. Cf. Rom 6.4.
8. See *Sermon* 103.4.
9. See *Sermon* 78.5 and n. 9.
10. Prv 4.27 LXX.
11. Mt 25.33.
12. Mt 25.34.
13. Ps 103 (104).2.
14. Mt 13.43.

they grow old. But the heavenly are clothed in a garment of heavenly light, and raised above the filth on earth, they do not ever become soiled with the passing of years, nor do they lose their luster because of any stain; but once the resurrection provides the clothes, they are worn in everlasting light.[15]

6. *But they went out of the tomb fleeing*, it says, *for fear and trembling overtook them* (v.8). An angel sits inside the tomb, the women flee from the tomb, because he has confidence from his heavenly substance, but they are in a panic from their earthly condition. The one who is unable to die is incapable of fearing the tomb. But the women both tremble because of what has happened, and as mortals they still have a mortal fear of the tomb.

This is why they say nothing to anyone: *And they said nothing to anyone* (v.8), because women are allowed to listen, but not to speak; they are allowed to learn, but not to teach, as the Apostle says: "Let the women be silent in church."[16] And so the same Mary afterwards both goes and gives the news,[17] but now not in the role of a woman, but of the Church, so that just as she is to be silent, on the one hand, as a woman, she is to give the message and speak, on the other hand, as the Church.[18]

7. *After this*, it says, *he appeared to two of them as they were walking* (v.12). Why not to three? Why not to four, but to two? Because here it is being shown that the faith in the Resurrection is to be preached to the two peoples, that is, to the gentiles and the Jews. From this, as we have said, it is thus being demonstrated that the one Church is being represented either in the two women or in the two disciples.[19]

---

15. That the manner in which the messenger of the Resurrection appears provides a glimpse of aspects of the resurrected state is also noted in *Sermons* 74.6 (FOTC 17.127) and 77.9.
16. 1 Cor 14.34.
17. See Mk 16.10.
18. For the view that the women who visited the tomb are types of the Church, see also *Sermons* 75.3 and 76.2–3. For a different typological signification, see *Sermon* 74.3 (FOTC 17.124–25).
19. Reading the textual variant *discipulis* (see PL 52.432) rather than Olivar's *populis*. On the two women as types of the two peoples, gentiles and Jews, comprising the one Church, see *Sermon* 75.3.

He appeared in another form (v.12). Let no one think that with his Resurrection Christ changed the form of his features, such that he who was himself with his wounds was different in his features. But the form is changed,[20] since from being mortal he becomes immortal, and from corruptible incorruptible, so that it is a case of having changed the substance, not of having changed the Person,[21] and of having acquired glorious features, not of having lost the recognizable characteristics of his features.

8. And so that this sermon may not, in its haste, avoid or pass too quickly over questions, we shall examine what follows in the next sermon[22] to the extent that the Lord discloses.

---

20. Chrysologus's language is somewhat confusing in that he states that Christ's "form" *(effigies)* is in one sense unchanged, but in another sense it has changed. That is, there are no quantitative changes in his outward manifestation, but there is now a qualitative change, marked by immortality and incorruptibility, which presumably explains the fact that the disciples did not recognize him in his risen state.

21. That is, Christ's human substance or nature has changed qualitatively: it is now immortal and incorruptible. See R. Benericetti, *Il Cristo*, 108–16, especially 114–16.

22. *Sermon* 83 (FOTC 17.133–37), where he interprets the latter portion of Mk 16.

SERMON 84

An Eleventh on the Lord's Resurrection[1]

N THE FORTY DAYS, during which it is related and believed that the Lord appeared in a different fashion to his disciples after his Resurrection, our words are focused quite fittingly on the readings themselves, on these very mysteries, and are based upon them, so that by the variety of evidence about the Resurrection our words may convert your grief at the Lord's Passion into perfect joy, dearly beloved; and so that he who in the past rose in our body through his own power, may now also rise in our hearts through faith.[2]

2. *And when it was evening on that first day of the week, and although the doors had been locked for fear of the Jews, Jesus came and stood in their midst* (Jn 20.19). *When it was evening:* it was evening more by grief than by time. It was evening for minds darkened by the somber cloud of grief and sadness, because although the report of the Resurrection had given the slight glimmer of twilight, nevertheless, the Lord had not yet shone through with his light in all its brilliance.

And although the doors had been locked for fear of the Jews. The extent of their terror and the disquiet caused by such an atrocity had simultaneously locked the house and the hearts of the disciples,[3] and had so completely prevented light from having any access that for their senses, overwhelmed more and more by

---

1. This sermon was preached during the Easter season, but greater precision is not possible. In later liturgical tradition this Gospel was read on the second Sunday of Easter. It is also unclear what sermons preceded and followed this one in the liturgical cycle. See F. Sottocornola, *L'anno liturgico*, 88 and 172–74. There is nothing textual to suggest, as A. Olivar does in *Los sermones*, 265–66 and 277, that this *Sermon* 84 followed *Sermon* 81 and preceded *Sermon* 78.

2. For other references to this recurring theme in Chrysologus's preaching, see *Sermon* 77.10 and n. 20.

3. See *Sermon* 81.2 for another reference to the state of the disciples' hearts.

grief, the murkiness of night increased and became more pervasive. No darkness of night can be compared with the gloom of grief and fear, because they are incapable of being tempered by any light of either consolation or counsel. Listen to the prophet: "Darkness has come over me and covered me."[4]

3. *And although the doors had been locked for fear of the Jews, Jesus came and stood in their midst.* I ask you, why is it doubted that divinity, which is without limit, was able to penetrate the hidden confines of the sealed sanctuary of a virgin's body preserved with her integrity fully intact, when, after the Resurrection, divinity, having acquired the density of our body in the mystery of the Incarnation, goes in and out through locked doors, and by such evidence shows that he is the Author of all creation, to whom creation offers no obstruction, but is obedient in every way?[5]

But if virginity is unable to refuse conception and birth to its Creator, if a locked door cannot deny an entrance and exit to its Creator, how could the stone in front of the tomb, no matter how large, no matter how much it bears the mark of Jewish malice, obstruct the Savior's Resurrection? But just as virginity and the door, both locked tightly, produce faith in his divinity, so too does the stone rolled back affirm faith in the Resurrection, which, when it was rolled back did not provide a way out for its Lord, but furnishes and allows a way in for our faith.[6]

4. *Jesus came and stood in their midst and said to them: "Peace be with you"* (v.19). The disciples' hearts were enduring continuous conflicts and battles between faith and doubt, despair and hope, and cowardice and bravery. And so he who can see what is hidden foresaw the warfare such thoughts would wage and used the first opportunity to restore peace to the disciples who saw him, so that he who had been taken from them in such ignominy as to have left grounds for conflict, when he was restored to their eyes would do away with the entire reason for their struggle.

---

4. Ps 54.6 LXX; Ps 55.5.

5. Other references to relating the Virgin Mary's sealed womb and the sealed tomb where Jesus' body had lain are found in *Sermon* 75.3 and n. 11.

6. That the stone rolled back reveals, but did not assist, the Resurrection, is a theme in many of Chrysologus's Easter sermons. See *Sermons* 74.5 (FOTC 17.126), 75.4, 77.7, and 80.3 (FOTC 17.129).

5. *The disciples rejoiced*, it says, *when they saw the Lord* (v.20). They *rejoiced*. To the extent that light is more appealing after darkness, that serenity is more appealing after a gloomy storm, to the same extent is joy more welcome after grief. *He said to them again: "Peace be with you"* (v.21). What does this repetition in bestowing peace mean, except that he wants the tranquillity that he had announced to their minds individually also to be kept collectively among them by granting peace repeatedly? He knew, at any rate, that they were going to have far from insignificant struggles in the future stemming from his delay, with one boasting that he had persevered in faith,[7] and another in grief because he had doubted.[8]

Therefore, in order to curtail the boasting and pride of the arrogant, and to heal and eliminate the sufferings of the one who had been infirm, he prevented warfare from arising by his command of peace. In his devotion and wise governance he ascribed whatever had transpired to the situation and not to the disciples, so that one might not refuse to give another what he, to whom all was owed, had furnished for the future. Peter denies,[9] John flees,[10] Thomas doubts,[11] all forsake him:[12] unless Christ had granted forgiveness for these transgressions by his peace, even Peter, who was the first in rank of all of them, would be considered inferior, and would perhaps be undeserving of his subsequent elevation to the primacy.[13]

6. *Just as the Father has sent me, I also send you* (v.21). The mention of his having been sent does not diminish him as Son,[14] but declares that what he wants to be understood here is not the power of the One who sends, but the charity of the One who has been sent, since he says: *Just as the Father*, not the Lord,

---

7. It is unclear to whom this refers—perhaps to the beloved disciple or one of the women present at the cross (see Jn 19.25–27).
8. See Jn 20.28.
9. See Mt 26.69–75 and parallels.
10. See Mk 14.51–52. See *Sermon* 78.4 and n. 8 for the identification of the fleeing youth with John.
11. See Jn 20.24–29.
12. See Mt 26.56 and parallels.
13. The term employed here is *primum*. For references in Chrysologus's sermons to Peter's privileged position of *principatus* (also translated "primacy"), see *Sermon* 78.7 and n. 14.
14. Chrysologus is eager to ward off any Arian view that would make the Son inferior to the Father. See *Sermon* 76.1 and n. 2.

has sent me, so *I send you* no longer with the authority of a Master, but with all the affection of a Lover. *I send you* to endure hunger, to suffer the burden of being in chains, to the squalor of prison, to bear all kinds of punishments, and to undergo bitter death for all: all of which certainly charity, and not power, enjoins on human minds.

7. *Whose sins you forgive, they are forgiven, and whose sins you retain, they are retained* (v.23). He gave power to forgive sins, he who by his breathing upon them poured the Spirit in their hearts and bestowed the One who forgives. *And he breathed on them and said: "Receive the Holy Spirit. Whose sins you forgive, they are forgiven them"* (vv.22–23). Where are those who declare that sins cannot be forgiven human beings by human beings? Where are those who oppress people such that once they fall because of the devil's influence, they are never to arise? Where are those who out of their mean spirit take away and refuse a cure for infirmities and medicine for wounds? Where are those who thwart sinners by shamelessly promoting despair of their being forgiven and of returning?[15]

Peter forgives sins, and welcomes penitents with complete joy, and firmly maintains that this power has been granted by God to all priests.[16] For after his denial Peter would have lost the glory of being an apostle as well as life, if he had not had a fresh start through penitence. And if Peter returned by means of penitence, who can survive without penitence?

8. But when Thomas had heard from his fellow disciples that they had seen the Lord, he responded: *Unless I see the nail-marks and put my hand into his side, I shall not believe* (v.25). Why does Thomas seek this kind of basis for faith? Why is he so harsh in his investigation of the Resurrection of One who suffered with such loving devotion? Why does the hand of a faithful disciple[17] in this fashion retrace those wounds which an unholy hand inflicted? Why does the hand of a dutiful follower strive to re-

---

15. On this topic of forgiveness of postbaptismal sins, see the Introduction, FOTC 109.20 and n. 100, and F. Sottocornola, *L'anno liturgico*, 206, n. 12.
16. The Latin is *sacerdotibus*, meaning primarily but probably not exclusively "bishops."
17. Literally, "the faithful right hand" *(devota dextera)*.

open the side which the lance of an unholy soldier pierced? Why does the harsh curiosity of a servant repeat the tortures imposed by the rage of persecutors? Why is a disciple so inquisitive about proving from his torments that he is the Lord, from his pains that he is God, and from his wounds that he is the heavenly Physician?[18]

The power of the devil has crumbled, the prison of hell has been thrown open, the shackles of the dead have been broken, the graves of those who have risen have been torn asunder,[19] on account of the Lord's Resurrection the whole condition of death has been rendered insignificant, the stone has been rolled back from that most sacred tomb of the Lord,[20] the linen cloths have been taken off,[21] and death has fled before the glory of the Risen One, life has returned, and flesh has arisen incapable of further harm.

So why, Thomas, do you alone, a little too clever a sleuth[22] for your own good, insist that only the wounds be brought forward in testimony to faith? What if these wounds had been made to disappear with the other things? What a peril to your faith would that curiosity have produced? Do you think that no signs of his devotion and no evidence of the Lord's Resurrection could be found unless you probed with your hands his inner organs[23] which had been laid bare in such a way by the cruelty of the Jews?

Brothers, his devotion sought these things, his dedication demanded them, so that in the future not even godlessness itself would doubt that the Lord had risen. But Thomas was curing not only the uncertainty of his own heart, but also that of all human beings; and since he was going to preach this message to the gentiles, this conscientious investigator was examin-

---

18. See R. Benericetti, *Il Cristo*, 235, n. 16, for a lengthy but not exhaustive list of Christ as *medicus* in Chrysologus's preaching.
19. See Mt 27.52.
20. See Jn 20.1, as well as Lk 24.2 and synoptic parallels.
21. See Jn 20.7.
22. The Latin expression is *callidus explorator*. Chrysologus uses it to refer to the devil in *Sermon* 11.5 (FOTC 17.59).
23. For similar language denoting the physicality of Christ's risen body, see *Sermon* 81.5 and n. 12.

ing carefully how he might provide a foundation for the faith needed for such a mystery.[24] Certainly at issue is prophecy more than hesitation; for why would he be seeking such things unless he had come to know by the prophetic Spirit that the only reason that the Lord had kept his wounds was as evidence of his Resurrection? And so, the request that he made because he was late was something that in the end he provided spontaneously for others.

9. *Jesus came*, it says, *and stood in their midst, and showed them his hands and side* (vv.19–20). For he who had entered through locked doors and was understandably thought by his disciples to be a spirit,[25] could prove to them in such doubt that it was he himself in no other way than by the very suffering of his body, by the very marks of his wounds. And so he came *and said to Thomas: "Take your finger and examine my hands, and put your hand into my side"* (v.27), so that these wounds, which you are opening[26] and which have already shed water for the baptismal bath and blood for the redemption of humanity,[27] may inundate the whole world with the faith.

10. *Thomas said in response: "My Lord and my God!"* (v.28) Let the heretics come and listen, and as the Lord has said, let them not be unbelievers, but believers.[28] Notice that not only his human body but also the excruciating sufferings his body endured in punishment show that Christ is God and Lord, as Thomas proclaims. [And truly he is God, who comes to life out of death, who rises up from his wounds, and who, even though he has endured such great and terrible things, lives and reigns, God forever and ever. Amen.][29]

---

24. For Thomas's "curiosity" as providential for the spread of the Gospel, see also Gaudentius of Brescia, *Sermon* 17 (PL 20.961–62).

25. Or "ghost" *(spiritus)*. See Lk 24.37.

26. *Aperiente* can also mean "revealing," as in Thomas's efforts in evangelization.

27. See Jn 19.34.

28. See Jn 20.27.

29. This concluding doxology appears to be a later addition and hence not authentic. As Olivar notes (CCL 24A.523), however, all the manuscripts he consulted contained this final sentence. It may well have been added to signal the conclusion of the sermons on the Lord's Resurrection. See A. Olivar, *Los sermones*, 179.

SERMON 85

On the Middle of the Fifty Days[1]

LTHOUGH SOME THINGS SEEM hidden by the depth of their mystery, nevertheless, no solemnity which the Church observes is fruitless. Commemorating a divine feast does not depend on the disposition of our wills, but it must be celebrated in view of its own merits. A true Christian spirit has never entertained the idea of putting up for discussion feasts which have solid grounding in the tradition of the Fathers and in the very seasons themselves, but desires to treat them with due reverence and speak of them with nothing but respect.[2]

2. *In the middle of the festival*, it says, *Jesus went up to the Temple* (Jn 7.14). What temple? "You are the temple of God, and the Spirit of God dwells in you."[3] The Lord today goes up to the temple of our heart, he who so mercifully came down in our bodily form. And how God goes up to the apex of the human heart, the blessed prophet explains when he sings: "Blessed is

---

1. This sermon and the next one are entitled *De Medio Pentecosten(-es)*, literally, "On the Middle of Pentecost." "Pentecost" refers not to the feast at the end of the fifty-day Easter season, nor to a subsequent season of Pentecost, but to the fifty days of the Easter season itself, the middle of which was marked with special solemnity in Ravenna, as this and the next sermon attest. It is a feast that seems to have originated in the east and perhaps been introduced to northern Italy via Ravenna, but was not very extensively observed. Since Jesus' Ascension was not observed as a separate feast at this time in Ravenna, it is likely that when it was introduced, it eventually eliminated the need for this observance, which made some references to the Ascension, at the midpoint of the Easter season. See A. Olivar, "San Pedro Crisólogo y la solemnidad *In medio Pentecostes*," *Ephemerides Liturgicae* 63 (1949): 389–99; A. Olivar, *Los sermones*, 347–50; and F. Sottocornola, *L'anno liturgico*, 190–97.

2. The allusion here to resistance to this feast echoes some of the complaints in *Sermon* 73.3 surrounding the liturgical observance of the one-year baptismal anniversary; see also n. 1 to *Sermon* 73.

3. 1 Cor 3.16.

the man whose help is from you, O Lord; you have gone up to his heart."⁴

And so, *in the middle of the festival the Lord went up to the Temple,* he who was about to furnish us with the perfect festival from heaven. Whatever sublime dimension, whatever tendency toward heaven was contained in human hearts, the weight of the Lord's Passion had bent it all the way down to hell. For certainly it is for that reason that Christ remains and lingers on the earth during the forty days.⁵ And if one may say so, he delays his Father's plan, and he keeps his Father's embrace in abeyance, until in every way he should raise up and remold everything unto the glory of his Ascension.⁶ So, that person who does not have Christ ascend to his temple here does not ascend to heaven with Christ.

3. *He went up to the Temple and was teaching* them, *and the Jews marveled and said: "How does this man know his letters, since he has not been taught?"* (vv.14–15) Well do they marvel that Christ knows what he has not learned, since they themselves are proven not to know the precepts of the Law which they have learned and teach, when the Lord says: "You are a teacher in Israel, and you have no knowledge of these things?"⁷ The Jews, who are so rebellious, marvel, they do not want to believe, they know how to⁸ marvel, they refuse to understand, but they do have the power to be ignorant! The Jews marvel as they say: *How does this man know his letters, since he has not been taught?*

That a virgin gave birth, you disparage, you do not marvel; that God is perceived and functions in our body, you deny and refuse to admit; that the blind man sees, that the deaf hears, that the lame walks, that the dead rises,⁹ and that Christ utters all the secret mysteries of God, do you not marvel at these? Is

---

4. Ps 83.6 LXX; Ps 84.5.
5. See also *Sermon* 84.1 for another reference to the forty days during which the risen Christ appeared to his followers.
6. That Christ's Ascension transports humanity into heaven is a theme found in *Sermon* 168.6 and in some of the sermons on the Creed, such as *Sermons* 57.9 (FOTC 17.108), 58.8 (FOTC 109.223), 61.8 (FOTC 17.114), and 62a.7 (FOTC 109.247).
7. Jn 3.10.
8. Reading *norunt* in PL 52.440 instead of *nolunt* in Olivar's CCL text.
9. See Mt 11.5 and Lk 7.22.

this the only thing that causes you to marvel, namely, that he knows although he has not been taught? This is he who has not been taught, but has bestowed knowledge. He it is who has created the intelligence through which letters are fashioned. Does an expert in the Law wonder why the Author of all things has not been taught his letters? It is clearly because God, the Origin of all, is in your midst, he who brings into existence what was not; since he has not been taught, he teaches.

SERMON 85A

[A Second] On the Middle of the Fifty Days[1]

T IS FITTING THAT we have made our way to gather at the midpoint of our great solemnity, since Jesus, our God and our Lord, the Consecrator of all feasts, proceeded, at the halfway-point of a festival, to go up to Jerusalem.[2] For just as an avid traveler aiming for his destination is ever so happy to call to mind how much of his journey he has already completed, and he is thereby made stronger to complete what remains and has all his strength renewed, so now with solemn joy and devotion we observe this day which tempers and moderates the ardor of our anticipation, so that with our minds refreshed we may arrive at the very grace and happiness of the Holy Spirit. This day has even greater appeal to us, because even though we might be unwilling,[3] nevertheless, it has drawn us most happily toward the sacred feast of Pentecost.

So it is, brothers, so it is the entryway of our city, which has deserved to have doorkeepers who are so great and so holy that they keep it bolted from enemies, shut from the wicked, opened to the good, and allow the citizens complete access. So

---

1. On the authenticity of this sermon, see A. Olivar, "San Pedro Crisólogo y la solemnidad *In medio Pentecostes*," 392–99, and *Los sermones*, 347–53. On this feast at the midpoint of the Easter season, see *Sermon* 85, n. 1. Both these sermons are uncharacteristically brief. It is possible that in both cases what we possess is only a fragment. However, both sermons as they have come down to us do have their own integrity, in that it does not seem that anything is missing in spite of some obscurities, especially in this *Sermon* 85a. There are other sermons in Chrysologus's corpus that are quite brief, such as those on certain feasts, on saints, or on his consecration of a fellow bishop. Given the negativity among his people to this particular feast, the brevity here may be a sign of his prudence in not overtaxing a congregation that was less than enthusiastic to begin with!

2. See Jn 7.14.

3. Similarly, a resistance to this particular feast is also noted in *Sermon* 85.1.

SERMON 85A

let us celebrate this delightful day in honoring the saints[4] with our spirits eager and our minds enraptured. "Let heaven be glad and earth rejoice,"[5] "let the mountains" leap "like rams, and the hills like the lambs of the flock";[6] "let the rivers clap their hands, as well as the sea and all that is in them."[7] Let all the elements resound in a harmonious melody in the praises of God; may God in all his glory hasten to us and prompt us to extol the Holy Spirit.

4. It is unclear to what this refers. There was a feast honoring St. Mark on April 25 in Rome dating from the sixth century, but it seems unlikely that Ravenna would already be celebrating this in Chrysologus's era. See H. Leclercq, "Marc (Procession de Saint-)," in *DACL* 10 (1932): 1740–41.
5. Ps 95 (96).11.   6. Ps 113 (114).4 and 6.
7. Ps 97 (98).8 and 7.

SERMON 85B

On the Day of Pentecost[1]

THE PRESENT FEAST, brothers, has received its name from the number, than which there is no other number more sacred in God's sight or more holy in the eyes of the Church, as the Holy Spirit has shown by his arrival. *When the days of Pentecost were completed*, it says (Acts 2.1). Seven weeks, you understand, provide an image of the sevenfold Spirit; the lamp with seven lights[2] in the tabernacle of old prefigures the illumination of the holy Church.[3] Seven days bring the world to completion by the action of God,[4] and by means of weeks and ten-day periods[5] the number seven contains the entire mystery of our salvation.

And so the Lord declares in response to Peter's question that sin must be forgiven not only seven times, but seventy times seven times,[6] the number which the evangelist Luke indicated by counting the succession of the seventy generations that produced the Lord.[7] For although the human being sinned against God from the beginning, as often as he was counted worthy of pardon he was allowed to continue to be born and live even in spite of his sinning. Certainly if penitence for remitting sin had ceased, not salvation but punishment would have been his due. But he attained true forgiveness then

---

1. On the authenticity of this sermon, see A. Olivar, *Los sermones*, 354–57. This is the only extant sermon by Chrysologus on the feast of Pentecost itself.

2. See *Sermon* 134.1 (FOTC 17.221) where the seven sons of the mother, all of whom were martyred by King Antiochus as described in 2 Mc 7.1–42, are referred to similarly as a lamp with seven lights.

3. See Ex 25.37.   4. See Gn 2.1–2.

5. See *Sermon* 12.3 (FOTC 109.59).

6. See Mt 18.22. See *Sermon* 139.7 for more on the significance of the number seven.

7. See Lk 3.23–38.

when Christ by means of the mystery of the number just mentioned[8] assumed man to free humanity from the stain of its sins.

That most illustrious number, which is completed by the addition of one day, makes all things perfect, because all perfection concludes in unity. From one and through one all things are, and the origin of everything comes from one. The number forty lifted us in our lowliness up to heaven; the number fifty, as we learn today, has imparted divinity onto the earth. How happy is the business which the holy Church has been granted to transact by means of numbers! The number forty, just as the faith contained in the Scriptures teaches, has put an end to the human race's captivity by virtue of the Lord's Ascension;[9] the number fifty has restored to all the liberty for which they had longed by virtue of the coming of the Spirit. Listen to the Apostle as he says: "Where the Spirit of the Lord is, there is liberty."[10]

2. The Holy Spirit has filled every house today,[11] in which dwell people "from every nation under heaven."[12] This is that house, brothers, where from every nation and tribe[13] the grace of the Holy Spirit has gathered us, and, having abolished every distinction of status, nationality, and gender, Christ has appeared as One through "all and in all."[14] Truly in this house what the divine Scriptures promise is fulfilled, in which diverse nations and peoples, in which princes, the powerful, all the lofty, and the poor without being scorned are gathered into one.

3. Standing here is the most pious imperial family,[15] serving

---

8. Literally, "written above" *(suprascripti)*, perhaps indicating that the sermon was written down and intended for publication on Chrysologus's part. See A. Olivar, *Los sermones*, 252, n. 57.

9. See Acts 1.3; Ps 67.19 LXX; Ps 68.18; Eph 4.8. This may indicate that there was still no separate feast commemorating the Ascension in Ravenna at this time, but it was included in the celebration of Pentecost. See *Sermons* 85 and 85a for references to the Ascension on a feast at the midpoint of the Easter season. See also F. Sottocornola, *L'anno liturgico*, 196, n. 48.

10. 2 Cor 3.17. 11. See Acts 2.2.
12. Acts 2.5. 13. See Rv 5.9.
14. Col 3.11.
15. Chrysologus also preached *Sermon* 130 in the presence of the imperial family. For more on Chrysologus's involvement with the civil rulers, and Galla Placidia in particular, see Introduction, FOTC 109.8–11.

the One, so that they may reign over all; bowing their heads to God, so that all nations may bend their necks to them; offering gifts to God alone, so as to obtain tribute from all peoples. They are here, strong in faith, secure in their innocence, prudent in their simplicity, rich in mercy, wealthy in love, awesome in their kindness, and what matters most, reigning thanks to their unchangeable communion;[16] they ennoble the rich but do not despise the poor, since they know that what has been lacking in the poor person is his wealth[17] and not his humanity; they know that he has lost nothing of the image of God, but rather the goods of this world; and they know that they can supply the rest, if the human being, who is the work of God, is to be kept alive.

16. That is, with God and in the Church.
17. As an example that those who are poor in wealth suffer no liability in God's sight, Jesus' first followers, Peter, Andrew, James, and John, are described in just this fashion in *Sermon* 28.1 (FOTC 109.115).

SERMON 86

*Sermon on Zechariah, After the Most Blessed
Bishop Peter of Ravenna Was Silent*[1]

ORLDLY SPEECH, SINCE it issues forth from human intelligence, serves and complies with what is instinctively human; but divine speech is in the power of the One who gives it, not the one who utters it. You have heard how Zechariah, that shining light of the high priesthood, while he was praying, became mute.[2] The father of the voice was silent, of the one who said, "I am the voice of one who is crying out in the desert."[3] The begetter of the cry became mute, and the one who had gone in to offer responses, when he went out offered only silence. So you see that my silence, which earlier made you sad, came from an ancient priestly custom, not from some brand new affliction.[4]

When he realized that his tongue was tied and that it had blocked the entryway for his speech, he ordered with a nod[5] that no one should inquire about the reasons for his silence, since he who had learned enough to know that it was a heavenly mystery had not learned how to speak about it. But this was only for the time being, since the priest's faculty of speech is being delayed, not withdrawn; it is being kept hidden, but not de-

---

1. In December some time prior to Christmas this sermon was preached immediately after *Sermon* 35 and probably followed by *Sermon* 91. See *Sermon* 35, n. 12 (FOTC 109.152), as well as F. Sottocornola, *L'anno liturgico*, 73, 97, 99, and 303, and A. Olivar, *Los sermones*, 261–62 and 266–68. Other comments are offered in V. Zangara, "I silenzi," 225–28. For a differing opinion on the liturgical season in which this sermon was preached, see R. Benericetti, *Il Cristo*, 146, n. 42.
2. See Lk 1.20–22.
3. Is 40.3; Mk 1.3.
4. *De novitatis incursu* could also be translated as "from some new fad that I had inflicted upon you." The reference is to his sudden silence that abruptly ended *Sermon* 35 (FOTC 109.152).
5. See Lk 1.22.

nied; it is held in suspense by the mystery, not banished. And so, the fact that Zechariah himself is silent is not a punishment, but a sign; at issue is not earthly weakness, but a heavenly secret.

God, who implants the word, gives the power to speak, makes a person speechless, and commands silence. Divine discourse is master, not servant, since the Word is God;[6] and so he speaks, not when he is ordered, but when he orders; not when he is asked, but when he bestows it; not when he is compelled to do so, but when he comes. Therefore, brothers, when he comes, listen, and when he does not come, be patient, and when he bestows himself, receive him, and when he refuses himself to you, pray, because the teacher[7] receives what the listener deserves.

Therefore, that sermon in the past was suspended as much on your account as on mine, so that our sense of shame might say no more about the woman's hemorrhage, the cause of her shameful wound, and her modesty to such an extent that the matter about which she said nothing would also remain concealed by our silence.[8] But let us return to what we began to say.

2. The water in Jerusalem flows in abundance when the angel stirs it up, not when the thirsty person comes for a drink.[9] So the words of the priest abound, because God grants it, not because the priest is giving a speech. This is why Zechariah himself, who was speaking prophecies to the people, is silent to himself, so that we might not be ungrateful to God, if on one single occasion he has willed that we be silent, to whom he has always generously bestowed his word uninterrupted. Zechariah is not offended at receiving the word from his son to whom he had given the light of life.[10]

And you, my children, pray for a voice for us, so that you may be able to hear a sermon. Restore my joy, so that you may possess your customary happiness and fulfill what the Apostle

---

6. See Jn 1.1.
7. That is, Chrysologus himself.
8. See *Sermon* 35 on Mt 9.20–22 (FOTC 109.149–52).
9. See Jn 5.4.
10. See Lk 1.63–64. This is a reference to John the Baptist, Zechariah's son.

said: "Who is the person who makes me happy, if not the one who is saddened by me?"[11] And so, may he come, may blessed Zechariah come into our midst, who by being speechless comforts us with the example of his piety, and by his silence does not allow us to be saddened by our silence. May he come, may the forerunner of silence come, he who is the mirror of the priesthood, the example of sanctity, the first of the Evangelists, the last of the prophets.[12]

3. *In the days when Herod was king of Judea*, it says, *there was a certain priest named Zechariah* (Lk 1.5). If there should be a priest under such a king, evils are tempered; solace is always present in grief; nor is there a comforter lacking for the one who has a persecutor at his heels. *In the days when Herod was king of Judea, there was a certain priest named Zechariah.* Until the time of Herod the sanctity of the priesthood, the dignity of the elders, and the piety of the fathers governed the Jewish nation; the authority was the divine Law, ambition had no power there, nor did rashness or presumption, because everything was regulated by divine, not by human, decree.

But Herod came from a foreign nation[13] and usurped the kingdom, he violated the priesthood, he disturbed the proper order,[14] he subverted the good morals, he rejected the elders, he corrupted the youth, he mingled the tribes, he ruined their pedigree, he defiled the race, and he completely uprooted whatever divine and human norms there were. But all this took place after the time of the saintly Zechariah; therefore, so that nothing like that would be believed to have occurred in the case of Zechariah, the evangelist is compelled to state the matter as follows:

4. *In the days when Herod was king of Judea, there was a certain priest named Zechariah of the class of Abijah* (v.5). Since up to his time the priestly race continued to be transferred from great-

11. 2 Cor 2.2.
12. That is, John the Baptist.
13. See Flavius Josephus, *The Jewish Antiquities* 14.7.3, where he states that Herod was born to a Roman father named Cassius and an Arab mother named Cypros.
14. Chrysologus repeats this particular accusation against Herod in *Sermons* 89.4 and 127.3.

grandfathers, grandfathers, and fathers, the time established by the Law and all the norms governing sacrifice were preserved, inasmuch as the merit and life of the priest overcame the impiety of the king, the iniquity of the age, the madness of ambition, and the fury of presumption. But let us listen to what follows.

5. *It happened that when he entered the Temple to offer incense, the whole multitude was praying outside at the hour of incense* (see vv.9–10). *At the hour of incense*, brothers, the sun was already setting on the Jewish Temple, so that in the morning it would rise on the Church; the evening of Jewish teaching was approaching, because the dawn of the Gospel was imminent; and day was fading for the Law, so that it might shine with all its brilliance on grace.

This is why *at the hour of incense*, that is, in the final period of observing the Law, Zechariah by the Spirit of prophecy sprinkles incense, offers prayers, pronounces petitions, utters solemn vows, makes mention of the time, asks again for what has been promised, and makes entreaties for the Christ. *And the whole multitude was praying outside.* He pleads for the people who were standing outside to be allowed in, because those whom the Law brought as far as the doorway, grace allows into the Temple.

6. *There appeared to him an angel*, it says, *standing at the right side of the altar, and when Zechariah saw him he was greatly disturbed, and fear fell over him* (vv.11–12). So it is no wonder if the priest is disturbed, if the teacher is stunned, if the high priest is afraid; if he does not have the least little thing to say when he sees the greatest of matters; if he abandons words, when he looks at signs. And lest Zechariah seem to be the only person to have been afraid, listen to what another prophet says: "Lord, I have heard your renown, and I was afraid; I have contemplated your works, and I trembled."[15] Who does not tremble when addressing God? He does not know where his words come from. And what about us? Now let us explain why the priest is silent.

7. *And the angel said in response: "I am Gabriel, who stand in the*

---

15. Hab 3.2.

presence of God, and I have been sent to tell you these things and to give you this good news. But now you will be silent and unable to speak" (vv. 19–20). Why blame a person for his silence, if the power of the one in command orders silence? Therefore, the fact that we who are of so little account were silent, attribute not to our forgetfulness, but to the occasion; to divine involvement, not to some human reason. So let us not be sad, because, if God so grants it, a moment's silence will be compensated for by a prolonged discourse, and our little bit of sadness will be turned into great joy. I give thanks to my God who has seen to it that what I lost in speech I have gained in love. For how great your charity is towards me, your pallor revealed, your shouts bore witness, your tears manifested, and your abundant prayers made clear.[16]

16. This is a rather touching description of the bond of affection shared by Chrysologus and his people.

SERMON 87

A Second ‹on Zechariah›[1]

IF THE LIGHT HAS been kept dim by excessive pain and a long illness, unless it is allowed back in gradually, the light becomes an enemy, when of course sunlight was created for the benefit of the eyes and to be pleasing to the eyes, and it is by means of them, as we are well aware, that sunlight is either transmitted or denied to the rest of the body. So too when minds have been kept in the dark through suffering a lengthy bout of unbelief, if faith suddenly shines with all its brilliance, the darkness of unbelief grows even more pervasive, unless instead the clarity of faith is restored little by little.[2] By a longstanding habit nature always either progresses or regresses.

This is why the Lord, in order to illumine the mystery of the Virgin birth for hearts by that time blinded by the dark cloud of faithlessness, arranged beforehand for a conception from what was a hopeless and aged sterility. Consequently, whoever saw bodily members that had withered away from a long old age come back to life, and, after the passage of a great many years of life, begin to bloom again in the prime of puberty, and the very nature that was in the evening of life awakened to signify that the one being born would be the Lord's servant; whoever saw these things would then be in a position to believe that after birth the flower of purity, the honor of bodily integrity, the distinction of chastity, and the seal of virginity could remain

---

1. (Angle brackets here indicate an addition to the title in Olivar's CCL text.) This sermon was preached in December some time before Christmas. See nn. 5 and 6 below.
2. This emphasis on the capacity of human vision to absorb only a little light at a time is given also in *Sermons* 64.1 (FOTC 109.255) and 146.1 (FOTC 17.238).

SERMON 87

and be preserved by the Creator when he himself would come forth from the womb.

2. The image we presented at the beginning had to do with eyes which were made weary by a lengthy illness in which we indicated that human eyes which are unfortunately accustomed to the night and darkened, are only gradually opened and drawn back to the light. To illustrate that the very authority about which we are now speaking fits and corresponds with this image, the Lord lit a lamp containing his light and sent it on ahead in John, so that after having received a glimmer of the light they might now be capable of tolerating the very radiance of the divine Sun, and take in the very splendor of divinity, as he says about John: "He was a burning lamp."[3]

The Lord intended that John might break open the dense darkness of the night with a gentle light, so that he himself might restore the day that does not know night to those who now long to come into light everlasting. This is how a dimly shining star makes the Magi, who were still inhabitants of the night[4] and entirely lacking in sight, used to the light, and gradually draws them to the very source of light and days. Brothers, since the seasons like a four-horse chariot persevere in running the laps of the entire year, and invite us again to the feast of the birth of our Lord,[5] and are already restoring our joy, it is certainly fitting that we now speak about the birth of John and about the pregnancy of a barren woman.

Then by these brief remarks about believing we may be able to make our way amid the lights of winter,[6] which are dim in the midst of clouds and fog, and, by the guidance of a star going before us and illuminating our way, to arrive where the childbirth is without labor-pains, where the One who is brought to birth is himself the Creator of his mother, and where the One who is being born is the very Origin of the one who bore him.

3. *There was a certain priest named Zechariah*, the evangelist

---

3. Jn 5.35.
4. The Magi are described with the same language in *Sermon* 157.1.
5. This is a clear indication that this sermon was preached sometime in December shortly before Christmas. See F. Sottocornola, *L'anno liturgico*, 263–64.
6. This is another indication of the seasonal context of this sermon.

says, *and his wife was Elizabeth, and they had no children, since Elizabeth was barren, and they both were advanced in years* (vv.5, 7). Barrenness is compounded by extreme old age, and the body's natural capacity provides absolutely no grounds for any hope of conceiving a child; and so that not even any thought at all of a child would remain, they had arrived at that age when the heat for procreation had ended, and the mortal chill of sterility had already taken over their organs. The father himself recognized therefore that a human being could no longer be born of a human being bereft of such human capabilities. And so in this way, brothers, belief is sown in the hard hearts of human beings, and faith is planted there, and therefore everything is believed to have been accomplished by God, since it was nothing that a human being could accomplish.[7]

4. Zechariah, it says, *entered into the Temple of the Lord to offer incense* (v.9). Appropriately it said that he *entered into the Temple*, and not "entered the Temple," because he himself was a temple of God, on fairly intimate terms at that, bearing within the purity of his heart all the mysteries of the Law, and offering in sacrifice, not so much incense, as undefiled prayer. For indeed God finds greater satisfaction in his own work than in human work, and the oil from an Arabian tree provides an aroma that does not please him as much as the sanctity that comes from a sincere heart and breast.

5. *An angel appeared to him*, it says, *on the right of the altar of incense* (v.11). It would have sufficed for it to say, *An angel appeared to him*. Why does it specify: *on the right of the altar?* So that you the listener understand that there is in the holy angels nothing from the left,[8] as Scripture says: "The Lord knows the ways that are on the right."[9] *An angel appeared to him:* whom by this time every human option had failed, so that John would be born of a barren mother before Christ would be born of a virgin. It was said concerning John: "See I am sending my angel."[10]

---

7. The same point is made in *Sermon* 89.7.
8. The Latin term for "left" is *sinister*, which also implies "unfavorable" and "perverse."
9. Prv 4.27 LXX.
10. Mal 3.1; Mt 11.10. The Latin *angelus* also means "messenger."

Happy is that nature which has declined so much in old age, that its newfound growth must be attributed to God. Happy is that nature which has exchanged deprivation by sterility for virginal fertility. Happy is she who brought to life in one birth everything she used to lament was deteriorating throughout the whole world, and she became the mother of a living offspring, who before was the pitiable source of offspring subject to death, giving birth to suffering with suffering.[11] She produced with a groan an offspring with groans in his future, and with the danger entailed in pregnancy, she brought forth a human being subject to dangers, so as to announce death at the very moment of birth, unceasing in her prayer with lamentations and tears for her children, since she knew that by such sorrows she was producing children who were going to die.

Therefore, by being barren nature was actually spared more distress, so that she would not be more intensely distraught by her very fertility, since she would produce more tears than children. And so it was that for so long a time she kept beseeching and begging her Creator with her tears, her grief, her moaning and groaning, since she understood that it was her fault that this had happened to her, and that it had not been ordained by the Creator in his great kindness at the time of creation.

This is why the Lord, who established nature himself, took the route of being conceived of a virgin and born of a virgin by invisible tracks and an unknown path, and traveled the journey of human birth with divine, not human, steps, so that by his birth he would from the very beginning liberate that very nature from the slavery of death, to which it had been so wretchedly consigned, and so that having cleansed the fountain he might restore the heavenly purity of the stream. Rightly then does John leap in his mother's womb,[12] since he was counted worthy, before his birth,[13] of knowing the liberation of his origin, and worthy of recognizing it before he lived.

6. At the hour of incense sterility becomes fertile[14] through

---

11. See Gn 3.16.
12. See Lk 1.41.
13. Literally, "before he was": the Latin verb is simply *esse*.
14. The Latin *aperitur* implies that sterility is given an "opening" to bear a child.

an angel, a conception is ordered, a child is promised, and within the confines of a sacred place a sacred birth is being prepared. This is why, while still in the womb and while the structure of his bodily members is almost formed, John speaks as a prophet by moving his body before he manages to use his voice.[15]

7. But in our desire not to prolong this sermon but to bring to a close our remarks on the profound and marvelous matters of this very extensive reading, so that I not neglect what most deserves mention, in our next sermon,[16] God willing, we shall examine what follows.

15. The Latin *perveniat ad vocis officium* bears the additional meaning of "attaining his function as voice," that is, as the "voice" preparing the way for Jesus.
16. This promised sermon is most likely *Sermon* 88 (FOTC 17.137–43), where Chrysologus begins by mentioning that he is now paying the debt that he owes his congregation and preaches on the verses of Lk 1 that immediately follow those treated in this *Sermon* 87. See F. Sottocornola, *L'anno liturgico*, 90, and A. Olivar, *Los sermones*, 267–68.

SERMON 89

A Fourth <on Zechariah>[1]

LL THINGS THAT HAVE been created by God are good for us, very good indeed, as Scripture says: "And God saw all the things that he made, and they were very good."[2] Therefore, all things that have been created by God are good, very good indeed. But between the vices and the virtues there are intermediate goods such that while the knowledgeable take from them material for teaching, the ignorant find there a cause for error. For the wise certainly come to know the Creator from contemplating creation; the foolish, while they think that mere creatures are the creators, cannot know the Creator. That is why the gentiles made the sun, the moon, the stars, gold, stones, wood into gods for themselves, things which Christians know have been assigned to serve them.

And it is no surprise that creation is one of these intermediate goods, since believers have Christ, the very Creator of all, as their salvation, but unbelievers have him as their downfall, as the evangelist says: "He has been appointed for the downfall and the rising of many."[3] In addition, some encounter the apostles for their death, others encounter them for their life, as

---

1. (Angle brackets here indicate an addition to the title in Olivar's CCL text.) The liturgical season for this sermon is a subject for debate. A. Olivar, *Los sermones*, 266–68, believes that this, like the sermons surrounding it in the Felician collection, was preached in December prior to Christmas, with Lk 1.5ff being the Gospel. F. Sottocornola, *L'anno liturgico*, 90–96 and 303–4, is of the opinion that it was preached on the feast of John the Baptist's martyrdom, probably June 24, with the Gospel of the day being either Mt 14.1–12 or Mk 6.17–29. Given Chrysologus's intention, voiced in this sermon, to treat the death of John, Sottocornola has the stronger argument for a liturgical context other than one immediately prior to Christmas.
2. Gn 1.31.
3. Lk 2.34.

Paul attests when he says: "To certain ones as a fragrance of death unto death; to others, moreover, as a fragrance of life unto life."⁴ Therefore, even the readings from the Gospel become for the good an opportunity for knowledge that saves, but for the wicked an opportunity for error.⁵

2. Previously⁶ when the very blessed evangelist mentioned that John the Baptist had been locked up in Herod's prison, killed on account of the adulteries of Herodias, beheaded as a dancing girl's reward, we have recognized that some had become upset about why God had handed over a holy man to an impious one, a virgin to an adulteress, a messenger⁷ to a dancing girl.⁸ Brothers, we have given a full treatment in another sermon⁹ of the virtues of John and the crimes of Herod; now let us speak about what the reason was for the prison, what the need was for incarceration, and what benefit there was from John's death. John could not die in a common fashion since he was born for a unique privilege.

When Christ was born as God in the flesh, John was begotten as an angel on earth, so that earthly functions would be mingled with heavenly functions, just as divine affairs were mingling¹⁰ themselves with human ones, and God would not be

---

4. 2 Cor 2.16.

5. On this same point, see, e.g., *Sermon* 52.1 (FOTC 109.202–3). For other references on this theme, see A. Olivar, "Els principis exegètics de sant Pere Crisòleg," in *Miscellanea biblica B. Ubach*, ed. Romualdo M. Díaz (Montserrat: Abadía de Montserrat, 1953), 434–36.

6. Probably a reference to a previous sermon, although F. Sottocornola, *L'anno liturgico*, 91, believes that this refers to the proclamation of the Gospel text on John's martyrdom in the current liturgy right before Chrysologus began this sermon.

7. Or "angel." See n. 23 below.

8. See Mt 14.1–12 and Mk 6.17–29.

9. Chrysologus preaches on John the Baptist's martyrdom in *Sermons* 127, 173, and 174, but it is unclear to which one if any of these he is referring here. At the beginning of *Sermon* 127 Chrysologus mentions the turmoil people feel when great vice overcomes great virtue, a point to which he alludes in this *Sermon* 89, but it certainly does not definitively indicate that his reference here is to *Sermon* 127.

10. *Se . . . miscebant:* although this text does not refer explicitly to the two natures in Christ "mingling together," Chrysologus does on other occasions use such language. Although inadequate by the Chalcedonian standards of a later decade, his terminology does not necessarily deny that the two natures remain

SERMON 89

without an angel on earth, nor would the Lord be without due celestial homage. But let us listen to the account of John's birth, so that we may be able to ascertain the reasons for his death.

3. *In the days when Herod was king of Judea,* it says, *there was a certain priest named Zechariah of the class of Abijah, and his wife was a descendant of Aaron, and her name was Elizabeth. Both of them, moreover, were righteous in the sight of God, proceeding blamelessly according to all the commandments and precepts of the Lord* (Lk 1.5–6). Whenever great orators who excel in their talent prepare to tell of the virtues of illustrious men, they mention their grandparents and great-grandparents, so that the dignity of their ancestors may result in the honor of those presently living, and the praise of their fathers may redound to the glory of the sons.[11]

Native glory is greater than any that is acquired. What comes from one's origin takes precedence over any subsequent achievement. It is more blessed to be endowed with glory than to acquire it.[12] This is why the evangelist, in order to extol John's glory, tells the lineage of Zechariah his father and of Elizabeth his mother, he mentions his ancestors, he writes of their merits, he speaks of their renown, he establishes their status, he tells of their life, he publicizes their eminent traits, and he commends their holiness.[13]

4. *It was,* he says, *when Herod was king of Judea* (v.5). He mentions the time of the infamous king who violated the sacred custom of the priesthood, disturbed the proper order,[14] undid what had been established, and eliminated what had been decreed. And what adds to Zechariah's merit is that although Herod was widening the scope of his foolhardy ventures against

---

unaltered in the one Christ. In Chrysologus's defense, see R. Benericetti, *Il Cristo,* 99–101.

11. On panegyric as a rhetorical form that lauds its subject by glorifying his or her ancestors, see Quintilian, *Institutio Oratoria* 3.7.10.

12. In ibid. 3.7.12–16, Quintilian disagrees by considering one's accomplishments more important than one's lineage.

13. A similar encomium of John's glorious ancestors is found in Ambrose, *Expositio Evangelii secundum Lucam* 1.15–16 (CCL 14.14).

14. Chrysologus levels the same charge against Herod in *Sermons* 86.3 and 127.3.

almost everyone, he ventured nothing against this man and was overcome by his virtues, such that the succession of the priesthood was preserved undefiled for the glory of his offspring.

And his wife was a descendant of Aaron (v.5). Aaron was the first high priest, when the priesthood originated;[15] so for this reason, with all his merits left unmentioned, she is called his daughter. In memory of him she manifested in herself the sanctity which as the devoted guardian of her illustrious lineage she most gloriously transmitted to her son. But the evangelist records the praises of this special mother:

5. *Both of them*, he says, *were righteous in the sight of God* (v.6). It is a new kind of happiness, it is an unparalleled marriage, when one mind abides in two people, one holiness in two. What differed in gender agreed in mind, and what was double to behold was one in conduct; and virtue made equal those whom nature had rendered unequal.[16] *Both of them*, it says, *were righteous in the sight of God.* To be pleasing in the judgment of human beings, to be righteous in the eyes of human beings derives from superior human virtue and achievement; in the sight of God, who examines hearts, who scrutinizes thoughts, and who sees how minds operate, to be righteous does not derive from human achievement, but from a divine gift.[17] If one is great who does not sin in the flesh, how great is the one who is sinless in his heart? So John was born of more than the flesh of those who in the sight of God had sinned neither in heart nor in body.

6. The evangelist said in addition: *Proceeding blamelessly according to all the commandments and precepts of the Lord* (v.6). *Proceeding:* one proceeds who does not stand in the crossroads of sinners, who realizes that he is a foreigner in this world, who fearlessly enters the austere dwellings of the virtues, and who as a tireless traveler climbs the mountains of the precepts and the hills of the commandments, in order to enjoy fully the presence of God his Parent in the happiness of his heavenly homeland.[18]

---

15. See Ex 28.1 and Lv 8–9.
16. Chrysologus makes the same point in *Sermon* 91.2.
17. The necessity for divine grace in order to be made righteous before God is given even greater emphasis in *Sermon* 91.3.
18. See *Sermon* 91.4 for the same exegesis of "proceeding."

Proceeding according to all the commandments and precepts. They proceeded according to all of them: something no one has done, or few at any rate. *According to all the precepts and commandments.* Who is unaware of smoke and passes through the fires of the desires? Who has never fallen and manages to avoid the slippery spots of life? Who proceeds unharmed through the raging waters of the vices? Who in the course of his journey encounters all the business of the flesh, the situations in life, and the activity of the world without incurring blame, since the very act of being born is full of crying and complaints?[19]

For indeed the one giving birth complains on account of the pain, and the one who is born complains by crying on account of his nature. But in Zechariah and Elizabeth guilt dies, blame disappears, and every accusation has been removed, since a place was being prepared in them from which perfect holiness would be born. But now let the reading itself make this clear.

7. *And they did not have a child*, it says, *since Elizabeth was barren* (v.7). This barrenness was not something accursed, but mystical, in which giving birth was not taken away, but delayed, and this barrenness was prevented from producing a child not permanently, but only temporarily; it was being cultivated by time, it was being preserved by virtue;[20] it was being ripened by age, it was developing in its old age, so that complete fertility would be its compensation issuing in a unique son, since a vast number of the virtues were being gathered together and coming to birth in the one child. Blessed is that barrenness which was being preserved for a live birth and was awaiting John, for whom, since all the privileges of being the first child were his due, the dignity of the first-born would not be lost.

And both were advanced in years (v.7). They *were advanced*, they did not regress. Old age has come alive in the holy ones; it is not failing, but it is advancing. Or what fails those to whom increments of the virtues are constantly added?[21] Therefore, in Zechariah and Elizabeth there is numbness: their reproductive

19. In this section Chrysologus repeats the word *querela* with both its meanings: "blame" and "complaint."
20. On this same point, see *Sermon* 91.5.
21. See *Sermon* 91.5.

organs are numb, the flesh grows cold, the bodily members are asleep, the time is gone by, their life is passing away, everything having to do with the human order and marital relations is dying out, so that by a divine gift rather than by ordinary reproduction from human beings[22] an angel[23] would be born.

8. We had made the promise to disclose from John's birth the reasons for his death,[24] but because today's sermon has drawn us out this far, and since the verses that follow are necessary for us to demonstrate this satisfactorily, may what has just been said count as giving his birth due glory, and may we not displease you if we postpone what we owe, but do not refuse it. A postponement for the debtors is more favorable to the creditor. So wait for what the debtor promises, and wait without concern, because what has been promised cannot be denied, when the benefits that had been denied are paid back so bountifully to a barren woman.[25]

22. A point that was also made in *Sermon* 87.3.
23. The Latin *angelus* means both "angel" and the more generic "messenger." See n. 7 above.
24. At the end of section 2 above.
25. This promised sermon on John's martyrdom could be one of the three sermons on this theme mentioned above in n. 9. F. Sottocornola, *L'anno liturgico*, 111, believes that it could well be *Sermon* 127, but it seems more likely that *Sermon* 127 may have *preceded* this *Sermon* 89, for reasons given in n. 9. It is quite possible that the sermon subsequent to this one is not extant. See also A. Olivar, *Los sermones*, 266–67.

SERMON 90

A Fifth <on Zechariah>[1]

HAT WE ARE LIFTED up when the saints fall down, and that we are made firm when the saints tremble, the hesitation of the priest Zechariah has shown us today. When he does not trust in the promises of God but debates about them,[2] and does not accept the divine works on faith, but investigates them with human reasoning, he pays for the sin of disbelief by being condemned to a long period of silence. He had heard from the angel: *Your prayer has been heard, and your wife Elizabeth will bear you a son* (Lk 1.13). He then said in response: *How am I to know this? I am an old man, and my wife is advanced in years* (v.18).

As much as he had lost hope of posterity because he was so far into old age, had he not learned just as much by his lengthy experience in life that God considers nothing impossible? He who had been a priest for so long had read and knew as a veteran high priest that while nature could be restrained by law,[3] the Author of nature could not be restrained, and that while time could limit the human being, it could not limit its Creator.

He knew that the bodies of Abraham and Sarah were decrepit[4] from extreme old age, and prevented from bearing the

---

1. (Angle brackets here indicate an addition to the title in Olivar's CCL text.) This sermon, which begins by commenting on Lk 1.18 (after a brief reference to Lk 1.13), was probably preached next after *Sermon* 88 (FOTC 17.137–43), which concludes with a commentary on Lk 1.17. These sermons were delivered in December before Christmas. See F. Sottocornola, *L'anno liturgico*, 96.

2. The contrast between trusting and debating or arguing is also noted in *Sermons* 49.3 (FOTC 109.189–90) and 61.3 (FOTC 17.112).

3. That is, by the natural law. In *Sermon* 44.4 and 6 (FOTC 17.97 and 98) Chrysologus also makes reference to the natural law and the Author of nature.

4. Literally, "dead" *(mortuis)*.

name of father and mother because of their very well publicized sterility, and that Isaac had burst forth to produce descendants in abundance in the Israelite people.[5] The deficiency of nature was not as detrimental to him as it was beneficial to be born by the kindness of the Author, and not of nature. Zechariah had learned that God had given to Rebecca and Anna, who had been childless for so long and had been out of favor with nature for so long, what barrenness had denied.[6]

2. So, having been instructed in such great matters, why is it that he says: *How am I to know this? I am an old man, and my wife is advanced in years?* Brothers, human nature is quite anxious near God, quite feeble near the divine powers, and in the matter at hand it does not find itself to be in the condition it thought it was earlier. The human being lacks sufficient knowledge of himself before proving himself within the situation and putting himself to the test in such instances.

He seeks heaven, he seeks the heights, he searches out the celestial realm, he moves heaven, he strikes at heaven; but when he has moved heaven, he is unable to bear heaven's weight. He strives to climb to the pinnacle of faith, he yearns to penetrate heaven by his own power, but when he has begun to proceed with human steps along the celestial paths, when he glances down at his own nature, he does not have as much confidence about the distance already traveled as he has fear about falling headlong. Thus when blessed Peter imitates God in walking across the water, and as a trailblazer he treads heavy-footed on the fluid path, he prays out of fear of sinking before rejoicing about what has already been granted to him.[7]

So now let us turn to Zechariah. Over a long period of time he used to lament that the devil was able to reign through death on account of one man's offense, and that human beings were born to suffer labors, groans, and dangers. He continually lamented his unfulfilled desire to have children, although it was a troublesome prospect in that they were destined to die.

5. See Gn 21.1–5.
6. See Gn 25.21 and 1 Sm 1.
7. See Mt 14.25–31. For a similar description of this incident, see *Sermon* 50.1 (FOTC 109.193).

Furthermore, he was lamenting the fact that he stood in the front line of the battle against sins, that he was besieged by throngs of vices, that he was always shaken and battered by the attack of ailments.

He could see in the distance the standards of the virtues, the hope of the Law, the freedom stemming from grace; nevertheless, none were able to arrive there by their own strength; people willed the good but did not do it, and they hated sins but did not conquer them. God ought to show mercy now, he ought to come to the aid now of those held captive in these ways. Therefore, when this high priest struck the ears of God with a constant complaint like this, with a lamentation of this sort, God took it upon himself to establish a wonderful proof of his answer to the one who made such a devout and just request for an offspring of his own. It was the sort of proof by which he could believe that God gives life to the dead and renders salvation to the hopeless, once he had given a child to decrepit[8] old age, a son to hopeless sterility, as the words of the Gospel reveal, when they say:

3. *Your prayer has been heard, and your wife Elizabeth will bear you a son* (v.13), "who will be a messenger of this redemption and a forerunner of this salvation; he will approach God, but not like you with words, nor will he try to influence him with his groans, nor, as you have done, will he need to gain our assistance, but he himself has been given a place in our order, and has been endowed with the honor of an angel. With his hand he will hold God who is greatly desired by all,[9] but never recognized by him, invisible even to the angels themselves; he will clasp him to his bosom, and then with happy arms hand him over to be seen by the world, and with his very blessed hands he will point him out so that he will come into the full view of human eyes.

"Your son will make God known to everyone, he will lead the Lord to share life with the lowliest of his servants, he will have the Judge associate with the accused, and so testify to the fact that the Magistrate has taken upon himself the person of the

---

8. Literally, "dead" *(mortuae);* see n. 4 above.
9. See Hg 2.8.

guilty. And thus he will show that the sentence which condemned humanity is about to come to an end, since the One who is brought to trial and takes the course he does for the sake of pardon is the very One who was about to hand the accused over to be punished.

"And so that this mystery of awesome mercy would be evident, Zechariah, your son submerges his Lord in the baptism of repentance, and washes him for the forgiveness of sins, because the Fountain wanted to be washed, the Advocate wanted to receive pardon, and the Judge himself wanted to undergo his own sentence, so that he would not condemn the accused, nor inflict vengeance upon the guilty.[10] He ascends the cross, he tastes death, he endures being buried, he enters hell, since he wanted to be punished rather than punish, and wanted to be loved rather than feared."[11]

4. But, brothers, when Zechariah heard that he had been counted worthy of so great a mystery by his prayers, he was terrified when he considered this very matter, he was disturbed by the thought of this very mystery, and he did not believe that he deserved anything so great, and he doubted that God was coming down for such great and awesome activities. This is why he says: *How am I to know this? I am an old man, and my wife is advanced in years* (v. 18). That is to say: just as my human condition does not permit me to have a son, so too God's eternal Majesty does not allow him to be born and die. Since his lack of trust was a pardonable matter, the angel inflicted upon him a punishment that was merely a sign, and he did not brand him with the stigma of unbelief. It is not an issue of unbelief, but of caution to be slow to believe lowly things about God and to be even slower to entertain dishonorable ideas about God.

5. The angel went on to say: *I am Gabriel* (v. 19), so that from such a great name and from the merit of so distinguished a servant the high priest would consider and believe how trustwor-

---

10. See Mt 3.13–17 and parallels.
11. For other references in Chrysologus's sermons to what he sees as one of the fundamental reasons for the Incarnation, suffering, death and Resurrection of the Son of God, see A. Olivar, *Los sermones*, 362. For other ancient authors, see *Sermon* 72b, n. 15.

thy and reliable the promise was. *I am Gabriel, who stand in attendance before God and have been sent to you* (v.19). By saying his name, he points out his merit; when he mentions that he stands in attendance, when he mentions that he has been sent, he acknowledges that he is a servant, so that the prestige of the name would not obscure the One to whom reverence was due. *I am Gabriel*, he says, *who stand in attendance before God, and I have been sent to speak to you, and to bring you this news* (v.19).

Truly, "Great is the Lord, and of his wisdom there is no measure."[12] He cures the afflicted of his wound, he fortifies the faltering in suffering chastisement, from punishment he produces evidence for faith with the words: *You will be speechless* (v.20), so that from yourself and in yourself you may acquire a standard for believing,[13] and from an example that strikes close to home you may believe that God can do what he promises. For when God wants, he closes your vocal organs, and when he wants, he opens up your mouth for speaking; so too when he wants, he surely can make a woman fertile, and when he makes a promise, he can make barren someone else who used to be fertile;[14] when he wants, he is able to bestow the capacity of bearing children; when he wants, he is able to deny nature's compliance.

Therefore, the angel acted so that by such evidence the high priest would learn not to say any longer: *How am I to know this?* (v.18) since he could verify it by pointing to all of creation. He who had read that "the sky, the earth, the sea, and all that are in them"[15] came to be out of nothing,[16] ought to have believed that he could make what he wants out of something, and could render to the despairing what he promises: he who had made everything out of what did not exist, has no difficulty in making whatever he wants out of something that already exists.

6. *And the people were awaiting Zechariah, and they were wondering about what was delaying him in the Temple. But when Zechariah came out he was unable to speak*, it says, *and they realized that he had*

---

12. Ps 146 (147).5.
13. *Regulam credendi.*
14. See 1 Sm 2.5.
15. Ps 145 (146).6.
16. For other references to *creatio ex nihilo* by Chrysologus, see *Sermon* 46.6 and n. 12 (FOTC 109.180).

seen a vision. But he made signs to them, it goes on to say, *since he remained mute* (vv.21–22). The high priest goes out bearing in his mouth an indication of barrenness, carrying in his heart an image of a conception, such that when the mother would give birth to her son, the son would give him his voice, at that moment the father would mystically generate speech, and at his birth the son would grant pardon to his father before he would wash away the age-old sins of the peoples. And since the one who did not believe was speechless, rightly does the prophet boast that he believed, by saying: "I believed, and therefore I have spoken."[17]

Brothers, faith gives speech, while lack of faith refuses to speak.[18] So if, brothers, as I have said,[19] when the saints fall down they lift us up, and when the blessed tremble they make us strong, let us conclude that nothing is ever impossible for God,[20] and let us not inquire into how he is going to do what he promises; in his case to have willed it is to have done it, and to have promised it is to have granted it.

17. Ps 115 (116).10.
18. A similar treatment of faith speaking and lack of faith being silent is found in Ambrose, *Expositio Evangelii secundum Lucam* 1.42 (CCL 14.27).
19. At the very beginning of this sermon.
20. See Gn 18.14 and Lk 1.37.

SERMON 91

A Sixth <on Zechariah>[1]

THOSE WHO KNOW HOW to dig gold out of the earth, when they discover a rich vein, devote to it whatever skill and effort they have. And because we have seen that a heavenly treasure lies buried in holy Zechariah, let us direct toward him my entire homily and your entire attention, so that what is acquired by our common effort may be our common gain.[2]

2. *In the days when Herod was king of Judea*, it says, *there was a certain priest named Zechariah of the class of Abijah* (Lk 1.5). Of this we have spoken already.[3] *And his wife was a descendant of Aaron* (v.5). Thus the evangelist begins, so that in the priest's wife, with her priestly lineage intact, his nobility would be made evident. *Both of them*, he says, *were righteous in the sight of God* (v.6). *Both righteous*, since there was one righteousness in the two. *Both righteous*, because the union between them was based not on their love, but on their holiness as a couple. *Both righteous*, since although they were unequal in gender, they were judged equal in merits. *Both righteous*, since just as there was one flesh in the two, so there was one spirit in the two.[4] Let married couples imitate them, so that those whom affection joins together, virtue also may unite.[5]

---

1. (Angle brackets here indicate an addition to the title in Olivar's CCL text.) This sermon was preached in December before Christmas. See F. Sottocornola, *L'anno liturgico*, 97 and 303, and A. Olivar, *Los sermones*, 266.

2. See *Sermon* 139.1 on the same notion of digging for gold as an image for applying oneself to access the profundities of Scripture. The same metaphor is used in this way by John Chrysostom in his *Homily on Genesis* 5.1 (FOTC 74.66).

3. Very likely in *Sermon* 86. See F. Sottocornola, *L'anno liturgico*, 97, and A. Olivar, *Los sermones*, 267.

4. The same point is made in *Sermon* 89.5.

5. There appears to be a typographical error in Olivar's CCL text, which has *inungat* instead of *iungat* (see PL 52.456). G. Banterle and C. Truzzi noted this

3. *Both of them*, it says, *were righteous in the sight of God. Both righteous in the sight of God:* and what about the passage that says: "No living person will be counted righteous in your sight"?[6] Perhaps in the sight of human beings one may be thought to be righteous, since human beings, as aware as they are of sins of the body, are equally unaware of vices of the mind. But in God's sight, before whom the secrets of the heart are laid bare, by whom hidden thoughts do not go unnoticed, who is judged innocent and righteous?

Is there a human being who does not sin in his heart, who does not have a bad thought, who is not guilty of harboring doubts, who does not incur blame through fear? Moses doubts, Aaron goes astray, Peter denies:[7] so who is righteous? And how were they *both righteous in the sight of God? In the sight of God,* yes, but by means of God. *Both righteous in the sight of God,* not by their effort but by grace.

Listen to the Apostle: "They are justified gratuitously through the grace of Christ."[8] And again: "Not from ourselves; it is God's gift. Not from our works, lest anyone boast."[9] Yet again: "What do you have that you have not received; but if you have received it, why do you boast as if you did not receive it?"[10] Therefore, this is more or less what the evangelist is saying: not that they did not have it, but that they received it; not that it was earned, but that it was bestowed.[11]

4. *Both of them,* it says, *were righteous in the sight of God, proceeding blamelessly according to all the commandments and precepts of God* (v.6). It said, *proceeding,* in order to show that they had progressed in the virtues, that they had not stood still, and that they had walked in the path of righteousness, they had not sat down, nor had they remained at a standstill in following the

---

in San Pietro Crisologo, *Sermoni e Lettera a Eutiche* (Rome: Città Nuova Editrice, 1997), 2.213, n. 3.
   6. Ps 142 (143).2.
   7. See Nm 20.12; Ex 32; Mt 26.69–75 and parallels.
   8. Rom 3.24.
   9. Eph 2.8–9.
   10. 1 Cor 4.7.
   11. The necessity and gratuity of grace are likewise mentioned in *Sermon* 89.5.

commandments, but they had reached the point of complete compliance with the commandments. *Proceeding blamelessly according to all the commandments and precepts of God.* Brothers, blessed are those not pierced by guilt nor wounded by any offense; but blessed are these who have been untouched by blame.[12]

Proceeding blamelessly according to all the commandments and precepts of God. If childhood, if adolescence, if young adulthood has been blameless, where is all the blame, and what sort of blame is there, against their old age? If there is this kind of beginning, what will the ending be like? That they climbed the peaks of the precepts and the hills of the commandments and did not falter in any way is a sign of unparalleled grace and unique happiness.[13]

5. *And they did not have a child,* it says, *since Elizabeth was barren* (v.7). It did not say, "They did not have children," but: *They did not have a child,* because he who was going to be born from such as these was going to be unique. Listen to the Lord as he says: "There is no one greater among those born of women than John the Baptist."[14] *Since Elizabeth was barren:* barren in body, but fertile in virtues; slow to conceive, but not slow before God; sealed shut, not to an offspring, but for a time; not refused a child, but preserved for a mystery.[15]

And both, it says, *were advancing in years* (v.7). *Advancing:* thus is described the mystery of an old age which does not yet cease being meritorious, is not failing with age, but advances; nor does it feel any decline in body since it obtains an increase in virtue.[16] Brothers, the holy Elizabeth's ability to bear a child has not been taken away, but merely delayed until the time of sensuality, bodily passion, conjugal necessity, the pursuit of pleasure, the sense of desire, and everything that disturbs, weighs down, and burdens the human conscience should pass away.

---

12. See *Sermon* 89.6 on the same topic.
13. For the concept that the state of sinlessness is "happiness of the first class," see also *Sermons* 34.1 (FOTC 109.144) and 167.6.
14. Mt 11.11 and Lk 7.28.
15. See *Sermon* 89.7, which makes the same point.
16. This same theme is developed in *Sermon* 89.7.

88   ST. PETER CHRYSOLOGUS

For the house of sacrifice, the inn of sanctity, the lodging of the preparer[17] for Christ, the dwelling of an angel, the royal court of the Holy Spirit, the temple of God[18] was being cleansed over a long period of time. "You are the temple of God," the Apostle says, "and the Spirit of God dwells in you."[19]

And so at the moment every kind of blame having to do with the body has been allayed, and they have become blameless in every way, just then barrenness flees, old age comes back to life, faith conceives, chastity gives birth, and there is born one who is greater than a human being,[20] equal to the angels, the trumpet of heaven, the herald of Christ, the mysterious agent of the Father, the messenger of the Son, the standard-bearer of the celestial King, the pardon of sinners, the chastisement of the Jews, the summons of the gentiles, and, to put it accurately, the clasp of the Law and grace, which fastened the high priest's double robe[21] which his holy father wore on his body.

6. The evangelist thus describes the virtues of the father and mother, so that from the merits of his parents the dignity of the offspring would be recognized, and so that he who in his birth surpassed the law of human generation may be shown to be greater than a human being. But if he is going to be the forerunner, let John now be born, because the birth of Christ is at hand;[22] let the new bearer of light[23] arise, because the radiance of the true Sun is now bursting through; let the herald cry out, because the Judge draws near; let the trumpet resound, because the King is coming; and because God is about to make his entrance, let the angel[24] now precede him. But because a

---

17. *Metatum metatoris:* other early Christian references to John as *metator* are noted in A. Olivar, *Los sermones*, 403–4.

18. Some of the same descriptions of and titles for John as noted in this and the following paragraph are also found in *Sermon* 127.2.

19. 1 Cor 3.16.

20. See Mt. 11.11 and Lk 7.28.

21. Likewise, Origen in his *Homily on Leviticus* 6.3.3–5 (FOTC 83.121–22) interprets allegorically the "double cloak" or "two tunics" the Israelite priest wore (see Lv 8.7) as the Law and the Gospels.

22. A reference to the proximity of Christmas.

23. Literally, "a new Lucifer" *(novus lucifer)*, likely a reference to the planet Venus, which appears in the sky before the rising of the sun. See F. Sottocornola, *L'anno liturgico*, 226.

24. *Angelus* also means "messenger."

human being is not sufficient to relate what is beyond humanity, let the angel now speak of the virtues of the angel who is going to be born.

7. The angel said to Zechariah: *Do not fear, Zechariah; your prayer has been heard. Elizabeth your wife will bear you a son, and you will call his name John; joy and exultation will be yours, and many will rejoice at his birth. For he will be great in the sight of God, he will not drink wine and strong drink, he will be filled with the Holy Spirit while still in his mother's womb, and he will turn many of the children of Israel to the Lord their God; and he will go before him in the spirit and power of Elijah, in order to turn the hearts of fathers towards their children and the unbelievers to the wisdom of the righteous, to make a people completely prepared for the Lord* (vv.13–17).

There is no place for human language, and the praise lavished by the preacher is made silent, when by the message of an angel John's glory is proclaimed, his virtue resounds, his fame is highly lauded, and there is nothing that a human being can add in his regard on whom God has conferred everything. *He will be filled with the Holy Spirit*, it says, *while still in his mother's womb.* You see how John reached heaven before he touched earth; he received the divine Spirit before having a human one; he acquired divine gifts before bodily members; he began to live for God before living for himself; rather, he lived for God before God would live for him, according to what the Apostle says: "It is no longer I who live, but Christ is living in me."[25]

In the sixth month he leaps in his mother's womb, and he announces that Christ has come into the womb of the Virgin.[26] He is an eager messenger who was intent on making an announcement before living. He is an impatient guide who reached the King before reaching his body; he took up arms before his bodily members; he sought the battlefield before the light of day; and in order to win victory over the world he won victory before he would be born. Without internal organs himself he gives his mother's internal organs a jolt; and because his body was still slowly being formed, he fulfilled his duty of evan-

---

25. Gal 2.20.
26. See Lk 1.26, 36, 41, and 44.

gelizing with his spirit alone. What am I to say? Before being the forerunner of Christ, John was his own forerunner![27]

8. One and the same Holy Spirit fills the hearts of father, mother, and son,[28] so that the song of the Lord's birth would ring out of one organ of holiness. And it is no wonder, brothers; there is always festivity to honor royal births, and a sweet and harmonious melody to celebrate them. So let us, brothers, let us glorify Christ's birth with hymns, and let us honor it with gifts, because a Christian only pretends to believe, if what an astrologer does,[29] he does not do.

---

27. Chrysologus is fond of underscoring John's vigorous activity even before leaving Elizabeth's womb. See *Sermons* 68.11, 69.6, and 72.3 (FOTC 109.279, 284, 294) and *Sermons* 70.3 and 88.4 (FOTC 17.120, 141).

28. See Lk 1.41 and 67.

29. See Mt 2.11. As above in n. 22, this is another allusion to the upcoming feast of Christmas.

SERMON 92

A Seventh <on Zechariah>[1]

RADUALLY DO THE WORDS of the Gospel elevate us to what is more lofty and raise us to the heights. And it is no wonder, brothers, if the celestial chariot carried Elijah up to heaven,[2] when daily[3] the fourfold transport[4] of the Gospels takes the human race aboard and conveys it to the kingdom of heaven.[5] See how it has now brought us along, brothers, from a barren woman's delivery to the Virgin's delivery, and from the birth of John it has made us very close at hand to the birth of our Savior.[6] But for the moment let us still be patient[7] and listen to the rest of the account about the high priest Zechariah,[8] so that on our royal journey we can reach the cradle of our King,[9] since the very reason that we have taken a secure seat in the heavenly chariot was to avoid the anxious moments and difficulties that shortcuts bring.

---

1. Angle brackets here indicate an addition to the title in Olivar's CCL text.
2. See 2 Kgs 2.11.
3. For evidence that *cotidie* is not necessarily to be taken literally as "each day," but more generally as "frequently" or "regularly," see F. Sottocornola, *L'anno liturgico*, 144–46.
4. Literally, "four-horse team" or "chariot" *(quadriga)*. See *Sermon* 170.4 (FOTC 17.279) for a reference to chariots of the apostles.
5. For more on this image of the chariot, see F. Sottocornola, *L'anno liturgico*, 224–27, especially n. 16.
6. This implies that this sermon was preached in December shortly before Christmas.
7. F. Sottocornola, *L'anno liturgico*, 262 and n. 22, suggests that the call for patience may be on account of Chrysologus's continuing to speak about Zechariah rather than the account of the Annunciation in Lk 1.26–38 that his congregation had been anticipating!
8. This sermon follows either *Sermon* 90 (see A. Olivar, *Los sermones*, 267–68) or *Sermon* 91 (see F. Sottocornola, *L'anno liturgico*, 97–99) both of which ended their discussion prior to Lk 1.23.
9. This is another reference to the upcoming feast of Christmas. In *Sermon* 140a.1, for example, preached during the Christmas season, Chrysologus mentions that he and his congregation have now "reached the cradle."

2. And so we heard read: *And the days of his service were completed, and Zechariah went back home* (Lk 1.23). Thus the whole tribe used to assist at the one Temple, and thousands of priests used to serve there, on account of the fact that the observance of the priestly office had been divided up among their very large number, assigned for time periods, and distributed by turns, so that the large crowd of them would not become jumbled and disturb the order of the priesthood, nor would one by functioning continually prevent another from carrying out his official obligation.[10]

3. *But after this his wife Elizabeth conceived* (v.24). It was in their power to have intercourse, and allowance was made for them to procreate, since they were still under the Law, which was the time of adolescence; religion[11] in its infancy was as of yet only drawing near. The Law, brothers, prohibited what was illicit, it did not deny what was licit; it held within the home, it was unable to grant anything above the home; it governed nature, it did not elevate the human being above nature. The Law was the gateway of faith, the herald of grace, the forerunner of the Gospel, the tutor of religion in its infancy. To the priesthood it permitted as a concession the chastity of legal marriage, in order to announce that the glory of perpetual virtue would come in the priesthood of grace.[12]

So, in accord with this indulgence Elizabeth, who was already decrepit[13] in old age, revives for a holy pregnancy, and her bodily members, dry and withered with wrinkles, produce living marrow making her internal organs fertile. Also that very time of life, that very time which had come to an end, is summoned back to her body, and the shelter of her womb which had dissolved in her very old age is suddenly restored to its youthful form. The order of things is astounded, the force of custom is overmatched, nature itself is amazed, and from the way the dwelling has been made ready the merit and dignity of

10. See 1 Chr 24.
11. That is, Christianity.
12. Chrysologus uses *sacerdotium* and *pontificatus* interchangeably here and in the previous section. This particular reference seems to be alluding to the office of Christian priesthood being reserved for celibates.
13. Literally, "dead" *(mortua)*.

the resident become known. But John found it quite marvelous that his sojourn was spent in a normal womb, after learning that his time had run out, that nature had refused him, but that he was welcomed thanks to that gift granted by the Creator and not by his mother.

4. *And she kept herself secluded for five months and said: "The Lord has done this for me"* (vv.24–25). It is well that she acknowledges that the Lord did it all, since she saw that none of this was conferred on her through human means. *And she kept herself in hiding for five months.* That is, even though what she had was a gift from God; nevertheless, it was not characteristic of her period in life. *She kept herself secluded for five months.* The old woman blushes about being pregnant, the aged woman is bashful about her first pregnancy, and inasmuch as she is with child in her extreme old age she stays in seclusion, so that laughter about her fertile old age would not add to the shame of her barrenness.

But that a conception by one who is elderly and aged is grounds for laughter, Sarah makes evident, who was barren and old like her.[14] When she realized that the Lord was permitting her to become pregnant and to be given a son, now that her life was almost over, she herself laughed about her pregnancy. In addition, that the combination of her being grey-haired and yet swollen and heavy with child could be a cause for laughter by everyone is attested even by the very name of her child, as Scripture says: "And he called his son's name Isaac, which means laughter."[15] She said in addition: "The Lord has made me laugh."[16] This is why Elizabeth wants to conceal the sacred mystery by saying: *The Lord has done this for me,* such that her modesty at just now conceiving a child bothers her for whom the distress of never becoming pregnant over so long a period of time caused turmoil.

5. The father is speechless from his punishment, the mother hides out of modesty. O how great is the silence[17] in which the

14. *Sermon* 90.1 also makes the comparison with Sarah.
15. Gn 21.3 Vg. See also *Sermon* 154.1 (FOTC 17.259–60).
16. Gn 21.6.
17. In *Sermon* 127.2 John himself is called the "silence of the prophets."

voice[18] is born! The father is speechless from his punishment, the mother hides out of modesty. O how still and quiet it is where the trumpet which is about to resound through the ages has its beginning! The father is speechless from his punishment, the mother hides out of modesty. O what a mystery that produces the herald of the divine Judge![19]

6. *The Lord has done this for me in the days in which he has seen fit to remove my disgrace among human beings* (v.25). The honor of marriage, yes, the dignity of matrimony is the procreation of dear children; for it is quite hard and sad both to lack the reward of virginity and not have the solace of sons and daughters; to endure the burdens of matrimony and not to enjoy the fruit of matrimony. This is why the holy, barren woman rejoices that her disgrace has been removed from her by saying: *The Lord has done this for me in the days in which he has seen fit to remove my disgrace among human beings.* That is, this is regarded as wretched in the eyes of human beings, but there is no guilt in the eyes of God, where it is no fault of the parent, but is evidence of the One who denies them. Certainly if some bodily infirmity is the reason for this, something beyond one's control is at issue, not one's will.[20]

7. But right now let all idle, carnal thoughts be removed, let all feeble sensory knowledge be cast aside, and let whatever ideas that are based entirely on human capability be excluded; let the eyes of the heart open up to faith, let the ears be unblocked, and let the pace of the mind run and charge ahead, so that we can reach the mystery of the virginal conception and penetrate the sacred mystery of the virginal birth.[21]

---

18. See Mt 3.3 and parallels.
19. John is also referred to as the herald of the Judge in *Sermons* 88.3 (FOTC 17.140), 91.6, and 127.2.
20. A similar point is made in *Sermon* 41.2 (FOTC 109.164–65).
21. Yet another reference to the fact that Christmas is fast approaching!

SERMON 94

A Second <on the Meal of the Pharisee>[1]

INCE IN THE LAST sermon we made our way through the first sections of today's reading, and we were equally amazed with what fervor, with what faith, with what daring, and with what great yet unusual homage the sinful woman touched the feet of the Savior himself, now let us listen to what the Pharisee said silently and what response Christ made, who hears even matters kept in silence.

2. The Pharisee, it says, *said to himself: "If this man were a prophet, he would certainly know who and what kind of woman this is who is touching him"* (Lk 7.39). O Pharisee, what you are seeing is not ignorance, but power; it is a case of divine judgment, not human error. *If this man were a prophet, he would certainly know who and what kind of woman this is who is touching him.* Pharisee, you are mistaken: he would not have been able to know more if he had been a prophet, because prophecy does not depend on a human being's choice, but on a divine gift. And so, a prophet does not know as much as he wants, but only as much as he who bestows prophecy grants.

If this man were a prophet, he would certainly know who and what kind of woman this is who is touching him. The touch of a bad woman burns up the person who is her partner in sin, defiles a person who is on her level, brands one who is suspect, and disgraces a person of bad will. But the sinful woman is made good, she is made holy, and she becomes innocent when she touches the Bestower of pardon.

Dung comes into contact with the sun, but it does not con-

---

1. (Angle brackets here indicate an addition to the title in Olivar's CCL text.) This is the second of three sermons preached consecutively on Lk 7.36–50. See sections 1 and 8 of this sermon. *Sermons* 93 (which precedes this one) and 95 (which follows) are translated in FOTC 17.143–51.

taminate it.² When wounds are handled by doctors, their festering does not infect them. Although the accused may touch the judge, he is unable to stain him as he makes his entreaty. Thus when a sinner touches the Lord, he does not make God dirty, but he is both freed from all sin and all at once snatches holiness in its entirety.³ The woman who had suffered from the hemorrhage proves this, since while touching the fringe of the Lord's clothing, she did not defile the fringe, but she herself was freed at that very moment from the filth of her long-standing affliction.[4]

3. *If this man were a prophet, he would certainly know who and what kind of woman this is who is touching him.* The Pharisee would believe that Christ was a prophet if he saw what was right before his eyes and what was known to the peoples. What do you suppose he will believe when he realizes the next moment that [Christ] beholds what is in his mind, that he judges his heart, that he looks into his conscience, and that he is aware of his thoughts? Do you suppose that perhaps then he will acknowledge him as God whom now after such great acts of power he does not even consider to be a teacher?

If this man were a prophet, he would certainly know who and what kind of woman this is who is touching him. The woman had a wound, she knew it, and so in this manner she was looking diligently for a physician for so severe a wound. The Pharisee, injured by the disease of unbelief, in a fever with the flame of pride, through his delirium did not know that he was insane. This is why Christ decided to cure him first, where a disease was raging unrecognized, so that the heavenly Physician would cure two sick people with one medication. *When the Pharisee who had invited him saw this, he said to himself* (v.39). Because the Pharisee had kept his thoughts to himself, Christ responded out loud to him, and while he laid bare the secrets of the Phar-

---

2. On this rather unusual image, see *Sermon* 35.2 and n. 2 (FOTC 109.150).
3. The general theme of God's not being harmed by coming into contact with human beings for the purpose of healing them of their afflictions and sins is found also in *Sermons* 35.2 (FOTC 109.150) and 36.1 (FOTC 17.76).
4. See Mt 9.20–22 and parallels. Chrysologus preaches on this story in *Sermons* 34–35 (FOTC 109.144–52) and *Sermon* 36 (FOTC 17.75–80).

isee's heart, he shows that he himself is the Author of all prophecy.

4. *Jesus*, it says, *said in response: "Simon, I have something to say to you"* (v.40). To you who need healing, but do not know how to look for healing; you who call God your Teacher, and disregard what God teaches; you fail to recognize that the one who professes to be a disciple of a teacher but does not follow his instruction gives great offense to his teacher. For just as the goodness of the disciple brings praise to the teacher, so the teacher is blamed when the disciple ignores what he teaches. *Simon, I have something to say to you.* He answered: *Teacher, speak* (v.40), and not: "God, speak." Right now you will realize that he is God whom you are calling "Teacher."

5. *"There were two people,"* he says, *"who were in debt to a certain moneylender. One owed five hundred days' wages, the other fifty. Since they did not have the means to repay him,"* he says, *"he wrote off both the debts. So who loves him more?"* He answered: *"I imagine the one for whom he wrote off the greater debt."* And the Lord said: *"You have judged correctly"* (vv.41–43). You have heard how the heavenly Creditor takes charity as payment for the whole debt,[5] and as the addition to all that was lent out he exacts and demands as interest only love. The debtor must be punished who neglects to pay back his obligation when love is all that is required.

Do you want to know, O man, what you owe to God? That you have been created is credit from God; that you are capable of reason is a loan from God; that you possess the ability to distinguish good from evil is something you have received; and that you pledged to follow completely the rule for living according to the bond[6] of the Law as God drew it up, you are not able to deny.

Meanwhile you act like a pig and wallow in mud through the vices of the flesh, and living like a beast on all fours, you are de-

---

5. The Latin clause *caelestis creditor totum debitum caritate conpensat* could perhaps also bear the meaning, "the heavenly Creditor in his charity remits the whole debt," but since the customary meaning of *conpensat* is "equalizes" or "balances," I take the "charity," like the "love" in the next clause, as belonging to the debtor and paid to the Creditor.

6. See Col 2.14.

prived of the reason with which you were endowed;[7] in the raging waters of your sins you confuse good with evil because you have lost the ability to distinguish between them, and you squander the substance[8] of the divine Law. Therefore, captivated by worldly pleasure, you have become a lamentable debtor of a glorious loan. Regarding one who fails to reap any profit in the virtues, the interest compounded from sins is multiplied.

6. But although you have fallen in this matter, although you have fallen headlong into these calamities, take care that you do not lose hope, O man; you still have the means to make amends to your very merciful Creditor. Do you want to be absolved? Then love. "Charity will cover a multitude of sins."[9] What is worse than the sin of denial? And nevertheless, Peter managed to wipe this out solely by love, as the Lord attests when he says: "Peter," "do you love me?"[10]

Of all the precepts of God, love holds the first place: "You shall love the Lord your God with all your heart, with all your soul, with all your mind, and with all your strength."[11] So, man, love God, and love him totally, so that you may be able to overcome and wipe out all your sins without distress. It is a cushy military assignment and an easy struggle when one gains a victory after all one's sins solely by love, as is clear from what follows.

7. *Turning to the woman*, it says, *he said to Simon* (v.44). Why is it that Christ turned to the woman but spoke to Simon? Because when he looks at the penitent he is reprimanding her detractor. *He said to Simon: "I entered your house, and you did not give me any water for my feet, but she has wet my feet with her tears and dried them with the hair on her head. You did not give me a kiss, but she, from the moment I came in, has not stopped kissing my feet. You did not anoint my head with oil, but she has anointed my feet with*

---

7. Chrysologus's language here is reminiscent of his description of the Prodigal Son in *Sermon* 1.5 (FOTC 17.28–29).
8. See Lk 15.13.
9. 1 Pt 4.8.
10. Jn 21.17. In commenting on this same account from Luke, Ambrose too brings in Peter (as well as Paul) as a sinner who loved much. See his *Expositio Evangelii secundum Lucam* 6.22 (CCL 14.182).
11. Mk 12.30; see Dt 6.5.

ointment. Therefore, I say to you: her many sins are forgiven her, because she has loved much. But the one to whom less is forgiven loves less" (vv.44–47).

It has been demonstrated that love wipes out and washes away all sins. But what[12] does he mean by saying: *The one to whom less is forgiven loves less?* Is it that one must sin the more in order to obtain a greater amount of love? Far from it![13] Charity helps concerning past sins, but it does not absolve future sins. Charity is unable to sin when it loves. Charity is not charity if it commits an offense. The charity of God is the guardian of holiness.

8. Brothers, if we know that we are sinners and we do not want to be sinners, let us pour our tears onto Christ's feet, let us wipe them with our hair, let us plant our kisses, let us pour out the oil of piety in complete devotion, so that it might be said to us: "Your many sins are forgiven you, because you have loved much." Let us imitate this woman who we see has not only been freed from her sins, but has even reached the very pinnacle of holiness. But inasmuch as today's sermon on charity has delayed us, we shall with God's help fulfill our promise and make clear next time who this woman is.

12. Reading *quid* in PL 52.466 instead of *qui* in Olivar's CCL text.
13. See Rom 6.1–2.

SERMON 97

A Second on the Tares[1]

INCE THE HASTE OF our previous sermon[2] was unable to penetrate the whole mystery of the last parable in deference to the fatigue we all felt,[3] let us now explain what remains as far as the Lord reveals it.[4] *He proposed to them,* it says, *a parable in these words: "The kingdom of heaven is like a person who sowed good seed in his field. But when people were sleeping, an enemy came, and sowed tares in the midst of the wheat, and went off"* (Mt 13.24–25).

But when people were sleeping: the one who plots ambush lurks by night. He flees those who keep watch by day, and assails those who sleep; one who is strong seeks and provokes a conflict in the open and with everybody ready, and he wants to gain victory in full view of everyone. It is a clear indication of weakness to attack those who are asleep. *But when people were sleeping, an enemy came.* One who is evil is always foolish as well. What does this enemy do? Granted that the servants were sleeping: but do you really think that the Lord too was asleep? Granted that slumber closed the eyes of the servants after their labors: but do you really think that any weariness had also overtaken the eyes of the One in charge?

---

1. The title is reconstructed from *Sermon* 96 (see CCL 24A.592).
2. *Sermon* 96. See F. Sottocornola, *L'anno liturgico,* 101 and 289, who suggests that perhaps this *Sermon* 97 was preached on September 16, the feast of St. Euphemia, to whom there is a brief reference in section 3 below. See also A. Olivar, *Los sermones,* 246 and 268. Another possibility is mentioned in *L'anno liturgico,* 300–301, namely, that her relics, some of which were believed to be in Milan and Aquileia somewhat earlier, may also have been at hand in the church where Chrysologus was preaching on this occasion.
3. Chrysologus mentions this same *communem laborem* in *Sermon* 96.7 (FOTC 17.156).
4. The same notion that the homilist depends on what Christ reveals for any insight expressed in the homily is noted with almost the same terminology in *Sermon* 4.5 (FOTC 17.43).

O enemy, you fugitive from the light, you kept awake, you labored, but you did not manage to stay hidden! For while the servants were sleeping, the Lord himself saw you. You deserter of heaven, you took precautions, you did your deed, but you did not succeed. God cannot lose what he himself guards. You author of deceit, you are fighting the Lord and not fighting against his servants by trying to have the result of your deceit ascribed to their negligence. He saw you, indeed he did, he who is a witness to all deceit and labor. Therefore, both the fruits of their labors await the servants, and the punishments for his wickedness await the deceiver. They will carry grain to the heavenly granary, but you will carry your sheaves of tares for yourself to Gehenna.

2. *But when people were sleeping, an enemy came, and sowed tares* (v.25). For what purpose? So that the Lord's harvest would perish. And what benefit will the enemy gain from this, except that the spirit of envy reckons damage to human beings as a benefit to himself, and thinks that he has acquired what human beings have lost? And so, as we have said, the devil for this reason carried out this scheme under the cover of darkness so that the blame for the tainted harvest might fall on the servants, and they might pay the penalty from the very place where they had hoped for a reward.

And so the servants, waking up in fear, tremble with great anxiety about what had happened, afraid that the sprouting of the tares would be their undoing who had nothing on their conscience except having sown good seed. This is why they came before their Lord before he heard about this, so that while secure in their innocence they might not be found guilty on account of their silence. When an innocent person is accused of a charge, in his eagerness to be acquitted, he pursues and prods the investigator.

3. *But when the stalks had grown, and had produced ears, then,* it says, *the tares appeared* (v.26). What lies hidden in a stalk, is manifested in the ear, and what is concealed in the seed is revealed in the fruit. Thus those whom we suppose are equal as believers we find to be unequal in faith. Thus the harvest of judgment reveals those who as sprouts of the Church stay hidden, accord-

ing to that saying of the Lord: "By their fruits you will recognize them."⁵

Many blossoms hold out promise of abundant fruit, but, put to the test by gusts of wind, very few persevere and bear fruit. And so in a time of peace the Church seems to have many who believe in Christ, but when the storm of persecution blows, there are few who are found to bear fruit in martyrdom. But Saint Euphemia yielded more fruit than she promised in her blossom, since with the blossom of her virginity intact she managed to bear copious fruit in martyrdom.⁶

4. *The servants of the head of the household*, it says, *came and spoke to him* (v.27). They came, brothers, in mind, not in body; it is not a matter of location, but of faith. They spoke, not with the cry of their voice, but with the silent pain of their heart: *Did you not sow good seed?* (v.27) It was you who sowed, not we. What we do through you we always attribute to you our Author; and by your action come to our aid in those matters which you command us to do.⁷ Therefore, if in your graciousness you make us sharers in your work, do not fix the blame solely on us for the tares arising.

In any event, Lord, either we are preserved in innocence with you, or you are tainted with guilt with us. We could not begrudge our own work, nor could we sabotage something over which we sweated so much. You have what you will, from wherever you will, when you will; we have nothing apart from your grace, thanks to which we stand, "we live, we move, and we have our being,"⁸ and without which we fall flat, we fade away, and we perish.

---

5. Mt 7.20.
6. On St. Euphemia of Chalcedon, martyred in 303, see Asterius of Amasea, *Homily* 11 in *Homilies I–XIV*, ed. C. Datema (Leiden: Brill, 1970), 153–55. See also G. Lucchesi, "Eufemia di Calcedonia, santa, martire," in *BSS* 5 (1964): 154–60. On her connection to Ravenna, see G. Cortesi, "Le chiese ravennati di S. Eufemia e la loro problematica," in *Corso di cultura sull'arte ravennate e bizantina* 25 (1978): 77–91. According to Agnellus, *Liber Pontificalis* 1, Apollinaris, the first bishop of Ravenna, was said to have celebrated the first baptisms in Ravenna on the spot where a basilica in her name would later be erected.
7. See Augustine, *Confessions* 10.29.40 (FOTC 21.298–99, trans. V. Bourke): "Give what you command, and command what you will."
8. Acts 17.28.

Therefore, did we work so hard at all this for ourselves just to have it destroyed? But while we were sleeping, you, the only One who does not sleep,⁹ you saw who did this. And if you saw, you, O just Judge,¹⁰—and who knows what happened? The One who keeps awake, not the one who sleeps, that's who—therefore, point him out so that you may thereby make our relief as great as the anxiety you see in us now.

5. The Lord *said: "A person who is an enemy has done this"* (v.28) A person who is an enemy has done it; then why, Lord, when you saw it, did you permit it? Why? Because the One for whom nothing can be lost is unable to fear deceit; and because it is more significant to discern deep meanings than to prohibit a mystery; it is greater to restore what has been destroyed than to spare it from injury; likewise it is necessary that there be tares, so that those of proven goodness may be made manifest. *A person who is an enemy has done this.*

6. *And his servants said: "Do you want us to go and gather up"* the tares (v.28)? As devoted servants they promise to be tireless in their labor and do not endure seeing, even for a short time, any blemish in their master's harvest. But the Lord, who is not bothered by the passing of time, and who can eliminate the damage to his harvest when he wills, forbids them by saying: *No* (v.29). And why he prohibited them from doing this, he explains next: *It is possible that in pulling up the tares you might uproot the wheat as well* (v.29).

Were they such inexperienced farmers, so unqualified for the task, and so unable to distinguish the one from the other that in pulling up the tares they would uproot the wheat as well? Where are the prophets who prophesy through the Spirit of God? Where is Peter, to whom the Father gives a revelation?¹¹ Where is Paul, in whom Christ works and speaks?¹² Where are all the saints, where are those who are saints to be sure, but servants as well, who know as much as the Bestower of knowledge has granted to each one?

7. But you say: there was nothing concealed here; there was

---

9. See Ps 120 (121).4.
11. See Mt 16.17.
10. See 2 Tm 4.8.
12. See Gal 2.8 and 2 Cor 13.3.

nothing concealed there, since one thing was seen in appearance, another thing was possessed in the blossom; and what today were tares, tomorrow would be made into wheat; and what in the present was wheat, in the future would be changed into tares. So today one is considered a heretic who tomorrow becomes a believer; and one who in the present is seen to be a sinner, in the future takes his place among the righteous.

This is why he referred both of them to the harvest, that is, until the judgment would leave room for his divine patience and until there was time for us to repent, so that the one who converted from evil to good would be counted among the Lord's wheat, to be gathered into the heavenly granary; and so that the one who became an unbeliever after being a believer would be consigned to the fire of Gehenna. And why should I say more? If the patience of God did not come to the aid of the tares, the Church would not have either Matthew as an evangelist after having been a tax collector,[13] or Paul as an apostle after having been a persecutor.[14]

And so Ananias was seeking to uproot the wheat on that occasion when he was sent to Saul and made this complaint about Paul: "Lord, how great are the evils which he did against your saints!"[15] What he means is, "Uproot the tares! Why send a sheep to a wolf? Why send a devoted servant to the insolent? Why send such a preacher to a persecutor?" But Ananias had seen Saul, while the Lord was seeing Paul. When Ananias was calling him a persecutor, the Lord already knew him as a preacher; and when he was judging him to be tares destined for hell, Christ already had a hold on him as a chosen vessel, wheat for the heavenly granary. Do you not know, he says, "that he is a chosen vessel of mine?"[16]

13. See Mt 9.9.
14. See 1 Cor 15.9.
15. Acts 9.13.
16. Acts 9.15.

SERMON 99

A Fourth on the Same[1] *<or on the Parable about the Yeast>*[2]

T IS FITTING THAT the sequence of the reading has reached the point today where the woman in the Gospel, the holy Mother, our Mother,[3] received yeast from the Lord, so as to lift and raise this temple[4] up for us today into so great a mass of holiness. Thus the Lord began: *To what shall I compare the kingdom of God? It is like yeast which a woman took and hid in three measures of flour, until all of it was leavened* (Lk 13.20–21).

The good Lord, Christ, the Lover of his own, tells a number of parables about his kingdom and varies the analogies. He does not take them from something mysterious, nor does he fashion them from heavenly material, but he draws them from daily experience, he derives them from everyday life, so that what is profitable for all may be accessible to every type of human being, in accord with what the prophet says: "Hear this, all you peoples, listen all you who inhabit the world, every earthborn creature and child of human beings, both rich and poor together."[5]

---

1. Namely, on the tares.

2. (Angle brackets here indicate an addition to the title in Olivar's CCL text.) Given the reference in section 2 to the parable of the mustard seed, it is likely that this sermon was delivered next after *Sermon* 98 (FOTC 17.156–60). *Sermon* 98 ends with a promise to explain the subsequent parable (on the yeast) in the next sermon—this *Sermon* 99 presumably. See F. Sottocornola, *L'anno liturgico*, 101, and A. Olivar, *Los sermones*, 182 and 268–69.

3. This Mother is both Mary (see section 5) and the Church (see section 6).

4. This reference to a "temple" may indicate that this sermon was preached at the time of the dedication of a church, perhaps that of St. John the Evangelist in 432, or to the spiritual temple, constituted by those recently baptized. If the latter, then the season was probably Easter, but there are no further clues in this sermon as to whether either of these scenarios is the case. See F. Sottocornola, *L'anno liturgico*, 101–2.

5. Ps 48.2–3 LXX; Ps 49.1–2.

If he introduced anything from the mysteries of divinity, anything from the inner sanctum of royalty, anything from the secret chambers of the rich, the poor person would not understand it, common people would not grasp it, simple folk would not comprehend it. But now he speaks of what is known to the rich and familiar to the poor, out of the circumstances of life itself that all share in common, because when God calls, it is the human being who is sought, and there is no distinction of persons in God's call. But let us return to the parable that was read.

2. *To what shall I compare the kingdom of God?* (v.20) By saying this he keeps the minds of his listeners in suspense, and he leaves them speechless and completely bewildered as to what can be compared to the kingdom of God, to God's reign, and while they wander in their thoughts imagining many wonderful things, the Lord of heaven finds an example of his kingdom that he adapts from the dwelling of the poor, from the hand of the woman who bakes bread, as he says: *It is like yeast which a woman took and hid in three measures of flour, until all of it was leavened* (v.21).

Just beforehand he compared his kingdom to a mustard seed,[6] now he likens it to yeast; earlier he mentions that a man took a mustard seed, now he asserts that a woman took yeast. Earlier he says that a man planted a tiny seed which grew into a large tree, just now he mentions that a woman hid a small amount of yeast which made the whole mass expand. Truly, as the Apostle Paul has said: "Neither is man without woman, nor is woman without man in the Lord."[7]

The different parables lead the diverse sexes to the one kingdom, nor does the Christian calling separate man from woman, since God joins them,[8] nature unites them, and their appearance, marvelously similar, makes them alike, and their bodily form matches them together. God ordains that one person be two and the two be one,[9] the other person being considered as one's self in the marriage bond, in such a way that

---

6. See Lk 13.19. 7. 1 Cor 11.11.
8. See Mt 19.6. 9. See Gn 2.24 and Mt 19.5.

neither is one's individuality abandoned nor is the union confused.

3. But why does the Lord produce these parables of his kingdom by means of a man and a woman? Why does he adapt such great majesty to such lowly and ill-matched examples? Brothers, a precious mystery is concealed in this lowliness, as the Apostle says: "This is a great mystery: I am talking now about Christ and the Church."[10] A precious mystery is concealed in this lowliness, in these comparisons the fundamental interaction of the human race is being conducted.

Through man and woman the condition of the world, which has been prolonged through the ages, is being brought to resolution. Adam the first man and Eve the first woman had sinned at the tree of the knowledge of good and evil;[11] they are led to the tree sprouting from the mustard seed in the Gospel so that the mustard tree, while closing their eyes with the very harsh eye-salve made from its seed, might open those eyes which the seductive tree had closed by opening them.

The wholesome tree with its fiery-tasting flavor was meant to heal the mouths which the taste of the poisonous tree had infected;[12] this tree with its hot food was to set the conscience on fire with burning zeal for repentance, after the other tree had succeeded in numbing the conscience now all stiff and frozen. Here nakedness no longer even feels cold or ashamed,[13] where pardon covers the whole human being, and the clothing of faith makes him warm. But this is the benefit granted the woman from the mustard seed which the man had taken; but what benefit is granted the man from the yeast which the woman took, let us examine more diligently.

4. *The kingdom of God,* he says, *is like yeast which a woman took and hid in three measures of flour* (v.21). The matter is drawn from everyday life: a man plants a mustard tree in the field; a woman attends to yeast at home; she provides bread for food; since

---

10. Eph 5.32.
11. See Gn 2.17 and 3.11.
12. On the senses of sight and of taste causing harm to Eve, see also *Sermon* 27.4 (FOTC 17.73).
13. See Gn 3.7, 10.

labor awaits the man outside, domestic concern keeps the woman occupied inside. This is why Sarah, a barren old woman, after working the yeast in this way, out of three measures offers three hearth cakes as hospitality to the Lord,[14] and she serves it with mystical devotion, so that the world, barren as it was as a result of its very old age, might place the yeast of faith in three measures, that is, in the equality of the Father, Son, and Holy Spirit, and serve its Lord three cakes by its confession of the Trinity.[15] Then in exchange for this service it would be made fruitful and produce a complete stock of Christian offspring.[16] But let us return to the matter before us.

5. The woman took the yeast of faith from God, after she had taken the yeast of infidelity from the devil. She hid it in three measures, that is, in three periods of human history, namely: from Adam to Noah, from Noah to Moses, and from Moses to Christ,[17] in order for that woman, who had corrupted the whole mass of the human race by the yeast of death in Adam, to restore the whole mass of our flesh in Christ with the yeast of the resurrection; so that the woman who had prepared the bread of sweat and tears might bake the Bread of life and salvation, and might truly be through Christ the mother of all the living,[18] she who in Adam was the mother of all the dead.

For it was indeed for this reason that Christ willed to be born, that just as death came to all through Eve, so life might return to all through Mary.[19] Mary is the one who brings to fulfillment what this yeast signifies, she manifests what is being represented, she validates the image as she receives the yeast of the Word from the celestial realm, and she moistened[20] hu-

14. See Gn 18.6.
15. A similar Trinitarian interpretation of the Matthean parallel to this Lucan text (Mt 13.33) appears in Hilary of Poitiers, *In Matthaeum* 13.6 (SC 254.300–301).
16. See Gn 18.10–14.
17. A different division of salvation history is mentioned in *Sermon* 59.9 (FOTC 109.228): "before the Law, under the Law, and under grace."
18. See Gn 3.20.
19. The Eve-Mary antithesis is also developed, for example, in *Sermons* 74.3 (FOTC 17.124–25) and 77.4.
20. In *Sermon* 146.7 (FOTC 17.241) Chrysologus engages in wordplay, noting that the same term *Maria* is both the name of Jesus' mother and the word

man flesh in her virginal womb—yes, indeed, in her virginal womb—forming it into a completely heavenly mass.

6. But now let us disclose what allegorical meaning remains in this parable. The woman who took the yeast is the Church; the yeast which she took is the mystery of heavenly teaching; the three measures in which she is said to have hidden the yeast are the Law, the Prophets, and the Gospels,[21] where the divine meaning is hidden and concealed in mystical language, so as to be evident to the believer, but hidden from the unbeliever.[22]

But his statement: *Until all of it was leavened* (v.21), means what the Apostle says: "Our knowledge is partial, and our prophesying is partial; but when what is complete comes, what is partial will cease."[23] In the sprinkling now is the divine knowledge: God moistens, he lifts up hearts, he increases intellectual abilities, and by means of his teachings he enlarges, he arouses, and he expands them so that they advance in heavenly wisdom. The whole thing rises:[24] when? When Christ comes.[25]

---

meaning "seas." It is not impossible that he has this notion in mind when he speaks here about Mary providing "moisture."

21. This same allegorical interpretation is found in Hilary of Poitiers, *In Matthaeum* 13.5 (SC 254.298–301), and Ambrose, *Expositio Evangelii secundum Lucam* 7.188 (CCL 14.279). Elsewhere in Chrysologus's preaching there are similar references: in *Sermon* 106.6, to Christ's search for good fruit through the Law, the Prophets, and his own bodily Presence; and in *Sermon* 98.6 (FOTC 17.160), to his kingdom which, symbolized by the mustard seed, took root in the patriarchs, was born in the prophets, grew in the apostles, and became a great tree in the Church.

22. A similar point about one of the reasons for the deeper meaning of Scripture is made in *Sermons* 96.1 and 132.2 (FOTC 17.152, 216).

23. 1 Cor 13.9–10.

24. Or "is leavened" *(fermentatur)*.

25. *Veniente Christo*. On the terms *advenire* and *adventus* in Chrysologus's sermons, see F. Sottocornola, *L'anno liturgico*, 273–78.

SERMON 99A

Against the Pharisees; On the Gospel Text: A Certain Pharisee Asked Jesus to Dine with Him, and Jesus Cured the Man with Dropsy[1]

HE AUTHORITY OF TODAY'S reading makes it very clear that today we speak against the Pharisees not with enthusiasm, but with grief, and not out of the prejudice that stems from hatred, but because we are spurred on by the truth. *And it happened*, it says, *that when the Lord had entered the house of a certain leader of the Pharisees to eat a meal on the Sabbath, they themselves were watching him closely* (Lk 14.1), in a spirit of treachery, not with a kind disposition.

When he had entered the house, it says. In the house there was a trap, in the greeting a trial, in the seat at table a snare, in the food there was deceit, in the bread a sword, in the cup poison, in the fellowship a bier, in the conversation entrapment. And if the table of the Pharisees is like this, what can their school be like? If it is even right for that to be called a table which was entirely a forge for wickedness and a kitchen of malice. There jealousy was burning, envy was inflamed, anger was being cooked up, pretense provided the seasoning, and all the courses of slander were being made ready.

And, nevertheless, there that Lamb of God was eating, not to be fed, but to be killed, just as if he knew none of this. He certainly was eating, brothers, not as if he were ignorant of this, but so that at least by his companionship, by their very intimacy and the gracious way in which he dined together with them, their ferocity might be tamed, their anger soothed, their envy extinguished. Then by his very humaneness these men might now return to being human again, they might acquire some af-

---

1. On the authenticity of this sermon, especially on stylistic and literary grounds, see A. Olivar, *Los sermones*, 340–44.

fection, they might notice his gracious charm, they might welcome their Parent,[2] they might recognize his kindness, they might acknowledge his powers, they might love his curative treatments, and they might desire, and not attack, his acts of healing.

2. *And it happened that when the Lord had entered the house of a leader of the Pharisees, there was a certain man with dropsy there before him* (vv.1–2). *When he had entered,* it says, *the house of a leader.* In the head there was a disease which was running and winding its way within all the bodily members, through the recesses of the marrow, deep down through the internal organs, through the channels of the veins, and, steadily increasing, it was overflowing and spreading into the skin itself, to such an extent that by its taking possession of the whole body it was turning it into a pool of dropsy. So Christ had come there not to dine, but to cure.[3] But now let our sacred reading bring to center stage the disease of dropsy itself, namely, the leader of the Pharisees, so that the leader of disease, the master of illness, the head of pestilence, who did not see himself in front of the table, might in any event see himself in front of Christ's[4] table.

3. *And there was a certain man with dropsy there before him.* Why *before him,* and not "before them"? Because the Lord saw in front of him what those who were afflicted by that very disease did not then see in themselves. For there was standing before the Lord the dropsy of the Pharisees; there was standing a drunkard's thirst, a glutton's hunger, water that was on fire;[5] there was standing there a complete picture of the Pharisee's heart full of disease, empty of virtue, overflowing with wickedness, thoroughly devoid of wisdom. A man with dropsy was standing before the Lord; there was standing the meal of Christ, the feast of God, the Savior's dish, and utensils that were

---

2. Other references in Chrysologus's sermons to Christ as Parent are indicated in R. Benericetti, *Il Cristo,* 236, n. 23.

3. See *Sermon* 93.1–2 (FOTC 17.143–44), where Christ came not to dine but to bestow divine mercy.

4. The text has the possessive adjective *suam* here, but given the sense of this sentence and the following section, the reference must be to Christ.

5. Chrysologus speaks similarly in *Sermon* 172.5 where hypocrisy, the dropsy of the Pharisees, increases rather than quenches their thirst.

of divine power, and not of the human will; because Christ's nourishment came not from human food, but from curing human beings and healing their infirmities.[6]

4. *And in response,* it says, *the Lord said to them* (v.3). It does not say that he spoke, but that he responded. But to whom did he respond, since no one spoke? The Physician responded to the infirmity, since the person with the infirmity was not looking for a Physician. And so he speaks to those who are learned in the Law, he speaks to the Pharisees, in whom could be found the infirmity with all its distress, the disease in its complete manifestation, and the pestilence in all its virulence.

In response he said to them: "Is it permitted to cure on the Sabbath?" (v.3) The Author of the Sabbath asks what was permitted on the Sabbath; and so the very One who had given the command inquires as if he did not know what he commanded. Brothers, he asks, not as One who does not know, but as One who is teaching.[7] For he was asking as a teacher, he was interrogating as Lord, he was investigating as God what benefit his teaching had brought his disciples, their obedience had brought human beings, and his instruction had brought his servants.

Is it permitted to cure on the Sabbath or not? (v.3) The fact is, he had prohibited sinning on the Sabbath, not curing; what he had not allowed was eagerness to do evil, not eagerness to do good; the kind of attentiveness to the flesh that he had forbidden was extravagance, not acts of healing; he had abolished works of human servitude, not works of divine beneficence; and he had consecrated that day as one in which the human being would be freed from earthly labors and available solely for God and for himself.

5. *He said to them: "Is it permitted to cure on the Sabbath?" But they said nothing* (vv.3–4). For they were silent just like beasts lying in wait for their prey; but they said nothing, eager to witness an offense, but not eager to witness a cure. The one who sees being done what he thinks is forbidden, and says nothing,

---

6. See section 2 above and n. 3.
7. For the view that Christ's questions are asked not out of ignorance but for a pedagogical reason, see also, for example, *Sermons* 64.4 (FOTC 109.258) and 176.5. For other examples, see R. Benericetti, *Il Cristo,* 263–64.

SERMON 99A

is already making an accusation while saying nothing. A friend, yes, a friend, hastens to prohibit what is wrong, not to publicize it. But they said nothing in order for God to be at fault, virtue to be found guilty, deliverance[8] to be accused falsely, and the perfect model of pardon to be indicted. This is how the eye sees when it has been wounded by envy's arrow; this is how one who is an enemy of God and adverse to truth makes an accusation.

But because a dedicated physician often cures a sick patient against his will,[9] Christ took hold of the man with dropsy and sent him off healed, because as soon as Christ grasps someone, the infirmity entirely loses its hold. God came to the man, and immediately the disease left the man. Therefore, the one who is unwilling to be held by God is willing to be held by every sickness. This is why the prophet sings as follows about the Lord holding him: "You have held my right hand, you have guided me according to your will, and you have received me with glory."[10]

6. Why need I say more, brothers? If Christ had not cured the man with dropsy at that time on account of the Sabbath, he would have abolished the Sabbath's meaning. But the Sabbath yielded to its Author, through whom it had been established for the avoidance of offenses and for healthy pursuits. But because the Pharisees were unable to understand the devotion God has for human beings, they are sent off to beasts of burden,[11] so that they might grasp the meaning from dumb animals, since in their pitiful state they failed to perceive what was made manifest so often and in such varied ways to them by Christ's miracles.

---

8. The Latin is *salus*, meaning both "healing" and "salvation."
9. See *Sermon* 50.4 and n. 14 (FOTC 109.195–96) on Christ the Physician often having to provide a treatment to which the patient is not inclined.
10. Ps 72.24 LXX; Ps 73.23–24.
11. See Lk 14.5.

SERMON 100

On the Syrophoenician Woman

ODAY WHEN BLESSED MARK commends the prudence of the Syrophoenician woman, when he tells of her faith, and when he extols the ardor of her belief, he creates no small question for those who listen attentively when he says: *And Jesus set off from there and went away to the regions of Tyre and Sidon; he entered a house and wanted no one to know it, but he was unable to stay unnoticed* (Mk 7.24). *He wanted, but was unable.* To want and to be unable is not characteristic of divine majesty, but it is characteristic of human weakness. For Scripture says: "Everything that the Lord wanted, he did in heaven, on earth, in the sea, and in the depths."[1] And the Apostle says: "Who resists his will?"[2]

The will that is not free and absolute is subject to constraint, and the will that is under the duress of considerable difficulties diminishes the freedom of the one whose it is.[3] The leper says to the Lord: "If you want, you can make me clean";[4] yet the evangelist says: *He wanted, but was unable.* What is blessed Mark doing here? Must the faith of the woman be extolled to the point that the power and will of the Lord be lessened? Or is her faith so keen that even though the Lord is unwilling she is able to search out what is divinely hidden?

Similar to this passage, it seems to me, is the one in which the Lord wishes to disclose and display the faith of the woman with the hemorrhage to manifest his own power, when he asks: "Who touched me?" To this the disciples say: "A crowd of people presses against you, and you ask: 'Who touched me?'"[5] It seemed to

---

1. Ps 134 (135).6.   2. Rom 9.19.
3. On this point see also *Sermons* 41.2 (FOTC 109.164) and 92.6.
4. Mt 8.2 and parallels.   5. Mk 5.31.

the disciples that all were touching the Lord by putting pressure upon him solely with their bodies, that in such an onrush of flesh all were indistinguishably joined together as one. At the same time he who had perceived it differently was inquiring about something else; he knew that this woman had reached his divine majesty, had penetrated his power with her mind, not her body, not with an ordinary touch, but with faith. So it is not man, but God; not flesh, but spirit who cries out: "Who touched me?" so that the miraculous deed might reveal the One whom his humanity was keeping concealed at that time.[6]

2. But let us examine more closely what *he wanted* and what *he was unable* mean. Mindful of his promise, Christ had come first for the salvation of the people of Israel, so that what he had promised to Abraham and his offspring,[7] to David and his posterity[8] he would faithfully render and fulfill. But because they showed themselves to be unworthy by their lack of faith, the gentiles' faith obtained, seized, and extracted what the unbelief of the Jews rejected and lost.[9]

Listen to what he says: "I have been sent only to the lost sheep of the house of Israel."[10] But the sheep, now having contracted rabies from their contact with wolves, and more ferocious in their own savagery than the wild beasts themselves, have always wanted to mangle and do violence to their Shepherd; and so Christ *was unable* to accomplish what he wanted, not on account of his own lack of power, but on account of the wickedness of those that were lost; and what he had taken away from one group he was forced to confer on another group, as he says himself: "The kingdom of heaven suffers violence, and those who do violence snatch it away."[11] The gentiles' faith did violence in order to seize the Father's inheritance, to snatch the whole of that very inheritance, just as he has demonstrated more clearly in the present reading.

---

6. For more on Chrysologus's treatment of this account, see *Sermon* 36.2 (FOTC 17.76–78).
7. See Lk 1.55.
8. See Ps 88.36–37 LXX; Ps 89.35–36; and Ps 131 (132).11–12.
9. See Acts 13.46.   10. Mt 15.24.
11. Mt 11.12.

3. *As soon as a woman whose daughter had an unclean spirit heard about him, she came in and fell at his feet. She was, however, a gentile, a Syrophoenician, and she implored him to cast the demon out of her daughter.* He said to her: *"Let the children be fed first. It is not right to take their bread and cast it before dogs"* (vv.25–27). He did not say that it is not right to cast bread before dogs, but *it is not right to take it from the children and cast it before dogs,* because to give dogs bread, even if it is not of direct human benefit,[12] is, nevertheless, an act of human reason. While their masters are asleep the dog is the guard by night, and by being ever watchful the dog makes the presence of a stranger known, bothers a thief, and resists a robber, so as to arouse the concern and anxiety of the servants.

But who in fact took the bread away from the children, when so many times and in such ways he offered, he granted, and he supplied it to them? But in their wickedness they tried to trample underfoot what was offered, and not to receive it for sustenance. And yet, a dog full of faith and full of longing, hastened to lap up what had been broken up and trampled underfoot by the children. This is why she said in response:

4. *For the dogs under the table eat the children's crumbs* (v.28). It is fitting that she who confessed that she was a dog is transformed into a human being; and it is right for those who were unwilling to be sons to be changed into dogs. It is fitting that she, who is praised for her insight and humility in having cast herself down under the table, is adopted, exalted, and honored at the table as a child.[13] It is right that she, who understood and acknowledged that by her own merits she was barely deserving of scraps, now feasts on the full loaf of bread. And why should I say more? So it is on account of his justice that the Lord was both unable to give to the Jews and unable to refuse the gentiles.

12. The Latin is *humanitatis.*
13. Olivar's CCL text has the masculine *filium,* while PL 52.481 has the feminine *filiam.* Hence, the gender-inclusive "child."

SERMON 102

On the Centurion's Servant[1]

HE FACT THAT, while dwelling in our body, Christ did not raise all the dead nor heal all the sick, let us attribute to a lack not of power but of time. If at that time he had shone upon the whole world with the full brightness of his power, he would have both done away with the time for faith and kept no glory in reserve for his second coming. But now he has regulated the signs of his miraculous powers in such a way as to provide evidence of his divinity, to bestow the fullest possible grounds for believing, and to take away any excuse from the cunning for disbelief, just as today the centurion, of whom the evangelist makes mention, has demonstrated by his faith and foresight.

2. *The servant of a certain centurion,* he says, *who was very dear to him, was faring badly and was dying* (Lk 7.2). This centurion was a Roman, but he himself was a Christian even more by bearing fruit one hundredfold,[2] he was in the service of God more than of this world, and while courageous in human warfare he stood his ground even more bravely in keeping peace with God.[3] *His servant, who was very dear to him, was faring badly and was dying.*

---

1. On opposing opinions entertained by A. Olivar and F. Sottocornola on whether or not this sermon was preached next after *Sermon* 15 on the same account in Matthew's Gospel, see *Sermon* 15.7, n. 15 (FOTC 109.74). Olivar's contention that it did seems more compelling. Sottocornola, for his part, in *L'anno liturgico,* 290–93, states that *Sermons* 101–6 were likely delivered at the end of the year, largely because in them Chrysologus refers to the end of the world, yet Sottocornola does concede that in this *Sermon* 102 there is only one slight reference to such a theme—the mention of Christ's second coming in section 1.

2. In a similar fashion to *Sermon* 15.2 (FOTC 109.70), there is a wordplay here between *centurio* and *centesimo.*

3. Similar praise for the centurion is found in *Sermon* 15.1–2 (FOTC 109.70–71), on the account in Mt 8.5–9.

He had a servant indeed, and truly mortally ill; but how dear the servant was who was valued so highly!

So let us investigate who this servant is who was dear to him. If the soul is in charge, the body serves; and nothing is more dear to the human being than his body. This servant who was dear to that centurion was ill to the point of death. The body born from infirmity, for as long as it lives, is ill to the point of death. So the centurion was asking for Christ alone to come to the aid of his mortal body by bestowing everlasting life.

3. *When he had heard about Jesus*, it says (v.3). *When he had heard about Jesus.* Unless the hearing of faith[4] had already come, the salvation of the body would not have resulted. Therefore, *he sent elders of the Jews to him* (v.3). A gentile sends Jews to Christ. So also for us, since the hearing of faith has already come, life of the body is soon to follow. *He sent elders of the Jews to him,* and to those ensconced in the Law he who was without the Law reveals the Author of the Law. So let no one be surprised if a gentile, that is, a Christian, invites, or accompanies, or leads a Jew to Christ. *He sent elders of the Jews to him, asking him to come and heal his servant* (v.3).

4. *When they had come, they appealed to him in these words: "He is worthy to have you grant this to him. For he loves our people, and he himself built a synagogue for us"* (vv.4–5). The Jews make an appeal for a gentile, but they make no appeal for themselves; and they show a great deal of concern for the salvation of someone else's servant, yet they show none for the salvation of their own children. They say: *He is worthy to have you grant this to him.* If the one who listens, believes, and sends people to Christ is worthy, how unworthy is the one proven to be who comes to Christ, sees, yet does not believe![5]

For he loves our people. He loves your people whom he makes so compliant to Christ; but you hate them whom you render so defiant towards Christ. Or how does a Christian not love your

---

4. See Rom 10.17.

5. The Latin is *venit, vidit, non credit,* recalling the words of another famous gentile who was high-ranking in the Roman military—the memorable *veni, vidi, vici* of Julius Caesar. See Suetonius, *De Vita Caesarum* 1.37. The latter two of Chrysologus's series of verbs are reminiscent of Jn 21.29 (Vg): *Quia vidisti me, Thoma, credidisti; beati qui non viderunt, et crediderunt.*

people, who by confessing Christ as one born of your people, exalts and extols to heavenly glory all that has to do with your people. *For he loves our people, and he himself built a synagogue for us.* You have heard that a synagogue is always demolished, and lies in continual disrepair, and does not rise up to become a celestial structure, unless a Christian architect makes it conform to the measurements of the Church's elevation.

5. *Jesus*, it says, *went with them* (v.6), but they did not go with Jesus, whom they did not accompany in spirit; nor were they with him since they were separated in heart, although they were together in body. *And now when he was not far away* (v.6). From where? From the gentile. To the very extent that the Jews were separated from Christ, just so closely was Christ joined to the gentiles. *And when he was not far away, the centurion sent friends to him* (v.6). The one who earlier had sent Jews, now sends friends, so that by calling them friends he shows that the others are enemies, which the Apostle attests when he says: "Enemies for your sake."[6]

While the Jews are envious that the gentiles have believed, they have lost all that had to do with both the Law and grace. *He sent friends to him.* What friends? Listen to the Lord addressing his apostles: "I no longer call you servants,"[7] but "friends." Just as faith promotes servants to the level of friends, so faithlessness reduces sons to penal servitude.

6. *He sent friends to him saying: "Lord, do not trouble yourself."* Why? *"Because I am not worthy to have you come under my roof"* (v.6). You see that Christ was leading the Jews more than being led by the Jews, so that they would hear that a centurion had reverence for God, that a gentile had respect for the Law, that a soldier had the benefit[8] of grace, that a Roman had the teaching of faith, that in the chill of paganism there was the Christian warmth, that in an earthly heart there was a secret from heaven, and that while fully serving this world he had full knowledge of the Sovereignty above.

Lord, do not trouble yourself. That is to say: God, why do you trouble yourself with a human body, why do you exhaust your-

---

6. Rom 11.28.   7. Jn 15.15.
8. Literally, "stipend" or "salary" (*stipendium*).

self with earthly labor, and tire yourself out with a lengthy journey? Why do you travel through various places, since you are everywhere in your entirety, and you hold and possess all creation within you? *Lord, do not trouble yourself; I am not worthy to have you come under my roof.* Brothers, what is the roof that either makes a person worthy or renders him unworthy, that may either attract or repel the approach of the Divine? Brothers, this roof is our body[9] which harbors the soul, which conceals the abode of the spirit, which covers the dwelling place of the heart, and which restricts the freedom of the mind by preventing it from seeing heaven.

So the centurion considers it to be something unworthy for Christ to come under this roof, that is, for divine majesty to enter into a human body. "I am not worthy to have you come under my roof." But since God, when he wills, makes what is human become divine, and, when he sees fit, changes what is of our flesh into his own Spirit, he does not disdain either dwelling in the flesh or coming under the roof of our body.

7. *For this reason,* he says, *I did not consider myself worthy to come to you myself* (v.7). Both these statements demonstrate his respect and devotion in that he regards it as something unbecoming for God to come to him, and knows that he is not worthy to approach God. Who comes before a judge without having been summoned?[10] Who approaches a king when he is not bidden? All the more so does one not come before God unless called! "Those whom he called," it says, "he also justified."[11] So the centurion does not flee from the coming of the Lord, nor does he decline Christ's presence, but he ensures that what is operative is the grace of the One who calls,[12] and not the rashness of one who is presumptuous. For what God can do, he brings to mind and expresses with a human example by saying:

---

9. For the idea that the roof is the human body, and that the human body is intended to be the temple of God, based presumably on 1 Cor 3.16 and 2 Cor 6.16, see *Sermons* 12.3 and 15.4 (FOTC 109.58, 72–73).

10. Similar rules of prudence and etiquette are noted in *Sermons* 93.3 and 109.3 (FOTC 17.144, 173).

11. Rom 8.30.

12. The gratuitousness of God's call is also mentioned in *Sermon* 2.4 (FOTC 17.32).

SERMON 102

8. *For I also am a man placed under authority, having soldiers under me; and I say to one: "Go," and he goes; and to another: "Come," and he comes; and to my servant I say: "Do this," and he does it* (v.8). That is, if I am placed under authority, and by merely the power of my word I make my subjects obey me, how are you, who are subject to no one, and to whose authority all things are subject, how are you not able to command cures, issue healings, and order acts of power by your word? Or are you unable to restore with a word what you have made with a word? "He spoke," it says, "and they were made; he gave the order, and they were created."[13] Or can you not repair one thing from another, you who provided all things from nothing?[14] *So say the word, and my servant-boy will be healed* (v.7). This fulfilled what the prophet sang regarding God: "He sent forth his word, and he healed them, and delivered them from their corruption."[15]

9. Brothers, when this centurion says: *I am not worthy to have you come under my roof* (v.6), he is a type of the Christian people, who judge that they do not deserve the bodily presence of Christ, but merely by the word alone, by the message, and the hearing of faith, they hear, believe, and receive for their own health all the miraculous deeds of the Lord. For his statement: *I say to one: "Go," and he goes; and to another: "Come," and he comes; and to my servant: "Do this," and he does it* (v.8), is thus indicating the rejection of the Jews, the calling of the gentiles, and the obedience of the Christian people. *I say to one*, that is, to the Jew, who does not believe: *"Go," and he goes; and to another*, that is, to the gentile, who has come to believe: *"Come," and he comes; and to my servant*, that is, to the one who is now a Christian: *"Do this," and he does it.*[16]

---

13. Ps 148.5. In *Sermon* 15.5 (FOTC 109.73) Chrysologus uses this same biblical reference to point out that God, who created all things by his word, now in Christ would heal by his word.

14. Also in *Sermons* 25.1, 46.6, 48.3, 49.4, and 103.1, for example, Chrysologus emphasizes *creatio ex nihilo;* for the first four of these references see FOTC 109.106, 180, 185, and 191.

15. Ps 106 (107).20. Chrysologus also juxtaposes this and the previous text spoken by the centurion in *Sermons* 15.5 (FOTC 109.73) and 112.5 (FOTC 17.183–84).

16. Chrysologus gives a very different allegorical interpretation to these same words in *Sermon* 15.6 (FOTC 109.73–74).

Let us pray, brothers, that we may deserve to be Christians not merely in name, but in faith, and that we may not merely hear what is commanded, but that we may do what we have heard. Since, just as carrying out what has been commanded characterizes a devoted servant, so not having carried out what has been commanded characterizes a defiant servant. *So say the word, and my servant-boy will be healed* (v.7).

10. *When he heard this*, it says, *Jesus marveled* (v.9). The Creator of marvels marvels. The Maker of ears, as though he does not know what he has not heard, is thus amazed at what he has heard. But while he marvels that a gentile has believed to such a degree, he rebukes the Jews for their unbelief. *And so to the crowds that were following him he says* (v.9), or rather he reprimands the Jews who remain, in these words: *Never have I found such great faith in Israel!* (v.9) It is true, brothers; faith lives and thrives only among the gentiles; signs and miracles seem boring and are of no benefit to the Jews.

SERMON 103

When He Raised the Widow's Son from the Dead[1]

ODAY BY TELLING US about the widowed mother's only son, fully bound with the burial wrappings and placed on the doleful bier, with multitudes in attendance while already on his way to the prison of the grave, and by announcing that he was restored to life by Christ,[2] the blessed evangelist has made all our hearts tremble, he has excited our minds, and has astonished us by what we have heard. Granted that the gentiles marvel at this, the Jews are astonished, and the world becomes frightened. But why do we marvel, since we believe that all the dead from time immemorial are to be awakened from their graves at the mere voice of Christ?

"The dead," says Isaiah, "will come forth, and those who are in the tombs will rise."[3] And the Lord says: "The hour will come when the dead will hear the voice of the Son of God, and those who are in the tombs will rise."[4] In addition, the Apostle says: "In an instant, in the blinking of an eye, at the last trumpet, the dead will rise imperishable, and we shall be changed."[5] "At the last trumpet." What is this trumpet, which wages war on the underworld, dislodges tombstones from the graves, signals life for the dead, and bestows the victory on those who rise to perpetual light? What is it?

It is what the Lord said previously: "The dead will hear the voice of the Son of God." This trumpet is not a horn of wood or

---

1. With its references to the upcoming feast of Christmas in section 6 as well as the overall theme of the general resurrection at the end of time, this sermon was delivered in December. See F. Sottocornola, *L'anno liturgico*, 102–3 and 290–91.
2. See Lk 7.11–17.
3. Is 26.19.
4. Jn 5.28–29.
5. 1 Cor 15.52.

bronze that gives a grim bellow to soldiers by a breath compressed through its hollows, but from the heart of the Father and the mouth of the Son it peals forth a summons to life both to those in the underworld and to those up above[6] simultaneously. "And at the last trumpet." The trumpet which in the beginning called the world forth out of nothing,[7] is the same one which on the last day will call the world back from destruction; and the trumpet which in the beginning raised the human being out of mud, is the same one that in the end will raise the human being up again out of dust.[8]

2. Brothers, thus we believe that the trumpet of the divine voice called out over the formless void, put the world together, arranged the elements, marked off the world, hung the sky over it, made the earth secure, put limits on the sea, submerged the underworld, gave everything its place, and commanded their harmonious interplay; thus it ordained that the universe be continually compliant.

And so that the world would not be a horrible wasteland,[9] God made winds to suit it, and established dwelling places: in heaven he put the angels who are purely spiritual beings, on the earth he set various kinds of earthly beings in place, in the air he provided creatures with wings for flying, in the waters he made the small as well as the large, so that a vast multitude of living beings would thrive; and in a marvelous fashion he bound the structure of the world together out of its separate parts in such a way that their intermingling did not do away with what made each distinct, nor did the distinctiveness of each thing tear apart their unity. And so it is that the link between day and night has been so arranged that work originates from rest, and rest from work.

Thus the sun and the moon in turn circle the boundaries of the world, such that the sun with its augmented light increases the brightness of the day, and the moon with a nearly equal

---

6. That is, those on the face of the earth.
7. For other references to *creatio ex nihilo* in Chrysologus's preaching, see *Sermon* 102.8 and n. 14.
8. See Gn 2.7 and Dn 12.2.
9. See Gn 1.2.

gleam does not leave the nighttime hours completely in the dark. Thus the stars in their course rise at various times, so as both to signify the seasons at night, and to give guidance to those who are traveling. Thus the seasons come even as they go, they begin to exist even while they cease. Thus seeds germinate, grow, sprout, mature, grow old, droop, die, and again are buried in the fertile furrows, dissolve through the beneficial process of decomposing, return from death into their own life, and revive from corruption into their usual form.

3. And if, brothers, the voice of God, the trumpet of Christ, throughout the course of days, months, seasons, and years, calls, retracts, brings out, brings back, restores, orders to be, causes not to be, consigns to death, and restores to life, why might it not be able to do once for us what it always does for everything else? Or does the divine power lose its strength only when it comes to us, solely for whose benefit God's majesty has performed everything that has just been mentioned? O man, if all these things come back to life again from their death for you, why will you not come back to life from your death for God? Or are you the one and only example of something perishing which God created, when it is on your account that all creation daily subsists, is moved, is changed, and is renewed?

4. Brothers, I say this not desiring to make void the power of Christ's miracles, but I urge you, that by the example of one individual who rises we may be roused to faith in the resurrection of everyone, and may believe that the cross is the plow of our body, faith is the seed, the grave is the furrow, dissolution is the bud, and expectation is the season. Thus when the spring of the Lord's coming has smiled upon us, then our bodies will rise up in full bloom to the harvest of life. They will no longer know either old age[10] or any end; they will not suffer the sickle, nor will they feel the threshing-flail, because after the chaff of old age has been plucked out in death, they will arise like fresh fruit in their new and glorified bodies.

5. If Christ was so moved at the tears one widow shed at a

---

10. On the resurrected body as youthful and vigorous (indeed as a 30-year-old!), see Augustine, *The City of God* 22.15 (FOTC 24.462).

certain moment that he stopped to meet her on the road, that he dried the streams of grief dripping from her eyes, that he drove death away, that he brought the man back, that he resuscitated a body, that he restored life, that he turned mourning into joy, and that he transformed funeral mourning into a birthday celebration, and if he gives back to the mother the child of her womb alive from the dead, what will he do now?

How he will be roused through and through at the constant tears of his Church,[11] at the blood and sweat of his bride! For the Church pours forth continual tears through those who make supplication, and she sweats sacred blood through her martyrs, until Christ returns and, to the eternal joy of this heavenly Mother, ushers from the mortal bier to everlasting life her only son, that is, the Christian people, whom so many ages bear off to their death.

6. But since the time of Christ's birth is coming, and Virginity is about to bring to light the heavenly miracle of producing a child, and it is no longer a star that announces the birth of the divine King, but the very ascent of the sun,[12] let us all hasten to offer adoration, and with holy gifts let us acknowledge that our God and King has come forth from the temple of the Virgin. Let us offer gifts, because a public offering is always made for the birth of a king. Let us offer gifts, because utterly irreverent is the one who adores with empty hands. The Magi attest to this, who were weighed down with gold, aflame with frankincense, and hallowed with myrrh when they bent down before Christ's cradle.[13]

What kind of message is being sent if the Christian fails to do what the Magi did? What kind of message is being sent if on the joyful occasion of Christ's birth the poor man weeps,[14] the cap-

---

11. Ambrose, *Expositio Evangelii secundum Lucam* 5.92 (CCL 14.164–65), in commenting on this same Gospel passage finds the widowed mother to represent Mother Church lamenting the impending spiritual death of any of her children who are guilty of grave sin. (There is a typographical error in the CCL 14 text: *ecclesiae* should read *ecclesia;* see SC 45.216.)

12. Apparently meaning that with Christmas the days start to become longer. See F. Sottocornola, *L'anno liturgico,* 227 and n. 17.

13. See Mt 2.11.

14. So, too, Gaudentius of Brescia uses the feast of Christmas to spur his people on to give alms to the poor. See his *Sermon* 13 (PL 20.933–43).

tive groans, the stranger laments, and the pilgrim wails? The Jew always honored the heavenly feasts with a tenth of his possessions;[15] what does a Christian think about himself if he does not honor the feasts with even a hundredth?

7. Brothers, do not think that I say this out of rhetorical excess,[16] and not out of a feeling of grief. I grieve, yes, I do grieve when I read that the Magi made Christ's cradle overflow with gold, and I see that Christians have left the altar of Christ's Body empty.[17] And at this time especially, when the hunger of the poor is of devastating proportions, and when it is so lamentable that the large number of captives continues to expand.[18]

Let no one say, "I have nothing," since God is asking you for what you have, not for what you do not have, since he approves of and accepts the widow's two copper coins.[19] Let us be devoted to the Creator, so that creation may be devoted to us. Let us support our neighbors in their tribulations, so that we may be freed from our tribulations. Let us fill the altar of God, so that a full harvest may fill our barns. It stands to reason that if we do not give, we ought not to complain that we do not receive.

15. See, e.g., Dt 14.22. For other affirmations of Judaism by Chrysologus, see Introduction, FOTC 109.16–17.
16. The Latin is *declamantis studio*. Elsewhere too he uses similar language avowing his avoidance of rhetorical display. See *Sermons* 5.8 (FOTC 17.51), 112.1 (FOTC 17.181), and 127.10. For a similar claim to eschew oratorical excess, see Jerome, *Homily* on Psalm 7 and *Homily* on Psalm 77 (FOTC 48.26 and 81).
17. F. Sottocornola, *L'anno liturgico*, 141, believes that this is a reference to a procession during the liturgy whereby gifts for the poor were brought to the altar.
18. The exact date and circumstances to which Chrysologus refers here are unclear. It is possible that the reference to captives refers to prisoners of war as a result of the invasion of Attila and the Huns in the late 440s. The "hunger . . . of devastating proportions" could be an allusion to the famine of 439 or that which occurred a decade later. See Introduction, FOTC 109.13; A. Olivar, *Los sermones*, 235–37; and A. H. M. Jones, *The Later Roman Empire 284–602*, Volume 1 (Oxford: Blackwell, 1964), 192–94.
19. See Mk 12.41–44; Lk 21.1–4.

SERMON 104

On the Rich Man Whose Field Yielded a Fruitful Harvest[1]

AS OFTEN AS THIS rich man comes into our midst, against whom through so many ages, throughout all the world, and all the time the voice of God cries out in accusation, on all these occasions the deceptive allurement of riches is put to flight, the raging fire of greed is extinguished, and the rabid fury of avarice is alleviated. For today the Lord Jesus has begun in this fashion: *The field of a certain rich man yielded a fruitful harvest, and thinking within himself he said: "What shall I do, since I have no place to store my harvest?" And he said: "This is what I shall do: I shall demolish my barns, and build larger ones, and I shall store up all my produce, and I shall say to my soul: Soul, you have an abundance of goods in reserve for many years; rest yourself, eat, drink, and be merry." But God said to him: "You fool, this night they claim your soul from you; but these things which you have procured, whose will they be now?"* (Lk 12.16–20).

2. He is a wretch whom fruitfulness has made sterile, abundance has made anxious, prosperity has made inhuman, and riches have made indigent! A kind field sustained an unkind master, and what the earth poured forth in abundance, he locked up and stored with tight security, so that he who was unwilling to be generous with his own goods was really a guardian of someone else's goods. Ungrateful to God, worthless to himself, an enemy of the poor, a disgrace to the rich, and one who kept nature imprisoned!

3. *The field of a certain rich man yielded a fruitful harvest, and he was thinking within himself* (vv.16–17). As if anyone can think

---

1. F. Sottocornola, *L'anno liturgico*, 103 and 290–93, is of the opinion that *Sermons* 101–6 were all preached near the end of the year because of eschatological references contained therein. In section 5 of this sermon there is a reference to the heavenly Judge by whom the stingy rich man stands condemned, and in section 7 a mention of everlasting life to follow this present life.

outside himself! But this one was thinking within himself who, after he conceived in his heart his godless plan, left himself no pity, no mercy. *Thinking within himself he said,* making use of himself as a worthy adviser because he could not have the comfort of having a partner in his wicked design. *And he was thinking within himself.* An unholy mind did battle with holiness, and was suffering a war within, since he had lost the peace and quiet of mercy.

4. *And he was thinking within himself: "What shall I do?"* (v.17) *"What shall I do?"* are the words of one who asks a question. And whom do you suppose he was asking? There was someone else in him, because the devil had already taken possession of the core of his being; and the one who had entered Judas's heart,[2] had a hold on the inner recesses of his mind. *What shall I do since I do not have?* (v.17) You have heard how the rich man has not. Listen to him cry: *I have not.* It is true that the one who is always seeking always has not; and the one who searches for storage in this way has no place for storage. But let us listen to what his internal adviser responded to him.

5. *I shall demolish my barns* (v.18). The one who was concealed has become very much apparent, because the enemy always begins with destruction. He sees to it, indeed he does, that you demolish what you possess, and that you make no changes to what you desire. You wretched rich man, ignorant about your present goods, you very foolishly debate about future ones; how much better it would have been if you had transferred your present goods to the homeland for your soul! But now the chains on your barns have choked the throats of the poor, have shackled the necks of strangers, and have pulverized the stomachs of the hungry. For this reason the groans of the poor go before you, and pale faces follow to accuse you; a throng of wailing parents assails you, so that you may be condemned by the heavenly Judge and have your fill of punishment for having locked yourself out from the abundance[3] of your barns by refusing access to others.

6. The rich man *was thinking within himself.* It was right that

2. See Jn 13.2 and 27; Lk 22.3.
3. Chrysologus employs a wordplay in juxtaposing *satietatem* ("fill") with *satiatem* ("abundance").

the following response was given to him by the One who "knows the thoughts of human beings, and that they are vain":[4] *You fool, this night they claim your soul from you, but what about these things which you have procured?* (v.20) *Fool* is the right word, since everything there had to do with the earth, leaving nothing for heaven; since everything there had to do with the flesh, leaving nothing for the heart. *Fool* is the right word, since he had made very extensive plans to store up provisions for a soul that was soon going to depart.

This night they claim your soul from you. It is appropriate on this night since he had fled the light of mercy and subjected himself to the darkness of avarice by saying: *Eat, drink* (v.19). But that those who drink are children of the night, and not of the day,[5] the Apostle makes clear as follows: "And those who get drunk are drunk at night."[6] He makes his way through the gloom, he is consumed in darkness, since he has consigned to the locked doors of his barns and stored away the necessities of life. *They claim your soul from you.* Why didn't he say that the One who had given him wealth "claims," instead of: *they claim?* Because God claims and leads back the souls of the saints, but the ministers of Tartarus[7] claim and carry off the souls of the unholy.

7. *And thinking within himself he said: "What shall I do, since I have no place to store my harvest?" And he said: "This is what I shall do: I shall demolish my barns, and build larger ones; and I shall say to my soul: Soul, you have an abundance of goods in reserve for many years; eat, drink, and be merry."* And [God] says: *This night they claim your soul; but the things which you have procured, whose will they be?* (vv.17–20) Therefore, this rich man was so thwarted that he suffered a greater loss in terms of what he was planning than in what he had procured, and the saying of the prophet was fulfilled: "Their spirit will depart and return to the earth; on that day all their plans will perish."[8] He made plans con-

---

4. Ps 93 (94).11.   5. See 1 Thes 5.5.
6. 1 Thes 5.7.
7. That is, the abode of the dead, which is personified, for example, in *Sermon* 65.6–9 (FOTC 109.263–66).
8. Ps 145 (146).4.

cerning what he would leave after him, not what he would send ahead of him.⁹

Therefore, according to the Apostle: "They became nonsensical in their thinking, and their hearts were darkened in stupidity; while they considered themselves to be wise, they have become fools."¹⁰ To this one it is said: *You fool!* And when he has been roused from the sleep of this present life, he finds that in that everlasting life he has nothing in his hands, just as the psalmist said: "They slept their sleep, and all the men found no riches in their hands."¹¹

So keep awake, you rich, in good works, and be asleep to bad works, insofar as your hand is never empty to the poor person, so as to be always full for you; because as much as the rich man in his generosity pours out to others, equally generous is what flows back to him in steady streams. So be rich in mercy, if you want to be always rich. And then your barns will be larger, then they will be full, if they are not empty out of stinginess or locked up out of greed.

---

9. That is, sending it on ahead in the hand of the poor person. See, for example, *Sermons* 7.6 (FOTC 109.38–39), 22.3 (FOTC 17.67), and 29.1 (FOTC 109.121).
10. Rom 1.21–22.
11. Ps 75.6 LXX; Ps 76.5.

SERMON 105

On the Infirmity the Woman Had for Eighteen Years[1]

ODAY THE CURE WORKED by Christ has given a marvelous display of divine power, has laid bare how cunning the devil is in his trickery, and has freed a woman who was afflicted by a long-lasting and mysterious malady, as the evangelist says: *Jesus was teaching in a synagogue on the Sabbath, and there was a woman present who had a spirit that kept her infirm for eighteen years, and she was stooped, and was in no way able to look up. When Jesus had seen her, he called her and said to her: "Woman, you are freed from your infirmity." And he laid his hands on her, and immediately she stood up straight and gave glory to God* (Lk 13.10–13).

2. *She had a spirit that kept her infirm, and she was stooped* (v.11). The malady was evident, but the author of the malady was not. All saw her distress, but they did not see the source of the distress. Her pain was apparent, but in that very pain her torturer lay hidden within. One could see that her body was bent over, but what was weighing her body down and making it bent went unseen. In the midst of her townsfolk the woman was bearing her enemy, but her townsfolk could see[2] no way of driving the enemy out. The crafty work of that most wicked spirit was thought instead to stem from the nature of her body, such that the cunning marauder held her captive by deception since he was unable to hold her by strength alone.

3. The devil would be nothing, if only human beings were

---

1. F. Sottocornola, *L'anno liturgico,* 103 and 292, n. 23, suggests that *Sermons* 101–6 may have been preached at the end of the year because of the eschatological references they contain. One such reference comes at the conclusion of section 9 of this sermon.

2. Reading the textual variant *videbant* rather than *videbat* in Olivar's CCL text. See PL 52.492.

more careful and cautious. For when did he ever have sufficient strength to prevail over the human being except by craftiness, or by lying, by treachery, by fraud, by deception, by malice, by employing the vices, and by sins in full frenzy? He always examines human wills, and without question flees from good wills, but complies with bad wills, in order to be the servant of wickedness, the procurer of sins, and the very parasite of the vices. And since on his own he is powerless, he lords it over the most despicable minds with the most despicable bondage.

Thus he deceived Eve with a lie,[3] thus he ensnared Judas with greed,[4] thus he made the Jews blind with envy, thus he engulfed the pagans in the darkness of the error of idolatry, thus he has confused peoples with his display of material extravagance, and thus he has taken possession of little children with the deception that they will not know healing. And so let us listen to what he has contrived in the case of this woman who was present.

4. *There was a woman present*, it says, *who had a spirit that kept her infirm, and she was stooped, and was in no way able to look up* (v.11). You see that this woman was sighing on account of being weighed down under the burden of a very wicked spirit, which always weighs down human beings under the burdens of sins, and keeps them stooped down to the earth, so that they not see heaven, not know celestial realities, not hope in God, and not return to their freedom by means of their Creator, but so that with their head bent over, eyes fixed downwards, and face cast down, they be always held captive under the yoke of the ancient enemy.

Thus was that tax collector weighed down who was unable to raise his eyes up to heaven, but he kept beating his breast in awareness of his sin; and since there was no room for denial, he was searching for room for mercy by saying: "God, have mercy on me, a sinner."[5] Lending his support to this notion, the most blessed prophet sang as follows: "My iniquities have descended on my head, and like a heavy burden they have pressed upon me."[6]

---

3. See Gn 3.1–6.
4. See Lk 22.3–6.
5. See Lk 18.13.
6. Ps 37.5 LXX: Ps 38.4.

And so as to reveal the author of that very burden, he makes this point elsewhere: "The hairy head of those who walk in their sins."[7] Because they do not resist sins, but walk in them, the devil both rides and runs over their head, such that those who on their own eagerly rush into evil are led under the devil's impulse to things that are even worse, as the Apostle says: "You were proceeding as if you were being led."[8] But let us examine what spiritual meaning still remains to be considered in this account.

5. *And there was a woman present who had a spirit that kept her infirm for eighteen years, and she was stooped, and was in no way able to look up.* Who is she, whose time of infirmity is even enumerated? Who is she, whom the cunning illness was so eager not to lift up from the earth, but to keep stooped down toward the earth? Who is she? She is the one who is now the holy Church,[9] the Mother of holy children, whom, as the Apostle says, "the spirit of this air, the spirit of disobedience,"[10] the spirit of error,[11] kept harassing with spiritual difficulty, and by laying upon her a variety of burdens was keeping her prone and prostrate on the earth so effectively that she never used to raise her gaze to heaven.

6. But why is it that she who is a type of the Church is found to be stooped over in the synagogue? Why is it? It is because, while she flees from the sacrileges of the pagans and turns away from the burdens of idolatry, she incurred and had to bear the heavier onus of the synagogue, as the Lord attests when he says: "Woe to you, scribes and Pharisees, you bind up heavy loads, and place them on people's shoulders, but you yourselves are not even willing to lift a finger the least bit to budge them."[12] Therefore, also blessed Peter says: "Do not place heavy burdens on the necks of your brothers, which neither we nor our ancestors were able to bear."[13] This is why Christ cries out in his de-

---

7. Ps 67.22 LXX; Ps 68.21.   8. 1 Cor 12.2.

9. Another reference to this woman as a type or "figure" of the Church is found in Ambrose, *Expositio Evangelii secundum Lucam* 7.173 (CCL 14.274).

10. Eph 2.2.

11. See 1 Jn 4.6.

12. See Lk 11.46 and Mt 23.4. In *Sermon* 96.2 (FOTC 17.153) Chrysologus joins Lk.11.52 and Mt 23.13 in a similar fashion.

13. See Acts 15.10.

sire to relieve human beings of their burdens: "Come to me, all you who labor and have been burdened. Take up my yoke, because it is easy."[14] When he says "all," he is clearly calling both the Jews and the gentiles.

7. But why is this woman's illness protracted for eighteen years? It is because if the Ten Commandments of the Law had not come to be joined to the grace of the number eight,[15] never would the holy Church, never would this woman have reached the fullness of time, the day of salvation, the acceptable time,[16] or the presence of her Savior. But even the kind of healing indicates the fact that this woman was a figure of the Church, in the following way:

8. *He called her to himself,* it says, *and laid his hands on her* (vv. 12–13). Thus the one who has been found worthy of becoming a Christian and each day sees others becoming Christians is fully aware that the Church is always being healed. For in order that a pagan who had been stooped under his sins be enabled to stand up straight toward heaven, first of all the evil spirit must be expelled from the pagan through the imposition of hands.[17]

But why did he who had expelled demons with a mere word

14. Mt 11.28–30.
15. In *Sermon* 126.9, in considering the number eighty (ten times eight), Chrysologus employs the same language and the same theme, namely, that the number ten refers to the Decalogue in the Mosaic Law and the number eight *(ogdoas)* refers to grace. The same numerological exegesis is found in Ambrose, *Expositio Evangelii secundum Lucam* 7.173, 274, but he specifies that the number eight represents grace because it stands for the "fullness of resurrection." The idea seems to be that the number eight is both a number of perfection, but also Sunday, the day of Christ's Resurrection, is occasionally referred to as the "eighth day." That some early baptismal fonts, including Ravenna's, were octagonal is further attestation to this connection with Jesus' Resurrection. On early Christian references to Sunday as the eighth day, see T. Carroll and T. Halton, *Message of the Fathers of the Church,* vol. 21, *Liturgical Practice in the Fathers* (Wilmington, DE: Glazier, 1988), 35–46. On an octagonal baptismal font in Ravenna, see A. J. Wharton, "Ritual and Reconstructed Meaning: The Neonian Baptistery in Ravenna," *The Arts Bulletin* 69 (1987): 358–75, esp. 363–64 and 368–69; and F. van der Meer and C. Mohrmann, *Atlas of the Early Christian World,* trans. and ed. M. F. Hedlund and H. H. Rowley (London: Nelson, 1958), 129.
16. See 2 Cor 6.2.
17. On recent scholarship concerning the significance of this reference to liturgical practice in Ravenna, see A. Olivar, *Los sermones,* 185. Another reference to the rite of exorcism in initiating one coming from a gentile background is found in *Sermon* 52.4 (FOTC 109.204–5).

and had cured all infirmities with merely a command lay his hands on this woman? Why does he change the process of healing, unless it is because he is then at that moment curing all in that one woman, or rather because he did not take the Church to himself, until first cleansing her of the devil through the imposition of his hands and making her a Christian, and in addition by the mystical sign of this present healing creating and instituting the healing of those who would become Christians?

9. But the leader of the synagogue is indignant because Christ is healing on the Sabbath,[18] and today the Jew is tormented with the rage of jealousy concerning the healing of the Church. He interprets matters having a heavenly meaning in an earthly sense, and supposes that the Sabbath has been consecrated for beasts of burden and not for human beings, since he quickly runs to the aid of an ox or ass that is in danger on the Sabbath, yet he does not[19] grant any pity or mercy to a human being dying on the Sabbath.[20] His foolishness is such that he both violates the Sabbath when a beast is at issue, and violates the essence of holiness when it is a human being at issue. He dictates God's Law to God, and he recasts how God's Sabbath is to be observed to such an extent that what God had compassionately conceded to the Jew in return for his earthly labor and physical work, "they have twisted like a treacherous bow,"[21] they who in this way turn the most upright precepts of the Law against the God of the Law.

O Jew, God has ordered you to rest from human concerns,[22] so that at least on one day, at least on the Sabbath you might pause and have concern for your salvation; and you, O Christian, be sure to keep the Lord's Day for the Lord, if you wish to see that other Day of the Lord,[23] and if you wish to possess with the Lord's help everything that belongs to the Lord.

18. See Lk 13.14.
19. There is an omission of *non* in Olivar's CCL text; see PL 52.494.
20. See Lk 13.15.
21. Ps 77 (78).57.
22. See Ex 20.10 and Dt 5.14.
23. This is a reference to the Lord's second coming, providing eschatological incentive for being present at the Sunday liturgy!

SERMON 106

On the Fig Tree to Be Chopped Down[1]

JUST AS A SKILLFUL teacher strikes at the intellects of students who are inexperienced in listening and slow to understand by employing various teaching techniques, and arouses and enkindles their talents, so does the Lord with a variety of parables and diverse metaphors call together and invite the sluggish and slow minds of the peoples to listen to the Gospel. For indeed the Lord begins today as follows: *A certain person had a fig tree planted in his vineyard, and he came to look for fruit on it, and did not find any. So he said to his vinedresser: "Look, it has been three years now since I have been coming to look for fruit on this fig tree, and still I have found none. Cut it down; for why does it take up space on the land?" But he said in response: "Lord, let it be for this year, until I dig around it and apply manure, and see if it bears fruit, but if not you can cut it down then"* (Lk 13.6–9).

2. *A certain person had a fig tree planted in his vineyard.* I ask you, what is so plain, what is so clear, what is so ordinary, what is as familiar to peasants as it is pertinent to the sophisticated, as the kind of parable that he has set before us, which comes from general experience, instructs everyone with its language, and attracts everyone by its example? An unfruitful tree is a burden to the sod, wastes space, drains the strength of the earth, causes damage to the farmer, is a nuisance to its owner, and so it is beneficial to cut it down, it is advantageous not to have it.

So too the human being who squanders the gift of nature, the blessing of his soul, the benefit of reason, the excellence of

---

1. This sermon may have been preached at the end of the year since there are some eschatological references: in section 4 to Christ's second coming, and in section 7 to the last judgment. See F. Sottocornola, *L'anno liturgico*, 103 and 293, n. 23.

intelligence, the judgment of his mind, his artistic talent, and his good upbringing, and invests them in unfruitful and empty endeavors, robs his Author of fruit, and is of no use to his Cultivator. Just as the tree deserves to be excised from the earth, so does this person deserve to be excised from life.

And just as is the case that, if an unfruitful tree is in a vineyard, while it extends its lethal shade over all the vines underneath it, it becomes hostile not only to itself, but also to vine branches that are fruitful, so too is it the case that, if a slothful and lazy human being happens to be in authority over peoples, he becomes harmful not only to himself, but to the masses, while by his example he corrupts and ruins those who follow him.[2] But let us listen to why the Lord told this parable.

3. After the numbness of winter has passed, while the fig tree blooms with unripe figs and gives the appearance of fruit in its blossoms, it deceives those who are unaware and deludes the inexperienced. For soon it sheds its unripe figs, and it manages to burst forth with sluggish buds, and the tree which seemed to be ahead of all the rest is later than all the rest in bearing fruit.[3] So it is right that the synagogue is compared by the Lord to the fig tree,[4] since it was heated by the warmth of the Law and for a time flourished as a prefiguration of the fruits of the Church.

For indeed since it was firmly grounded by having the Patriarchs as its roots, since it was raised high with its priestly stalk, since it spread out diffusely with the prophets as its branches, and since it was full of the unripe figs of the Jewish observance, it was flourishing at that time with the sole hope that it would bear fruit through Christ, or rather, that it would later bear Christ himself as its fruit, as the psalmist says: "I shall place one of the offspring of your womb upon your throne."[5]

---

2. It is unclear whether Chrysologus had a particular ruler in mind. Given his laudatory comments about the imperial family elsewhere, if he was making an accusation against someone, it may well have been against a lesser figure like Boniface or Aetius, who was responsible for some of the civil unrest under which Italy suffered in the fifth century. See A. Olivar, *Los sermones*, 237.

3. A similar discussion of the natural properties of the fig tree is given in Ambrose, *Expositio Evangelii secundum Lucam* 7.162 (CCL 14.269–70).

4. The fig tree of this parable is also presented as a symbol for the synagogue in Ambrose, *Expositio Evangelii secundum Lucam* 7.160–72 (CCL 14.269–73).

5. Ps 131 (132).11.

Therefore, the holy ones, who were aware of this, derived the hope of fruit from the blossom, and drew consolation in the present from the future, since they saw even then that the eternal succeeds the mortal, the everlasting succeeds the transitory, grace succeeds the Law, the Church succeeds the synagogue, the heavenly succeeds the earthly, the divine succeeds the human, Christ succeeds all; because with long-lasting patience they confidently awaited his arrival, they rejoiced with the joy that faith provides once he had come. Among these holy ones was that Simeon who, when he had been promised "that he would not see death until he saw the Christ of the Lord,"[6] exclaimed: "Now, O Lord, you let your servant go in peace according to your word, because my eyes have seen your salvation."[7]

4. But the ignorant, while placing their trust in the entirety of the Law, were neither concerned about awaiting Christ, nor deserving of accepting or recognizing Christ; and they were just as deceived by the little buds of the Law as the inexperienced are deceived by the fig tree with its unripe figs. This is why the Lord sends to the fig tree those who desire to know the time of his future coming, as he says: "When you see that the fig tree produces its unripe figs, you say that summer is near. And when you see the things about which I am speaking, know that the kingdom of God is near."[8] You see that the fig tree does not signify present events, but thus indicates future ones. But now let us attend to the parable before us point by point.

5. *A certain person had a fig tree planted in his vineyard* (v.6). The synagogue is the fig tree, the owner of the tree is Christ; the vineyard in which the tree is said to have been planted is understood to be the people of Israel, as Isaiah the prophet thus says: "The vineyard of the Lord of hosts is the house of Israel."[9] *He came*, it says, *to look for fruit on it, but did not find any* (v.6). Christ came, and he found in the synagogue not any fruit of faith, because it was all overshadowed by the deception bred by faithlessness.

---

6. Lk 2.26.
7. Lk 2.29–30.
8. Lk 21.30–31.
9. Is 5.7.

Christ came to the fig tree, to which we read that Adam had fled in his nakedness after his sin, as it says in the Book of Genesis: "And they realized that they were naked, and they took fig leaves, and made loincloths for themselves."[10] So Christ came to the fig tree, in order to find Adam and cover his nakedness with the holy garment of his Body, since the fig tree was not concealing Adam's shame, but was arousing it. This fig tree, that is, the synagogue, was baring the private parts of his body by its circumcisions; it was not covering them.[11]

6. *He came to look for fruit*, it says, *and did not find any. So he said to his vinedresser: "Look, it has been three years now that I have been coming to look for fruit on this fig tree, and still I have found none; cut it down"* (vv.6–7). The vinedresser, who is ordered to cut down the barren fig tree, is the angel in charge of the synagogue, who secures a reprieve by his intercession, since he is unable to make any excuse for its failure to produce fruit.

But this statement of his must not be overlooked: *Look, it has been three years now*. The three years are the three periods through which Christ came to the synagogue in search of fruit, that is, through the Law, through the Prophets, and through his own bodily Presence,[12] so that the barren fig tree, which already denied fruit to God on the grounds that it was not needed, would not refuse food that was needed at any rate for the Man, for the One who hungered, for Christ to eat. But now let us listen to what the vinedresser responded.

7. *Lord, let it be for this year* (v.8). The vinedresser begs that an

---

10. Gn 3.7.
11. In Ambrose, *Expositio Evangelii secundum Lucam* 7.164–65 (CCL 14.271), are found some similarities to Chrysologus's interpretation: a mention of Adam (and Eve) and their fig leaves, and a reference to the synagogue not bearing fruit. But, in contrast to Chrysologus, Ambrose refers explicitly to Christ as the new Adam looking for fruit rather than leaves, and his anti-Jewish remarks are less virulent. Indeed, in section 166 (271–72), Ambrose is rather laudatory about circumcision.
12. A similar delineation of three moments of divine revelation is given in *Sermon* 99.6, where Chrysologus refers to the Law, the Prophets, and the Gospels. See also *Sermon* 99, n. 21. In Ambrose, *Expositio Evangelii secundum Lucam* 7.166 (CCL 14.271), the three years also represent three periods when Christ came—to Abraham, Moses, and Mary—which Ambrose further explains as in the seal of circumcision, in the Law, and in Christ's Body.

additional year in the era of the Gospel be granted, about which Isaiah says: "Announce a year of favor from the Lord and a day of vindication."[13] For what reason? *Until I dig around it* (v.8). He wants to dig all around it with the apostolic plowshare,[14] because it failed to respond to the cultivation supplied by the Law's cutting blade.[15]

And I shall apply manure (v.8). If this manuring was necessary for so great a root, when the tree was nurtured with heavenly rain which made the holy sod so fertile, then it did not deserve to bear fruit. The sterile fig tree, the pitiful synagogue, is manured by the pity of the gentiles, so that aided by the vilest of applications that tree might return to fertility, which after such great and unsparing attention failed to bear fruit. If after this it remains as sterile as ever, it will then be cut down as hopeless and useless, not by the sickle of the vinedresser, but by the ax of the Lord himself.

And so he did not say: "In the future I am going to cut it down," but *you will cut it down* (v.9), in accord with what John says: "Already the ax is in place at the roots of the trees. For every tree that does not bear fruit will be cut down and cast into the fire."[16] So after the cultivation that occurs in the era of the Gospel, the ax of the Last Judgment will cut down the trees that have not borne fruit, and the final conflagration will take them and burn them to ashes.

13. Is 61.2 and Lk 4.19.
14. Ambrose, *Expositio Evangelii secundum Lucam* 7.168 (CCL 14.272), refers similarly to the "apostolic spades."
15. A similar failure is noted regarding the "plowshare of the Law" in *Sermon* 137.1.
16. The reference is to remarks by John the Baptist in Mt 3.10 or Lk 3.9.

SERMON 110

A Third <on the Apostle>[1]

TO LEAD THE FIRST and the last, both the Jews and the Greeks, to salvation, the blessed Apostle always holds up high the one and only standard of faith; whoever does not deserve to have and to hold it will not be able to possess the glory of being triumphant in heaven. This standard alone, brothers, is what precedes into battle the ranks of those who fight against faithlessness, it points out who the King is, it unites allies, and it terrifies the unholy enemy by the mere sight of it. And so he begins today: *The fact that it was credited to him as righteousness was not written, however, for Abraham's sake but for ours, who believe in him who raised Jesus our Lord from the dead* (Rom 4.23–24).

2. You see, brothers, that while people of an earlier age believe in the future events, while those of a later era believe in the past events, thus by the one way of faith both[2] attain to salvation; while they confessed that Christ would come, we now confess that he has come; they marvel and yet believe that he was going to come down and even to die in a human fashion; we boast that he has died and has risen.[3] And why should I say more, brothers? This mystery of salvation was denied to the eyes of those who came before as well as of us who have come later so that it would be entirely a matter of faith.

---

1. (Angle brackets here indicate an addition to the title in Olivar's CCL text.) *Sermons* 108–18 and 120 are all on St. Paul—his letter to the Romans and First Corinthians. All but three have already been translated in FOTC 17.166–208. The particular liturgical season in which these sermons were preached is unclear. While these sermons do not form a series as a whole and many of them were delivered in different years, it seems likely that *Sermons* 110–13 were preached one after the other. See F. Sottocornola, *L'anno liturgico*, 104–8.

2. Reading *utrique* in PL 52.503 instead of *utique* in Olivar's CCL text.

3. See Gal 6.14.

3. But concerning his statement: *The One who raised Jesus our Lord from the dead* (v.24), lest anyone believe that this action was done by another, he himself is the One who made and raised up his own Body, as he said: "I have the power to lay down my life, and I have the power to take it up again."[4] For the Resurrection could not have been raised by another, nor could Life[5] have been brought to life by another, nor could the One who was going to bestow these things on everyone be without them himself. Indeed, the Fountain does not thirst, nor does Bread hunger, nor does the Sun lack light, nor does Rest itself grow tired.

4. *He was handed over*, he says, *for our offenses, and he rose for our justification* (v.25). He was handed over for offenses, not so that this Life which was unable to die might be punished, but solely that the offenses which had banished us from life would be blotted out. *And he rose for our justification.* As long as the condemnation remains, the condemned person is unable to be justified.

Therefore, since the sin of our first parent had doomed us by giving death the right to hold us under its sway, Christ, our heavenly and true Parent, by having removed our condemnation to death by means of his own death, justifies us by his Resurrection,[6] so that it would not be the guilty, but their guilt, that would perish; and so that the punishment itself, that is, death, which had been ordered to strike down the guilty, would rightly fail and lose the power that was its trademark. Why did that cruel and unholy one dare to lay hands on the innocent One, the Judge himself? And so Paul added:

5. *Therefore, since we have been justified by faith, let us be at peace before God* (Rom 5.1). That is to say: let it cease, let the mother of dissensions cease, let the enemy of tranquillity, let the hostile attack on peace cease! Let the Jew not be exalted because of the Law, let the gentile not be haughty on account of any natu-

---

4. Jn 10.18.
5. See Jn 14.6. In *Sermon* 40.3 (FOTC 17.87), Chrysologus emphasizes that Christ as the "Life" made the decision and had the power to lay down his own life, whereas here he stresses that he was the agent of his own Resurrection.
6. A similar reference to Christ as Father, in the sense of being the source of new life as the new Adam, is found in *Sermons* 7.1 (FOTC 109.35) and 72b.5.

ral capacity, and let the philosopher not be made proud by his frothy and inane opinions. Let no one boast about his merits, let no one boast about his works, because it is the peace of God that has re-established and restored life, which the first transgression had removed, and our furious attacks on one another had kept even farther away. Therefore, *let us be at peace before God.* Let the earth not rebel against heaven, let the flesh not revolt against the spirit, but let everything have the humility to be united in the everlasting glory of heavenly peace.

6. *Through this we have access* (v.2), since he himself has become the Way for us.[7] *Faith in this grace* (v.2): the guide along this way is faith, brothers. *In which we stand, and we boast in our hope of the glory of the children of God* (v.2): we stand, to be sure, by faith, not bodily; and we boast in hope, not in already having received the reality. *But not only this, but we also boast of our tribulations, knowing that tribulation produces patience, but patience produces character, and character produces hope, and hope does not disappoint* (vv.3–5). See how through these stages of life the just man is given the strength to become the perfect man:[8] through tribulation, patience, character, and hope.

Brothers, tribulation, so to speak, first shakes and agitates the just man in his infancy. But when it discovers that he is patient, tribulation then educates in greater matters the adolescent who is already of good moral fiber. *Patience produces character* (v.4). Patience, brothers, is what proves that a young adult is fit for the virtues of Christ. *But hope does not disappoint* (v.5). Hope is what perfects the man, and is tireless in guiding him to measure up to the fullness of Christ.[9] It characterizes perfect virtue that what you do not have in reality you possess on the strength of hope.

7. *Since charity has been poured forth in our hearts* (v.5). And in order to show the nature of divine charity which has been poured forth upon us, he added: *For why did Christ die at the appointed time for the ungodly, while we were still infirm? For hardly ever does someone die for a righteous person. But perhaps someone might*

---

7. See Jn 14.6.
9. See ibid.

8. See Eph 4.13.

dare to die for a good person. God, however, proves his charity toward us, since, while we were still sinners, Christ died for us (vv.6–8).

If Christ loved the human race to such a degree that he was willing to die for the ungodly and for sinners, what, we ask, is he going to bestow upon the righteous? What? His life, his kingdom, his glory. From you he received death, which loomed over the earth for the ungodly. He keeps in store for you what he has always possessed in himself and through himself and continues to possess in heaven.

So let us say with the prophet: "What return shall I make to the Lord for all the blessings he has given to me? I shall take up the cup of salvation."[10] That is, I also shall die for him. But is there any similarity? He of his own accord dies for the ungodly and the sinner; but I find it difficult to die for a righteous and good person. I find it difficult, because it is not so much my will as it is inevitability that leads me to death. Listen to what he says to Peter: "But when you grow old, another will gird you and lead you where you do not want to go."[11] In adversities, brothers, what is inevitable cannot be compared with something we will.[12] To acquiesce is something inevitable, to will is a matter of virtue.[13] To the one who wills it, death itself has been made submissive, since death has always prevailed over the unwilling.

And nevertheless, brothers, since the human being cannot return anything approximating God's charity, let him give what he can, since he has been received according to what he has: lacking in glory, dead to life, ruined for salvation. Let us boast, brothers, about the sudden change in this enterprise, since death, which used to be the only complete compensation for goodness among human beings, through Christ has become a testimony to God's charity.[14]

10. Ps 115 (116).12–13.
11. Jn 21.18.
12. On this same topic, see also *Sermons* 38.2 (FOTC 17.83) and 41.2 (FOTC 109.164).
13. But, on making a virtue out of a necessity or an inevitability, see *Sermon* 42.5 and n. 24 (FOTC 109.171).
14. See Rom 5.7–8.

SERMON 113

A Sixth <on the Apostle>[1]

WHEN THE BLESSED APOSTLE asks about what is well known, and inquires about what is evident, he is of course rebuking and scolding those who corrupt the words of God by the interpretation they give, and they think up a justification for their offenses from the very place where they ought to have received instruction in the virtues. And so he began today as follows: *What shall we say? Shall we continue in sin in order that grace abound?* (Rom 6.1) He had said earlier, brothers: "Where sin has abounded, grace has abounded all the more."[2] And the reason that he has begun in this fashion—and for the sake of that divine and unparalleled[3] teaching he joins ranks with the ignorant, as it were, by asking a question—is that he might give a response filled with the erudition of heavenly wisdom.

2. "For if where sin has abounded, grace has abounded even more,"[4] *what then shall we say: shall we continue in sin in order that grace abound?* (v.1) If mercy's inclination is toward those who commit transgressions, if there is plentiful grace for sinners, if God's generosity is oriented toward the unrighteous, and certainly if future goods are procured by present evil deeds, why should we take the difficult road of the virtues, why should we undertake the hard labor of acquiring righteousness, why should we continually endure the torments of preserving our innocence among the wicked? Let the crimes of human beings

---

1. (Angle brackets here indicate an addition to the title in Olivar's CCL text.) On this sermon's place within Chrysologus's preaching on St. Paul, see *Sermon* 110, n. 1.

2. Rom 5.20.

3. Perhaps this is an allusion to Cicero, *Philippic* 2.15.39, where Pompey is described as "that unparalleled and almost divine man."

4. Rom 5.20.

increase, so that heavenly benevolence may overflow, just as he said: "Let us do evil so that good things might come";[5] let us *continue in sin so that grace may abound* (v.1)!

3. Brothers, the same person, namely, the Apostle himself, who asks the question, makes this response to it: *Far from it! For how shall we who have died to sin live in it?* (v.2) When he says, *Far from it!* he has thereby denounced the thinking and the reasoning of the foolish. Indeed the physician is not beneficial to the wound, but to the cure and the healing; he rejoices, not in a festering sore or in diseases, but only in good health. So too is it with God, who on account of the massive extent of the wound has applied a massive and strong dose of medicine; and he has bestowed grace not on the sin, but on the human being; he has rained down the shower of his mercy not to multiply but to blot out offenses.

Let no one, let no one, I say, be so glad about his illness that he wishes to continue in his wounded state. The one who is always hesitant about being cured is ungrateful to the physician, and a foe to his cure, nor does he ever really desire to be healed, and he wants the grace of God to abound for his sins in such a way that he wants to pile up sins on top of sins. Wretched is the one who with such a wish strives to be guilty by means of pardon! We must flee, brothers, we must flee this madness which even after the cure is held captive by the love of diseases. For more often than not it is a recurring illness that is the lethal one.

4. But by his statement: *We who have died to sin*, he is alluding to the present time, since he has said that we have died to sin; he did not say that already in its entirety sin has died to us; because, although sin itself, as far as carrying out any action, is defunct for the saints and the faithful, nevertheless it lives and rages furiously right up to the moment of our death. But then sin itself will die in us "when this corruptible body will put on immortality," and "the words written in Scripture" will be fulfilled: "'O death, where is your sting? Where, O hell, is your victory?' The sting of death is sin."[6]

5. Rom 3.8.
6. 1 Cor 15.54–56.

But that one lives for sin, who, as Paul says in what follows,[7] is a slave to his lusts, and is subservient to deplorable urges, who complies with the vices, who yields to offenses in his unhappy state of constant captivity, who thinks that what has to do with sin is part of his nature, and who treats the disease, which is an accident,[8] as though it were the product and favor of his Creator. And so in order to expose the ignorance of such people he said in addition:

5. *Or do you not know that all of us who have been baptized in Christ have been buried with him through baptism into his death?* (vv.3–4) Let the faithful listen and learn how the three days the Lord spent in the grave are represented by the triple immersion in Baptism; let them rejoice that they have risen with Christ, although not yet in body, yet already by newness of life; let the whole human being be a dwelling of the virtues, who had earlier been a cistern of the vices, and, as Paul said, *as Christ rose by the glory of the Father, so too let us walk in newness of life* (v.4). Whatever has to do with his powers, Christ refers to the Father's glory; and the human being, who has nothing of his own, takes pains to claim for himself that he has risen by means of Christ.

6. But his remark: *Let us walk in newness of life*, confirms what we said earlier, that, although not yet changed in body, nevertheless the person is to proceed as already entirely changed in life: let him know himself, let him have dominion over the elements, since he used to serve the elements up until this time on account of ignorance;[9] let him give his own property away for glory, he who formerly in his foolishness used to steal the property of others; let the one who used to practice illicit acts of the flesh hold with disdain even the bodily acts that are permitted; let the one who up to this time was in his wickedness trying to destroy innocence, die more gloriously on behalf of innocence.

---

7. See Rom 6.6, 12–16.
8. "Accident" in the philosophical sense, as not being an inherent part of one's essence or nature. On evil or sin as an accident, and neither something created by God nor a substance, see also *Sermons* 11.2 (FOTC 17.57) and 111.2 (FOTC 17.176). In addition see Introduction, FOTC 109.18 and n. 90.
9. See Gal 4.3.

And why should I say more? If from the old human being one has already been made a new human being,[10] let him transform the raging whirlpool of his vices into a fountain of the virtues.

7. All the way through to the end of the reading the blessed Apostle keeps stating and asserting this point: that the one who follows the pattern of innocence given by the risen Christ, who imitates his life, and who strives to implement his holiness, is able to live with Christ[11] and to reign with Christ. As for his remark: *That the body of sin might be destroyed* (v.6), let it be destroyed, brothers, in action but not in substance, in deed but not in form, since he wants to make the human being lost to sin, but not to God, since he says: *Consider yourselves to be dead to sin, but alive for God* (v.11); and he strives with all devotion to restore the human being to heavenly freedom, brothers, when he says: *Do not let sin reign in your mortal body* (v.12). And again: *Sin will not have dominion over you* (v.14).

He did not say: "It does not approach you," nor: "It does not arouse, it does not entice"; but: *Do not let it reign*, do not let it have dominion. Let the battle joined by the wicked realm of sin bring glory to the conqueror, let its struggle and defeat make the victor triumphant, and at long last let it grieve that it is being tread underfoot by those who were formerly its slaves and now completely safe. Let the cruel tyrant bemoan the fact that he has been cast under the feet of those who used to be his captives, and let that old enemy bewail the fact that he has reached the point where those over whom he had been triumphant for so long are now triumphant over him.

10. See Rom 6.6.
11. See Rom 6.8.

SERMON 118

An Eleventh <on the Apostle>[1]

INCE THE WHOLE HOPE of the Christian faith has its foundation in the resurrection of the dead, and so that no one may dare to have doubts about it, today we have had a very lengthy reading proclaimed to you from blessed Paul as he affirms this with his authority, with facts, and with examples; our sermon is unable to find anything which it might be able to add to what he has said. But because you, my dear ones,[2] always demand the ministry of our office, with the ardor of the resurrection itself we are eager to repeat these same matters and to tread in these very tracks more vigorously.

2. Brothers, it is always a pleasure to speak about the resurrection, it is a perpetual delight to hear about the resurrection, since it is always unpleasant to die, but always a delight to live. Therefore, may the resurrection always echo in our mouths, may the resurrection always make its way into our mind's hearing, so that death, which always besieges our senses with its terror and lamentation, may be cast out from our senses.

And so the farmer sings of a plentiful harvest and of bountiful feasting so as not to feel the toil and sweat of the plowshare which lie ahead of him; so too the sailor makes a melody about ports and profit so as not to be afraid of shipwreck or other haz-

---

1. (Angle brackets here indicate an addition to the title in Olivar's CCL text.) See *Sermon* 110, n. 1, regarding Chrysologus's preaching on St. Paul. A. Olivar, in *Los sermones*, 270–71, believes that *Sermon* 118 followed next after *Sermon* 117, because at the close of 117 (FOTC 17.202), Chrysologus promised that he would preach a complete sermon on the resurrection. But the fact that the biblical text occasioning *Sermon* 118 was from an earlier section of 1 Cor 15 than was *Sermon* 117 makes Olivar's contention highly unlikely. The sermon promised in 117 is probably not extant.

2. Literally, "your charity" *(vestra caritas)*. See A. Olivar, *La predicación cristiana antigua* (Barcelona: Herder, 1991), 882.

ards of the sea; thus the soldier repeats a refrain about booty and triumphs so as not to fear wounds nor be afraid of blows from a sword.[3] Therefore, may the Christian await, sing, and think about the resurrection with his mind, mouth, and eyes, so that he can despise and tread underfoot all fear of death.

3. Death, brothers, is the mistress of Despair, the mother of Unbelief, the sister of Corruption, the parent of hell, the wife of the devil, the queen of all evils, who is so insatiable and so deliberate in her attacks against the whole human race that she first sends ahead Despair to murmur and seduce on her behalf as follows. And so Despair[4] says: "O man, why are you wasting your time? Look, Death, your mistress, is coming, and she is going to reduce your soul to nothing and consume your flesh with decay and your bones with aging, so as to make you, who did not exist before your birth, nonexistent after death. So, you who are about to die, do not delay paying for yourself what you owe to your various stages in life before you die: spend your childhood in games, spend your adolescence in delights, spend your youth in pleasures, spend your old age with me, so that you will not imagine that you have no reason to have despaired of hope."

4. After her she sends her daughter Unbelief, who makes the following threats: "Are you thus disposing of your life as if you are not going to die, as if you will avoid death? O man, faith is deceiving you; you trust faith, which promises future blessings in order to take away present ones; and pledges that there are all sorts of unseen things after death, in order to remove the things that do exist before death. Who has come from there, or what wise person believes in things that have been promised for so long but never fulfilled? Oh, if only you would eat and drink! Eat and drink, for tomorrow you will die."[5]

5. Third, she directs Corruption, her sister in wickedness,

---

3. Somewhat similarly, in *Sermon* 10.1 (FOTC 109.52) Chrysologus mentions that the difficulties faced by both sailors and soldiers are made more tolerable by singing. In *Sermon* 14.1 (FOTC 109.66), as the soldier is fortified by the blast of the trumpet, so the soldier of Christ is heartened by the singing of a psalm.

4. For a similar personification with discourse, see *Sermon* 65.6–9 (FOTC 109.263–66) regarding Tartarus.

5. See Is 22.13 and 1 Cor 15.32.

with such fury that she assaults, lays hold of, and seizes what can be seen of human beings throughout their graves, and revealing her ultimate prisons she points out those who lie there bound and immobile, and in order to throw all the senses of the human being into turmoil with complete horror and complete fear, she oozes decay, she belches gore, she strews stenches, and she proclaims that she has supplied worms from herself as countless butchers to one human body.

6. Why should Christians not trust Despair or Unbelief? They are the way Death wages war; with these generals and with these tactics in a battle of this sort she captures, crushes, and kills all those whom nature brings forth into the present life. She holds sway over kings, she conquers peoples, she routs nations. It has never been possible to bribe her with wealth, or to move her by entreaties, or to soften her by tears, or to conquer her by strength.

Brothers, how wrong those authors have been who have tried to write about the good of death.[6] And what is so surprising about that? In this case the worldly-wise think that they are great and remarkable if they convince simple folks that the thing that is the greatest evil is the greatest good. Quite correctly does Scripture say about this lot: "Woe to those who call evil good and good evil; woe to those who put darkness for light and light for darkness."[7] And truly, what deception would be beyond them, what blindness have they been unable to induce, when they have succeeded in making the undiscerning believe that it is an evil to live and a good thing to die? But these things, brothers, truth dispels, the Law banishes, faith attacks, the Apostle censures, and Christ blots out, who, while restoring

---

6. For similar sentiments, see *Sermon* 101.4 (FOTC 17.162). For two representatives of the classical Latin tradition on this topic, see Cicero, *Tusculan Disputations* 1.34.82–35.85 and 1.48.116, and Seneca, *De Consolatione ad Marciam* 22–26. For two other early Christian Latin writers on this topic, see Lactantius, *The Divine Institutes* 3.19 (FOTC 49.216–20); Ambrose, *On the Death of His Brother Satyrus* 2.18–35 (FOTC 22.204–11); and Ambrose, *Death as a Good* (FOTC 65.70–113). Lactantius is closer to Chrysologus's thinking on this matter. Ambrose, especially in the latter work, draws a great deal from the Platonic tradition on this topic—specifically, from Plato, Philo, Plotinus, and Porphyry—and is far more willing than Lactantius and Chrysologus to speak of death as a good.

7. Is 5.20.

the good that life is, discloses, condemns, and banishes the evil of death.[8] And so the Apostle began:

7. *But I remind you, brothers, of the gospel which I preached to you, which you in turn received, in which you also are standing, by means of which you likewise are being saved; you must hold to it in the manner in which I preached it to you, unless you have believed in vain. For I have handed on to you as of the utmost importance that Christ died for our sins, that he was buried, and that he rose on the third day in accord with the Scriptures* (1 Cor 15.1–4).

The gospel which I preached to you, which you in turn received: God's generosity enriches the one who is going to live, not one who is going to die. Otherwise for what purpose does someone receive something good, if the recipient is not going to survive? *In which you also are standing:* surely the one who stands is someone who lives forever, since the one who is going to die lies prostrate forever. *In which you likewise are being saved:* whoever dies perishes; it is always the case that one who is saved is someone who stays alive. *You must hold to it in the manner in which I preached it to you, unless you have believed in vain:* not only, brothers, has one believed in vain, but that person has also lived in vain, if he believed that he was born for the sole purpose of perishing.

8. O man, is there anything in your life that rises that does not fall? Anything that falls that does not rise again? Day rises in the morning, late in the night it is buried, and again it rises in the morning. The sun is born each day, dies each day, and rises again each day. As the seasons pass, they perish; as they return, they come back to life. Therefore, O man, if you do not trust God, if you do not follow his Law, if you do not agree with what you hear, at least trust your eyes, and at least follow the elements which continually preach to you your resurrection.[9]

9. Even if these realities are of no help, let ones that are un-

---

8. For Chrysologus, death is an undeniable evil, as his reading of Rom 5.12 assures him (see his *Sermon* 111 on this text in FOTC 17.175–80), although it has been conquered by Christ.

9. Elsewhere, too, Chrysologus points to indications of the resurrection from the rhythms of nature. See *Sermons* 57.15 (FOTC 17.109), 59.16 (FOTC 109.229), 103.2–4, and 176.4. For examples in other writers, see *Sermon* 59, n. 25 (FOTC 109.229).

der your control and are raised from death by your action teach you that you can be raised by God's action. Go to the seed with the Apostle as your guide; take a dried-up grain of withered wheat, lifeless and motionless; put your plow to work, dig up the earth, make a grave, bury the wheat, see how it withers and dies, swells with moisture, decays, and disintegrates; and when it finally reaches the point in sum and substance where Despair, Unbelief, and Corruption were attacking you earlier, at that very moment and all of a sudden it comes back to life in the form of a bud, it sprouts up into a blade, it grows into a stalk, it matures into a grain, and it recovers all of its own appearance and form that you were lamenting had perished. The purpose of this, O man, is for the wheat to teach you not so much to eat as to savor the mystery,[10] and to compel you not so much to labor as to believe.

10. Let us be silent about the rest, because the blessed Apostle, with eloquence that is straightforward, abundantly clear, and divine, indicates from what source, when, how, and through whom death has come.[11] O man, receive faith, since it is given for free; believe in the resurrection, because he who promises it charges no price.

---

10. The expression "savor the mystery" is an attempt to render *sapere*, which means both "to be wise" and "to taste."
11. See 1 Cor 15, especially vv.21–22.

SERMON 121

On Lazarus and the Rich Man[1]

OU HAVE HEARD TODAY, brothers, the end-result of poverty, and you have learned what is the outcome of wealth from the Lord's words. *There was a certain rich man, and he was dressed in purple and linen, and he used to feast sumptuously every day. And there was a certain beggar named Lazarus, full of sores, who used to lie at his entryway, desiring to eat the crumbs that fell from the rich man's table; even the dogs used to come and lick his sores. It happened,* he said, *that the poor man died and was carried by the angels to the bosom of Abraham. The rich man, however, also died, and was buried in hell* (Lk 16.19–23).

2. Look, brothers, at what a lamentable reversal of circumstances: the angels carry the poor man, and hell swallows down the rich man! See, brothers, how the poor man in death has completely surpassed the rich man, and in the one action of being raised on high, the poor man has eclipsed the rich man in all his pomp and glory. Why does their burial so deceive people's eyes? Why are the pompous funeral rites so untrue?

Here the whole city goes out to pay its respects to the rich man while his corpse is transported for burial; the poor man journeys all alone; just two sympathetic pall-bearers carry the poor man, not four of them, as is customary for a dead man, but two are assigned to carry him on one pole, as though being pressured into throwing away some burdensome thing. It is fitting that the services of the angels, it is fitting that divinely mandated acts of respect were bestowed upon him right away,

---

1. *Sermons* 121–23 form a continuous series, delivered at successive liturgies. Since *Sermon* 122.1 (FOTC 17.208–9) refers to the feast of St. Andrew celebrated on that day (November 30), these three sermons then were preached from late November through early December. See F. Sottocornola, *L'anno liturgico*, 108–9, and A. Olivar, *Los sermones*, 271–72.

for whom even the final expressions of human courtesy were so cruelly denied. A throng of slaves in mourning precedes the rich man's corpse, a multitude of angels singing psalms leads the way before the poor man's bier. The rich man's body clothed in gold lies enclosed inside a marble tomb; the poor man's flesh rests in unadorned mud, and by being placed directly in the earth it escapes the worms' bites, and it keeps decay and stench from setting in.

But let us inquire, brothers, into what was the fault, the offense, the wicked deed of the rich man that consigned him to the torments of hell, and, in the face of his sentence of condemnation, caused his verdict to be sung by so many generations as the judge himself[2] pronounced it, as the Lord says:

3. *There was a certain rich man, and he was dressed in purple and linen, and he used to feast sumptuously. And there was a certain beggar named Lazarus who used to lie at the rich man's entryway, and he desired to eat the crumbs that fell from the rich man's table* (vv.19–21). Is it merely the fact of riches in and of themselves that is the cause for guilt? Must clothes, for example, just by being what they are, be condemned in God's sight? Are feasts merely in themselves warrant for punishment, such that not only do they receive no recompense for being something good, but they even suffer and deserve the same destruction as everything else that is evil? Or is being a beggar so praiseworthy and holy in and of itself, and are sores so sacred as to be whisked off by the hands of the angels into the bosom of holy Abraham?

And so it is quite strange, brothers, that Abraham, who formerly had been rich, now spurns the rich man—Scripture says so: "And Abraham was very rich"[3]—and one whom he had as his equal in earthly wealth he now condemns and allows to suffer punishment, particularly since the word of God does not say a thing about any good deeds done by this poor man or any evil deeds by that rich man.

So why does Abraham now embrace the poor man, and re-

---

2. From the following section as well as the next homily (see *Sermon* 122.4 [FOTC 17.210]), it is evident that Abraham is the judge in question.
3. Gn 13.2.

fuse and resist the rich man? Or how did Abraham's wealth render him innocent, while the rich man's wealth made him guilty? How did it promote Abraham to the rest which all the saints enjoy while consigning the rich man to the abyss where all the wicked suffer? But lest what I have to say weary your mind and keep you listening in suspense for too long, we must hurry up and resolve this conundrum.

4. Abraham, brothers, was rich not for himself but for the poor person, and he was eager, not to amass wealth, but to give it away, and he exerted more and more energy in storing his resources in the lap of the poor person instead of in barns, as is abundantly clear from the whole course of his life.[4] For as a foreigner he labored continually, so consequently as a foreigner he knew what it was to be a foreigner. And since he stayed under a tent, he did not allow any stranger to stay without a roof over his head, and as a guest himself he always received every guest.[5] Exiled from his homeland and homeless himself, he was both a home and homeland for all.[6]

Recognizing that he was not placed here as a possessor, but as a distributor of divine bounty, in whose mind dedication toward another was dearer than his own life, he appoints himself as a new kind of warrior against death in order to vindicate the oppressed, to release captives, and to rescue those who were at the very point of death. Abraham welcomed and attended to his guest, he did not sit down,[7] and he did not take his place at table with his guest, but he waited upon him. When he saw a foreigner Abraham did not consider himself to be the master; he himself served the meal after very carefully directing his wife to do some fairly elaborate cooking, and he, who entrusts himself and all his property to his household servants, actually has difficulty handing this task over to his wife as competent as she was.[8]

---

4. Similar praise of Abraham is found in *Sermon* 28.2 (FOTC 109.116–17) and elsewhere.

5. That Abraham as a foreigner was acutely attuned to the needs of guests is mentioned also in *Sermon* 66.2 (FOTC 109.268).

6. See Gn 12.1–10 and 18.1–5.

7. There is a wordplay in Latin which the English does not capture: *adstitit, non adsedit*.

8. See Gn 18.6–8.

And what more should I say, brothers? So holy was his hospitality, and so holy were the hands by which it was always provided that, as a result, he invited God himself to his home and prevailed upon him to be his guest;[9] he came to Abraham, to the refreshment of the poor, to the shelter of strangers, he who will acknowledge in the future that he was the One welcomed in the stranger and the poor person, when he will say: "I was hungry, and you gave me to eat; I was thirsty and you gave me to drink; I was a stranger, and you welcomed me."[10]

5. *But it happened that the poor man died, and was carried by the angels to the bosom of Abraham* (v.22). It is appropriate, brothers, that he now welcomes all the saints to his peace, and in the very blessedness of heaven he carries out the office of steward, since, while always welcoming foreigners and the poor here, he became worthy of welcoming God himself with the angels, and seeing God as his guest under his own tent, whom he always recognized as his Benefactor. And truly, brothers, he would have thought that his state of beatitude was deficient, if in the very glory of heaven he no longer served in the holy ministry of hospitality, and if he enjoyed the divine gifts all by himself, who in this life considered himself cruel if he refused anyone human goods.

Abraham, brothers, always runs to meet those who come from a distance, he even calls back and implores those who pass by, with great pleading he prevails upon those who are unwilling to come to his table, he always places before his guest the best and fattest offering from his herds, and he always called for bread kneaded by his wife's hands and freshly baked, bread which his unending kindness certainly would not allow to be cold or a day old.

6. But that other rich man, or rather that one who was held captive by his riches, who was the servant of wealth and shackled by his very property, a completely immovable tomb of ostentation, in whom even the slightest bit of pity had neither been seen nor heard, disdains not merely the person, not

---

9. See *Sermon* 66.2 (FOTC 109.268) on this same point.
10. Mt 25.35.

merely the poor man, but disdains even mercy itself to Lazarus as he lies in such a state at his entryway. With purple, with linen, with fine clothing, and with exquisite dining the cruel soul was feeding his heart that was hard as iron.

God, that eager Seeker of human salvation, in his desire to soften that soul, cast before his entryway not Lazarus so much as the very crucible of pity. I said "crucible" on account of his heart that was hard as iron. And so, the beggar Lazarus is positioned and presented before his pitiless eyes, and so that the rich man be able to give, the rich man's wealth grows greater and greater. But the rich man, harder than steel, either shamefully squandered or cruelly hoarded whatever addition God made to the rich man's wealth for the support of the poor man.

Furthermore, in order not to be silent, but rather to shout forth, in order to admonish the rich man, in order for the famished, poor man to make it evident that the only thing he was asking for was bread, and in order to prevail upon the spirit of the wealthy man to bestow merely the bare minimum, God saw to it that the poor man increased in hunger.

7. *He desired*, it says, *to eat the crumbs that fell from the rich man's table* (v.21). But the rich man who was stuffed with the various dishes of food was belching his indigestion to heaven, so that he would not hear the cry of the poor man lying in such distress on the ground. And so, because the cry issuing only from one mouth was of no avail before such impenetrable ears, God opened the whole body of the poor man with wounds in order to open the rich man's heart, so that the poor man would have as many mouths to admonish the rich man as he had wounds. The inner organs break through, sores develop, gaping wounds expand, pus flows forth, and all the flesh of the poor man presents a spectacle of pity, so that the one whom the cry of the hungry man had not moved, at least the sighs of pain, the groans, and the full ensemble of these afflictions might shake up. But the rich man "with a haughty eye and an insatiable heart"[11] scorned hearing, seeing, and noticing all these things.

God still looks for a way for the rich man to be freed from

---

11. Ps 100 (101).5.

his obstinacy. He dislocated the poor man's hands from his joints, so that he would not shoo the rich man's dogs away, which he was going to feed from his own wounds for the sake of the rich man's wound, and in a new manner, brothers, the order of compassion is transformed: the beggar's compassion becomes the way that the greedy man's lack of compassion is disclosed. The rich man does not feed the poor man on the crumbs that fall from his table, and Lazarus the poor man, because he did not have anything else, compassionately provided for the dogs from his own flesh. You wretched rich man, if you refused to give bread, why weren't you at least willing to drive the dogs away?

But your dogs are gentler than you, or rather you are crueler than your dogs, for while you act cruelly they show restraint, since they do not offer their teeth to bite, but their tongues to serve, such that like a sponge they do not hurt his wounds, but they wipe them clean. O rich man, in your dogs pity has conquered hunger, but in you overabundance has not overcome pitilessness. That the dogs did this out of a desire to soothe him is evident from what we see them doing on a daily basis. For dogs always soothe their own wounds by licking. The dogs care for the poor man as nature teaches them, and man neglects man[12] with nature itself accusing him of this grave offense. It is true, yes it is true, that since the rich man is unable to give even crumbs, in his avarice he is always in need.[13]

8. What I have yet to say must be postponed, brothers, because we have used up the time for speaking, and the section of the reading that is most important for us to address is still to follow.[14]

---

12. The Latin is *homo hominem neglegit*. A more extended treatment of "man's inhumanity to man" is given in Augustine, *Sermon* 65.1.2–2.3 (PL 38.427). See especially Paulinus of Nola, *Letter* 25*.2 *(homo hominem non fuerat misertus)*, in CSEL 29.231. In this section of the letter, Paulinus is commenting on this same parable and like Chrysologus indicates that the dogs are more humane to Lazarus than is the rich man.

13. *Semper avarus eget:* an exact quotation from Horace, *Epistles* 1.2.56.

14. Chrysologus preaches on this same Gospel text in the next three sermons. *Sermon* 122 is translated in FOTC 17.208–13.

SERMON 123

A Third on the Same[1]

T IS A CHARACTERISTIC of a shameless debtor either to postpone what is due or to deny what he has promised; an honorable one, by contrast, makes good on both pledges without delay and readily.[2] We have promised to address everything that remains about that rich man who, while clearly treating Lazarus brutally and harshly, is even more brutal and cruel to himself. Up to this point both the holy evangelist and our sermon, as far as it was possible, indicated what the rich man said to Abraham.[3] This is what was said: *And lifting up his eyes, while he was in torment, he saw Abraham from afar, and said: "Father Abraham, have mercy on me, and send Lazarus to dip the tip of his finger in water and cool my tongue, because I am in agony in these flames"* (Lk 16.23–24). To which Abraham now responds:

2. *My son, you received good things in your life* (v.25). O wondrous pity! He still calls a son the one whom he notices has degenerated so much by his own cruelty. O unparalleled benevolence! He still calls a son the one whom he sees is a vassal of hell, an offspring of punishments, by now the lowest slave in Gehenna. But he calls him a son, in order that his son's lack of pity become clearer and clearer, since the pity manifested in the father's words perdures even toward such as him.

"You call me father, and I call you son, so that you may grievously lament that you have lost what was yours by birth. I still call you a son, so that you may weep more bitterly that you have

---

1. This sermon on Lazarus and the Rich Man follows *Sermon* 122 and was preached in late November or early December. See *Sermon* 121, n. 1.
2. The preacher as debtor in owing a sermon he had promised is a common theme in Chrysologus. See, e.g., *Sermon* 36.1 (FOTC 17.75).
3. See *Sermon* 122 (FOTC 17.208–13). The "promise" referred to is stated in 122.8 (213).

lost what grace and nature had given to you, since it is equally sorrowful to have lost what one used to have as it is painful not to have had it at all. I call you a son, so that you may understand that what you are suffering is the result of your sentence, and not of wrath. I call you a son, in order for my patience to last for me and your punishment to last for you."

3. But this one, brothers, knows that he is not a son since he confesses and considers himself to blame for what he has lost from the nature of so devoted a father. He certainly then would have reflected his lineage if he had been devoted, hospitable, merciful, and compassionate toward the poor man. The one who does not do the works of his father denies his lineage, as the Lord teaches in the following: "If you were the children of Abraham, you would be doing the works of Abraham."[4] The one who can make the unassailable claim in his defense of doing his father's works attests to the veracity of his lineage. But what does Abraham say?

4. *My son, you received good things in your life.* Here in sum is the offense of this rich man, namely, that since he received good things, how guilty he is for appropriating what was not his due. If the one who locks up what is his, if the one who does not give generously what he has received, is so villainous, how culpable then is the one who guards his own goods jealously and seizes what belongs to another!

Brothers, let us give what is ours, if we can even call it ours; nevertheless, let us give what we consider to be ours, let us keep away from what belongs to another, let us shun any designs on what does not belong to us. Certainly, if we have taken something from someone, let us return it with all haste, lest, when we leave everything here, we be brought there poor in substance and rich in offense face-to-face with that rich man.

Nevertheless, let the rich man learn: he received good things, but did not become their sole proprietor.[5] You see, brothers, that the rich man's thoughts are exposed by what holy Abraham says, that his judgment is found to be faulty, that

---

4. Jn 8.39.
5. Chrysologus engages in wordplay here: *recepit bona, non accepit.*

his understanding is censured, since he believed that whatever he possessed thanks to the Lord's generosity, was not just given to him, but was due him. Realize the state of his judgment and the direction of his heart when he believed that God was in his debt, and, wicked in his wealth, held his Lord liable to his interest charges.

He was ignoring the fact that the Lord, although he walked this earth as a poor man, nevertheless ascended wealthy into heaven, and he lent, he did not borrow, when he gave five talents to one, two to another, one to yet another,[6] from whom he even promises that he will exact interest, and not pay it out, when he says to the servant: "You worthless, lazy servant, would that you had given my money [out on loan], and I would have come and collected it at least with interest!"[7] Therefore, this rich man is even more wicked, since he was not kind toward another, and, although he received good things, he did not receive good things for good deeds, but in his unworthiness he received good things for bad deeds.[8] But let us move on to Lazarus, and find out what the meaning is of the following:

5. *And Lazarus likewise* received *bad things* (v.25). And let it suffice for his credit, let it redound to his glory, if he did not do good deeds, but received bad things. Clearly that person is blessed, brothers, who has faith and trust in accepting good things from God while receiving bad things. Blessed is the one who always considers himself in debt to God. Blessed is the one who always repays his debts to God.[9] Certainly if he is unable to do so, at least let him tearfully beg with all humility that his debts be forgiven him, in words coming from the Lord himself: "Forgive us our debts."[10] Blessed is the one who discharges his debts to God, even when he does not know that he has incurred them, as the prophet instructs quite profoundly when he says: "At that time I restored what I did not take."[11]

Blessed is the one who always accuses himself before God, so

6. See Mt 25.15.
7. Mt 25.26 and 27; Lk. 19.23.
8. The same point is made in *Sermon* 66.4 (FOTC 109.269–70).
9. See below, section 7.   10. Mt 6.12.
11. Ps 68.5 LXX; Ps 69.4.

that God might excuse him, as Scripture advises in this fashion: "The just man from the start is his own accuser."[12] And if he is just, why does the just man accuse himself? "Because there is no one alive who will be just in your sight."[13] Perhaps a human being may boast before a human being about righteousness, about innocence, about merit; before God the one who brags about his innocence and who boasts about his righteousness is not a human being. A case in point is that Pharisee who, when he was not praying, but counting up, calculating, and belching out his acts of righteousness, left in a worse state in comparison with the tax collector who was made righteous.[14] But let us move forward.

6. *Now, however, this one is comforted*, he says, *but you are tormented* (v.25). You see, brothers, so understand, brothers, from what has been said, that although there are separate places there, nevertheless, there was still only one region of the underworld to hold both the just and the unjust, and although there was already a great abyss, nevertheless, not yet did a heavenly dwelling keep them apart; although a grim chasm divided them, nevertheless, not yet did any inhabit the height which had been assigned to the angels in heaven.[15] A flaming sword, as the Lawgiver relates, kept revolving before the entryway to paradise,[16] so that no human being might return there, so that no human being would gain access there; the gates of the netherworld were bolted shut by bronze doors and iron bars,[17] so that no way out would be available to those souls which had been cast down there from above.

Furthermore, the bond of our father's debt which consigned each one to death continued to be written down by the pen of his blame and the ink of his guilt, and the great amount of interest accrued through the ages kept compounding to the detriment of his offspring, and there was no one suitable to en-

---

12. Prv 18.17.   13. Ps 142 (143).2.
14. See Lk 18.9–14.
15. See also *Sermon* 66.5 and n. 13 (FOTC 109.270).
16. See Gn 3.24.
17. A description of a similar fortification composed of bronze and iron is found in Virgil, *Aeneid* 7.609–10.

ter paradise, to extinguish the flame which had been divinely mandated, to open the gates of the underworld which had been bolted by heaven's decree, or to cancel the bond[18] which continued to be locked up in the ark of the Law as God had commanded.

This is why the Lord himself came on the scene, he who had banished the first man, that is, the insubordinate servant; the Lord himself, who had bolted paradise, who had locked up the netherworld, descended in the fullness of his power to the earth and below the earth, in order to extinguish the flames and to destroy in an instant what had been kept secure. This is why he carries his cross as a battering ram[19] as he is about to enter the netherworld, in order to crush and shatter the very gates of Tartarus which were fortified with bronze and iron. From his side he poured water out[20] in order to mark the way to paradise, to extinguish the fire of the underworld on the saints' side, to wash away and completely dissolve the ancient bond of debt, and to remit by suffering what he had imposed by his command.

7. Recognize this, brothers: be glad, brothers, that after the triumph of Christ the prison of the saints has been broken open, and the netherworld no longer exercises any jurisdiction over the saints, since Christ[21] penetrated all the way to the netherworld in order to free the just, not the unjust.[22] Let us realize, brothers, how great a benefit Christ has provided, or rather, how without Christ no one possessed salvation, since, besides the wretched dissolution of their bodies, the souls, too, of the saints were being held in confinement in the underworld. Therefore, Lazarus was blessed, who owed everything to God, in order not to owe anything to sin! He was blessed who

---

18. See Col 2.14.
19. In Ravenna in the Archbishop's Chapel, now part of the Archbishop's Museum, there is a mosaic dating from the sixth century depicting Christ as a warrior bearing his cross as a kind of battering ram. It is at least possible that the artist may have had this reference from Chrysologus in mind.
20. See Jn 19.34.
21. Reading *Christus* (see PL 52.539) rather than *Christi*, apparently a typographical error in Olivar's CCL text.
22. See *Sermon* 66.5 (FOTC 109.270) on this same theme.

here received so many evils, in order to possess there every good thing!

8. And Abraham said in addition: *Neither is anyone able to cross from here to you, nor can anyone pass from there* (v.26). It is frightening, brothers, it is very frightening to hear these words, which reveal that after they die and once they have been consigned to penal custody in the underworld,[23] such people are unable to be transferred to the peace of the saints, unless, now that they have been redeemed by the grace of Christ, they are set free from this desperate state by the intercession of the holy Church, so that what their sentence of condemnation refuses them, the Church may obtain, and grace may supply.[24]

9. Nevertheless, this rich man still makes his request: *Father Abraham.* With no one to blame but himself, he who has thus lost both father and homeland still calls upon his father. *Father Abraham:* this wretch tells a lie even as he is being punished. *Father Abraham, send him to my father's house* (v.27). If he speaks the truth in calling him his father, then who is the other father about whose house he is inquiring? Can he possibly believe that he has Abraham, though absent, as his father even when he recognizes that by his own actions he has lost him in person? And so, does he believe that the house of that other father is kept intact for him by the favor of Abraham, whose bosom he sees is refused him there, and whose rest he sees is flatly denied him?

Father Abraham, send him. Whom? Lazarus, of course. Where? *To my father's house.* Now too late the rich man invites Lazarus to his father's house, not out of mercy but out of his own misery; he invites Lazarus, whom for so long he did not welcome as he was lying in such misery at his entryway, and under the pretext of pity he wants Lazarus to go back to his old wounds and his groans of the past, since he failed in his first petition to call him

---

23. This provisional penal custody is not as severe as what awaits the damned after the Last Judgment. See *Sermon* 122.5 (FOTC 17.211).

24. On the power that intercessory prayer by the Church was believed to have, see J. Ntedika, *L'évocation de l'au-delà dans la prière pour les morts: Étude de patristique et de liturgie latines (IVe–VIIIe s.)* (Louvain and Paris: Nauwelaerts, 1971), 84–135 (103–5 on Chrysologus). See also *Sermon* 103.5.

down to his own torments. Earlier he said: "Send him to me";[25] now he says: "Send him to my brothers." The impetus behind the unhappy man's grief and actions is his unwillingness to see in a happy state the one whom at one time he had determined to be unhappy.

10. "Send him to my brothers." Where? *To my father's house.* For what purpose? *I have five brothers,* he says, *so that he may bear witness to them not to come to this place of torment* (v.28). How can someone have concern for someone else when he is so blatantly unconcerned for himself? He is shameless and presumptuous in attempting to procure an opportunity for repentance for others when he has been so shortsighted and so cruel to himself in failing to provide for his own need for forgiveness. *Send Lazarus; I have five brothers.* And do you think that Lazarus can accomplish anything for your five brothers when he had no success with you as he cried out for so long, employing his whole body with so many wounds? Rightly did Abraham respond to him:

11. *They have Moses and the prophets, let them listen to them* (v.29). Let Lazarus rest after such great labors, and, as far as you are concerned, weep for your own punishments which you deserve to suffer. But the Lord God some time ago had regard for your brothers and for all people, and not on the strength of your advice, but out of his own generosity provided for their salvation: he gave the Law through Moses, he bestowed prophecy through Elijah. Therefore, let them listen to them, so that they not experience your torments.

12. The rich man replied: *No, Father Abraham, but if someone rises from the dead, they will believe him* (v.30). Abraham gave this response to him: *If they do not believe Moses and Elijah, neither will they believe even someone who rises from the dead* (v.31). No truer words could be spoken, brothers: the person who has refused to believe in the One speaking from heaven through the Law, the One coming from heaven in Christ, will surely be unworthy of believing in One who returns from the dead.

It is Christ himself, brothers, our God and our Lord, who

---

25. See Lk 16.24.

spoke from heaven to Moses, it is he who spoke on earth in an earthly body, he who returned from the dead with his earthly body. Nevertheless, that rich man's brothers, who are understood to be the Jewish people, refused with unyielding obstinacy to believe in him who told them what blessings there are in heaven and what evils there are in hell.

13. Certainly, brothers, the time prevents us from telling now who the rich man is or who Lazarus the poor man is or who the rich man's five brothers[26] are, nor does it permit us to reveal what spiritual meaning lies concealed in this narrative.[27] But since we have been instructed by Christ as to what their future holds and what awaits the unjust in hell, let us act, indeed let us hasten, by word, deed, and mercy, so as to be able to seize the heavenly goods and, out of great fear, avoid and sidestep evils.

26. From sections 11 and 12 above and from *Sermon* 66.7 (FOTC 109.271), Chrysologus indicates that the five brothers signify the Jewish people.
27. In *Sermon* 124.9, just when it appears that Chrysologus is going to reveal what the spiritual meaning of this parable is, he instead confines himself to moral exhortation!

SERMON 124

A Fourth on the Same[1]

ACH TIME THE RICH man in his purple is set before us by God, and each time the poor man, wounds and all, is presented to us, on every such occasion the arena of mercy is opened before us, and the racecourse of pity is revealed to us,[2] so that from a heavenly perspective we may be able to notice in how short a time the poor man attained such a glorious palm of victory and the rich man came to such a devastating end.

2. *There was a rich man,* it says, *and he was dressed in purple and linen, and he used to feast sumptuously every day. And there was a certain beggar named Lazarus who used to lie at his entryway, desiring to eat the crumbs that fell from the rich man's table* (Lk 16.19–21). The rich man was dressed in purple, the poor man in black and blue; the rich man in linen, the poor man in filth; the rich man with gold, the poor man with a stench. The poor man used to perspire from his wounds, the rich man from his ointment; the poor man had a foul air about him, the rich man a fragrant

---

1. A. Olivar, *Los sermones,* 271–72 and 277, contends that this sermon on Lazarus and the Rich Man was the fourth one in a series after *Sermons* 121–23. He does not supply much justification for his position. F. Sottocornola, *L'anno liturgico,* 109, on the other hand, claims that this sermon was preached in a different year from the series 121–23. In particular, *Sermon* 123 promised that the next sermon would be on the allegorical meaning of the characters in this Lucan parable (123.13), but this promise is not fulfilled in this *Sermon* 124, but instead is purposely omitted (see the beginning of section 9), after much of the same ground is covered as in the previous three sermons. One cannot conclude with certainty that this sermon did not immediately follow *Sermon* 123, but Sottocornola's reservations do seem more plausible. In any event, it is likely that this *Sermon* 124 was preached in late November or early December. See *Sermon* 121, n. 1.

2. Chrysologus employs similar language in describing the plight of the woman with a hemorrhage. See *Sermon* 33.4 and n. 12 (FOTC 109.141).

one. The rich man used to recline on a soft, feathered couch, the poor man used to lie on the very hard ground.

The rich man used to belch up his sumptuous meals, the poor man used to cough up pus. The rich man kept pouring wine, the poor man his tears. When he could eat no more, the rich man would throw away his bread, but the poor man who was starving didn't even have any crumbs. From his trays of food the rich man used to feed his dogs who kept barking at the poor man, while the poor man used to keep the rich man's dogs fat from his own wounds.

And, in short, we have read that everything that was good came the rich man's way, and everything that was bad came the poor man's way; nevertheless, such adversities did not crush the poor man, nor did all this prosperity do the rich man any good; in fact, poverty propelled the poor man to philosophy,[3] pain to virtue, being despised to being patient, an unavoidable condition to one that was freely willed,[4] hunger to fasting, thirst to endurance, death to life, punishment to reward, earth to heaven, indigence to the kingdom; so too his purple drove the rich man to pride, his linen to extravagance, his wealth to inhumanity, his abundance to heartlessness, his ointments to rottenness, his splendor to blindness, his loftiness to devastation.

Therefore, adversities neither straighten out the lazy nor overcome the strong, since it is neither one's material prosperity nor poverty, but one's character[5] that either leads the grateful to their reward or leads the ungrateful away to their punishment.

3. The poor man, full of sores, is stationed at the rich man's doorway, but this occurs not by some human coincidence, but by God's design, in order that the contest between the rich and the poor man play itself out on earth and have its audience in heaven. God was watching, the angels were watching the unique competition between the rich and the poor man. The

---

3. That is, to have his soul ordered and in harmony, with his reason in control of his appetites.

4. On this topic, see *Sermon* 110.7 and nn. 12 and 13.

5. The Latin is *animus*, indicating the inclination, disposition, or vibrancy of one's mind or soul, and hence "character."

rich man stood all decked out in the armor of his riches, and, by contrast, the poor man was lying clothed only in his very flesh, unless you consider as his breastplate the one wound he had over his entire body.[6] The rich man was being protected by throngs of servants; the poor man, his skin torn away, was being prodded by his stinging pain. The rich man was hurling spears of heartlessness, while Lazarus was repelling them with his shield of compassion. The rich man was brandishing his cruelty to wound the poor man, while Lazarus was thwarting the rich man's sword by remaining fully alive from such a wound.

Why should I say more? The poor man was victorious, who earlier moved fully into his soul while his body was fading away, and with his flesh trampled underfoot, but fully armed from above, he made his ascent into the spiritual realm, so that the rich man's cruelty would find no place to strike.

4. For the reason that God had arranged for the rich man and the poor man to be always in the sight of one another was that they both might provide a cure for each other's particular affliction. The poor man was sick in body, the rich man in mind. This is why the poor man's cure was continually delayed, so that the rich man would accept from the poor man the medicine from his wound, compunction from his groans, repentance from his tears, an example from his patience, mercy from his hunger, understanding from his thirst; in short, fellowship in heaven from compassion on earth.

Clearly the purpose was that the rich man would be grateful to God for having been favored with such blessings, when the rich man saw that the poor man was steadfast in his gratitude to God amidst all the evils he endured. And so it was right that he who lay prostrate was being carried by the angels, that he who was grieving was being comforted in the bosom of Abraham, and that he always live unto God since he did not know how to live for himself in this world.

5. *It happened*, it says, *that the poor man died, and was carried by the angels to the bosom of Abraham. The rich man, however, also died,*

---

6. Earlier Zeno of Verona had used similar language to describe Job as an individual whose entire body was covered by one enormous wound. See *Tractatus* 1.15.1.5 (CCL 22.61).

and was buried in hell (v.22). The wretch had his soul buried before his body, and he was not delivered to bodily peace before being delivered to the punishment of the grave, in order to live and be punished forever, since he was once and for all dead to life. *And he was buried in hell. And he saw Abraham from afar and Lazarus in his bosom* (vv.22–23). How great a reversal of circumstances! How low has the rich man sunk! How high has the poor man ascended! There he looks up at the one whom he had looked down upon here below;[7] and from hell he sees in the bosom of Abraham the one whom from his haughty couch he refused to look at lying prostrate before him.

6. *Father Abraham, have mercy on me!* (v.24) He foolishly seeks from his father the mercy which he had denied to his brother. *Have mercy on me!* What can mercy do for him to whom everything has ended in punishment? Or what help can supplication before his father obtain for him whose accuser has his place in his father's bosom? Lazarus clings to his father's breast, and strikes all the chords of fairness in his holy heart, so that he maintains his role as father of a good son, but as judge of a bad one.[8]

7. *Father Abraham, have mercy on me, and send Lazarus to dip the tip of his finger in water and cool my tongue, because I am in agony in these flames* (v.24). *Send Lazarus*, so that he who is the reason for my agony, may now be a minister of refreshment and offer merely the tip of his finger as a relief, even though at the time when he lay prostrate I refused him the comfort[9] of my entire hand.

And send Lazarus to dip the tip of his finger in water and cool my tongue. And so he thirsts for a drop, he who poured out vats of wine, leaving the poor man thirsty; and he supposes that he can put out the flames of Gehenna with what drips from a fingertip, when he did not put out the fires of drunkenness by drinking large quantities all day long; but he asks that he be given this drop to cool him down, which he had denied to the poor man when he was parched.

7. On this same point, see *Sermon* 66.2 (FOTC 109.268).
8. For a similar description, see *Sermon* 122.4 (FOTC 17.210).
9. Reading the variant *solacium* rather than *solacii* in Olivar's CCL text.

This is the drop, O rich man, which made you cruel; this is the drop which, since you refused it, made Lazarus's mouth dry, because even a drop is enough to cool down the poor man, or a crumb—*desiring*, it says, *to eat the crumbs which fell on the ground* (v.21). Bread was being squandered, wine was being spilled, and what the poor man was being refused at the end of his life was going to waste on all the rich man's ostentatiousness.

8. *And send Lazarus to dip the tip of his finger in water and cool my tongue.* The tongue is the head of evil in the head: it disparages the one in need, it insults the poor man, it snarls at pity, it carps at mercy; and appropriately it holds the first place in Gehenna, it leads the way in suffering, and is foremost in being punished, because it prohibited mercy although it had been given the authority to grant it.[10]

9. And although the progression of the reading both compels me to tell, and summons you to hear, who the rich man decked out in purple is, who Lazarus the poor man is, who the five brothers of the rich man are, and how the rich man experiences the agonies of Gehenna before Judgment Day, my grief, however, prevents me from telling you.

The rich man died, it says, *and was buried in hell* (v.22). And if the prison of Tartarus lies under the earth, if there is burning heat, if there is an underworld with unending torment, if there is a grim attendant to drag us away to these punishments after our labors in this world, why are we surprised? Where are we? What is this somnolence that deludes us? What is this lethal forgetfulness that has its hold on us? Why do we not have as our only concern to despise all else and to escape from such evils, lest by living for this world and by being concerned about other matters we suddenly be dragged away to suffer such enormously terrible and cruel punishments?

And if we have the possibility of ascending on high, and if we have the opportunity of living in heaven, if the bosom of Abraham has been made ready to provide rest for all who are good,

---

10. Similar reasons why the tongue feels the torment most acutely are mentioned in *Sermon* 66.3 (FOTC 109.269).

if Peter has been stationed at the gates of heaven,[11] if Lazarus is in the bosom of so great a father, and since there is certainly no doubt about the location of the regions, the persons, and the names just indicated, why do we not exchange earth for heaven? Why do we not purchase what is eternal with what is transitory? Why do we not use what is going to perish to buy what lasts forever, so as to avoid the punishments of hell and to be able to see, to grasp, and to possess in abundance these realities about which, even given our obvious limitations, we are eager to hear?[12]

11. See Mt 16.19. The role of St. Peter as heaven's gatekeeper is noted also in *Sermons* 154.3 (FOTC 17.261) and 172.4. For similar references in other patristic authors, see A. Rimoldi, *L'apostolo San Pietro* (Rome: Gregorian University, 1958), 309–14.

12. Chrysologus has another exhortation as well as an excoriation of moral lethargy in *Sermon* 66.9 (FOTC 109.272–73).

SERMON 125

On the Unjust Steward[1]

SALT[2] INDEED IS A HEALTHY SEASONING for all food, if it is used in limited amounts; otherwise, used immoderately, both the salt itself is ruined, and it destroys what it seasons. For an excessive amount makes bitter what a moderate amount could have made tasty. So too the reasoning faculty that is in us, if it should have moderation, provides flavor, gives birth to understanding, produces prudence, enlarges the heart, increases ability, gives mature expression to what must be said, puts eloquently what must be heard, becomes delightful to itself, and becomes perfectly delightful for those who partake of it. And certainly that reasoning faculty will be sweet as honey which will let nothing bitter come out of its mouth.

2. We have made these introductory remarks, so that our reasoning may be kept within the bounds of moderation in interpreting the Gospel, so as not to ruin the food of life, the divine nourishment, the heavenly flavor, but so as to preserve them for us with most judicious sobriety, according to the words of the Apostle: "To know no more than it is right to know, but to know in sobriety."[3] But now let us listen to what the Lord has said.

---

1. The reference to the parable of the Prodigal Son in section 5 suggests that it was the Gospel at a liturgy a short time earlier. Since the parable of the Prodigal Son was read during Lent, it is likely that this *Sermon* 125 was also Lenten. See F. Sottocornola, *L'anno liturgico*, 64–65 and 109–11. A. Olivar, *Los sermones*, 271–72, suggests that the reference to the Prodigal Son means that Lk 15.11–32 was also read in addition to Lk 16.1–9 at the same liturgy when this *Sermon* 125 was preached. Given how very brief the reference to Lk 15 is in this and the subsequent *Sermon* 126, Olivar's hypothesis seems unlikely.

2. The "salt" metaphor is also employed in *Sermon* 120.1 (FOTC 17.203).

3. Rom 12.3.

3. *There was a certain rich man* (Lk 16.1). And who was this man if not Christ? Who is rich except the One who in our poverty kept possession of all the riches of creation? *There was a certain rich man.* He often used to say this to the Jews,[4] so that they would understand that the opulence of divinity belonged to him even in the poverty of his humanity. He was rich, indeed he was, he was rich in his majesty while being poor in the eyes of the Jews. And how was he not rich who had angels to attend him,[5] the powers to obey him, and the elements to serve him, and seeing that things that did not yet exist were created at his bidding, and came to pass at his summons?[6]

4. *There was a certain rich man, and he had a steward* (v.1). Who is this, if not the human being to whom the possession of the world had been completely entrusted for cultivation? *There was a certain rich man, and he had a steward, and a charge against him was brought before him* (v.1). As if he did not foreknow, as if he did not foresee, he to whom secrets are known, and before whose eyes even what is hidden is laid bare.[7]

And a charge against him was brought before him. Therefore, was it a rumor[8] that he believed, did he come to know it because of news spread by a rumor? Far from it! But at issue was that those things which he knew, which he was concealing out of kindness, he then began to investigate since the earth was making the accusation—"The cry of your brother's blood is shouting out of the earth."[9] The earth is shouting, heaven is shouting, the angels were grieving, since by then the whole story was circulating all around the world.

5. *And a charge against him was brought before him that he had squandered his property* (v.1). Earlier we read that this man's younger son had squandered his property,[10] now it is asserted that the steward had squandered his goods. Just as the same

---

4. See Lk 12.16; 16.1 and 19.
5. See Mt 4.11 and Mk 1.13.
6. See Rom 4.17.
7. See Heb 4.13.
8. Chrysologus mentions the noun "rumor" *(fama)* because it is the root of the verb "to bring a charge" *(diffamo)*. Such an etymology does not work in English, because "defame" has a more pejorative implication.
9. Gn 4.10.
10. See Lk 15.13. Likewise, an allusion to the Prodigal Son is made in *Sermon* 126.5, also on the unjust steward.

Christ is God and man, and the same is father and head of the household, correspondingly it is the same person who is both steward and son. Here we have diverse circumstances, a change in names, but no difference in persons.

6. *And a charge against him was brought before him that he had squandered his goods, and he summoned him* (vv.1–2). He summoned him by means of the Gospel. *And he said to him* (v.2). And what does he not do by means of the Gospel, by means of which he criticizes behavior, he lays bare what was hidden, he exposes one's conscience, he reproves offenses, he enumerates sins, and to the one who persists in them he threatens punishment, although to the one who changes his ways he promises pardon in return? *And he summoned him, and said to him: "What is this I hear about you?"* (v.2) He ascribes what he knows to what he has heard, because he does not wish to hasten the sentence against the guilty, and he calls into his presence the convict as if he were only accused, since he is so eager to forestall condemnation with pardon. *What is this I hear about you?*

7. *Give an account of your stewardship; you will no longer be able to be a steward* (v.2). Why does he join such severity with such kindness? Why does he remove him from stewardship before receiving his report? *Give an account; you will no longer be able to be a steward.* As man he now asks for an account, as God he announces what is now at hand and what will be. *Give an account; you will no longer be able to be a steward.* He asks for an account, not to exact, but to forgive. He asks, in order to be asked; he asks here, so as not to ask there; he asks in this age, so as not to ask at the judgment; he is in a hurry to ask, in order that the time of punishment not preclude time to make amends.

Give an account of your stewardship; you will no longer be able to be a steward. Why? Because the end of your life and the moment of death are coming; already attendants from heaven are ready to bind you, already judgment is beckoning; so hasten, in order not to lose time to make amends, you who have lost the time to do good deeds.

8. *Give an account.* That is to say: "Settle your account, settle your business, so that you do not have to pay back what belongs to me; you will settle it, however, if you now stop squandering it.

I assumed your prior debts, when I assumed[11] you; I paid them off, when I absolved you. As your Advocate I was present to be heard on your behalf; although I am the Judge[12] I stood trial, I was found guilty by those judged guilty by me; although free of punishment, I underwent punishments, and did not avoid being sentenced by those who were condemned; I the conqueror of death accepted death, I the destroyer of hell entered the underworld, not only to wrest you from your punishment by these means, but also to raise you to my dignity. So see to it that although the period of your stewardship has left you excluded, you be now included among the recipients of my everlasting gift." But now let us give our full attention to the response made by the steward.

9. *He said to himself*, we are told: *"What shall I do?"* (v.3) "What shall I do now?" The human being always desires to do good at that moment when death takes away any opportunity to do it. *He said to himself*, it says. He is asking himself for advice, it says, since he had no source outside himself from which to obtain any help. *He said to himself*. He pricks his heart, he vexes his mind, he puts all his innards into turmoil, in order to extract from himself the sort of repentance that he could offer on his own behalf.

10. *I am unable to dig* (v.3). It was not strength that he had been lacking, but sufficient time to complete the labor. *I am unable to dig, I am embarrassed to beg* (v.3). He is afraid of shame at the future judgment, in which there is no longer time to make a petition, but only to be punished, and where the guilty one turns a brighter red from his conscience than he does from the fire of Gehenna. *I am embarrassed to beg.* And who is not embarrassed at having to beg in heaven? He is a wretch whom this transitory life had as a rich man, but everlasting life will possess as a beggar, and Tartarus will keep him naked when heaven could have received him and maintained him in opulence!

11. The present example refers to the people: that it would

---

11. The Latin is *suscepi*. For Chrysologus's christological use of this term, see R. Benericetti, *Il Cristo*, 97–99 and 260–62.

12. For other references to Christ as Advocate and Judge in Chrysologus's sermons, see R. Benericetti, *Il Cristo*, 235.

be good for us, very good indeed, if each one of us should apply these matters to ourselves, if we should relate them to ourselves, who must recognize that we are stewards on the earth, and not think of ourselves as sole proprietors; recognizing that we have received the ministry of temporary superintendence and that we have not acquired any perpetual right of possession; we must be on our guard lest a report of mismanagement of property go ahead of us to the head of the household, in line with what the Apostle has said: "The sins of certain people are evident and go ahead of them to judgment; for others, however, their sins follow them there."[13]

He does not reach the intended outcome of his life, who loses the opportunity for good stewardship but instead is loudly denounced for having squandered what had been entrusted to him. From this, yes, from this comes a premature demise, from this comes a death earlier than expected, from this comes the bitter summons, from this comes an even harsher reckoning for one's self, as the prophet cries in lamentation: "Unjust and deceitful men will not live half their days."[14]

But when sickness reminds us of our summons, when a fever is so severe that it keeps us from our stewardship, when the force of pain compels us to hurry up and render an account of our stewardship, would that we pursued the course of action and reasoning that this present steward did, would that we turned toward the counsel of our soul, to compunction of heart, to repentance of mind, to mercy for support, to compassion for protection, and to confession[15] for assistance!

We would certainly make petition about the bonds of our debts to the Lord, and to receive pardon we would pay off, even if not the whole amount, at least half, just like that steward, so that we who are called to account for being unjust stewards in squandering the goods entrusted to us, would by our pious deceit acquire in the end the praise of the Judge himself—*And he praised his unjust steward*, it says (v.8).

13. 1 Tm 5.24.
14. Ps 54.24 LXX; Ps 55.23.
15. This *confessio* includes both a "confession" of unworthiness and a "profession" of faith in God.

12. And since the conduct of the steward in the Gospel creates no small question, inasmuch as we read that he was guilty of many offenses but became acceptable because of one deceitful action, why it is that he became acceptable and even who he is, we shall discuss more fully in the next sermon,[16] with God's help.

16. *Sermon* 126.

SERMON 126

A Second on the Same[1]

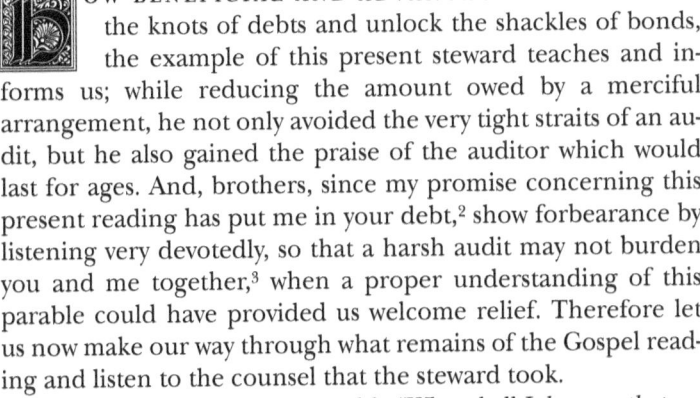OW BENEFICIAL AND ADVANTAGEOUS it is to untie the knots of debts and unlock the shackles of bonds, the example of this present steward teaches and informs us; while reducing the amount owed by a merciful arrangement, he not only avoided the very tight straits of an audit, but he also gained the praise of the auditor which would last for ages. And, brothers, since my promise concerning this present reading has put me in your debt,[2] show forbearance by listening very devotedly, so that a harsh audit may not burden you and me together,[3] when a proper understanding of this parable could have provided us welcome relief. Therefore let us now make our way through what remains of the Gospel reading and listen to the counsel that the steward took.

2. *He said to himself,* we are told: *"What shall I do, now that my master is taking my stewardship away from me? I am unable to dig, I am embarrassed to beg. I know what I shall do." And so, after summoning his master's debtors one by one, he said to the first: "How much do you owe my master?" He answered: "One hundred jugs of oil." He said to him: "Take your bill, and sit down quickly, and write down fifty." Then to the next one he said: "And you, how much do you owe?" He answered: "One hundred measures of wheat." He said to him: "Take your invoice, and write down eighty." And the master praised the steward for having acted prudently* (Lk 16.3–8).

---

1. This sermon on the Unjust Steward was preached next after *Sermon* 125. See *Sermon* 125, nn. 1 and 16.

2. On the preacher being in debt, in that he owes a sermon he had promised his congregation, see, e.g., *Sermon* 123.1 and n. 2.

3. On interpreting the Scriptures as a cooperative venture between the preacher and the congregation, with the latter contributing their undivided attention, see Introduction, FOTC 109.25–26, and, as another example, *Sermon* 139.1.

3. Certainly now it is clear, certainly now it is evident that there continues to be a great number of questions in the Gospel readings which remain obscured with their divine mysteries and veiled with heavenly meanings, and that what is uttered by the mouth of Christ concerning celestial secrets is not easily accessible to the human intellect. *And the master,* he says, *praised the unjust steward for having acted prudently* (v.8).

I ask you, what does an earthly mind grasp in this text? What does ordinary hearing grasp and understand from this?— Where a plan of clever deceit between the steward and his master's debtors is praised; where the honor of the debtor is removed, where decency is taken away, where innocence is violated, where respect is dead and buried; where the steward, at the time when he must give an account, is more eager for deceit than he was panting after a lifestyle of extravagance during the period of his stewardship; where at the very moment of the audit he was furiously engaged in disposing of more of what belonged to his master, than he wasted and exhausted during the days of his employment; and he who had earlier reduced the property by squandering it, by reducing the debts did even more damage; and he has no concern about how he might be able to make up the difference, but he keeps scheming about how he might be able to lessen what remained.

4. He said to a debtor: *How much do you owe my master?* (v.5) He did not say: "How much do you owe me?" By speaking in this fashion he was addressing the conscience and bringing to light the intention of the debtor. And why is it that without any regard for the master the debtor conspired with the steward to commit such deceit? *"How much do you owe my master?" He answered: "One hundred jugs of oil." "Take your bill, and write down fifty"* (vv.5–6). The steward conspired to commit such deceit, and the result was that he lost all credibility by cutting the bill in half. *How much do you owe my master?* Both of them knew that the heavenly Creditor was present always and everywhere, and he could not be hindered by their deceit; but not even under the watchful gaze of his Lord does a person stop what he is doing, once he has begun to steal.

Nevertheless, granted that it is a human custom for a debtor to seek profit by acting deceitfully, and for a steward to look after his own interests by stealing in this fashion: but again I ask, why does the Lord approve of deceit, why does he praise thievery, and why does he extol falsehood? What is wickedness he calls prudence, and he judges to be an act of mercy what offers to many people the worst example of falsehood. So let it have this meaning on the fleshly level, but now for us to understand it spiritually let the elucidation that God provides begin to shine.

5. The parable which previously had provided us food for thought in the person of the younger son[4] has been reiterated in the steward. The gentiles are called an unjust steward from the mammon of injustice—*Make for yourselves*, he says, *friends from the mammon of injustice* (v.9)—since they had abandoned the Creator and handed themselves over completely to slavery to mammon. Whoever is free from captivity to this mammon, and is no longer weighed down under the cruel burden of money, stands securely with his vantage point in heaven, and from there looks down over the mammon which is holding sway over the world and the worldly with a tyrant's fury.

It holds sway over nations, it gives orders to kingdoms, it wages wars, it equips warriors, it traffics in blood, it transacts death, it threatens homelands, it destroys cities, it conquers peoples, it attacks fortresses, it puts citizens in an uproar, it presides over the marketplace, it wipes out justice, it confuses right and wrong, and by aiming directly at morality it assails one's integrity, it violates truth, it eviscerates one's reputation, it wreaks havoc on one's honor, it dissolves affections, it removes innocence, it keeps compassion buried, it severs relationships, it does not permit friendship. And why should I say more? This is mammon: the master of injustice, since it is unjust in the power it wields over human bodies and minds.

6. Therefore, the steward of this mammon, representing the gentile people, guilty of squandering his property so irresponsibly, is summoned by the Lord by means of the Gospel to give an account of his stewardship, that is, of the good he has by na-

---

4. See Lk 15.11–32. There is also a reference to the parable of the Prodigal Son in *Sermon* 125.5.

ture. It is said to him: *You will no longer be able to be a steward* (v.2), at the time when the end of the world is being announced to him. And at last he believes, as the Apostle says, that the form of the world is passing away,[5] that the period of human stewardship is expiring, and returning to his senses[6] he asks what he ought to do.

He said to himself, we are told: *"What shall I do?"* (v.3) His heart groaned, his mind was in torment, but faith furnished the answer, belief provided the sage[7] advice that as steward he should now return to his true Master, and that by disbursing the mammon he would become victorious and force that cruel master to serve him, so that what had been the means of perdition would become conducive to salvation.

7. Therefore, the steward, formerly a pagan,[8] now a Christian, makes his way to his Master's first debtor. To whom? The Jew. He interrogates the debtor. He asks, "What?" and "How much?" as though he did not know the amount of the debt. The bearer of the bill, thanks to the Gospel, already knew the answer, but by asking such questions he was seeking an acknowledgment.

Accordingly the debtor acknowledges both what and how much he owes when he says: *One hundred jugs of oil* (v.6). Why not a mass of silver or gold? Why not one hundred ten, or ninety, but one hundred? So that both from what was owed and from the amount owed a heavenly mystery might be revealed. The Jew owed oil, which by means of the Law's bond he had taken to anoint kings, prophets, and priests as a prefiguring of Christian chrism, until he would come into the presence of the very Leader[9] of kings, prophets, and priests, to whom the full

---

5. See 1 Cor 7.31.   6. See Lk 15.17.
7. The Latin is *salutare,* denoting something beneficial and healthy both temporally and eternally.
8. The Latin is *gentilis.*
9. Namely, Christ. On this same theme, see Pelagius, *De vita Christiana* 1.1 (PL 40.1033). On these two texts as referring to the postbaptismal chrismation or confirmation ritual in the west, see D. Van den Eynde, "Notes sur les rites postbaptismaux dans les Églises d'Occident," *Antonianum* 14 (1939): 260–66; on references pertaining to northern Italy, see idem, "Les rites liturgiques latins de la confirmation," *La Maison-Dieu* 54 (1958): 68–69; on this anointing as signifying the prophetic role of Christians, see É. Lamirande, "L'idée d'onction

hundredfold amount of chrism was to be given and poured out in its entirety.

But since the debtor, by breaking the contractual agreement, and so that he would not have to repay the debt, behaved wickedly and killed the Creditor, the legal contract itself, that is, the Law, came into the gentiles' hands, so that the Jew, summoned by means of the gentile, would pay off the interest in penance because he changed the debt into an offense.[10]

8. So you see that the steward does not encourage deceit, but repentance; he is anxious that mercy be sought, he is not inciting another to falsehood when he says: *Take your bill, and sit down quickly, and write down fifty* (v.6). David makes clear that the number fifty pertains to mercy, when he sings out in Psalm Fifty: "Have mercy on me, O God, according to your great mercy."[11] The number fifty reveals mercy,[12] in that the Law prescribes that the fiftieth year, which is the jubilee year, wipes out and dissolves the fetters of all debts and all contracts.[13]

Therefore, this steward intends for the Jew, who because of what was written in the Law was being held captive and stung by debts he could not pay, to be made solvent by means of Christ's mercy. The Jew owes oil, since, as the Apostle says, by the barrenness of unbelief he had dried up in himself the abundance of the fertile olive tree.[14] Therefore, now that it is also cultivated with the heat of Gospel faith it produces Christian branches, and comes back to life in the fullness of grace.

9. *Then to the next one he said: "And you, how much do you owe?" He answered: "One hundred measures of wheat"* (v.7). After the grain of wheat, which is Christ, has been planted in the earth, that is, our flesh,[15] and has been made fruitful to yield a plenti-

---

dans l'ecclésiologie de saint Augustin," *Revue de l'Université d'Ottawa* 35 (1965): 113*–15*.

10. For a somewhat similar allegorical interpretation of the parable of the Prodigal Son as signifying the interaction between gentile and Jew, see *Sermon* 5.7 (FOTC 17.50–51).

11. Ps 50.3 LXX; Ps 51.1.

12. Further spiritual significance of the number fifty is indicated in *Sermons* 85b.1 and 139.7.

13. See Lv 25.8–55.   14. See Rom 11.16–24.

15. In *Sermon* 67.7 (FOTC 17.117), Chrysologus refers to Christ as "Bread sown in the Virgin, leavened in the flesh," with eucharistic overtones.

ful harvest for heaven by means of the Lord's burial, as a result the human being now owes a hundredfold return to his Author—"Unless the grain of wheat falls to the earth and dies," it says, "it will remain only a grain of wheat."[16]

Therefore, since the steward is aware of this, he shows considerable foresight when he says: *Take your bill, and sit down, and write down eighty* (v.7), because, just as the number fifty conveys mercy, so too does the number eighty prefigure the fullness of faith and grace. This is the number that,[17] as a reader who is quite familiar with the Law and quite devoted to studying the Gospel understands, is made up of the Ten Commandments of the Law and grace's number, eight.[18] And so, when he speaks in this fashion, the steward is urging the debtor, by writing down eighty, to reach a settlement by grace for what he was unable to repay by nature. Therefore, it is right that this steward earns the praise of his Lord, since in these bills it was not deceit but salvation that he had in mind.

10. But what he meant by: *The children of this age are more prudent regarding their own generation than are the children of light* (v.8): is that those who were the children of this age, that is, the gentiles, have now become God's chosen ones, and those who were the children of God, that is, the Jews, have now been left behind[19] among the children of this age. *Regarding their own generation:* in which they have been reborn, not in which they were born—"Let these things be written," it says, "for another generation."[20] "Another" refers to "this generation of those who seek"[21] the Lord.

11. But may the God of knowledge and illumination illumine your hearts,[22] and fill the recesses of your mind to capacity with all his knowledge.

16. Jn 12.24.
17. Reading the variant *quem* instead of the *quam* of Olivar's CCL text.
18. For similar remarks about the number eighteen (eight plus ten), and especially the significance of the number eight for Christians, see *Sermon* 105.7 and n. 15.
19. To capture Chrysologus's wordplay one might say that the gentiles are the elect *(electi)*, and the Jews are derelict *(relicti)*.
20. Ps 101.19 LXX; Ps 102.18.   21. Ps 23 (24).6.
22. See 2 Cor 4.6.

SERMON 127

On the Birth[1] of St. John the Baptist[2]

ODAY WHILE THE VIRTUE of John and the ferocity of Herod are related to us, our innards were shaken, our hearts trembled,[3] our sight grew dim, our mind became dull, our hearing deserted us. For is there anything within human sensation that remains undisturbed when a large amount of vice destroys a large amount of virtue?

2. Herod, it says, *apprehended John, and had him bound, and put in prison* (Mt 14.3). John was the school of the virtues,[4] the instructor of life, the model of sanctity, the pattern of morality, the mirror of virginity, the epitome of purity, the example of chastity, the way of penitence, the pardon of sins, the discipline of faith. John was greater than a human being,[5] equal to the angels, the apex of the Law, the seed of the Gospel, the harbinger of the apostles, the silence of the prophets, the lamp of the

---

1. That is, the "birth" unto eternal life, a common expression for martyrdom.

2. This sermon, together with *Sermons* 89, 173, and 174, deals with the death of John the Baptist. It may have been preached next after *Sermon* 89. These sermons were likely delivered on or near the feast of John's martyrdom, probably June 24. See F. Sottocornola, *L'anno liturgico*, 111 and 303–4. For more on the liturgical context of this sermon and *Sermon* 89 and whether they were preached consecutively, see *Sermon* 89, nn. 1, 9, and 25. Because the authenticity of this sermon has been contested by some scholars, A. Olivar, in *Los sermones*, 189–95, gives an extended treatment of its manuscript tradition and provides numerous textual references from this sermon to argue that both in style and in content it is properly attributed to Chrysologus.

3. A similar reaction by Chrysologus and his congregation is noted in *Sermons* 89.2, 174.1 (both treating John the Baptist's martyrdom), 103.1, and 151.1. Similar terminology is also used in *Sermon* 143.8, describing the Virgin at the Annunciation.

4. Chrysologus uses similar terminology to describe the human body (*Sermon* 12.3) and the cross (*Sermon* 54.4), where the virtues are both learned and practiced; see FOTC 109.58 and 208.

5. See Mt 11.11 and Lk 7.28.

world, the herald of the Judge, the forerunner of Christ, the preparer for the Lord, the witness of God, the mediator of the whole Trinity.[6]

3. But Herod is the very one who desecrated the Temple, ruined the priesthood, disturbed its proper order, profaned the kingdom, corrupted anything that had to do with religion, the Law, life and morals, faith, and discipline.[7] Herod was ever an assassin toward his fellow citizens, a brigand toward people of any distinction, a ravager toward his allies, a robber toward those of his own household, a killer of the common folk, a murderer of his children, a slayer of foreigners, a parricide towards his own, drenching the land with gore in his bloodthirstiness.[8] And so it is that he gulped down the hallowed blood of John from his enormous cup of cruelty. But now let the reading speak for itself.

4. *Herod,* it says, *apprehended John and had him bound.* He who had released sins' shackles is bound with the shackles of a sinner, so that pardon once shackled might not leave any room for pardon. *He had him bound and put in prison.* Herod, you are the one who committed adultery, yet John the Baptist goes to prison? Thus one who is guilty sits in the judge's place and passes judgment, the persecutor of innocence takes the place of a defender. I ask, where is truth to be found? Where is good reputation? Where is decency? Where is the good name of the public magistrate? In fact, where is God? Where is the human being? Where is decorum? Where is the law? Where are purely natural rights? Everything all at once has been thrown into turmoil, O Herod, because of the way you act, pass judgment, and give orders.

5. *He apprehended John,* it says, *and he had him bound, and put in prison.* Herod, you are being subpoenaed, his shackles place the blame on you, the prison accuses you, the harm done to

---

6. A similar listing of John's attributes is found in *Sermon* 91.5.
7. Many of the accusations listed in this paragraph are also mentioned in *Sermons* 86.3, 89.4, 152.4 (FOTC 17.256), and 156.5 (FOTC 17.267), albeit against Herod the Great (see the next note).
8. See Mt 2.16. Chrysologus confuses Herod Antipas, who put John the Baptist to death, with Herod the Great.

John publicly points to you. The one who looks for the reason for John's arrest finds in you what deserves punishment, and the cause for his distress about John. John, who is recognized throughout the world for his reputation, who is known for his virtue, who is widely renowned for his sanctity, by attracting to himself those who inquire into the harm done to him, sees to it that your incest becomes disclosed to all; he brings it about that you are put to shame in public, since a reproof in private was unable to reform you.

6. John kept after Herod with warnings, not with an accusation; he wanted him to mend his ways, not to perish; but Herod preferred to perish rather than to reform.[9] To those held captive by crimes the freedom of innocence becomes most odious. Virtue is antagonistic to the vicious, sanctity is detestable to the sacrilegious, chastity is inimical to the shameless, integrity is a punishment to the corrupt, temperance is a foe to the wanton; mercy is unbearable to the cruel, godliness to the ungodly, justice to the unjust.

The evangelist attests to this when he says: "John kept saying: 'It is not right for you to take the wife of your brother Philip.'"[10] This is the reason why John runs afoul. The one who warns the wicked is considered offensive. The one who rebukes those who are at fault is deemed blameworthy. What John had to say concerned the Law, justice, and well-being;[11] his remarks certainly were not spoken out of hatred, but out of love: but see what kind of a reward he received for his devotion from the ungodly one!

7. *Although he wanted to kill him*, it says, *he was afraid of the people* (v.5). It is easy for one to turn away from justice who is motivated by the fear, not of God, but of human beings. This fear can postpone the opportunity to sin, but cannot take away the will to sin. Therefore it is also the case that those whom fear delays from committing iniquity become even more eager for iniquity. It is only the fear of God which corrects minds, banishes

---

9. See also *Sermon* 174.5 on the opportunity for reform that John offered to Herod Antipas.
10. See Mt 14.4 and Mk 6.18.
11. Or "salvation" *(salutis)*.

offenses, preserves innocence,[12] and bestows an endless capacity for good. But let us hear about what the most blessed John actually suffered.

8. *On Herod's birthday*, it says, *the daughter of Herodias danced in the middle of his dining room, and it pleased Herod, and he made an oath promising to give her whatever she asked of him. But, having been advised earlier by her mother, she said: "Give me the head of John the Baptist on a dish." And the king was deeply saddened on account of the oath; nevertheless, because of those who were dining there he ordered it to be given to her, and sent to have John beheaded, and his head was placed on a dish and given to the girl, and the girl gave it to her mother* (vv.6–11).

9. You have heard, brothers, how great is the cruelty which is born from pleasure. *And his head was placed on a dish* (v.11). A house is transformed into an arena, the table turns into a theater, dinner guests become spectators, a banquet is changed into frenzy, a meal becomes a massacre, wine changes to blood, a funeral is held on a birthday, to mark one person's beginning is another person's ending, a banquet is changed into a murder scene, musical instruments ring out the tragedy of ages.[13]

A beast, not a girl, enters; a ferocious animal, not a woman, prances about; along her head she combs out her mane, not her hair; she stretches and contorts her frame, but it is her savagery that grows and intensifies, her cruelty that looms large, but not her body; this wild animal unequaled in ferocity[14] roars with her mouth, gnashes her teeth,[15] she is not struck by a sword, but wields it.[16] *Advised earlier*, it says, *by her mother* (v.8), and brandishing a lance from her mother's heart, as a new kind of beast, she disdains preying upon the body and proceeds to lop off the head itself.

---

12. *Fugat crimina, innocentiam servat.* This terminology is reminiscent of *fugat scelera . . . reddit innocentiam* in section 5 of the *Benedictio cerei* or Easter *Exultet* attributed to St. Ambrose, in *Studi e testi* 121.226. See *Sermon* 65, n. 17 (FOTC 109.266).

13. Similar in terminology and content is *Sermon* 173.7, also on John's demise.

14. See Ps 79.14 LXX.

15. Ps 34 (35).16.

16. A similar description is given in *Sermon* 174.2.

SERMON 127

10. But, lest anyone think that we want to hear ourselves talk about such things, we do not want to hear ourselves talk, but we want to cry out[17] so that the joys of your festivities be celebrated prudently, so that the parties that mark your birthdays maintain moderation in merriment, so that Christ may attend your feasts, that the banquet be held in the sight of the Author; may the very nature of the celebration to which we are invited be honored by decency; may the happiness of your table extend to the poor, may your household dance with the discipline of innocence. May debauchery depart, may dissipation be banished; may the plague of dancing girls, the bawdy songs of musicians, what fuels pleasures, what weighs down the belly, and what shipwrecks minds all be done away with, be wiped out with the feasts of Herodias, so that your joy at present may reach a happiness that lasts forever.

11. Today, brothers, we have directed our sermon to Herod, because the listener is well aware how great is the martyr's bliss, when he hears about the misery of the persecutor. Nevertheless, it is fitting for us to know both that John came to birth as a result of his death, and that Herod died as a result of how he spent his birthday.[18]

---

17. Chrysologus contrasts *declamare* ("making a rhetorical display" or "hearing oneself talk") with *clamare* ("crying out"). See also *Sermon* 103.7 and n. 16.

18. On this point, see also *Sermon* 174.6.

SERMON 128

On the Birth[1] of St. Apollinaris[2]

BLESSED APOLLINARIS,[3] the first in the priesthood, alone adorned this church with the exceptional honor of having one of her own martyred. It is fitting that his name was Apollinaris, since according to the injunction of his God he lost[4] his life in order to acquire it for life everlasting.[5] Blessed is he who so finished the race and so kept the faith[6] that he truly was found to occupy the first place among the believers. Let no one suppose that he is anything less than a martyr on account of his title as Confessor, since it is well known that it was God's will that he kept returning to the contest at least on a daily basis. Listen to Paul as he says: "I die daily."[7] To die once is too little for the one who is able to bring back again and again to his King a glorious victory over the enemy.

It is not death as much as faith and dedication that make one a martyr; and just as it is a mark of virtue to fall in battle, in conflict, for the love of the king, so it is a mark of perfect virtue to engage in combat for a long time and to bring it to its con-

---

1. As in the previous sermon, "birth" refers to being born into eternal life as a martyr.
2. This sermon was delivered on July 23, the feast day of St. Apollinaris, the first bishop and martyr of Ravenna. See F. Sottocornola, *L'anno liturgico,* 111 and 299.
3. For more on St. Apollinaris, see Introduction with pertinent footnotes, FOTC 109.2–4.
4. Chrysologus traces the etymology for Apollinaris to ἀπόλλυμι ("to lose"). In *Sermon* 154.3 (FOTC 17.260), Chrysologus again gives evidence of knowing Greek by mentioning that Stephen derived his name from a "crown." Other allusions to Greek in Chrysologus's preaching are noted in D. L. Baldisserri, *San Pier Crisologo, Arcivescovo di Ravenna* (Imola, 1920), 79.
5. See Jn 12.25.   6. See 2 Tm 4.7.
7. 1 Cor 15.31.

clusion. Therefore, the enemy did not make him a martyr, since he did not inflict death, but he proved him to be a martyr, because he did not remove his faith; the crafty enemy hurled the weapons that he could, and he aimed at him everything he had in his arsenal; nevertheless, he was unable to budge this bravest of leaders, nor could he tarnish his constancy. It is the highest honor, brothers, to despise this present life for the Lord's sake, if that is necessary, but it is also glorious even while living to scorn and trample underfoot the world and its ruler.

2. Christ was hastening to the martyr, and the martyr was hastening to his King. It is appropriate that we said he "was hastening," in conformity with the words of the prophet: "Rise up, run to meet me, and see."[8] But so that the holy Church retain for herself her defender, she runs eagerly to Christ, so that she may both preserve the crown of righteousness[9] for the victor, and may furnish for herself the presence of her warrior in time of war.

The confessor often used to shed his blood, and with his wounds and with faith in his heart he kept bearing witness to his Creator. Casting his gaze toward heaven he despised both the flesh[10] and the earth. Nevertheless, the Church still in her tender infancy conquered, held fast, and succeeded in delaying his martyrdom by her longing. I call it an "infancy," brothers, since it always obtains everything and fights more with its tears than by reason of its strength. For the determination and the sweat of the strong are not as powerful as the tears of children, because in the former case bodies are broken, but in the latter situation hearts are broken; by force of strength, judgments of the mind are influenced only with difficulty, but to children's tears, a devotion that is already disposed towards them yields completely.

3. And why should I say more, brothers? She has seen to it, Holy Mother Church has seen to it that she would in no way be separated from her high-priest.[11] He is alive here, here as a

---

8. Ps 58.6 LXX: Ps 59.4.   9. See 2 Tm 4.8.
10. Chrysologus's rhetorical skill is evident here: *Caelum suspiciens carnem dispiciebat.*
11. The Latin is *antistes,* one of several terms for a "bishop."

good shepherd he is at his post in the midst of his flock, and he is never separated in spirit, although in body he has temporarily gone ahead of us. He has gone ahead, I mean, in his earthly condition; in another respect, the very dwelling that is his body reposes among us.[12] The devil has been destroyed, the persecutor has met his end; here we have reigning and living the one who longed to be put to death for his King.

12. As noted in the Introduction, FOTC 109.3–4, the depiction of Apollinaris as a shepherd surrounded by sheep grazing around him, in the apse mosaic of Sant'Apollinare in Classe, the basilica built over his remains, may have been inspired by Chrysologus's words in this sermon. On archaeological findings regarding Apollinaris's remains and earlier basilicas, see M. Mazzotti, "S. Apollinare in Classe: Indagini e studi degli ultimi trent'anni," *Rivista di Archeologia Cristiana* 62 (1986): 199–219.

SERMON 130

On the Birth of a Bishop[1]

UST AS A LENGTHY anticipation of some great thing that was promised enkindles the spirit and wearies the mind, the awaited fulfillment of the promise stirs up all the senses and everything inside a person. This is why today, as Isaiah has said, Holy Mother Church[2] has appeared festive, full of joy, and all decked out; she has clothed herself with the cloak of her delight, and as a bride[3] she has put on her garland, and has arrayed and adorned herself with a variety of attire.[4] As the heavens shine with starlight, and as the earth blooms with its flowers, and as a garden makes its shoots spring up, so has she made her gladness spring up in the sight of all her children, since, according to the promise made to David, today a son has been born to her in place of her father.[5]

---

1. A. Olivar, *Los sermones*, 197–98, considers this sermon to have been preached on the occasion of Chrysologus's consecration of a suffragan bishop. I believe that it is actually his first sermon after being consecrated bishop himself, delivered as he takes possession of the diocese of Ravenna in the presence of Galla Placidia and the imperial court. Usually when Chrysologus consecrates a suffragan bishop, he concludes his sermon by welcoming the new bishop to speak immediately after him; see *Sermons* 130a.3 and 165 (FOTC 17.271). Such an invitation is conspicuously absent in this *Sermon* 130. See Introduction, FOTC 109.7–8, and, for yet another opinion regarding the occasion for this sermon, F. Sottocornola, *L'anno liturgico*, 112.

2. For other references to the Church as mother, see *Sermon* 73.3 and n. 17, and *Sermons* 128.3, 130a.1, 169.6, and 175.1 and 4.

3. On the Church as bride or spouse of Christ, see *Sermons* 22.6 (FOTC 17.69), 31.3 (FOTC 109.132), 61.13 (FOTC 17.114), 76.2, 98.6 (FOTC 17.159), 164.8, 103.5, and 175.4; in the latter two instances, the Church is described as both bride and mother.

4. See Is 61.10. F. Sottocornola, *L'anno liturgico*, 112, suggests that this may have been the text read at this particular liturgy.

5. See Ps 44.17 LXX; Ps 45.16. Chrysologus uses this same scriptural reference regarding a new bishop in *Sermon* 130a.2. On the interpretation of Ps 44 as signifying the Church's giving birth to new bishops (sons) who trace their suc-

He is not to weigh her down with a burden, nor frighten her with his authority, nor cause her anxiety or distress, nor disturb her with severity. Rather, he is to be faithful and dutiful in supporting her; make her thoroughly secure by his ever-vigilant care; attend to what is necessary through diligent labor; unite the household with his gentle guidance; be hospitable to guests; be solicitous of parents; comply with kings; collaborate with those in power; treat the elderly with reverence, the young with kindness, his brothers with love; show affection to children; offer willing service to all through Christ.

2. David said: "Hear, O daughter, and see."[6] Let me say: "Hear, O Mother, and see": "In place of your fathers, sons have been born to you."[7] May they be elders in their prudence,[8] fathers in their seriousness, sons in their charity, young[9] in their virtue, youthful in their pleasantness, infants in their innocence, "children as far as malice is concerned,"[10] ignorant of worldly matters, completely possessing now the kingdom of God, as the Lord attests when he says: "Let the little children come to me, for to such as these does the kingdom of heaven belong."[11]

Such does the bond of perpetual virginity produce, such does this heavenly union produce, unacquainted with sex, aware of conceiving, familiar with giving birth, unfamiliar with corruption, pure in modesty, with her virginity intact, chaste with children, prolific in her virginity.[12] While so dedicated a Mother as this today celebrates the birthday feast of one of her offspring, she opens her bosom, she makes her embrace spread far and wide, she shouts, she cries out with divine canticles, in

---

cession all the way back to the apostles (their fathers), see Augustine, *Enarrationes in Psalmos* 44.32 (CCL 38.316).

6. Ps 44.11 LXX; Ps 45.10.

7. Ps 44.17 LXX; Ps 45.16.

8. A similar reference to the new bishop as having the wisdom and discipline of old age, though young in years, is made in *Sermon* 130a.2.

9. That is, incorrupt. 10. 1 Cor 14.20.

11. Mt 19.14.

12. On the Church's chastely conceiving and bearing her episcopal offspring, see also *Sermon* 130a.1 and 175.4. The Church as virgin and mother gives birth to her sons in a manner analogous to that of Mary as Virgin and Mother giving birth to Jesus her Son.

order to summon everyone, to receive everyone, to clasp everyone to her breast of charity and have them rejoice with her.

3. Also present is the mother of the Christian, eternal and faithful Empire herself, who, by following and imitating the blessed Church in her faith, her works of mercy, her holiness, and in her reverence for the Trinity, has been found worthy of bringing to birth, embracing, and possessing an august trinity.[13] This is how the Trinity rewards those who are fervent in their love and zeal for him. She has been found worthy of giving honor to herself and rejoicing that the grace of God has made for her an object of devotion like him. She, their mother, has been found worthy of having her dignity redound to her children by means of the Mother.[14]

Pray, brothers, that, since our Christian rulers deign to share in our joys and be present at our solemnities with their pious devotion, all the priests may also with equal grace be devoted in offering supplication for them throughout the length of their days.

---

13. For other very laudatory remarks of Chrysologus towards the imperial family, see *Sermon* 85b.3. Similar language is used in *Sermon* 43.3 (FOTC 17.92) to describe John the Baptist, who, presumably at Jesus' Baptism, also "embraced and possessed" the divine Trinity. On Chrysologus's relationship with the Empress Galla Placidia, see Introduction, FOTC 109.7–12. The trinity at issue here most likely comprises her two children, Valentinian III and Honoria, and Galla's nephew Theodosius II. A. Olivar, *Los sermones*, 237–39, suggests that the third member (instead of Theodosius II) was Galla's granddaughter Eudocia.

14. Namely, the Church.

SERMON 130A

On the Ordination of a Bishop[1]

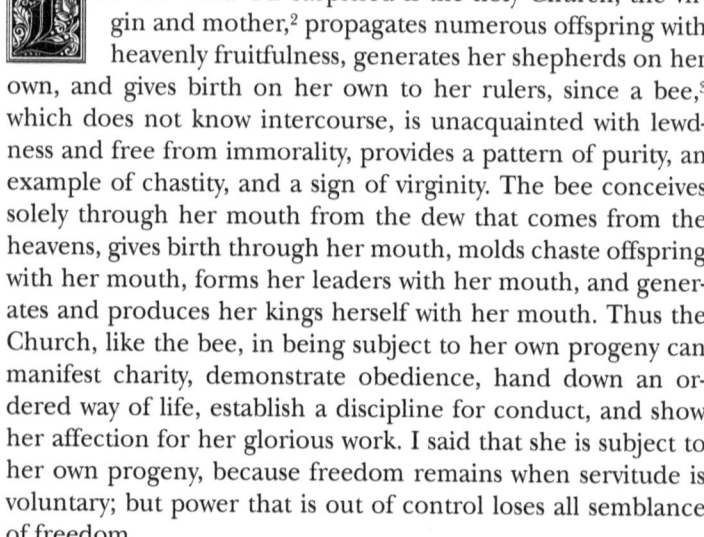ET NO ONE BE surprised if the holy Church, the virgin and mother,[2] propagates numerous offspring with heavenly fruitfulness, generates her shepherds on her own, and gives birth on her own to her rulers, since a bee,[3] which does not know intercourse, is unacquainted with lewdness and free from immorality, provides a pattern of purity, an example of chastity, and a sign of virginity. The bee conceives solely through her mouth from the dew that comes from the heavens, gives birth through her mouth, molds chaste offspring with her mouth, forms her leaders with her mouth, and generates and produces her kings herself with her mouth. Thus the Church, like the bee, in being subject to her own progeny can manifest charity, demonstrate obedience, hand down an ordered way of life, establish a discipline for conduct, and show her affection for her glorious work. I said that she is subject to her own progeny, because freedom remains when servitude is voluntary; but power that is out of control loses all semblance of freedom.

2. Therefore, it is right that the venerable Church, like that

---

1. Regarding this sermon's authenticity, see A. Olivar, *Los sermones*, 321–23.
2. See *Sermon* 130.1 and n. 2 for other references in Chrysologus's preaching to the Church as mother. On the Church's remaining a virgin while bearing episcopal offspring, see *Sermon* 130.2 and n. 12.
3. On ancient attitudes, pagan and Christian, about the bee, see L. Koep, et al., "Biene," in *RAC* 2 (1954), 274–82. As one example from classical literature, see Virgil, *Georgics*, Book 4, especially lines 197–202 concerning reproduction without intercourse. On the praises of the bee in Latin Christian thought, especially as an image of virginal procreation and begetting by means of the mouth, see, for example, *Benedictio cerei* or Easter *Exultet*, 7–8, in *Studi e testi* 121.227; see also *Sermon* 65, n. 17 (FOTC 109.266); Ambrose, *Hexameron*, 5.21.66–72 (FOTC 42.212–18); idem, *De Virginibus*, 1.8.40–44 (PL 16.210–11); and Prudentius, *Hymns for Every Day*, 3.71–75 (FOTC 43.18).

bee, by the testimony of her mouth[4] has selected for herself and generated herself her shepherd, younger than the rest, in order that, in the words of the prophet, a son might be born to her in place of her father: "In place of your fathers sons have been born to you. You will establish them as princes over all the earth."[5] I said "younger," not in wisdom, but in age. But regarding seriousness, knowledge, character, and discipline, he gives every indication of fullness of years.[6]

3. And since in describing the one brought to birth today we have used the metaphor of the bee, which by its voice moves the troops forward out of their camp, with its voice leads them to their own abodes, to the place of the most pleasant work and quiet, it is now appropriate for us to be silent, so that the newborn shepherd may use his own voice to give a clarion call on matters divine, so as to motivate the army of the Lord the moment he is born, and summon and bring them back right away to their own beehives, accompanied by the Lord. However, brothers, just as from the cradle itself through the very stages of life, so too has he ascended through the ranks of ecclesiastical office,[7] and since it would take too long for me to speak about it, as the evangelist has said, "He is of age, let him speak for himself."[8]

    4. This apparently refers to the voice of the people in the diocese in nominating and/or electing the new bishop.
    5. Ps 44.17 LXX; Ps 45.16. On interpreting this biblical text as a reference to the Church's giving birth to a new bishop, see *Sermon* 130.1 and n. 5.
    6. A similar idea is expressed in *Sermon* 130.2.
    7. Clearly, this newly consecrated bishop had "gone through the ranks" and held several other offices in the Church before being named bishop. On this terminology *(gradus ecclesiastici officii)* for the designation of degrees of ecclesiastical orders or ranks, see R. Gryson, "Les degrés du clergé et leurs dénominations chez saint Ambroise de Milan," *Revue bénédictine* 76 (1966): 119–22.
    8. Jn 9.21. At the end of *Sermon* 165 (FOTC 17.271), when Chrysologus consecrated another bishop, his final sentence replicates this one almost exactly. Both are obvious references to the practice of the new bishop "getting the last word" after the consecrating bishop concluded his remarks. Hence the brevity of Chrysologus's sermon on such occasions.

SERMON 131

*On the Gospel Where It Says: "If anyone keeps my word,
he will not see death forever"*[1]

E HAVE FREQUENTLY SAID that God is not seen with bodily eyes, that divinity is not contained in a carnal mind, that human reasoning does not grasp the Creator of the universe, but faith alone hears God,[2] a complete act of trust is needed to perceive him, and human observation, to the extent that it can, recognizes not how great he is, but that he is. And so Moses, who is raised from being a servant to the dignity of being a friend, from a man to a god, seeks the face of God, but does not find it; he asks, but he does not receive;[3] and he is admonished to look only at the back of God, so that the human being may seek to follow God, not precede him, and may not be presumptuous in seeking anything before God, but by worshiping him may come to understand that all things come after God.

2. God repeatedly manifests the form of a human being to human beings, and fits his own magnificent grandeur into the tiny space of our body, so that our weak eye may be able to gaze upon the presence of God, so that our limited vision may be able to perceive it. And so God comes to Abraham in the form

---

1. Jn 8.51. This sermon may have been preached during Lent. The only internal evidence is found at the end of section 8. But, additionally, from the extant sermons of Chrysologus, the few that are on the Gospel of John appear to have been delivered exclusively during Lent or Easter. Also, the particular Johannine text on which this sermon is based was in fact read during Lent in the churches of Rome, Milan, Aquileia, and Benevento. Finally, one collection of some of Chrysologus's sermons places this sermon in the middle of others that are definitely Lenten. See F. Sottocornola, *L'anno liturgico*, 79, 112–13, 218–19, and 432, n. 10.
2. See Rom 10.17.
3. See Ex 33.13–23.

of a human being, he approaches him by appearing as a stranger, and as is customary for a weary traveler he receives water for his feet; but he is also invited to eat and is filled with the beef and the bread that are set before him; and he so completely entrusts and devotes himself to accommodating human beings that when he is touched and seen he seems to be fully and truly human, and this on the very occasion when as true God he comes to bestow an offspring, to open up the womb to produce a child, in a hopeless situation where barrenness had perdured into extreme old age.[4]

3. Thus while Jacob is traveling, a fellow Traveler meets up with him and shows himself to be on an entirely equal level of interaction as a human being such that he who is God becomes completely engaged in wrestling the man who called out to him, and seems to be conquered[5] at that time with sinews or muscles, since he gives heavenly gifts and divine favors to the victor.[6]

Thus did Isaiah catch sight of God seated in the attire of a King,[7] in order to understand that if kings are not ruled by God the King, they themselves can rule as rulers over nothing,[8] since they are human beings. Thus does Daniel catch sight of God as a Father with snow-white hair, of a venerable old age, awesome in his antiquity, surrounded by angels, and seated on a fiery throne in judgment.[9] Thus does Daniel himself gaze upon the Son of God coming as Son of Man on the clouds of heaven, in order to understand that Christ was unknown earlier by those who were so faithless, but had always been known by believers.[10]

4. If human beings see God so many times looking like a human being, why is it that the Jew by looking only upon the man exasperates Christ so much, unless perhaps his appearance, honor, and truth is considered offensive? The evangelist today

---

4. See Gn 18.1–15.
5. Reading the variant *vinci* rather than *vincere* in Olivar's CCL text.
6. See Gn 32.24–29.
7. See Is 6.1 and 5.
8. *Nisi a deo rege regantur reges;* . . . *nichil regere posse rectores.*
9. See Dn 7.9–10.
10. See Dn 7.13–14.

has mentioned that Christ said: *If anyone keeps my word, he will not see death forever* (Jn 8.51). To which statement the Jews responded: *Now we know that you have a demon. Abraham our father and the prophets have died, yet you say: "If anyone keeps my word, he will not see death forever." Are you greater than our father Abraham and the prophets? Whom do you make yourself out to be?* (vv.52–53)

5. Look how faithlessness ensnares them all! Look how jealousy closes their eyes![11] When wickedness has been decided upon beforehand, look at how severely it distorts the heart's judgment! O how harshly does obstinacy do away with reason! Perverse human thinking is incapable of listening to something once it has decided to hate it. Goodness is detestable to the wicked, justice is odious to the unjust. This is why human beings are unable to foresee the truth in the midst of their lying. The mind in its capacity for judgment is unable to ascertain what is true while lies are being disseminated. The one who has set his course on error always hears what he wants rather than what is.

6. Christ had said: *If anyone keeps my word, he will not see death forever.* The Jew does not discuss what he has heard, and he looks for no interpretation of what has been said to him; he demands that the One who makes the promise prove what he[12] thinks is impossible. But as soon as his mind conceives them he brings forth blasphemies, he gives birth to insults, he spreads slander, and he strives with such malice to discredit the authority of the speaker that no one believes that the One who seems to be subject to the human condition so completely can at the same time grant eternal goods to mortals.

7. *Now we know that you have a demon.* A demon, since it is an author of evil, promises what is evil, not good; it is accustomed to kill, not to give life: it does not want human beings to be eternal, since it does not allow them to be even temporal beings. Therefore, Christ is not a demon, but he is God who restores the life which he had bestowed, and by his word he

---

11. Anti-Jewish rhetoric like this is found in *Sermon* 48.3 (FOTC 109.184–85). Similar in terminology and content is Cyprian, *Jealousy and Envy* 5 (FOTC 36.297).

12. Namely, the Jew.

makes human beings eternal, whom the devil by his influence had made temporal.

8. *Abraham*, it says, *and the prophets have died, and you say: "If anyone keeps my word, he will not see death forever"* (v.52). Let the believer listen, so that he may recognize by the revelation that comes from faith what the unbeliever is unable to hear, what one cannot see once he has plunged into the darkness of unbelief. Christ said: *he will not see death*. It stands to reason, O Jew, that your obstinacy seeks to tell what is false. When Abraham and the prophets heard the word, they were steadfast in keeping it, but, nevertheless, they died, but not forever. Therefore, when he says: *he will not see death*, and adds: *forever*, he is promising the resurrection, but he is not denying that they will die for a time.

O Jew, the ones whom death made come to an end in the present age, the resurrection remakes to last forever in the future. Listen to him saying this more clearly: everyone who believes "will not die forever, but will pass from death to life."[13] How then does he not die, since he passes from death to life? Therefore, he does die, everyone who is born out of the mortal condition dies, but he lives, yes, he lives, and he lives forever, everyone who is born out of the life-giving generation.[14]

9. But I say: why did the One who was able to remove death will that the human being pass through death? The physician who prevents diseases is more deserving of thanks than the one who administers medicine for diseases after the fact and not without pain. O Jew, Christ the Physician[15] would have done this too, if the patient had not been ungrateful to the Physician. He both gave life and warned the human being that death was coming. But the human being who had not experienced adversity was unable to maintain his prosperity. We cannot

---

13. Jn 11.26 and 5.24.
14. An allusion to Baptism. Chrysologus may be intending these remarks for those preparing for Baptism at the next Easter; this is the only internal evidence suggesting a Lenten context for this sermon. See F. Sottocornola, *L'anno liturgico*, 112–13.
15. For other references to this title for Christ in Chrysologus's sermons, see *Sermon* 50.4 and n. 15 (FOTC 109.195–96).

know how good the good is except by an awareness of evil. Therefore Christ will be glorified who both gave life which prior to then nobody possessed, and now restores it when it was lost, and the human being who is more conscious of his life will exercise more discretion in his own regard and be more grateful to his Creator.

10. *Are you greater*, it says, *than our father Abraham?* (v.53) Clearly greater, and greater to the degree that the Lord is greater than the servant, and God is greater than the human being, to the degree that the Maker is greater than what is made,[16] the Giver of life is greater than the dead, and he who raises up is greater than the one who is going to rise.

11. *Jesus answered: "Abraham exulted that he was to see my day: and he saw it, and rejoiced"* (vv.54, 56). *The Jews said: "Abraham died"* (v.52). In order to show them that Abraham was alive, he said that he had seen his day, that is, the day on which Christ was born to the world. The Creator of days is not constrained by the day, the Author of time does not know periods of time. But for the sake of the human being Christ was born a man and became subject to both day and time. *Abraham exulted that he was to see my day* (v.56). If Moses and Elijah are present on the mountain in order to catch sight of the promised Christ,[17] what prevents Abraham from being present when the Virgin gives birth, so that after waiting very patiently he might behold the blessing promised in his descendants,[18] that is, in his seed?[19]

12. *"I declare to you,"* he says, *"that before Abraham was, I am." They picked up stones to throw at him* (vv.58–59). If "all things were made through him, and without him[20] nothing was made,"[21] and he is the One to whom the Father said: "Let us make the human being in our image and likeness,"[22] how did Abraham

---

16. Reading the variant *factor facturae* rather than *factura factori* in Olivar's CCL text.

17. See Mt 17.3 and parallels.

18. The Latin is *gentibus*, which can also bear the meaning of "nations" or even "gentiles."

19. See Gn 12.7 and 15.18.

20. Reading *ipso* with the majority of the manuscripts rather than *ipsum* in Olivar's CCL text.

21. Jn 1.3.

22. Gn 1.26.

not see him? "Let us make the human being in our image and likeness." Regarding an angel and God, as the substance is different, so too is the image. Therefore, it is only to the Son that the Father can be speaking when he says: "Let us make the human being in the image and likeness of us,"[23] who have the same image and substance.[24]

13. *"Before Abraham was, I am."* They *picked up stones*, and building a tower,[25] in order to fall from a greater height,[26] they provided themselves stones; and the stones which these miserable creatures took did not kill God, but were the means by which they killed themselves. *Jesus hid himself* (v.59), not out of fear, but to pardon. God spares the sinner when he flees; by turning away, God wills not to destroy the rebellious.[27]

---

23. Chrysologus quotes Gn 1.26 in exactly the same way as previously; it is translated into English differently here so as to get across the emphasis on the *nostram* ("our," or, as here, "of us") that Chrysologus intends.

24. Chrysologus indicates here that he is aware of a certain Jewish exegesis of Gn 1.26 that interprets "us" as referring to God (the Father) and angels. See Introduction, FOTC 109.17–18 and n. 86. For references in other early Christian authors, see R. Benericetti, *Il Cristo*, 140, n. 7.

25. See Gn 11.4.

26. For other references to "the higher they are, the harder they fall," see *Sermon* 13.5 and n. 9, and *Sermon* 26.2 (FOTC 109.63–64 and 111).

27. For the belief that Christ's flight as an infant into Egypt was also providential for human beings, see *Sermons* 150.11, 151.7, and 153.3.

SERMON 136

In Praise of the Holy Bishop Adelphius[1]

THE HOLY SPIRIT OF Bishop[2] Adelphius and his reputation for great kindness have this noteworthy quality, that although rich, he enters the dwelling of the poor, and seats himself at the poor person's table, and makes himself at home with the humble, while his wealth, power, and prominent position resulted in making him unique. For among the greatest of his virtues this will of his must be mentioned, which spurned the haughtiness that comes from having others pay him homage, despised the reverence due to his august house, trampled underfoot as well his lofty rank of authority, and scorned taking his wealth to heart,[3] from which sources the greatest amount of pride always holds sway over the dispositions of human beings; this will of his stooped down to the extreme distress of the destitute, in order to lift up the poor person by his association with him.

Clearly blessed and completely free from any trace of the disease of arrogance is his spirit, which took the initiative of entering the poor person's lodging, in order to be a debtor be-

---

1. This Adelphius is likely the bishop of Aquileia who served in that capacity from 426 through 436. In his *monitum* to this sermon (CCL 24B.824), A. Olivar states that Chrysologus's excessive praise and deference toward Adelphius indicate that Chrysologus was a relatively new bishop at the time. Ravenna was probably not yet of metropolitan standing. See Introduction, FOTC 109.9–10 and n. 35. F. Sottocornola, in *L'anno liturgico*, 113–14, is of the opinion that this sermon dates to 430, just before Ravenna was elevated to metropolitan status. See also A. Olivar, *Los sermones*, 229–30 and 239, regarding the difference between this sermon, delivered when Chrysologus was a "simple bishop," and *Sermon 175*, preached when he was of metropolitan rank.
2. The Latin term is *antistes*, which signifies a metropolitan or archbishop. See R. Benericetti, *Il Cristo*, 60 and n. 28.
3. Olivar's CCL text has a typographical error: *conscientiae* should be *conscientia*. See PL 52.567.

fore being a bestower of kindness.[4] It is evident that he was eager to imitate God who when incarnate accepted human acts of service from others before lavishing divine blessings upon the human being.[5] This is what we perceive that Adelphius has done, present here before us and high priest[6] of the Most High God.

Although he is rich in words, full of knowledge, great in talent, and first in rank,[7] he has desired to experience what it is to be in need and to listen to our mediocre remarks, like that prophet who was hungry for the widow's last bit of food, and by his own hunger increased her children's[8] distress, starting up a new ministry[9] with his request, in order to bestow by making a request, to fill stomachs by being hungry, and by emptying out the barn to stuff it to overflowing with divine bounty for the indigent.[10]

2. And we, little children, are not sorry that we have given what we had, because, although the deed disturbed us for a time, the example encourages and consoles us. In a short time the meagerness of our talent, like the food of that widow, will improve, thanks to an increase coming from heaven at the word of this man of God, and from then on the storehouse of our heart will never be deprived of the substance of life, but our poverty and deficiency themselves will be abolished.

O happy stream,[11] that grows more abundant as it flows along, and with complete freedom acquires and absorbs more water in its current. See, he has come, and a shower from heaven has rained down upon your lofty spirits, and the river from on high with all its force has watered with its current the city of

---

4. This suggests that Adelphius is visiting Chrysologus in Ravenna.
5. Perhaps an allusion to Lk 2.7.
6. The Latin term is *pontifex*.
7. This phrase *(loco primus)* also appears to indicate Adelphius's superior status as a metropolitan over Chrysologus.
8. It apparently slipped Chrysologus's mind that the widow in question had only one child, her son.
9. Possibly an allusion to the ministry or office of widow in the Church.
10. See 1 Kgs 17.8–16.
11. In *Sermon* 173.2, Chrysologus likens his own words to a stream of refreshing water.

God that is within us,[12] in order that our land, dampened by divine dew, may bear fruit a hundredfold.[13] Open your minds, widen your hearts, and stretch out the lap of your intellect, so that whatever he pours out in abundance there from the treasure chests of heaven you may be able to possess for eternal glory and everlasting wealth.

12. See Ps 45.5 LXX; Ps 46.4.
13. See Mt 13.8.

SERMON 137

When John Flees to the Desert[1]

FTER THE FERTILITY OF the Jewish soil was depleted by being tilled continually by the plowshare of the Law,[2] blessed John flees to a desert in a gentile region, setting the brambles of sin ablaze with the fire of his spirit,[3] cutting down trees that bore no fruit with the ax of vengeance,[4] leveling the rough hills of pride, raising up valleys of humility by making the ground level,[5] with expert cultivation adjusting the whole surface of the land to the way the nutrients flow, to correspond with the course of the Jordan, and in so doing he prepares fallow land in abundance, and he makes it fertile for the seed of the Gospel.

2. *The word of the Lord*, it says, *came over John the son of Zechariah in the desert, and he went into the whole region of the Jordan* (Lk 3.2–3). *The word of the Lord came*, since "the Word became flesh and dwelt among us."[6] *Over John:* why not "to" John, but "over" John? It is because that which "is from above is over all."[7] *The word of the Lord came over John.* This is because John is the voice,

---

1. F. Sottocornola, *L'anno liturgico*, 114, suggests that this sermon could have been delivered in Lent for the following reasons: *Sermon* 167, on the parallel Gospel account in Matthew, is Lenten; the strong emphasis in this *Sermon* 137 on mercy and almsgiving to the poor is a popular Lenten theme; and the references to Baptism found here, customary during Lent, together with the promise at the end to explain the difference between the baptisms of John and of Christ in a subsequent sermon, constitute more evidence for a Lenten delivery.

2. Similar references to the failure of the Jewish "soil" to yield much fruit are made in *Sermons* 106.7 and 164.3.

3. It is unclear from the text whether the Latin word *spiritus* refers to John's spirit or to the Holy Spirit.

4. See Lk 3.9.

5. See Is 40.4 and Lk 3.5.

6. Jn 1.14.

7. Jn 3.31.

but God is the Word.⁸ *The word of the Lord came over John:* God came over John, the Lord came over the servant, the Word came over the voice.

3. But you say to me: why is it that the voice precedes the Word? It precedes, but it does not exceed it.⁹ He goes ahead to offer deferential service to the One who follows, not to signify his own authority. The voice itself is not the Judge, but it is the messenger of the Judge. The Word judges, the voice acts as herald; power resides in the One who gives the orders, not the one who cries out. But let the voice himself, the herald himself admit this, attest to it, and assert it, by crying out: "After me One is coming," he says, "who is more powerful than I."¹⁰ Why more powerful? It is because my task is to instill fear, but his is to pass judgment.

4. *He went into the whole region of the Jordan.* He went to the Jordan, because a water jar could no longer wash away the filth of the Jews, but only a river could—as is written in Scripture: "There were stone water jars," it says, "for the purification of the Jews."¹¹ He went to the Jordan, in order to give the penitents water and not wine to drink. *He went into the whole region of the Jordan, preaching a baptism of repentance for the forgiveness of sins* (v.3). Pardoning was within John's power, but not without repentance; there was forgiveness, but acquired by sorrow; there was a cure for the wound, but accompanied by grief; there was a baptism to remove the fault, but not to blot out the lingering sense of guilt.

And why should I say more? By means of John's baptism the human being was being purified for repentance, but not advanced to grace. But, by contrast, Christ's Baptism regenerates, transforms, and makes a new person out of the old one so effectively that there is no knowledge of the past nor any memory of the things of old in the one who out of his earthly condition

---

8. This contrast between John and Christ is frequently employed by Augustine. See, e.g., his *Sermons* 288.3–4, 289.3, and 293.3 (PL 38.1304–6, 1309, and 1328–29).

9. Chrysologus's rhetorical flair is evident here: *Praecedit, sed non praecellit.*

10. Mt 3.11.

11. Jn 2.6.

has been made heavenly,[12] and already possesses heavenly and divine blessings.

A case in point is the son, upon his return from a period of dissolute living, to whom his father gives the finest robe of immortality, puts the ring of liberty on him,[13] kills the fatted calf,[14] and changes the waters of repentance into the wine of grace, so that now cups of the undiluted wine of grace[15] may be served in abundance at the feast, so much so that the sober intoxication of the Lord's chalice eliminates pangs of conscience, the groans of repentance, and the weeping over sins, as the prophet says: "How splendid is your cup that intoxicates!"[16] For just as unseemly as earthly intoxication is, equally splendid and seemly is heavenly intoxication.[17]

5. *Therefore, he used to say to those who would come out to be baptized by him: "You brood of vipers, who instructed you to flee from the wrath to come? Therefore, bear fruits worthy of repentance, and do not start saying: 'We have Abraham as our father.' For I say to you that God is able to raise up children for Abraham from these stones. For the ax has already been set in place at the roots of the trees. Every tree that does not bear good fruit will be cut down and cast into the fire"* (vv. 7–9).

6. *Brood of vipers* (v. 7): he issues a reproof with an example, he chastises with a comparison, he reveals by means of an image, so that now he may prevail in changing, not merely the morals, but the very nature of the venomous offspring. *Brood of vipers:* inasmuch as those whom God had created human and had made children of Abraham, malice spawned and turned into vipers; and those whom an act of merciful kindness had

---

12. See 1 Cor 15.47–48.
13. Also in *Sermon* 5.6, on the Prodigal Son (FOTC 17.49), Chrysologus finds the robe to signify immortality and the ring liberty.
14. See Lk 15.22–23.
15. In *Sermon* 160.6 similar language is used together with the quotation of Ps 22 (23).5 to refer to the cup of Christ's blood in the Eucharist.
16. Ps 22 (23).5.
17. Both similar terminology and the notion that the eucharistic chalice confers spiritual inebriation and forgiveness of sins are found in Ambrose, *The Sacraments* 5.3.17 (FOTC 44.314). For other references in the Latin patristic tradition to this notion of spiritual inebriation, see H. J. Sieben, "Ivresse spirituelle," in *DSp* 7.2 (1971), 2317–20. See *Sermon* 147.6 (FOTC 17.246).

made and infused with the sweet delight of heaven, godlessness infected with a love for fatal vomit, inducing them to pour out the poison of serpents, and in an unspeakable example of cruelty to be conceived out of the death of their father, to be born from the death of their mother.

Brood of vipers, progeny ungrateful to nature, whose birth marks the destruction of their father, whose life is the death of its parent. *Brood of vipers:* it is said that at the time when it conceives, the viper takes the head of her mate into her mouth and then tears off his head, such that by means of her bloodstained kisses conception is not an act of affection, but a crime, and in this way she gives birth to children of her wickedness who are murderers according to the order of vengeance, not of nature. For the offspring, conceived out of the slaughter of their father, demand to be nourished by blood before milk, and seek vengeance on their mother.[18]

And so we are told that vipers destroy the womb and, although their organs are not yet fully developed, with the fury of an adult they crush the wicked dwelling where they were conceived, and consequently for them to live means never seeing their mother, the mother who bore such as these.

7. We have felt compelled to describe in greater detail the example and image contained in the metaphor which Saint John made, to make clear that the name given the Jews by him derives, not from slander, but from the truth. In so doing he makes clear, brothers, that the brood of vipers was the synagogue[19] and her children, to whom Christ came with a husband's love—as John says: "He who has the bride is the bridegroom."[20] It was Christ's head that was sought and demanded by the mouth amid Judas's hugs and bloody kisses,[21] when the words, "Crucify him, Crucify him!" were uttered.[22] And so, the

---

18. The image of the viper is also employed in *Sermon* 31.1, and references in other patristic writers are indicated in *Sermon* 31, n. 3; see FOTC 109.130.

19. *Sermon* 31.1, indicated in the previous note, contains similar anti-Jewish rhetoric.

20. Jn 3.29. This same quotation and the marital imagery applied to Christ's relationship to the Church are found also in *Sermon* 31.3 (FOTC 109.132).

21. See Mt 26.48–49 and parallels.

22. Lk 23.21 and Jn 19.6.

offspring conceived at the cost of such precious blood are armed right away to put their mother to death, with the result that after having burst the womb of the synagogue they run, upon hearing John's voice, to be regenerated as the brood of God.

8. *You brood of vipers, who instructed you to flee from the wrath to come?* (v.7) What is the wrath to come? It is that which has no end, which does not release the human being by death, but keeps him enchained, and no longer allows him to have any hope for pardon, once it has condemned him to the penal realm of Tartarus.[23] Admonished by the words: *from the wrath to come* and *brood of vipers*, they recognize their lineage and their sin, and so they said in response: *"What shall we do in order to be saved?" He said in reply to them* (vv.10–11).

What he is about to say, brothers, I am afraid to say, lest the number of my listeners who, I notice, are contemptuous he may make downright defiant. What shall I do? I am afraid to speak, but I cannot be silent.[24] My duty to be merciful prevents me from the one, but my duty to be of benefit urges me to the other: merciful, lest the listener incur guilt because of his contempt; of benefit, lest he never be told what he is supposed to do, and through my silence the teacher[25] prove harmful. I am going to speak, brothers, so that both the naked person may get dressed, and I may lay all I have out before you.

9. *The one who has two coats*, he says, *is to give to the one who has none; and the one who has food is to act in a similar fashion* (v.11). Do you think that the one who asks for one of the two coats is asking for too much? He is not asking for too much, because he is not asking for a jewel, but only for a coat; not for gold, but only for bread. And if the one who does not give one of his two coats is guilty, what about the one who refuses to give one yet has a closet full of them? The result of locking up his clothes

---

23. Tartarus is the realm of the dead, personified for example in *Sermon* 65.6–9 (FOTC 109.263–66).

24. Chrysologus uses almost exactly the same terminology in *Sermon* 67.1 (FOTC 17.115). For this expression in other Latin patristic writers, see J. H. Baxter, "Varia, I. Proverbs," *Archivum Latinitatis Medii Aevi* 4 (1928): 115.

25. Other references to the bishop as teacher *(doctor)* in Chrysologus's sermons are mentioned in R. Benericetti, *Il Cristo*, 60, n. 28.

and withholding his bread is that the poor person dies of hunger and perishes from the cold. Such a person buries his clothes, he does not store them away; he saves them not for the sake of precaution, but of the grave.

What one refuses to the poor he gives to the moths,[26] and with his clothes he is a devourer of the body, as the Lord says: "Their worms will never die."[27] The poor person's hunger has struck Christ, the pain of the human being has pierced God's heart, the groans of the captive have reverberated deeply within Christ, and contempt for the destitute has such far-reaching effects as to have hurt the Creator, as he himself acknowledges when he says: "I was hungry, and you gave me nothing to eat; I was naked, and you did not clothe me."[28]

10. *Tax collectors also came to him and said: "What shall we do?"* Let tax collectors listen: *Claim no more than what has been prescribed for you* (vv.12–13). He reveals what it is that makes a tax collector guilty: *Do not demand more.* The one who demands more is an extortionist, not a tax collector. Let him consider how guilty in God's sight is the person who seizes the goods of the downtrodden and the oppressed; by his extortion he oppresses and torments more and more, and for the one who has difficulty paying what he owes, he imposes the additional and further burden of something that person does not owe.[29]

11. There also came *soldiers who spoke.* Let soldiers also listen to what this teacher answered as well to the soldiers who questioned him: *"And what shall we do?" "Do not terrorize anyone, nor falsely denounce anyone; be content with your pay"* (v.14). The true soldier is not the one who terrorizes, but the one who defends; not the one who spreads slander, but repels it; who goes off to receive his wages from the King, and does not go off to rob a fellow citizen.

12. Blessed John taught divine matters in such a way as not to turn human ones upside down. He set the state on a firm

---

26. On this same point, see *Sermon* 7.6 (FOTC 109.38).
27. Is 66.24 and Mk 9.48.
28. Mt 25.42 and 43.
29. See *Sermon* 26.5 (FOTC 109.113) for another reference to Chrysologus's concern that the taxpayer not be overwhelmed.

SERMON 137

foundation, he did not tear it asunder. He demonstrated that what he taught had been ordained by God and had the power to produce and preserve justice. But we are now going to pass over in silence what the relationship is between John's baptism and Christ's Baptism, since it requires a more extensive treatment.[30]

30. This "more extensive treatment" is not extant.

SERMON 139

On the Gospel Where It Says: "If my brother sins against me"[1]

UST AS GOLD LIES concealed in the earth, so does the divine meaning lie hidden in human language.[2] And therefore as often as the Lord's words are revealed to us, the mind should be alert, the spirit attentive, so that the intellect may be able to enter the inner sanctum of heavenly knowledge. Let us hear why the Lord has begun speaking in this vein today.

2. *Take notice of yourselves* (Lk 17.3), he says. What is the meaning of this new kind of talk? Where is this unusual admonition heading? *Take notice of yourselves*, he says. That one takes notice of himself, who does not pay excessive, impudent, and unnecessary attention to someone else's actions. *Take notice of yourselves*, he says. The wandering eye, the extended gaze, the restless glance pays no heed to its own destruction, but falls over itself in running after someone else's failings; blind to its own sins, it brings another person's faults into broad daylight; unaware of the evils it has committed, it accuses and bears witness to the evils of others; with tepid indifference about its own guilt, it is all ablaze and hot on the trail of proving the guilt of someone else, even of one who is innocent.

And, in short, as the Lord has said, the eye does not see the beam in itself, but sees the speck in someone else's.[3] Isn't the eye the author of transgression—Scripture says, "She saw that it was attractive"?[4] Isn't it the entryway of death, the torch of

---

1. See Lk 17.3–4. Because of the eschatological overtone in section 8, F. Sottocornola, *L'anno liturgico*, 290–91, suggests that this sermon may have been delivered near the end of the year, in December prior to Christmas.
2. On this topic, see *Sermon* 91.1 and n. 2.
3. See Mt 7.3.
4. Gn 3.6.

envy,[5] and the furnace of jealousy? All aflame with desire doesn't it run more speedily through the actions of another than a fire runs through parched grass on earth? It is of God, it is of God's Providence that the eye that looks all around when it is open is narrowly compressed into the pupil, so that it look at what it sees with restraint and not look askance; that it may foresee, not forestall; that it look ahead, not look down;[6] that the eye be the window of the soul,[7] the mirror of the mind, the light of the body, the guide of the bodily members, not the entryway of the vices. But let us return to what we were saying.

3. *Take notice of yourselves*, he says. He said this to you as a group, not to you individually, because whatever notice a human being takes of another, he takes notice of himself; and as much as he will be on the lookout for another, that other person will be on the lookout for him, as becomes clear from the following.

4. *If your brother sins against you*, he says, *rebuke him, and if he repents, forgive him* (v.3). Come now, O man, and since God commands it, be God's deputy: forgive sins, be merciful regarding offenses, you yourself pardon any sins that have been committed against you, so that you do not now lose those features of divine power within you; whatever you do not pardon for another, you will refuse for yourself in that other person. *If your brother sins against you*, he says, *rebuke him.* Rebuke as a judge, pardon as a brother, because charity joined to freedom, and freedom mingled with charity both stifles fear and rouses one's brother.

A brother has a fever when he does harm to his brother, a neighbor is delirious when he does wrong to his neighbor, he does not know what he is doing, and he is a stranger to his own humanity; the one who does not show compassion and come to his aid, or who does not show patience and provide for his heal-

---

5. The Latin is *invidiae fax.* See Cicero, *Pro Milone* 35.98: *faces invidiae.*
6. Chrysologus's rhetorical artistry is evident here: *oculus in orbem . . . apertus artatur angustissimus . . . visum videat, non invideat; praevideat, non praeripiat; prospiciat, non despiciat.*
7. On the eye as the "window of the soul," see *Sermon* 52.1 and n. 3 (FOTC 109.202).

ing, or who does not grant him pardon to make him well, is not well himself, is sick and infirm, has no heart, and is shown to be without any human feeling. A brother raves: attribute it to sickness; a brother is doing crazy things: attribute what he is doing to the fever, and you will be unable to ascribe the wrong to your brother, and you will wisely place the blame on the infirmity, and you will grant pardon to your brother, so that his healing may redound to your glory, and his being pardoned may result in your being rewarded.

5. *If your brother sins against you,* he says, *rebuke him; if he repents, forgive him.* No one who hears this should take it upon himself to be severe in forgiving, and with vain presumption impose some legal burden on his brother who offends him, and thus imagine that it is a hard thing to forgive offenses. A human being should call to mind that he is a sinner and that he will sin, and then he will begin to love pardon, and not love vengeance. You hear that you have to forgive, and you do not hear that you have to be forgiven.

Tomorrow you too will sin against the one who sinned against you today; and your judge will be the one who earlier was a defendant before you, and he will render you pardon if you have given it; if you did not give it, he will either deny you pardon, or, if he does give it, he will put you under obligation more than just excusing you. Forgive the sinner, forgive the penitent, so that when you sin, the pardon you receive will be a recompense rather than a gift you do not deserve. Pardon is always good, but it is sweetest at the moment when it is needed. That person has nullified punishment, kept the judge at bay, and avoided judgment, who by forgiving another has already provided pardon for himself even before committing an offense.

6. *And if your brother sins against you seven times, and seven times a day returns to you and says: "I am sorry," forgive him seven times* (v.4). Why does he give a rule that restricts pardon, why does he set a quantifiable limit, and set definite boundaries for it? Does he employ his mercy so as to do damage to pardon? Does his favor operate by diluting pardon? If seven times, if eight times, is there a number that can exceed the favor? Is there

some amount which renders benevolence inoperative? And does one fault consign someone to punishment after he has been already pardoned for seven offenses? Far from it! The foremost moral obligation that must be understood is that it is a sin to have shown mercy and compassion less instead of more. For just as the one who has forgiven seven times is happy, so much happier still is the one who has forgiven seventy times seven times.

7. Peter, in failing to recall this command, asks the Lord: "'If my brother sins against me, how many times should I forgive him? Seven times?' The Lord answered: 'Not only seven times, but seventy times seven times.'"[8] Therefore the number that is prescribed does not restrict pardon, but extends its scope, and what he limits with a precept, he leaves limitless for the will, so that if you forgive as much as he commands, that indicates how obedient you are, but if you forgive more, that indicates how much your reward will be.

But the number seven, which seems to be small numerically, is discovered to be immense in its symbolism.[9] For the number seven progressing through the days makes the Sabbath, which the Lord blessed and allotted to resting, for himself from his own work as well as for human beings from their labor.[10] The number seven running through the weeks thus multiplies seven days by seven, such that it concludes on Pentecost, the solemnity which is full of mystery for us, and then pours forth the whole shower of the Holy Spirit with the sound from heaven upon the Church's harvest.[11] When the number seven hastens through the months, it consecrates for us the feasts of the seventh month with all the holiness of fasting.[12]

When the number seven traverses the years, it makes the seventh year which gives rest to the land, and absolves all the

---

8. Mt 18.21–22.
9. For more on the symbolism associated with the number seven, see *Sermon* 85b.1.
10. See Gn 2.2–3 and Ex 20.8–11.
11. On the Feast of Pentecost, see *Sermon* 85b, especially section 1.
12. This is apparently a reference to the practice of fasting during September, a custom of the church in Rome also adopted by Ravenna. See F. Sottocornola, *L'anno liturgico*, 439–42.

bonds that keep brothers in debt. When the number seven makes the cycle of a week of years, it ushers in the fiftieth year, which is called a jubilee year,[13] for pardon and forgiveness to be whole and complete, so that servitude might be removed, liberty restored, so that the records, or rather the tombs,[14] of promissory notes may be destroyed, so that the debtor may rise again, that what is owed may be buried, that the poor man's field may come back to him, and that every contract drawn up by a rich person's greed may perish.

8. And if the number seven, multiplied by seven through days, months, and years, has conferred so much forgiveness and pardon, let the Christian listener consider and attend to what the number seven multiplied seven times by seventy times seven can produce. Then the contract of credit and debt will certainly come to an end, then the whole state of servitude will certainly be abolished, then, yes, that freedom that knows no end will come, then their field will be returned for all eternity to those who will live forever.

There will come, yes, then there will come true forgiveness, when even the inevitable tendency to sin will be abolished, when uncleanness will perish and the world will then truly be called clean,[15] when life will return and death will not exist, when Christ will reign and the devil then will perish. Pray, brothers, that the Lord will also increase our faith so that we can believe and possess these realities.

---

13. See Lv 25.8–55. See also *Sermon* 126.8 regarding the mercy associated with the jubilee year. Ambrose, *Expositio Evangelii secundum Lucam* 8.23 (CCL 14.306), also refers to the jubilee year in commenting on this same Gospel account.

14. This expression is not as strange as it may appear: in English we speak of being "buried" in debt.

15. Chrysologus engages in wordplay here: *mundus . . . vocabitur mundus; mundus* as a noun means "world" and as an adjective means "clean." Likewise, see *Sermon* 167.6, and Augustine, *Sermons* 105.6.8 and 283.2.1 (PL 38.622 and 1286), and *Tractates on the Gospel of John* 38.6.1 (FOTC 88.108).

SERMON 140A

On the Nativity of the Lord[1]

Y EXAMINING THOROUGHLY AND over a long period of time the mystery of the Virgin's giving birth[2] and Christ's being born, we have at last become worthy to reach the sacred cradle of his birth; thus is it indicated to us today by the words of the Gospel. *It happened*, it says, *in those days that an edict went forth from Caesar Augustus that the whole world was to be enrolled. This first census took place* (Lk 2.1–2). When Christ was born there was a census of the whole world, since a census was owed to Caesar, but a pledge of allegiance[3] was owed to the Creator.

In a coin is the image of Caesar, in a human being is the image of God. And accordingly, the world is enrolled such that the likeness of the king is fashioned on the coin, and the image

---

1. For convincing evidence concerning this sermon's authenticity, see A. Olivar, *Los sermones*, 327–34. F. Sottocornola, *L'anno liturgico*, 130, believes that this sermon was preached on Christmas Day, and that the first sentence contains a reference to previous sermons delivered a short time earlier on the Annunciation, of which several have survived. V. Zangara, "I silenzi," 232–50, by contrast, argues that Chrysologus never preached on the actual day of Christmas, largely on the basis of *Sermon* 146.1 (FOTC 17.238) where Chrysologus speaks about being silent on Christmas Day itself. So, all the Christmas sermons of his that we possess, including this *Sermon* 140a, were actually delivered not on that day but on the days immediately afterwards. While in general Chrysologus may not have preached on Christmas Day, exceptions to this usual practice did occur. See, e.g., *Sermon* 140b and nn. 1–2. A. Olivar, *Los sermones*, 274, suggests that this *Sermon* 140a may have followed *Sermon* 140 (FOTC 17.226–29), where Chrysologus concludes by stating his intention to preach on Christ's birth from the Virgin, but most of the sequencing of the sermons concerning the Annunciation and the birth of Christ is almost impossible to ascertain, as the wide variety of scholarly opinions on this matter attests.

2. There is a grammatical error here. The text reads *virgineus partus*. Proper Latin grammar would require *virginei partus* (the genitive case).

3. The Latin is *professio*, used by Chrysologus both as "census" or "enrollment" and as "profession of fealty."

of God is refashioned in the human being;[4] and the coin is rendered to Caesar in such circumstances that the human being is rendered to God, and the statement which was spoken by the Lord is being enacted: "Render to Caesar the things that are Caesar's, and to God the things that are God's."[5]

2. *This first census,* it says, *took place.* It was first in terms of mystery, but not first in time; first in merit, not in order; first not in enrollment, but in faith. But since the world underwent Roman censuses long before this one, how can it be said that now the whole world was being enrolled for the first time, unless it is that divine realities are being mystically foretold by means of human ones?

3. *And so Joseph went up in order to be enrolled with Mary his betrothed wife* (vv.4–5). It is well put that he *went up,* because the way to divine realities is always a lofty ascent. He went up in order to be registered as betrothed, not as a married man; as a guardian,[6] not as a husband;[7] dedicated to the service of the offspring, not to intercourse with the mother; to record that the child in the womb was divine and not human.[8] Mary also went up, so that she would be registered as a maidservant rather than as a parent; to record that she had the symptoms of

---

4. This notion of the two images, one on the coin and the other in the human being, is also found in Chromatius of Aquileia, *Tractatus* 17.2.5 (CCL 9A.270).

5. Mt 22.21.

6. So too in *Sermon* 145.1 (FOTC 17.233). But in *Sermons* 140b.2 and 175.4, it is Christ himself who is called the Bridegroom and guardian.

7. See also *Sermon* 140b.2. In *Sermon* 175.4, Joseph is called a husband *(maritus)* "in name only." Such language does not necessarily mean that Chrysologus thought that Mary and Joseph were not really married. Chrysologus does employ the term *sponsus* ("betrothed") to describe Joseph's relationship with Mary. It is likely that Chrysologus assumed that a man who was called a *coniunx* and *maritus* (both meaning "spouse" or "husband") engaged in carnal relations with his wife, while such a connotation was not implied by the word *sponsus*. Since Chrysologus insists on Mary's perpetual virginity, Joseph could only have been her *sponsus* and clearly not her *coniunx* or *maritus*. See J. P. Barrios, "La naturaleza del vínculo matrimonial entre María y José según San Pedro Crisólogo," *Ephemerides Mariologicae* 16 (1966): 331–35.

8. Although such an expression appears to be monophysite, Chrysologus in other texts clearly affirms Christ's full humanity. At issue here is Christ's origin, which is divine rather than human, since Chrysologus vigorously affirms the virginal conception of Jesus such that his Father is God and not Joseph.

a pregnancy, but not the carnal knowledge;[9] that it was a divine gift and not a human act that made her heavy with child;[10] that, since the virginity of the mother remains, it is believed beyond any doubt and clearly shown that her child is the Creator's offspring.

4. *And while she was there, the days were completed for her to give birth* (v.6). That is, the days of the epochs of this world were completed rather than ordinary days; listen to the Apostle: "When the fullness of time came, God sent his Son,"[11] so that he would assume the infancy of the world. And thus it was that the first man fell while burdened by the weight of a command.[12] So too Noah's posterity tumbled headlong while aiming for the heights of heaven, and was thwarted by the fragmentation of languages.[13]

The Jewish people likewise fell prostrate on the ground while not strong enough to bear the burden of the Law, and preferred being compared with dumb beasts[14] to being put on the same level [with all other peoples] in terms of their ignorance of the Law. Rightly then does the Author of the times await the proper time of the world, and permit this age to be instructed over a long period, so that the world would be more mature to receive its Restorer even at this late hour, since earlier in its immature state it was unable to accept its Creator.[15]

5. *The days were completed for her to give birth, and she bore a Son, and wrapped him in swaddling clothes and laid him in a manger* (vv.6–7). He who encloses the world is enclosed in a womb; the Author of nature is born;[16] the Creator of human beings and of

---

9. The Latin is *conscientiam*, which can also mean merely "awareness." See also *Sermons* 141.2 and 146.3 (FOTC 17.230 and 239).
10. Literally, "that she was carrying a divine gift and not a human weight" *(se . . . portare divinum munus, non pondus humanum)*.
11. Gal 4.4.
12. See Gn 3.6.
13. See Gn 11.1–9.
14. See Ps 48.13 LXX; Ps 49.12.
15. In *Sermon* 147.8 (FOTC 17.246–47), Chrysologus mentions that the Incarnation occurred precisely when people's unfulfilled longing to see God over the course of time had finally brought them to the point of experiencing torment and fatigue.
16. On this same point, see *Sermons* 143.11 and 156.3 (FOTC 17.266).

periods of time becomes the Firstborn of humanity; the Treasure of heaven is clothed with the swaddling clothes of the indigent; he who makes thunderbolts fly gives an infant's cry;[17] in a manger lies the One to whom all creation lies subject.[18]

O man, do you not realize by what means Christ pursues you in order to call you back? He enters the womb in order to refashion you in the womb; he is born in order to make you reborn to immortality;[19] he becomes the Firstborn in order to offer you a share in the divine lineage.[20] Therefore, Christ is laid in a manger, and is placed before the very mouths of beasts, that they recognize their Creator by his fragrance, as it were. And so he is laid in a manger, that the words of the prophet be confirmed: "The ox knows its owner, and the ass its master's manger."[21] And likewise confirming what the psalmist said: "Human beings and beasts you will save, O Lord."[22] For human beings are called beasts,[23] since Christ says to them: "Take my yoke upon you, since it is easy; and my burden, since it is light."[24]

---

17. In *Sermon* 144.1, Chrysologus states that the "Word of God gives an infant's cry." See also *Sermon* 160.2. For a collection of Latin patristic texts on such paradoxes associated with Christ's birth, see A. Olivar, "*Iacebat in praesepio et fulgebat in caelo:* Un estudio sobre fuentes patrísticas de textos litúrgicos," in *Eulogia: Miscellanea liturgica in onore di P. Burkhard Neunheuser* (=*Studia Anselmiana* 68), ed. P. G. Farnedi (Rome: Ed. Anselmiana, 1979), 267–75.

18. See *Sermon* 69.2 (FOTC 109.282) also on this theme.

19. See also *Sermons* 117.4 (FOTC 17.201), and 143.9.

20. On this point, see, e.g., *Sermons* 31.3, 50.2, 60.14, and 71.2 (FOTC 109.132, 194, 236, 285–86), as well as *Sermons* 67.2 and 70.2 (FOTC 17.115, 119–20), and *Sermon* 148a.1.

21. Is 1.3. Other references to this biblical verse as indicating the astuteness of the animals in the stable are *Sermons* 141.4 and 156.8 (FOTC 17.231 and 269).

22. Ps 35.7 LXX; Ps 36.6.

23. See also *Sermon* 141.4 (FOTC 17.231).

24. Mt 11.29 and 30.

SERMON 140B

<A Second> on the Birth of the Lord[1]

ODAY[2] IN ORDER FOR me, brothers, to be able to proclaim the Nativity of the Lord in all its majesty, I need your prayers to obtain from the Lord the means to do this, that he himself put his word in the mouth of his priest, and that he who has today seen fit to enter a partnership[3] with our flesh may not refuse to do this favor for our mouth. For we are not striving, brothers, to reveal the ineffable mystery of the divine generation,[4] but we are eager to announce the great and wonderful joy of our salvation, just as the angel said: *See, I bring you news of great joy which is for all the people* (Lk 2.10).

May this conception, may this birth frighten no one today, brothers. For when virginity conceives, when purity gives birth, it is the power of God, and not pleasure, that is clearly at work.

---

1. (Angle brackets here indicate an addition to the title in Olivar's CCL text.) For Chrysologus's authorship of this sermon, see A. Olivar, *Los sermones*, 338–40. V. Zangara, "I silenzi," 246–50, contests this sermon's authenticity, in part at least because it contains clear reference to having been preached on Christmas Day itself, which he claims Chrysologus never did. The internal evidence of this sermon, however, attests to its authenticity, especially in the numerous terms and ideas employed that are prevalent in other sermons, particularly in those assigned to the Christmas season, which are indisputably by Chrysologus. See *Sermon* 140a, n. 1.

2. From references to "today" in section 1, it is evident that this sermon was preached on Christmas Day. See F. Sottocornola, *L'anno liturgico*, 130–31. On the extent of scholarly debate about the order of this and Chrysologus's other sermons during the Christmas season, see idem, 120–22. A. Olivar, *Los sermones*, 274, suggests that this *Sermon* 140b followed *Sermon* 140a, but that is not likely, especially since it would put 140a *before* Christmas Day.

3. The Latin is *commercium*; see R. Benericetti, *Il Cristo*, 101–3, on this text and other references to this term in Chrysologus's christological preaching.

4. Chrysologus probably means that he is not going to address how the Son was eternally begotten of the Father, inasmuch as he says below that "today . . . divinity did not have its start."

Listen to the angel's words: "The Spirit of the Lord will come upon you, and the power of the Most High will overshadow you."[5] Today, brothers, divinity did not have its start, but humanity is made new;[6] today[7] Christ was born, not for himself, but for me. So, "come to him and be enlightened, and your faces will not blush with shame";[8] because today, as the prophet has said, "He has placed his tent in the sun."[9]

2. What is being accomplished, brothers, is something divine and not human.[10] Never is the virginity naked which is adorned with the eternal cloak of its purity. The angel comes as forerunner[11] to the dwelling place of chastity, in order to prepare the royal court for the King, the temple for God, and the marriage chamber for the heavenly Bridegroom. For when the Lord was born, virginity was not lost but consecrated, which itself bore the Bridegroom and Guardian[12] of its purity.

Mary offers faithful service; pregnant, yet a virgin; a virgin, yet a mother; for it was barrenness, not purity, that she lacked. There stand at hand sanctity, sincerity, modesty, chastity, integrity, and faith,[13] and all the virtues were present together, so that the fearless maidservant would carry her Creator in her womb, and, while being the champion of her sex, she would know no pain or groans in giving birth to the Power of heaven.

---

5. Lk 1.35.

6. Chrysologus puts this antithesis eloquently: *non inchoavit deitas, sed humanitas innovatur.*

7. These two references to "today" provide clear indication that this sermon was delivered on Christmas Day.

8. Ps 33.6 LXX; Ps 34.5.

9. Ps 18.6 LXX; Ps 19.4. On the interpretation of the solar imagery of this psalm in a christological sense by Chrysologus and others, see R. Benericetti, *Il Cristo*, 148–50, and A. Rose, "Les cieux racontent la gloire de Dieu: Psaume 18,1–7," *Les questions liturgiques et paroissiales* 38 (1957): 299–304.

10. That is, the active role in Christ's Incarnation is taken by God. See also on this point, *Sermons* 62a.4 (FOTC 109.246–47), 148.1 and 3 (FOTC 17.247–48 and 250), and 153.1.

11. The Latin is *metator*, which includes also the idea of making preparations in advance. See *Sermon* 140.5 (FOTC 17.228), where it is rendered "harbinger," and, as a title for John the Baptist, *Sermon* 91.5 and n. 17.

12. Cf. *Sermon* 140a.3 and n. 7.

13. Chrysologus uses similar language in praise of the name "Mary" in *Sermon* 146.7 (FOTC 17.241–42).

Blessed is that fruitfulness which both acquired the honor of motherhood and did not lose the prize of chastity. Therefore, he does not disdain to inhabit what he deigned to fashion; he does not think that it is undignified for him to touch flesh since he had handled it in the past with his heavenly hand when it was in the form of dust.[14]

He has come to your face, O man, because you were unable to reach his face; and he who was invisible has become visible[15] for your redemption. The One besought by your ancestors has come. Listen to the voice of one who cries out: "Show your face, and we shall be saved."[16] The witness of innocence and defender of purity[17] stands at hand, and does not grieve that he has lost his bride, but exults in having recognized the Lord; he follows, not as a husband,[18] but as a servant, and he rejoices that he is paying homage to the One whom he observes all the angels serving.[19]

3. So, at the time of his birth Christ, through whom every place was created, finds no place in the inn;[20] and he who is Lord of all the world is born as though a foreigner,[21] to enable us to be citizens whose homeland is heaven.[22] He is wrapped in swaddling clothes[23] in order to restore in his own Body the unity of the human race that had been rent asunder, and bring to the kingdom of heaven the garment of immortality whole and entire, resplendent with the purple color of his blood. He is born, brothers, in order to improve the very nature which the first human being had corrupted. He lies in swaddling clothes,

14. See Gn 2.7.
15. On this point, see *Sermon* 50.1 and n. 2 (FOTC 109.193).
16. Ps 79.4 LXX; Ps 80.3. See *Sermon* 147 (FOTC 17.243–47) on the intense human longing throughout history to gaze upon God's face, which is only satisfied in the Incarnation.
17. A reference to Joseph, who is described in these or similar words in *Sermons* 145.1 (FOTC 17.233) and 175.4. See also Ambrose, *Expositio Evangelii secundum Lucam* 2.2 and 4–5 (CCL 14.31–33); Augustine, *Sermon* 225.2 (FOTC 38.190); and Prudentius, *The Divinity of Christ* 602–3 (FOTC 52.25).
18. On this point, see *Sermon* 140a.3 and n. 7.
19. See Mt 1.18–25 and Lk 2.13.
20. See Lk 2.7.
21. For similar paradoxes, see *Sermons* 50.3 (FOTC 109.194–95) and 79.5.
22. Chrysologus makes this point also in *Sermon* 50.2 (FOTC 109.194).
23. See Lk 2.7.

but he reigns in heaven; he rests humbly in a cradle, but he thunders amid the clouds;[24] he is placed in a manger,[25] because it is evident that "all flesh is grass,"[26] as Isaiah says. This is the grass, brothers, whose blossom is transformed into heavenly Bread, and by feasting on it we reach life eternal.[27]

    24. For other comparable antitheses associated with Christ's birth, see *Sermon* 140a.5 and n. 17.
    25. See Lk 2.7.
    26. Is 40.6.
    27. A similar likely eucharistic allusion is found in Ambrose, *Expositio Evangelii secundum Lucam* 2.43 (CCL 14.50), and another is even more explicit in Chromatius of Aquileia, *Sermon* 32.3 (CCL 9A.145). In one manuscript this *Sermon* 140b continues with an additional discussion of the flight into Egypt (Mt 2.14–15). Reasons for judging this concluding section as spurious can be found in A. Olivar, "Sobre un sermón de Epiphanía y un fragmento de sermón de Navidad atribuídos erróneamente a san Pedro Crisólogo," *Ephemerides Liturgicae* 67 (1953): 135–37.

SERMON 142

<A Second> on the Annunciation of the Lord[1]

OU HAVE HEARD TODAY, brothers, an angel having a discussion with a woman concerning the repair of the human being. You have heard that the purpose was for the human being to return to life by the same course by which he had fallen to his death.[2] An angel has dealings, yes, has dealings with Mary concerning salvation, because an angel had had dealings with Eve concerning destruction.[3] You have heard about an angel constructing from the mud of our flesh a temple of divine majesty with ineffable skill. You have heard that in a mystery that exceeds our understanding God was placed on earth, and the human being was placed in heaven. You have heard that in an unheard-of manner God and man were mingled[4] in one body. You have heard that the frail nature of our flesh was strengthened by the angel's exhortation to bear God in all his glory.

1. (Angle brackets here indicate an addition to the title in Olivar's CCL text.) This sermon was preached shortly before Christmas and is a continuation of another which is probably not among those that are extant and which concluded by commenting on Lk 1.30. See F. Sottocornola, *L'anno liturgico*, 115 and 119, and A. Olivar, *Los sermones*, 273.
2. On this notion of "recapitulation" in Chrysologus and other Latin Christian authors, see *Sermon* 77.7 and n. 11.
3. See Gn 3.1–5. On Mary as "new Eve" in Chrysologus's preaching, see also *Sermons* 74.3, 140.4, 148.5 (FOTC 17.124–25, 228, 251), 64.2 (FOTC 109.255), 77.4, and 99.5.
4. The Latin is *misceri*. Although after the Council of Chalcedon in 451 this term was deemed to be imprecise and tending toward a monophysite view of Christ, Chrysologus did not use it with the latter intention. Leo the Great in *Sermon* 23.1 (preached in 442) used the same term to indicate the union of the divine and human in Christ (see CCL 138.103; FOTC 93.88, where it is translated as "connected"). *Mixtio* is virtually equivalent to *commercium*, meaning "mutual interpenetration." See M. Herz, *Sacrum Commercium* (Munich: Karl Zink, 1958), 121–22 and 139; and R. Benericetti, *Il Cristo*, 99–103.

2. And so, in order that the fine sand of our body in Mary not give way under the excessive weight of the construction from heaven, and that in the Virgin the thin twig[5] not be broken which was about to bear fruit for the benefit of the whole human race, the voice of the angel spoke out right away so as to banish fear with these words: *Do not be afraid, Mary* (Lk 1.30). Before the matter at hand, the Virgin's dignity is made known from her name, for *Mary* in the Hebrew language is translated "Lady." Therefore, the angel calls her "Lady," so that any trepidation coming from being a servant may depart from the Lord's mother, since the very authority of her offspring caused and mandated that she be born and called a Lady.[6]

3. *Do not be afraid, Mary: you have found grace* (v.30).[7] It is true: the one who has found grace knows no fear. *You have found grace.* Before whom? *Before God* (v.30). Blessed is she who alone among human beings has been counted worthy to hear these words as applied to her ahead of everyone else: *You have found grace.* How much? As much as he had said just previously: the full amount.[8] And it truly is the full amount which rains down and over all creation in a drenching shower.[9]

4. *You have found grace before God.* When he says this, even the angel himself is amazed either that the woman has found so much, or that all human beings have found life through the woman. The angel marvels that God has come in his entirety

---

5. Chrysologus engages in wordplay here: *in virgine . . . virga.*

6. There is some question about the accuracy of this etymology from Hebrew, although the Hebrew *mar* does mean "lord." "Lady" is the feminine equivalent of "Lord" as the Latin makes clear: *domina* and *dominus.* See also Jerome, *Liber Interpretationis Hebraicorum Nominum* 62.19–20 (CCL 72.137), where Jerome states that "Mary" means *domina* in the Syrian language. Regarding Chrysologus on this topic, see H. Barré, "La royauté de Marie pendant les neuf premiers siècles," *Recherches de Science Religieuse* 29 (1939): 136; and B. Kochaniewicz, *La Vergine Maria,* 241–44 and 257–58. It is also noteworthy that in *Sermon* 146.7 (FOTC 17.241) Chrysologus finds significance in the fact that Mary's name in Latin—*maria*—is also the term for "seas," and he points to biblical references to seas whose waters impart life. There is a typographical error in Olivar's text: *suis* should read *sui,* modifying "offspring." See PL 52.579.

7. The Latin word *gratia* means both "grace" and "favor."

8. See Lk 1.28.

9. On a rain-shower as an image of the Incarnation, see *Sermon* 60.5 and n. 20 (FOTC 109.233–34).

within the confines[10] of the Virgin's womb, God, for whom creation, even when considered together in its entirety, is confining. This is why the angel lingers, this is why he mentions her merit when he calls the Virgin, mentions grace when he summons her, and has difficulty explaining the situation to her as she listens; it stands to reason that it is only with difficulty and a fair bit of anxiety that he finds the right words to help her to understand this. Consider, brothers, with what reverence and fear it is right and proper for us to take part in so great a mystery, when the angel does not dispel the fear of his listener without fear himself.

5. *And now you will receive in your womb* (v.31). It is well put that *you will receive* what flesh does not know, what your condition does not possess, what nature does not allow. *You will receive in your womb.* Who gathers a harvest before laboring and perspiring over the earth? Who obtains fruit before devoting and expending his energy on the plant? Who arrives at any place for lodging without traveling along the road? Who experiences a growth in nature apart from nature? Therefore, blessed, truly blessed indeed, is Mary, who obtained so glorious an offspring without the concerns associated with begetting, with none of the distresses connected with motherhood.

Blessed is she who received and kept the divine Child in her heart in such a way that she was unaware of it from all the external indications of her body. Blessed is she who thus committed and entrusted to her breast[11] alone what she had received from heaven by the message of an angel. It is a heavenly enterprise that is being carried out within the Virgin's house in such a way that the house itself does not notice it since it is kept locked with its bolts intact.

6. *You will conceive and bear a Son* (v.31). The One who goes in and out, and leaves no traces of his entrance or exit, is a divine, and not a human, inhabitant. And the One who keeps his mother a virgin at his conception, and leaves her a virgin at his

---

10. The "confinement" of God in the Incarnate Son is also noted in *Sermons* 50.3 (FOTC 109.194–95), 143.8, and 147.1 (FOTC 17.243).
11. On this point, see *Sermons* 140.5 (FOTC 17.228) and 143.8.

birth,[12] is not an earthly man, but a heavenly Man. So, let the law of our flesh yield its place, let our nature claim nothing here as its own, when for the divine offspring the law from heaven is established according to the divine nature. May our speaking about conception and birth not weary the mind of the listener, but may it stir up the Christian's understanding more than a little, when for a heavenly offspring divine signs of God's power are being accomplished.

7. *You will conceive and bear a Son.* He did not say "for you," nor did he say "your." Why? It is because *he will be called holy and the Son of God* (v.35). O Virgin, grace, and not nature, has made you a mother; God's merciful devotion wanted you to be called a "Mother," which your continence did not allow; in your conceiving, in your giving birth, purity grew, chastity increased, continence was strengthened, virginity was made firm, and all the virtues continued to thrive.[13] O Virgin, if everything is preserved for you, what did you provide? If you are a virgin, how are you a mother? If a bride, how a mother? By the action of the One who has added to all you have and has taken nothing away.

O Virgin, your Creator has had his beginning from you, your Origin arises from you, in your offspring is your Father, in your flesh is your God, and the very One who gave the world light has acquired the world's light through you. Therefore, having been advised by an angel, O Virgin, do not presume to call him your son, but as soon as you give birth, call him Savior, because virginity does not bear a son for itself, but bears a child for the Creator, and continence carries its Lord, not its nursling, as the angel says: *And you will call his name Jesus* (v.31), which in the Hebrew language means "Savior."[14]

12. See, for example, *Sermons* 62.8 (FOTC 109.242–43), 117.3 (FOTC 17.200), 148.1 (FOTC 17.247–48), and 148a.3 regarding affirmations of Mary's perpetual virginity.

13. Mary is also presented as an exemplification of all the virtues in *Sermon* 140b.2.

14. Regarding this etymology, see also *Sermon* 59.5 and n. 12 (FOTC 109.226–27), as well as *Sermons* 57.5 and 61.4 (FOTC 17.106–7, 113), *Sermons* 60.5, and 62a.2 (FOTC 109.234, 246), and *Sermon* 144.5. See also Augustine, *The Trinity* 13.10.14 (FOTC 45.389).

8. *But Mary said to the angel: "How will this happen?"* (v.34) Notice Mary asking a question, and if whoever asks expresses doubt, why is Zechariah the only one to incur blame as a skeptical interrogator?[15] It is because the One who knows one's deepest thoughts examined not the words, but the hearts; he judged not what they said, but what their intentions were. For what prompted them to ask their questions was dissimilar, and the way they presented themselves was entirely different.

She believed against nature, he doubts out of consideration for nature. She asks about how the whole matter will unfold, he insists that what God orders cannot be done. He is not willing to believe even with the inducement of prior examples, she is quick to believe even without the benefit of any precedent. She expresses wonder about a virgin giving birth, he is incredulous about a conception from wedlock. And so it is right that she speaks, that she acknowledges her God, and confesses that he is in her body; he is speechless until he should be proven wrong in denying that John would be born by bringing him to life from his own body.

9. *How will this happen?* Why do you ask? *Since I do not know man* (v.34). O woman, what man are you looking for? Is it the one whom you lost in paradise? Restore the man, O woman, restore the one placed here by God; restore from yourself the one whom you lost at your own hands;[16] disregard the order of nature, but recognize the order of the Creator. He will take and fashion a man from you, he who in the beginning fashioned you and took you from a man.[17]

Do not look for a man, let human work cease since divine skill is sufficient to restore the human being. This is why God himself came to you, because you were displeased that the human being had not[18] attained to God; no longer does flesh come to flesh, but *the Holy Spirit will come upon you* (v.35), since "what is born from flesh is flesh, and what is born of spirit is

---

15. See Lk 1.18–20. On this point, see *Sermon* 88.2 (FOTC 17.138).
16. A rather backhanded compliment to Mary as new Eve! See n. 3 above, as well as *Sermons* 64.4 (FOTC 109.258–59) and 80.3 (FOTC 17.129).
17. See Gn 2.21–22.
18. Adding the textual variant *non* to Olivar's CCL text.

spirit, since God is Spirit."[19] Therefore, the one who is born of the Spirit is indisputably God.[20]

10. *The Holy Spirit will come upon you, and the power of the Most High will overshadow you* (v.35). The power of God overshadows her so that human frailty may not collapse as it is about to bear God. *And the power of the Most High will overshadow you.* She is not to know the heat of our body, since the shadow of God's power protects her, nor is she to look for some earthly lodging tucked away in private, since she sees that she is wrapped all around in a cloak of heavenly splendor.

11. *For this reason the child that will be born from you will be called holy and the Son of God* (v.35). Let no one take "holy" in an ordinary sense here, but with that uniqueness with which the heavens resound: "Holy, Holy, Holy Lord God of hosts."[21]

12. Mary, however, is sent to Elizabeth,[22] a virgin to a barren woman, a child to an old woman, so that in their pious contest both may take something, both may equally obtain something: that the one may gain faith from a situation without precedent, and the other may gain virtue from the strictures of her situation.[23] When she heard these things Mary responded:

13. *I am the maidservant of the Lord; let it be done to me according to your word* (v.38). She who is called "Lady"[24] by the angel recognizes and acknowledges that she is a maidservant, because when a devout soul is blessed with honors it grows more reverent and increases in grace; it does not exult in arrogance, nor swell up with pride. *Let it be done to me according to your word.* She who puts her trust in the word is deemed worthy to conceive the Word—"In the beginning was the Word, and the Word was with God, and the Word was God"[25]—and she attains to the

---

19. Jn 3.6 and 4.24.
20. See R. Benericetti, *Il Cristo*, 176–78, regarding Chrysologus's "Spirit christology," although Benericetti seems to overstate his case in seeing references to "Spirit" in texts such as this one as referring not to the Holy Spirit but to the Son as agent of his own Incarnation.
21. Is 6.3.
22. See Lk 1.36–37 and 39–45.
23. Literally, "a virtue out of necessity" *(de necessitate virtutem)*. On this expression, see, e.g., *Sermon* 42.5 and n. 24 (FOTC 109.171).
24. See above, section 2.
25. Jn 1.1.

whole reality, since she gives her consent to the mystery with the hearing of faith.[26] How sinful is the heretic[27] who does not believe after the event, when he notices that she had such great trust before the event!

26. See Rom 10.17.
27. Perhaps an Arian who would not hold to the full divinity of the Word, or a Nestorian who would refuse Mary the title "Mother of God" (see *Sermon* 145.6, FOTC 17.235–36).

SERMON 143

<A Third> on the Annunciation of the Lord[1]

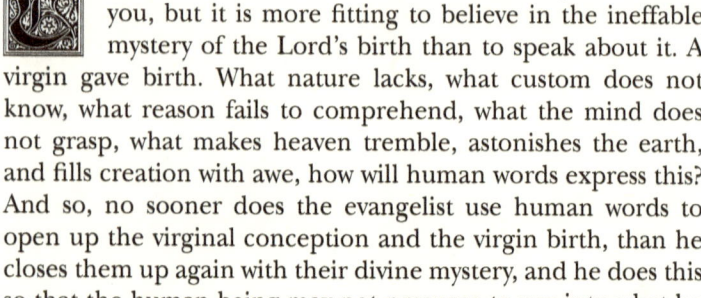ERTAINLY A SERMON ON the Nativity is owed to you, but it is more fitting to believe in the ineffable mystery of the Lord's birth than to speak about it. A virgin gave birth. What nature lacks, what custom does not know, what reason fails to comprehend, what the mind does not grasp, what makes heaven tremble, astonishes the earth, and fills creation with awe, how will human words express this? And so, no sooner does the evangelist use human words to open up the virginal conception and the virgin birth, than he closes them up again with their divine mystery, and he does this so that the human being may not presume to pry into what he has been commanded to believe. Who can approach the mystery of God, the virgin birth, the causes of events, the activity of the ages, the partnership[2] between divinity and flesh, and the mystery that man and God are one God?[3]

2. Thus the evangelist says: *The angel Gabriel was sent by the Lord to a town of Galilee named Nazareth, to a virgin betrothed to a man named Joseph, and the virgin's name was Mary* (Lk 1.26–27). *The angel was sent by the Lord.* When an angel is the mediator, let

---

1. (Angle brackets here indicate an addition to the title in Olivar's CCL text.) In spite of the title, which comes, of course, from a later editor, and the fact that the Gospel text on which this sermon is based deals with the Annunciation to Mary, this sermon was preached early in the Christmas season. It is likely that it followed *Sermon* 141 (FOTC 17.229–32) and immediately preceded *Sermon* 144. See F. Sottocornola, *L'anno liturgico*, 115–20; V. Zangara, "I silenzi," 232–40; and A. Olivar, *Los sermones*, 273.

2. The Latin is *commercium*, meaning also "mutual interpenetration." See *Sermon* 142.1, n. 4.

3. According to R. Benericetti, *Il Cristo*, 103 and n. 121, by this expression Chrysologus is not expressing a monophysite christology but rather the unity within Christ of the divine Son of God and his divinized humanity.

human conjecture cease. When the messenger is a heavenly one, let any earthly explanation be rejected. Let human curiosity fade when the envoy is celestial.

The angel was sent by the Lord. The one who is quite attentive in listening to who was sent and by whom avoids delving too much into the hidden ways of God.[4] The one who is worthy of knowing what God enjoins through the angel is the one who is afraid to know it. Listen to God as he says: "Upon whom shall I rest? I shall rest upon the person who is humble, meek, and who trembles at my words."[5] "Humble and meek": as meek as the person is who complies with orders, equally brazen is the one who argues about God's orders.

3. *The angel was sent to a virgin* (vv.26–27). This is because virginity is always akin to the angels. To live in the flesh apart from the flesh is not an earthly life, but a heavenly one. And if you want to know something, it is greater to acquire the glory of an angel than to possess it in the first place. To be an angel is a matter of happiness, to be a virgin is a matter of virtue. For virginity obtains by strength what the angel possesses by nature. Therefore, an angel and a virgin are each a divine rank, not a human one.

4. *The angel came and said to her: "Hail, full of grace, the Lord is with you, blessed are you among women"* (v.28). *Hail, full of grace, the Lord is with you.* You see with what sort of dowry the Virgin has been pledged.[6] *Hail, full of grace, the Lord is with you. Hail,* that is, "receive."[7] What? The dowry of virtue,[8] not of shame. *Hail, full of grace.* This is the grace that gave glory to heaven, God to earth, faith to the nations, an end to vices, order to life, discipline to behavior. The angel brought down this grace; the

---

4. The idea that the Incarnation is a matter so profound and mysterious that it is accessible only to faith, demands a reverent response, and must not be overly scrutinized, analyzed, or debated, is frequently reiterated by Chrysologus. In addition to his sermons, he also mentioned this in his *Letter to Eutyches* 1 (FOTC 17.286).
5. Is 66.2.
6. Namely, to Christ. See *Sermon* 140.2 (FOTC 17.227).
7. Chrysologus interprets the angel's greeting in the same fashion in *Sermon* 140.3 (FOTC 17.227).
8. The Latin *virtus* also connotes "strength" and "power."

Virgin accepted it and would in turn impart salvation to the world.

5. *Hail, full of grace.* Grace bestowed itself to individuals piecemeal, but to Mary the fullness of grace gave itself in its entirety all at once. "All of us," the evangelist says, "have received of his fullness."[9] Hence David too says: "It descends just like rain upon fleece."[10] When fleece is taken from the body, it does not know the body's suffering; so too when virginity is in the flesh, it has no knowledge of the vices of the flesh. And so a heavenly shower rained down on the fleece of the Virgin, falling ever so gently, and the whole wave of divinity hid itself in the absorbent fleece of our flesh, until that fleece would be squeezed on the yoke of the cross and pour out upon all the earth the rain of salvation—"and just as raindrops moisten the earth"[11]—in order that just the right amount of rain would water the tender buds of faith with its life-giving drops and not leave them dry.[12] *Hail, full of grace, the Lord is with you.*

6. *The angel was sent by the Lord.* And what does he say? *The Lord is with you.* And so he who had sent his messenger to the Virgin was with the Virgin. God preceded his messenger, but without departing from the Godhead. He who is present in all places cannot be confined any place, and he is everywhere in his entirety, without whom everything amounts to nothing.

7. *Blessed are you among women.* Truly blessed is she who has both retained the glory of virginity and achieved the dignity of motherhood.[13] Truly blessed is she, since she has both been deemed worthy of the grace of a conception from heaven, and won the crown of purity. Truly blessed is she who has both received the honor of having a divine offspring, and become the Queen of all chastity. Truly blessed is she who was greater than heaven, stronger than the earth, wider than the world, for she alone contained God, whom the world does not contain; she

---

9. Jn 1.16.   10. Ps 71 (72).6.
11. Ibid.

12. For other examples of early Christian christological and mariological interpretation of this psalm, see *Sermon* 60.5 and n. 20 (FOTC 109.233–34).

13. On the paradox of Mary being both virgin and mother, see also *Sermons* 58.5 and 59.7 (FOTC 109.223, 227).

carried him who carries the world; she gave birth to her Creator,[14] she nourished the One who nourishes all living things.[15] But let us see what the evangelist says.

8. When Mary saw the angel, he says, *she was troubled at his arrival* (v.29). The flesh was troubled, she was disturbed within, her mind trembled, she was astounded in the very depth of her heart,[16] because at the entrance of the angel the Virgin realized that God had entered. The temple of the human body was troubled, and the narrow confines were being shaken in that dwelling formed of flesh, since God in all his magnitude was establishing himself in the Virgin's breast,[17] and within the narrow boundaries of her breast such great majesty squeezed itself in.

9. But if it is acceptable, before penetrating the depths of the Christian faith, let us address those who regard the virgin birth, the great mystery of loving-kindness,[18] the restoration of human salvation, as an injury to divinity. God came to the Virgin, that is, the Craftsman to his work, the Creator to his creation. Since when does the restoration of a work not redound to the craftsman's honor? Since when is it not considered a glorious honor if the maker should repair what he made? To avoid letting what he has made go to ruin, is there anyone who does not renovate it when it grows old, and when it collapses does not set it up straight, and when it is falling into disrepair does not fix and improve it?

Therefore, what is being accomplished in the virgin birth is no injury to the Creator, but the creature's salvation. If God has made the human being, who blames him for having remade him? And why do we think it is proper that he fashioned the human being out of mud[19] but consider it improper that he did

---

14. The Latin word *genitor* means literally "begetter" or "father," suggesting that the eternal Son begot Mary inasmuch as the divine power to create belongs to him as God, equal to the Father.
15. On similar paradoxes, see *Sermon* 140.5 (FOTC 17.228).
16. The same sort of reaction is noted in *Sermon* 140.5 (FOTC 17.228). See also *Sermon* 127.1 and n. 3.
17. On this same point, see *Sermons* 140.5 (FOTC 17.228) and 142.5.
18. See 1 Tm 3.16.
19. See Gn 2.7.

the refashioning out of flesh?[20] What is more valuable, flesh or mud? Therefore, the more valuable the material of our restoration, the greater the glory.

10. Or when is God not the Molder of the human being in the womb? Listen to Job: "Your hands made me and fashioned me."[21] And later: "You caused me to coagulate like milk, you clothed me with skin and flesh, you put me together with bones and muscles, and you gave me life and mercy."[22] And David said: "You have formed me and placed your hand upon me."[23] And God said to Jeremiah: "Before you were conceived I knew you, and I sanctified you in the womb."[24]

So if he fashioned the features of Job in the uterus of the one who bore him, if he put David's members together in his mother's womb, if he sanctified Jeremiah while he was still inside his mother, if he filled John with the Holy Spirit in the womb of a barren woman,[25] what is so strange now if he has dwelt in the Virgin's womb? The very One who created woman from the side of a man[26] has recreated man from the womb of a woman, and has refashioned man from the body of the Virgin.[27] And so, O man, the very matter that seems new to you is considered old to God.

11. But you say: why was there need for God to be born,[28] since he has at his disposal the power to perform any action? Why? It is because by being born he had remade the nature which he had made through creation, because that nature which had been made to propagate life was propagating death.[29] Through the sin of the first man nature received a

---

20. A similar point is made in *Sermons* 141.3 and 148.1 (FOTC 17.230–31 and 248).
21. Jb 10.8.
22. Jb 10.10–12.
23. Ps 138 (139).5.
24. Jer 1.5.
25. See Lk 1.41.
26. See Gn 2.21–23.
27. See also *Sermon* 57.6 (FOTC 17.107).
28. That the Incarnation was not for any need or lack on God's part, but rather out of a will to save humanity, is a point made also in *Sermons* 148.1 (FOTC 17.248) and 148a.2.
29. For more on this issue, see *Sermon* 111.5 (FOTC 17.178).

lethal wound, and what was the beginning of life began to be the origin of death. So this is the rationale for the Nativity, this is what compelled Christ to be born, that the Nativity of the Creator would provide nature with a cure, and nature's healing would bring her children to life.[30]

30. On this same point, see, e.g., *Sermon* 156.3 (FOTC 17.266).

SERMON 144

<A Fourth> on the Annunciation of the Lord[1]

CONCERNING CHRIST'S Nativity, the loftiness of the matter and the magnitude of the mystery cause and compel us to delay our sermon. A virgin has given birth: who will speak of it? "The Word was made flesh";[2] who will tell of it? If the Word of God gives an infant's cry,[3] how will the human being brought to perfection by such means proclaim this verbally? As the star provided light at night for the Magi who were searching for him,[4] a teacher's[5] sermon about the Lord's birth furnishes as much illumination for those who listen, causing them to rejoice that they have found Christ, and not to presume to debate about it; to honor the infant with gifts,[6] and not to belittle him. But pray, brothers, that he who grew gradually in our body, may see fit to grow little by little in our discourse.

2. Today the evangelist related that the angel spoke as follows: *Do not be afraid, Mary, you have found grace before God* (Lk 1.30). *Do not be afraid, Mary.* Why? Because you have found something. The one who is afraid is not the one who has found, but the one who has lost something.[7] She found, yes, she found the grace of her heavenly offspring by conceiving, while not losing her distinction as a virgin by giving birth. *Do not be afraid,*

---

1. (Angle brackets here indicate an addition to the title in Olivar's CCL text.) This sermon was preached shortly after Christmas Day and followed *Sermon* 143. See *Sermon* 143, n. 1.
2. Jn 1.14.
3. On this and other paradoxes, see *Sermon* 140a.5 and n. 17.
4. See Mt 2:1–2, 7, and 9.
5. On references in Chrysologus's preaching to the bishop's function as teacher *(doctor)*, see R. Benericetti, *Il Cristo*, 60, n. 28.
6. See Mt 2.11.
7. Chrysologus makes this point, albeit much more tersely, in *Sermon* 142.3.

Mary. What is she afraid of, seeing that she conceives the One who keeps the universe secure, and gives birth to the One who is the joy of the ages? There is nothing to be afraid of when it is a divine and not a human enterprise; when one is cognizant of virtue[8] and not shame. What does she fear who receives the one who inspires fear in all things that are feared themselves? What does she fear who has the Judge of the case as her advocate, and who has Purity as witness to her innocence?[9]

3. *Do not be afraid, Mary, you have found grace before God.* The Virgin found within herself what "was in the beginning with God,"[10] the Word that is God, and she was made a great temple of God, although she was a small abode of humanity, and the magnitude of the Virgin's womb contained the One whom the small size of a human body could not contain.[11]

4. *Do not be afraid, Mary. And now,* it says, *you will conceive in your womb* (vv.30–31). *You will conceive in your womb:* out of respect it would have been sufficient to have said only *you will conceive.* Why is it that he added *in your womb?* It was to show that it was a true conception, and not a figure of speech; that it was an actual birth, and not a metaphor; to show that just as the true God was born from the true God,[12] so too from a true conception a true human body was born. In Christ's birth, brothers, bodily harm, but not bodily nature, was removed; the creature was not obliterated, but the fault was done away with. Therefore, it is a heresy that makes the false assertion that Christ took on a body made of air, and did not have flesh, but concocts the claim that he merely pretended to be a man.[13]

---

8. Or "power" *(virtus)* which comes from God in bringing about the virginal conception. See *Sermon* 140b.1.

9. In *Sermons* 140b.2 and 145.1 (FOTC 17.233), it is Joseph who is the witness to Mary's innocence.

10. Jn 1.2.

11. For other paradoxes associated with Christ's birth, see *Sermons* 140a.5 and 140b.3.

12. The Latin *de vero deo deus verus* is taken from the Nicene Creed. See N. Tanner, ed., *Decrees of the Ecumenical Councils*, vol. 1 (London and Washington, D. C.: Sheed and Ward/Georgetown University, 1990), 5.

13. In *Sermon* 58.6 (FOTC 109.223) Chrysologus also opposes a docetic christology that would deny that Christ really died. Chrysologus's reference to a "body made of air" echoes a charge against Marcion's teaching that Christ's

5. *You will conceive in the womb*, it says, *and you will bear a Son, and you will call his name Jesus* (v.31). What is "Jesus" in Hebrew, is called "sotir" in Greek, and "salvator" in Latin.[14] So it is right that everything is kept safely intact[15] for the Virgin who bore the Savior of all. *And you will call his name Jesus.* It is because in this name God is adored in all his majesty; the whole of those who abide in heaven, the entirety of those who dwell on earth, and all who are confined within the depths of hell fall prostrate in adoration before this name. Listen to the Apostle as he says: "So that at Jesus' name every knee should bend in heaven, on earth, and under the earth."[16]

This is the name that gave sight to the blind, hearing to the deaf, mobility to the lame, speech to the mute, and life to the dead, and the strength of this name has cast out[17] the devil and all his power from bodies that had been possessed.[18] And if the name is so great, how great must its power be? But who this One is who is called by this name, let the angel now say.

6. *And he will be called*, he says, *the Son of the Most High* (v.32). You see that what the Virgin conceives is no earthly offspring, but a heavenly one. It is the Virgin who gave birth, but God who acknowledged the Son as his own.[19] Therefore, all that a person ends up doing who debates about this Nativity from a human perspective is to take great pains to insult so great a Father.

7. *And the Lord will give him*, he says, *the throne of David his fa-*

---

flesh derived from "the stars and the air" *(sideream . . . carnem et aëream)*. See Ps.-Tertullian, *Adversus Omnes Haereses* 6.5 (CCL 2.1409).

14. And "savior" in English. On this etymology, see *Sermon* 142.7 and n. 14.

15. Chrysologus engages in the wordplay: *salva* and *salvator*. Mary's virginity is preserved "safely intact" because she is bearing the world's "Savior."

16. Phil 2.10.

17. Reading the variant *effugavit* instead of the *effugatur* of Olivar's CCL text.

18. See Is 35.5–6; Mt 11.5; Mk 7.37; Lk 7.22 and 10.17. A similar list of miracles accomplished by Christ is found in *Sermon* 150.10.

19. This is a way of asserting that it is God who is Christ's Father, based on the practice in the Roman world of the father picking up and accepting his newborn child, ensuring the baby's legitimacy and welcome into the family. Chrysologus may have had in mind the Gospel accounts of Christ's Baptism or Transfiguration where the Father proclaimed that Jesus was his beloved Son. See Mt 3.17 and 17.5 and parallels.

ther (v.32). From this the heretic produces his fog of unbelief, here he manufactures material for his error. "Take note," he says, "—these are not my words, but the angel's—*the Lord God will give him.* Is not the one who gives greater than the one who receives? And the one who receives something did not have it before receiving it." But, brothers, let us listen to these words not as unbelievers, but as believers, and may we have as evidence in support of faith what they have as the occasion of their error.

The Lord God will give him. Who is giving? Or to whom is he giving? Is it, at any rate, anyone other than God who gives it to man, divinity to flesh? *God will give him.* God who? Certainly the Word, which "was in the beginning"[20] always God. To whom is he giving? To the One who "became flesh and dwelt among us."[21] Listen to the Apostle as he says: "God was in Christ reconciling the world to himself":[22] indeed to himself, and not to another.

Therefore, this God, who was in Christ, was giving the kingdom to himself in Christ, and was conferring on the body which he had assumed what he had always possessed in his divinity, as is indicated by the angel's own words: *The Lord God will give him the throne of David his father.* You see that when he receives it, he is called Son of David; when he gives it, he is named Son of God; he himself said: "All that the Father has is mine."[23]

And what need is there to receive, when the power to possess already exists? He says: "All that the Father has is mine." Who receives what is his own? Or is it owing to the favor of the one who gives it if what is bestowed already belongs to the one who receives it? We acknowledge that he received it; but it is he who was born, who assumed flesh, who assumed infancy, who endured the cradle, who assumed life's various stages, who faced life's toils, who felt hunger, who experienced thirst, who did not avoid suffering so many forms of indignity, who mounted the cross, who underwent death, who entered the tomb.

20. Jn 1.2.
21. Jn 1.14.
22. 2 Cor 5.19.
23. Jn 16.15.

O heretic,[24] ascribe to this one anything that he received. Or do you suppose that he who received such indignities from human beings disdains receiving honor from God? Or do you think that he who was willing to suffer pain and death at the hands of his enemies considers it distasteful to have the kingdom conferred on him by the Father? O heretic, if only you understood that what has to do with indignity, infancy, stages in life, time, whatever is given or received, diminution,[25] and death is not predicated of divinity, but of the body, you would then inflict no indignity on the Son, and you would introduce no disparity into the Trinity.[26] But let us return to ourselves,[27] and let us speak now about what pertains to us.

8. *The Lord God*, it says, *will give him the throne of David his father, and he will reign over the house of Jacob forever, and of his kingdom there will be no end* (vv.32–33). He who was always seated with his Father in heaven has now received the throne of David on earth. He who has always reigned in his own right, has now obtained an eternal kingdom over the house of Jacob for us. Let us rejoice, brothers, because he who has reigned in his own right is about to reign for us.[28] Let us rejoice, because he will come to reign over the earth, so that we can reign with him.

Listen to the Apostle: "If we suffer with him, we shall reign with him."[29] He was born for us, and so he certainly will come to bestow the kingdom upon us, as he himself promises when he says: "Come, blessed of my Father, receive the kingdom that has been prepared for you from the beginning of the world."[30] He said: "for you," and not "for me."[31] He will come, in order to

---

24. As elsewhere in Chrysologus's preaching, the heretic in question is clearly Arian. See Introduction, FOTC 109.19–20.

25. On this diminishment of the Son as Incarnate but not in his divinity vis-à-vis the Father, see, e.g., *Sermons* 58.5 and 60.4 (FOTC 109.223, 232–33), and 148.1 (FOTC 17.248).

26. The disparity at issue is the radical subordination of the Son to the Father, characteristic of Arian theology.

27. That is, to us who assent to correct doctrine.

28. Chrysologus makes this same point when preaching on "Thy kingdom come" of the Lord's Prayer. See, e.g., *Sermon* 72.5 and n. 18 (FOTC 109.295).

29. 2 Tm 2.12. 30. Mt 25.34.

31. That Christ's coming was for the benefit of humanity and not for his own good is mentioned also in *Sermon* 140b.1.

be always with us, in order to be before our eyes, he who now is enclosed so tightly within our hearts. He will come, so that the ones whose glory comes from the kingdom may have confidence from their intimacy.

9. *And of his kingdom there will be no end* (v.33). You who believe that he will come,[32] rejoice, because he has promised a kingdom without end, where there is no one to replace you in your regal service, and where dignities last forever. But why is it that those who are ambitious for goods that will pass away are not ambitious for goods that will endure? Why is it, why is it, I ask, that they pay a high price for perishable honors, but want to receive eternal honors for free?

Brothers, one's status is prepared here, ranks are determined here, honors are assigned here; the one who has not received a testimonial letter[33] from putting his faith in the Gospel here, will not possess there the insignia of eternal dignities. Therefore, if such service is pleasing, and if we wish to serve forever, let us take up the arms of Christ, "let us stay awake and be sober,"[34] let us conquer the devil, and let us overthrow the vices, so that we can receive our rewards and crowns together.

---

32. For references in Chrysologus's sermons to Christ's second coming at the end of time, his *adventus*, see R. Benericetti, *Il Cristo*, 145, n. 40, and F. Sottocornola, *L'anno liturgico*, 273–78.

33. A letter of introduction that will ensure the bearer's admission, metaphorically speaking.

34. 1 Thes 5.6.

SERMON 148A

<A Fourth on the Nativity of the Lord>[1]

TO GIVE ADEQUATE EXPRESSION to what the magnitude of the mystery of salvation and the profound sacredness of the Lord's Nativity demand, no dutiful acts of homage nor words of praise suffice. Indeed, what will our feeble devotion offer in response to so great a gift and to such great grace, when the Only-Begotten Son of the Most High Father, coeternal with the Father, and inspiring awe in heaven, on earth, and under the earth,[2] willed to submit to being united[3] with a human body for the salvation of humankind? Or what tongue will be able to tell of it, what familiar experience can be drawn upon to inquire into it,[4] and, really, what human being will attempt to appraise it, in which he has God as his only source and witness? "For no one knows the Son except the Father."[5] How is frail humanity that is corrupted by sins able to make headway into the secret of the virgin birth?

---

1. (Angle brackets here indicate an addition to the title in Olivar's CCL text.) The parallels in both terminology and content between this sermon and some of the indisputably authentic sermons of Chrysologus convincingly demonstrate that he was also the author of this sermon. See A. Olivar, *Los sermones*, 324–27. F. Sottocornola, *L'anno liturgico*, 120, believes that this sermon was preached on Christmas Day. He does not, however, present any compelling evidence for his position. V. Zangara, "I silenzi," 244, is of the opinion, probably correct, that this sermon was preached shortly after Christmas. The one sermon we possess that was certainly preached on Christmas Day, and thus contrary to Chrysologus's usual practice, is *Sermon* 140b. For more on Chrysologus's custom of not preaching on Christmas Day, see *Sermon* 140a, n. 1, and *Sermon* 140b, nn. 1 and 2.

2. See Phil 2.10.

3. The Latin word for "being united" is *consortium*, which, taken literally, means "partnership." See R. Benericetti, *Il Cristo*, 94–95.

4. That the Incarnation is so novel that no implications or assessments can be drawn about it from ordinary human existence is a point made also in *Sermons* 148.3 (FOTC 17.250) and 153.1.

5. Mt 11.27.

2. And so he is born, yes, Christ is born, not out of a need to live, but out of a will to save.[6] He who bestows life upon the dead is born among the dead. Let us have no doubts that there came to pass what in the days of old and by the authority of the Holy Spirit Isaiah, the greatest of the prophets,[7] predicted would occur: "A virgin will conceive and bear a son."[8] That a woman gives birth is the assurance of the truth of the Incarnation; the reason why it is a virgin who bears the child is the eternal glory of the One who is born. Christ is born from an inviolate woman, because it was not right that virtue should be born through pleasure, chastity through lust, or incorruption through corruption.

The One who was coming to destroy death's ancient dominion would have been unable to arrive from heaven in a new dispensation,[9] and certainly as Lord of the universe he would not have been able to assume "the form of a slave,"[10] by which he was planning to redeem us, if the maidservant[11] had not given birth to him. Or else how would the Son of God undergo spittle, lashes, and the cross for us, if he had not offered himself as Son of Man?

3. Judea certainly knows no happiness, since she shuts out such great light for herself by her dark suspicions which lead her to make the false accusation of adultery; while not believing that a virgin has conceived, she alleges that her God's graciousness is really a sinful human act, and in the deadening gloom of her envy she proclaims as a vice what is actually a virtue.[12] But you pitiable human being, put your trust in him whose sole reason for being born was your salvation.

Consider carefully, brothers, what and how great is the

6. On this same point, see also *Sermons* 143.11 and 148.1 (FOTC 17.248).

7. In *Sermon* 57.1 (FOTC 17.103) Chrysologus calls Isaiah an evangelist as well as a prophet.

8. Is 7.14.

9. The Latin is *novus ordo*, terminology also employed in *Sermon* 40.4 (FOTC 17.88) to denote God's plan to save humanity in and through Christ. For more on this aspect of Chrysologus's thought, see R. Benericetti, *Il Cristo*, 225–30.

10. Phil 2.7.

11. See Lk 1.38.

12. On this objection, which probably did stem from some Jewish circles, see Introduction, FOTC 109.17–18 and n. 87.

blindness of the unbelievers, which says that Christ was not able to be born of a virgin, and in this heavenly birth looks for an ordinary human occurrence, and the creature puts God on trial by using laws which pertain to the created order. And so let human impiety bring nothing up for discussion about the Nativity of him who was compelled out of piety to be born for the human being. That the Son of Man and of God humbled himself in the flesh,[13] that a virgin conceives, gives birth, and remains a virgin after the birth,[14] derives from the power of heaven in all its mystery, and not from the order of mortal nature.[15]

13. See Phil 2.8.
14. On the threefold nature of Mary's virginity as formulated and discussed from the fourth century into the Middle Ages, see J. A. de Aldama, *Virgo Mater* (Granada: Faculty of Theology, 1963), 222–47. For other references in Chrysologus's sermons, see *Sermon* 142.6 and n. 12.
15. Chrysologus expands on this point with some of the same terminology in *Sermon* 146.2 (FOTC 17.238). A. Olivar notes that one manuscript has an additional section to conclude this sermon. Its language and style are not Chrysologus's, and hence the addendum is judged to be spurious. See A. Olivar, *Los sermones*, 326–27.

SERMON 150

On the Lord's Flight into Egypt[1]

F HUMAN LANGUAGE CANNOT explain the virginal conception and birth, if the human intellect does not take it in, and if the human mind does not grasp it, who is capable of speaking about God having fled as a Man? *An angel of the Lord*, it says, *appeared in a dream to Joseph, saying: "Take the boy and his mother, and flee to Egypt"* (Mt 2.13). If we have said that it was a matter of merciful kindness that Christ was born, what shall we say about the fact that we read that he fled? Perhaps, just as we said that he was born in order to restore our nature, we may say that he fled to call fugitives back. And really, if he himself wanders off in order to call back the sheep that was wandering amid the mountains,[2] how is it that he does not go into exile in order to bring back the peoples who were in exile?

2. *Take the boy and his mother, and flee to Egypt.* Why is it that a heavenly matter is treated in such a way that when a human being hears of it he is bewildered, his mind becomes tired, his understanding gets weary, his intellect becomes dull, his faith wavers, his hope falters, and his very capacity for believing begins to fail? *Take the boy and his mother, and flee to Egypt.* When a human being is in hot pursuit, God flees; when the earth gets violent, heaven trembles; when the dust flies, the angels are disturbed, and the panic of the Father is made manifest in the flight of the Son.

---

1. This sermon was preached some time after Christmas Day and in a different year from *Sermon* 151, since both sermons treat the same biblical text (Mt 2.13–15) in a similar fashion. See F. Sottocornola, *L'anno liturgico*, 122 and 233, and A. Olivar, *Los sermones*, 275. On p. 248, Olivar suggests that there may have been a feast in Ravenna shortly after Christmas dedicated to the flight into Egypt.

2. See Mt 18.12.

3. *Take the boy and his mother, and go off to Egypt.* When Saul was in hot pursuit, David took refuge in Judea, and that neighboring place received him;[3] the home of one widow was available for Elijah to hide out;[4] but there is no place for Christ in his flight, his province is of no avail, and his country offers no help. While he departs, no neighboring peoples, no bordering regions are available, but all he can manage[5] is a barbarous exile in the grim land of Egypt, foreign in appearance, language, and customs.

4. *Take the boy and his mother, and flee to Egypt.* If the refuge of the universe flees, if the help of all things hides, if the courage of everyone is afraid, if the defense of everything does not defend himself, why is human flight censured, or human trepidation rebuked, or human fear blameworthy? Why does Peter, who is afraid and denies, stand accused;[6] or John, who trembles and flees;[7] or all the disciples, since they desert out of fright?[8]

5. And granted, brothers, that these things happened: but why are they committed to writing, why are they mentioned in books, why are they recited through the ages, why are they noted in the daily readings,[9] why are they revealed to every people? Is it so that every language, place, age, and time might come to know that God was afraid? For just as when virtues are read aloud, they encourage our spirits to improve, so too when weaknesses are recited, they cast our spirits down. What, then, did the evangelist mean by writing these things for an everlasting remembrance?

It characterizes a loyal soldier[10] to keep silent about his

3. See 1 Sm 19.11–17.
4. See 1 Kgs 17.8–24.
5. Reading *procurat* (see PL 52.600) instead of *procuratur* in Olivar's CCL text.
6. See Mt 26.69–75 and parallels.
7. See Mk 14.51–52. On the identification of the young man who flees in Mk 14 with John, see *Sermon* 78.4, n. 8.
8. See Mt 26.56 and parallels.
9. For the view that "daily" *(cottidianis)* need not be taken literally as "every day" but rather in a more general sense as "regularly" or "frequently," see *Sermon* 92.1 and n. 3.
10. Another description of the proper conduct of the Christian as a loyal soldier is given in *Sermon* 68.5 (FOTC 109.277).

king's flight, and instead to tell about his steadfastness and speak of his virtues, but to be quiet about his fears, to reveal his courageous deeds, yet be reticent about his weaknesses, to blot out anything negative, to proclaim his victories, in order thereby to succeed both in breaking the enemy's resolve, and arousing the valor of his allies. Therefore, by mentioning such things, the evangelist seems to have aroused the barking of the heretics[11] and to have removed any defense from the faithful.

6. *Take the boy*, he says, *and his mother away, and flee to Egypt.* They are commanded to flee, not to set out;[12] they are constrained by necessity: they themselves did not will this; the angel bids them to make a secret journey: it is not a trip that they chose to take, such that traveling, always troublesome in itself, is even more troublesome on account of fear. So it is now the time for us to seek out the reason why these things have been written for us.

7. *Take the boy and his mother away, and flee to Egypt.* That one who is valiant flees in war is a matter of cleverness, and not fear. When God flees from a human being, it is on account of a mystery, not of fright.[13] When one who is powerful gets away from a weak person, he is not afraid of his pursuer, but he is bringing him out into the open. For the one who desires to record a public victory over his enemy wants to conquer in full view. He who wants to commit his triumph to the ages does not permit himself to engage in a hidden conflict. A secret victory and concealed valor leave no example for posterity.

8. The reason that Christ flees is that he yield to time, and not to Herod. For he who had come to bring back a victory over the enemy does not flee from death; he who had come to lay bare all of the devil's cunning and deceit does not panic at

---

11. The heretics at issue may be Arians who could interpret the account of Christ's flight as indicating his inferiority to the Father in terms of his divine power.
12. The Latin words *fuga* and *profectio* contrast running away or even backwards in flight versus moving forward and making progress. This same distinction is made in *Sermon* 151.1, which replicates much of the material in this section.
13. For other references to the benefit human beings receive when God flees, see *Sermon* 131.13 and n. 27.

human plots; nor was he afraid at that time when he was an infant, since he did not know how to be afraid as a Man, and was unable to be afraid as God. Brothers, if Christ had been slaughtered at that time among that number[14] of those who were being nursed, his death would have been a misfortune, with no involvement of his will; there would have been no virtue, but only distress; there would have been something unavoidable, and no place for his power;[15] and he would have had the reward of innocence, but not the glory of majesty.[16] And then what would become of that dictate uttered by God: "You shall not kill the lamb in its mother's milk"?[17]

9. *Herod*, he says, *is about to search for the boy* (v.13). Herod was searching, but by means of Herod it was the devil who was searching, since he saw that the Magi, whom he used to have as leaders in his errors, had fled from him.[18] If Christ, while still wrapped in swaddling clothes,[19] feeding[20] at his mother's breasts, speechless, whose actions went unnoticed, and who was not old enough to walk, if Christ transformed standard-bearers of the devil, that is, the Magi, into his own most loyal generals, the devil already had a preview of what Christ would be able to accomplish in the prime of his life. For this reason he incited the Jews and spurred Herod on, so that he, the crafty schemer, might overtake Christ in his infancy, which was already proving dangerous to him, prevent any future displays of his power, and remove the standard of the cross,[21] which would be deadly to him, but the greatest source of victory for us.

14. Literally, "that flock" *(illo grege)*, in accord with the scriptural quotation with which this section ends.
15. As God, Christ is never constrained by *necessitas* ("need" or "inevitability") but wills to manifest his *potestas* ("power"). On this point, see *Sermons* 148.1 (FOTC 17.248), 148a.2, and 153.8.
16. On what would have been lost had Christ been put to death prematurely, see *Sermons* 146.8 (FOTC 17.242–43) and 151.4.
17. See Ex 23.19, 34.26; and Dt 14.21. This is an allusion to Christ as Lamb of God (see Jn 1.29 and 36).
18. See Mt 2.12. Chrysologus's language is purposely ambiguous here, so as to indicate that the Magi fled both from Herod and from the devil, whom they had formerly served in their astrological pursuits.
19. See Lk 2.7.
20. Literally, "busy" *(occupatus)*.
21. On the "standard of the cross" and another harbinger of its power

The devil realized, he certainly realized that Christ with his teachings and acts of power would soon make life and the whole world new; since while still crying as an infant he had seized what was at the very summit of the world, according to the words of the prophet: "Before the boy knows how to call his father or mother, he will take the power of Damascus and the spoils of Samaria";[22] and as the Jews themselves attest, when they say: "You see that the whole world is going after him."[23]

10. Christ had promised through the Law and the Prophets that he would come in the flesh, that he would progress through the stages of life, that he would announce the glory of the kingdom of heaven, that he would preach the doctrine of the faith, that he would exorcize demons by merely the power of his word, that he would give sight to the blind, that he would make the lame walk, the mute speak, the deaf hear, that he would grant forgiveness to sinners, and life to the dead.[24] And so, for Christ to fulfill this as a Man, death was something that he postponed while he was an infant, but not something from which he fled.[25]

11. In conclusion, that his flight originated not out of a fear of danger, but out of the mystery of prophecy, the evangelist asserts when he says the following: *Take the boy and his mother, and flee to Egypt* (v. 13), and then: *In order that the Scripture be fulfilled: "Out of Egypt I have called my Son"* (v. 15; Hos 11.1). Christ, therefore, fled in order that the truth of the Law, the reliability of the Prophets, and the testimony of the Psalms would be firmly established, as the Lord himself said: "It was necessary that what was written about me in the Law, the Prophets, and the Psalms be fulfilled."[26]

---

earlier in the life of Christ, see *Sermon* 17.4 (FOTC 109.82). For references in other patristic authors to the *vexillum crucis*, see E. Skard, "Vexillum Virtutis," *Symbolae Osloenses* 25 (1947): 30.

22. Is 8.4.
23. Jn 12.19.
24. For a similar list of Christ's miraculous deeds and pertinent scriptural references, see *Sermon* 144.5 and n. 18.
25. For a similar reference to death being in the infant Jesus' remote rather than proximate future, see *Sermon* 151.4.
26. Lk 24.44.

Christ fled for us, not for himself;[27] Christ fled in order to ensure that the mysteries would be dispensed at the proper times. Christ fled in order that by his future acts of power he would both remove any grounds for excuse for the unbelievers, and offer incontrovertible evidence for faith for those who would believe. And, in short, Christ fled in order to give us confidence to flee, because in a persecution it is better to flee than to deny.[28] Accordingly, because Peter was unwilling to flee, he denied;[29] John, in order not to deny, fled.[30]

---

27. For another reference to Christ's infancy being for human salvation and not for his own benefit, see *Sermon* 140b.1. See also *Sermon* 144.8.
28. See Mt 10.23. A similar point about the occasional appropriateness of fleeing is made in *Sermon* 151.6.
29. See Mt 26.69–75 and parallels.
30. See Mk 14.51–52.

SERMON 151

A Second on the Same[1]

ODAY'S READING has troubled our hearts, shaken us in the depths of our being,[2] and has made us wonder if we were hearing correctly. *An angel of the Lord*, it says, *appeared to Joseph in a dream, saying: "Get up, take the boy and his mother, and flee to Egypt"* (Mt 2.13). When he was born, virginity did not resist him, reason proved no obstacle, and nature did not thwart him. Therefore, what power, what force, what peril could prevail over him so as to compel him to flee?

Take the boy and his mother, and flee to Egypt. It would have been more reverent to say: "Make your way to Egypt," so as to indicate a journey, but not a flight; something willed, not something done out of necessity; motivated by a considered judgment, not fear; a free human act, at least, if not a divine one. But now instead, a flight is mandated, mandated from heaven, mandated through an angel, so that fear seems to have taken hold of heaven before taking hold of earth.[3]

2. *Take the boy and his mother, and flee to Egypt.* Flee to Egypt, depart from your own people to foreigners, to the sacrilegious from the holy ones, from your Temple to the shrines of demons, to the land of idols from the region of the saints. Judea is so insufficiently extensive, the whole wide world is so confining, the Temple's sanctuary cannot hold them, the multitude of priests is of no avail, and the countless number of relatives cannot conceal them, that only the profane land of Egypt is conducive for hiding the Deity.

---

1. This sermon on the Lord's flight into Egypt, as with *Sermon* 150 but in a different year, was preached shortly after Christmas Day. See *Sermon* 150, n. 1.
2. For references to similar reactions, see *Sermon* 127.1 and n. 3.
3. Much of what is contained in this section is also found in *Sermon* 150.6.

The situation is so urgent, and so there is no time at all to consider the modesty of the Virgin, the weariness of the Mother, her sexual purity, Joseph's danger, the anguish of their being so far away, their separation from all their family, and, hardest of all, that they who were Jews were about to live abroad among gentiles, with whom they have nothing in common, or rather, who suffer overwhelming devastation[4] because they transgress the Law.

3. O how difficult! Living abroad is hard enough even among fellow-citizens and relatives. The one who experiences someone else's home thinks with longing about what his own home is like. And what has happened to that statement: "Lord, you have become a refuge for us,"[5] as well as: "God is our refuge and strength"?[6] If the refuge flees, if the strength is afraid, if the protection goes away, what life, hope, security, or defense is there? One widow was enough for Elijah against the plots of a free king;[7] all of Judea was not enough for Christ against the threats of the captive Herod.[8] Elijah consumed with fire from heaven those who had been sent to him;[9] Christ was saved only by fleeing.[10] Let this suffice as the extent of our complaints about Christ's flight.

4. Brothers, that Christ fled[11] had to do with a mystery, not fear; it was the liberation of the creature, not a peril to the Creator; it was a matter of divine power, not human frailty; of concern was not the death of the Creator, but the life of the world. For why would the One who had come to die flee death? Christ would have struck down any possibility for our salvation, if he had permitted himself to be struck down as a little child.[12] Christ had come in order to confirm by example what he had taught by precept, to do himself what he had commanded to be done, and to show that things which seemed impossible when they were heard were possible when they were seen.

---

4. Literally, "shipwreck" (*naufragium*).
5. Ps 89 (90).1. 6. Ps 45.2 LXX; Ps 46.1.
7. See 1 Kgs 17.8–16. 8. See Mt 2.13.
9. See 2 Kgs 1.9–12. 10. See Mt 2.13–15.
11. R. Benericetti, *Il Cristo*, 208–11, lists seven reasons that Chrysologus provides in *Sermons* 150–51 to justify Christ's flight into Egypt.
12. Also on this point, see *Sermons* 146.8 (FOTC 17.242–43) and 150.8.

He had come to impart knowledge of his divinity to the world by performing miracles, and to remove ignorance from a human race that did not know him. He had come to rouse the sluggish hearts of mortals to faith by his acts of power. He had come to overcome the devil by fighting him out in the open, so that he would be conquered by human beings and by divine decree, and so that he would be overthrown by a human example. He had come to fulfill the promises he had made that he would be present, in order to grant to those whom he had allowed to know him also to see him.

He had come so that the Jew would refrain from transgressing the Law. He had come to lead the gentiles to faith. He had come to select apostles to be teachers of the world, and to fill them with heavenly teachings, fortify them with powerful deeds, and arm them with miracles, so that they would subdue their aggressors with miracles, heal the sick with powerful deeds, and instruct the unlearned with their teachings. And, in short, he had come to destroy death by dying,[13] to break hell open by penetrating it, to unlock the tombs by rising, and by ascending to heaven to grant earthly beings access to heaven. All these things would certainly have been lost to us if Christ had not fled when he was in the cradle.

5. But you who are listening to me might say: since it could have been otherwise, why did he submit himself to such great and terrible wrongs? Why? First because the human being was not able to be saved except by one who was human, nor could human wrongs be taken away except by human wrongs. The one who wants to take care of someone else's situation makes that situation his own. The one who does not suffer with another is unable to take away the other person's sufferings.[14] Christ assumed[15] us in himself in order to give himself to us; he endured our sufferings in order to remove our sufferings.

6. The reason that Christ fled was to provide a standard for our flights during persecutions. When a martyr has been taken

---

13. For similar formulations, see *Sermon* 72b.5 and n. 19.
14. This same point is made in *Sermon* 50.1 (FOTC 109.193–94).
15. The Latin is *suscepit*. For Chrysologus's christological use of this term, see R. Benericetti, *Il Cristo*, 97–99 and 260–62.

into custody he must hold steadfast, but when he has not been taken into custody he must flee the persecutor, in order to grant the persecutor an opportunity to come to his senses, and not remove from himself the opportunity of making supplication, as the Lord says: "If you are persecuted in one town, flee to another."[16] The one who provokes a persecutor makes him such; the one who avoids the persecutor corrects him. Therefore, we must flee, we must not provoke them, if we want our persecutors to be saved, for whom we have been instructed to pray: "Pray," he says, "for those who persecute you."[17]

We must pray, we must flee, so that the one who rages through ignorance may be healed; and so that the one who suffers may come to the palm of victory on account of his patience, and may not come to peril on account of his rashness. Brothers, if the martyrs had not fled from Saul, they would not have made Paul a martyr.[18] Christ taught that this must be done, he left this as a precedent for us, so that since the Lord fled, the servant might not consider it beneath his dignity to flee.

7. And there is another reason why Christ fled, that as an infant he postponed the time of his suffering, and that he ascended the cross when he was more than thirty years old in his earthly[19] life, namely, that he who had made the human being fully equipped for life might refashion him for the fullness of life; and so that he might likewise hand over to heaven the one whom he had put on earth.

8. And that he fled to Egypt occurred for another reason: he fled to Egypt to reprimand the Jews for their faithlessness by means of the faith of the gentiles; for Egypt reverently received its Lord, whom Judea had put to flight, so that in its faith it would prefigure the Church and the gentiles that were about to be preferred to the synagogue and the Jews.

---

16. Mt 10.23. On this point, see also *Sermon* 150.11.
17. Mt 5.44.
18. See Acts 9.26.
19. Literally, "bodily" *(corporalis)*.

SERMON 153

A Second on Herod and the Infants[1]

ROTHERS, OUR HUMAN UNDERSTANDING cannot explain the mystery of the Virgin birth. What nature does not possess comes from the Creator, not from nature; it is the heavenly Spirit's work which flesh is unable to understand. Where there is no evidence of human involvement, there is the sign of God's action, as the prophet says: "The Lord himself will give you a sign: behold, a virgin will be with child."[2] Where there is nothing with which we are familiar here on earth, everything then is ordained by heaven. What does not come from the world cannot be grasped by the worldly wise.

When conception preserves the virginity of the mother, and giving birth leaves her virginity intact, the manner of generation is divine, not human.[3] God walks where no trace of any human traffic is found; custom loses its force when miracles are accomplished. Such signs show no respect for customs, uniqueness does not admit of a precedent, just as today's reading reveals when it tells about little children fighting divine battles.[4]

2. The whole cohort that arose alongside its King was eager to die before its King rather than die with him.[5] The sol-

---

1. The title of this sermon is reconstructed from *Sermon* 152 (see CCL 24B.949; FOTC 17.254–59). Both sermons were preached during the Christmas season, probably after the sermons on the flight into Egypt on a day specifically dedicated to the "Holy Innocents." The brevity of this *Sermon* 153 is consistent with the length of some of Chrysologus's other sermons on saints' feast days. *Sermons* 152 and 153 were preached in different years and not consecutively in the same year. See F. Sottocornola, *L'anno liturgico*, 122–23 and 234–36, and A. Olivar, *Los sermones*, 275.

2. Is 7.14.

3. On this point, see *Sermon* 140b.2 and n. 10.

4. See Mt 2.16–18.

5. Chrysologus's rhetorical flair is evident in the sentence: *Coorta regi cohors regi suo magis praemori quam commori tota gestiit.*

diers[6] dedicated to Christ began to fight before they began to live,[7] to do battle before playing, to shed their blood before drinking up all the milk from their mothers' breasts.[8] The ardent souls did not put up with any delays imposed on them by their bodies: rushing off from the lap into the raging troops of the enemy they receive courage before caresses, wounds before kisses, and the sword before ointment, so that they can inhabit heaven before earth, accept rewards of the spirit before the flesh, bring back triumphs for God before they stop having to be fed by human beings.[9]

Truly, truly, brothers, these are martyrs of grace: they confess while being silent, they fight although they do not know how, they conquer although unaware of the fact, and they die unaware, unwittingly they carry off the palms of victory, unknowingly they seize the crowns.[10] Therefore, just as the Virgin who knew no corruption received the honor of motherhood, so too infants who were unaware of suffering seized the palms and crowns of martyrdom.

---

6. The infants slaughtered by Herod are called "soldiers" also in *Sermon* 152.7 (FOTC 17.257–58).

7. See also *Sermon* 152.7 (FOTC 17.257). For other examples in Chrysologus's sermons of people who accomplished something memorable even before they really began to live, see *Sermon* 68.11 and n. 34 (FOTC 109.279).

8. On the juxtaposition of blood and milk, see *Sermons* 146.8 and 152.2 (FOTC 17.242, 255), and 172.3. See also Prudentius, *The Martyrs' Crowns* 10.700 (on a young Christian who was martyred), in FOTC 43, trans. M. C. Eagan (1962), 220. Eagan refers to Juvenal, *Satire* 11.68, who makes the same contrast but with a kid goat as the subject.

9. Chrysologus makes the same point in *Sermon* 152.7 (FOTC 17.257–58). See also Cyprian, *Letter* 58.6 (FOTC 51.167); Prudentius, *The Book of Hymns for Every Day* 12.125–32 (FOTC 43.89); Optatus, *Sermo: In Natali Sanctorum Innocentium* 4 (PLS 1.289); Augustine, *Sermons* 199.1 and 202.2 (FOTC 38.61, 73); Ps.-Augustine, *Sermon* 218.2 (PL 39.2150); idem, *Sermo: De Natale Domini* 2 (PLS 2.1341–42); Maximinus the Arian, *Sermo VIII: In Natale Infantum* (CCL 87.69–72); and Quodvultdeus, *De Symbolo* 1.15–18 (CCL 60.318–19). Many of these texts receive comment in F. Scorza Barcellona, "La celebrazione dei Santi Innocenti nell'omiletica latina dei secoli IV–VI," *Studi Medievali* (3d ser.) 15.2 (1974): 705–67 (743–46 on Chrysologus).

10. Ambrose, *Expositio Evangelii secundum Lucam* 2.49 (CCL 14.52–53), mentions that these infants, who had not yet attained the use of reason, still managed to confess and offer praise to God who accomplished his works within them.

3. But what do we say about the fact that the King himself, who ought to have stood fast, fled all alone and fled at the warning of his Father? This fleeing is a sign of the most intimate kind of love, it is not a sign of cowardly fear.[11] If Christ had stood fast, the synagogue would have them as sons, and the Church would not have them as martyrs.

11. On the propriety of Christ's flight into Egypt, see *Sermons* 150.11 and 151.7.

SERMON 155A

<A Second>[1] *on January First*[2]

NOW WE MUST HALT our playing of the trumpet of the Gospel,[3] now we must not speak about the Apostle's insights, in order for that prophetic song of lament to be the only sound that is heard, which says: "I became mute and was humbled, I kept silent about good things, and my grief was revived."[4] The grief of the Christian bishop[5] is revived when the error of the pagans does not wear out with time, nor is it dispelled by faith in all its brilliance. The days are now coming, the days that mark the new year[6] are coming, and the demons arrive with all their pomp, a full-fledged workshop of idols is set up, and the new year is consecrated with age-old sacrilege.

They fashion Saturn, they make Jupiter, they form Hercules, they exhibit Diana with her young servants, they lead Vulcan around roaring out tales of his obscenities, and there are even more, whose names must be left unmentioned, since they are hideous monsters; since nature does not produce such deformities, nor does creation have any knowledge of them, art takes great pains to mold them.[7] Moreover, human beings are

---

1. (Angle brackets here indicate an addition to the title in Olivar's CCL text.) On the authenticity of this sermon, particularly because of its similarity to *Sermon* 155 (FOTC 17.261–64) in both style and substance, see A. Olivar, *Los sermones*, 334–38.
2. Literally, the "Kalends of January" *(Kalendis Ianuariis)*, when this sermon was preached. See Introduction, FOTC 109.15–16 and n. 71.
3. For other patristic references to the *evangelica tuba*, see A. Olivar, *Los sermones*, 337, n. 31.
4. Ps 38.3 LXX; Ps 39.2.
5. The Latin term is *pontifex*.
6. Literally, the "Kalends" *(kalendae)*.
7. Much of the content and terminology in this section is also contained in *Sermon* 155.1 (FOTC 17.261–62).

dressed as beasts,[8] they turn men into women,[9] violate honor, mock good judgment, deride public criticism, ridicule the world with the world as their witness, and say that they are doing these things for amusement.[10]

2. These are no amusements, no, they are not; they are sins. A human being is changed into an idol; and if it is a sin to go to idols, what do you think it is to be an idol? O man, you have been made in the image of God;[11] whatever you wickedly introduce into yourself by your own depravity attempts and strives to insult God.[12] Clearly you may not have altogether intended it this way, but on the whole this is how God judges the matter: namely, that you are the reason for the continuation and present-day survival of the obscenity that characterized the centuries that were under the sway of those whose cult is perishing day by day.[13]

Indeed, there is not enough charcoal that can blacken the faces of such gods; and so that their appearance may reach the level of utter and complete terror, straw, skins, rags, and dung are procured from all over the world, and anything connected with human shame is put on their face. Among gods like these the one who is thought to be more magnificent is the one found to be more obscene among the obscene;[14] and the one who is considered the most magnificent of all is the one who can make monsters themselves marvel at his being so uniquely deformed.

The prophet's curse is fulfilled: "May those who make them

---

8. On this point, see also *Sermon* 155.6 (FOTC 17.264).

9. For a similar custom among Persian royalty that likewise elicits Chrysologus's ire, see *Sermon* 120.2 (FOTC 17.203–4).

10. In Ravenna on January 1 and January 3 people masqueraded as pagan deities and animals in what was called the *pompa circensis*, marking both public games *(ludi compitales)* and the inauguration of civic magistrates *(nuncupatio votorum)*. While Christians who took part saw such activity as harmless amusement, Chrysologus interpreted it far more negatively. See R. Arbesmann, "The 'Cervuli' and 'Anniculae' in Caesarius of Arles," *Traditio* 35 (1979): 111–13.

11. See Gn 1.26.

12. Chrysologus makes these same points in *Sermon* 155.4–5 (FOTC 17.263–64).

13. On this, see also *Sermon* 155.2 (FOTC 17.262).

14. See also *Sermon* 155.1 (FOTC 17.261–62).

become like them, as well as all those who trust in them."[15] And this is what Christians gaze at, what Christians look forward to, what they allow into their homes, what Christians welcome in their homes, while paying no heed to what the Apostle said: "That those who do such things deserve death."[16]

3. But you say: let those who make them die. Words do not excuse you since your will does not excuse you; a person is not innocent of this business when his consent implicates and entangles him in it. Listen to the rest of the verse: "Not only those who do them but also those who approve of those who do them."[17] In short, I beseech you, in the midst of evils cease doing evil. Believe me, believe me, I tell you, they would fade away to nothing if fake Christians were not going over to them.

Flee these things, keep yourselves and your homes off-limits to them, because God, who sees what is hidden,[18] surely cannot be deceived out in the open. "Leave, leave their midst," just as the prophet said, "and be separated from them, and touch nothing unclean";[19] so that at long last the ones who up until now have been deceived because we played along with them may return to their senses because of our zeal. And so, flee from these demonic activities, if you desire to hear about divine ones.

15. Ps 113B.8 LXX; Ps 115.8.
16. Rom 1.32.
17. Ibid. Chrysologus uses this text for the same purpose in *Sermon* 155.4 (FOTC 17.263).
18. See Mt 6.4, 6, and 18.
19. Is 52.11 and 2 Cor 6.17.

SERMON 157

A Second on Epiphany[1]

HE FEAST DAYS OF the Lord reveal their content by their names, for just as Christ gave the day of his birth by being born, and gave the day of the Resurrection by rising, so too he produced the day of his Illumination[2] by the light of wondrous deeds. The One who earlier when he was born concealed himself within a human body, later by his works revealed himself in heavenly mystery. Later in three different ways he appeared as God who earlier was seen as a man with an unparalleled birth. Rightly, therefore, is the present solemnity called by the name of Epiphany, in which the Deity, which was being kept hidden within our flesh from our gaze, now shone brightly.

This, brothers, this is the feast which was conceived on different occasions and bore three characteristic signs of the Deity. Through the Epiphany the Magi acknowledge Christ as God with mystical gifts,[3] and the worshipers of stars and inhabitants

---

1. This sermon was preached on the feast of Epiphany, a relatively new feast in Ravenna as compared with the more longstanding feast of Christmas. See F. Sottocornola, *L'anno liturgico,* 123–24 and 238–39. The fact that *Sermons* 156 (FOTC 17.265–70) and 158 mention only the adoration of the Magi and neither Jesus' Baptism nor the miracle at Cana, as do this *Sermon* 157 and *Sermon* 160, suggests that these latter two sermons were preached later in Chrysologus's episcopacy. See *L'anno liturgico,* 240–42. In pp. 243–50 Sottocornola compares the information about Epiphany in Chrysologus's sermons with material gleaned from other 4th–5th century Italian sources, and he concludes that Ravenna derived its celebration of Epiphany from other northern Italian churches rather than directly from the east.

2. This term implies that Chrysologus is drawing upon his knowledge of the Greek-speaking tradition of the east in his interpretation of Epiphany. See F. Sottocornola, *L'anno liturgico,* 239–40 and 250.

3. See Mt 2.11. Chrysologus makes this same point in *Sermon* 160.2 and his *Letter to Eutyches* 1 (FOTC 17.285).

267

of night find the Creator of light when it was pitch dark, to indicate that this comes from the grace of the Author, not the diligence of the seeker; that it is the gift, not of the star, but of God the Creator; that the credit goes, not to any creature, nor to human ingenuity,[4] but to God's generosity.

2. *Magi came from the east, saying: "Where is the newborn King of the Jews? For we have seen his star and have come to adore him"* (Mt 2.1–2). *We have seen his star.* And what is not his? The star belongs to him, he does not belong to the star. His is the star that received existence, but did not give it. The Author was in control of the star's rising; it was not in control of the Author's rising.[5] It is called his star not because it created him but because it was created by him;[6] it originated by his command, not by fate; not by computation, but by the Author; it was not something that would cause a rising, but that would undergo a setting. The star was not a lawgiver, but a sign-bearer,[7] producing not the arrangement of days, but light at night. The star guides one's journey, not one's life;[8] it was the Magi's companion, not Christ's relative; not a lady ruling with the Lord,[9] but a little maidservant of little servants.[10]

3. But someone asks: "Why Magi, why by means of a star, if there is no causal relationship or connection among the stars, one's origin, and one's nature?" Why Magi? Why a star? It is so that through Christ the very material of error would thus become the occasion of salvation, just as through Christ the cause of death became the cause of life. It is the singular characteristic of strength to throw the enemy into confusion by means of his own sword. Among the Magi it was ignorance and not their will that was to blame, and it was not their intention, but their

---

4. On the limitations of the Magi's ingenuity *(ars)*, see also *Sermons* 156.9 (FOTC 17.269–70) and 160.2.
5. "Rising" in the sense of "birth."
6. *Non a genesi sed a genitore.* The Latin in this entire paragraph is highly rhetorical.
7. *Non legiferam sed signiferam.*
8. *Ministra viae non vitae.*
9. *Dominantis domina.*
10. Remarks similar to this section are found in *Sermon* 156.7 (FOTC 17.268).

error that was at fault. To search for God while not knowing how to search is an incapacity rather than guilt.

Therefore, it was merciful that God both granted that he be found by those who were searching, and placed the blame on error. And so Paul by a similar kind of consideration was made a preacher out of being a persecutor, because through his zeal for the Law he was attacking the Law, and in his love for God he was sinning against God. This is why faith is attributable to Paul and lack of faith is attributable to his ignorance.[11]

4. But the listener says in addition: "Granted that the star shows the way to the Magi in their search not of its own accord, but at God's bidding, but where did they derive such great knowledge of mystical gifts? Where did they learn the great sacred symbolism of what they were offering?" Not from Chaldean ingenuity,[12] but from the ancient tradition of the sacred elders. These[13] were of Noah's race, of the sons of Abraham, who had learned through God and not through craft that Christ was born, and they had come to know by a profound mystery that this Man was God, a King, and that he was about to die. And so it is that they brought gifts in accord with the faith of their fathers, such that they knew enough to offer gold to the King, incense to God, and myrrh to the One about to die,[14] and by such gifts they showed appropriate reverence and honor. But let these remarks suffice as far as the Magi are concerned.

5. During Epiphany Christ at the wedding gave water the taste of wine, so that it was on account of power and not pleasure that Christ attended the wedding; not for the sake of courtesy, but of a miracle;[15] the reason for his action was to perform

---

11. See 1 Tm 1.13.
12. See the end of section 1 and n. 4.
13. That is, the Magi.
14. See Mt 2.11. Such symbolism is noted also in *Sermons* 158.10 and 160.2. This is also the interpretation given in Irenaeus, *Adversus Haereses* 3.9.2 (SC 211.106–7); Prudentius, *The Book of Hymns for Every Day* 83.69–72 (FOTC 43.87); Ambrose, *Expositio Evangelii secundum Lucam* 2.44 (CCL 14.50–51); and idem, *De Fide* 1.4.31 (CSEL 78.15). Augustine, *Sermon* 202.3 (FOTC 38.74), interprets the frankincense as an indication of Christ's priesthood; Leo, *Sermons* 31.2.2 and 36.1.2 (FOTC 93.134 and 156), finds myrrh to be a symbol of Christ's humanity (rather than mortality).
15. Chrysologus artfully juxtaposes *humanitatis* and *potestatis*.

a sign, not to fill his stomach; it was not to provide for drunkenness, but to manifest his divinity.[16] And so the very moment when he changed the nature of the water, he disclosed the Author, and the Creator of the elements was revealed by means of the transformation of the created entity.[17] Happy is that wedding, happy indeed, at which Christ is present, and which is consecrated not by dissipation, but by his acts of power![18] What then will not be transformed into grace, when water has been transformed into wine?[19]

6. During Epiphany Christ entered the basin of the Jordan[20] to consecrate our Baptism, in order that those whom he had assumed by being born on earth, he would raise up to heaven by being reborn;[21] that he would have free in himself those whom he had seen were captives when they were apart from him; that he would bring to life those whom guilt had made mortal; that he would make those live forever whom death had caused to live only for a time; and that those whom the devil had made exiles on earth, he would make his partners in heaven.[22] The reason, brothers, that the Holy Spirit descended and infused himself in full at that time, and that the Father proclaims from heaven: "This is my beloved Son,"[23] was that those[24] who had shared with the Son in the one activity of creating us would together impart the grace to restore us.

---

16. Chrysologus eloquently contrasts *ebrietatis* and *deitatis*.
17. See also *Sermon* 160.6 for this same interpretation of the revelation at Cana.
18. It is likely that Chrysologus intends both this meaning and that of moral "virtues" by using the word *virtutibus*.
19. See Jn 2.1–11.
20. See Mt 3.13–17 and parallels. See also *Sermon* 160.3. Thus the three revelations of Christ celebrated at Epiphany were the adoration of the Magi, the miracle at Cana, and his Baptism in the Jordan. For more on these three aspects of the feast, see n. 1 and, more generally, T. K. Carroll and T. Halton, *Message of the Fathers of the Church*, vol. 21, *Liturgical Practice in the Fathers* (Wilmington, DE: Glazier, 1988), 171–88.
21. For commentary on Christ's being reborn at his Baptism, see A. Olivar, *Los sermones*, 391, n. 17.
22. For some other references to such a "partnership," see R. Benericetti, *Il Cristo*, 94–95.
23. Mt. 3.17.
24. Namely, the Father and the Holy Spirit.

7. Thus it was that Christ was recognized as God at different times, but on one and the same day, by the Magi's gifts, by the transformation of the water, and by the voice of his Father as a threefold testimony, and that from the triple revelation of Christ the one hallowed feast of Epiphany was established.

SERMON 158

A Third on Epiphany[1]

WE OFTEN WONDER WHY Christ enters his world in such a way that he experiences the confines of the womb,[2] that he suffers the indignity of being born, that he endures being wrapped up in swaddling clothes, that he tolerates being helpless in a cradle, that he seeks with tears to be fed at the breasts, that he feels completely the stages[3] and constraints in life. And how else should he have come who willed to garner favor, to cast out fear, and to seek charity? Nature shows what every infant can do and accomplishes.

What fury does infancy not conquer? What ferocity does it not tame? What cruelty does it not restrain? What rage does it not calm? What power does it not overcome? What severity does it not soften? What hardness does it not break down? What love does it not demand? What affection does it not extract? What favor does it not exact? What charity does it not obtain? That this is so, fathers know, mothers recognize, all people attest, and human hearts bear witness. So then, he wanted to be born, who wanted to be loved, not feared.[4] And, nevertheless, listen to what success so charming, so devot-

---

1. This sermon was preached next after *Sermon* 156 (FOTC 17.265–70), which treats only the first two verses of Matthew 2 and in its closing sentence promises another sermon on the subsequent verses. F. Sottocornola, *L'anno liturgico*, 123–24 and 237, also suggests that this *Sermon* 158 was preached on the following Sunday. See also A. Olivar, *Los sermones*, 249 and 275–76. On how this sermon fits within Chrysologus's Epiphany preaching, see *Sermon* 157, n. 1.

2. On such "confinement," see also *Sermon* 142.4 and n. 10.

3. That Christ experienced the various stages of life is indicated also in *Sermon* 150.10.

4. For other references in Chrysologus's sermons and in other ancient authors to God's preference to be loved rather than feared, see *Sermon* 72b.4 and n. 15, and A. Olivar, *Los sermones*, 362.

ed,[5] and so dear an infancy achieves in the face of human malice.

2. *Upon hearing this*, it says, *Herod was troubled, and all Jerusalem with him. And gathering the chief priests and the scribes of the people, he inquired of them about where the Christ was to be born* (Mt 2.3–4). If Jerusalem, if the king, if the scribes, if the chief priests are so troubled at the infancy of Christ, what would they do if Christ had come at that moment as a fully grown man, endowed with wealth and a crowd of followers?[6] What if he had come with a suspicious lot and foreigners?

They[7] who have no consideration for the time in life, or one's age, or the poor person, or the parent, however, as soon as they hear that he was born, prepare to inflict death on the newborn, their guile on the innocent, wickedness on the holy One, swords on the naked One, soldiers on One who is all alone, murder on him as he gives a baby's cry, and punishment on him who pardons. And to mix violence together with blood, their bitter cruelty declares war on the cradle, attacks the breasts with weapons, strikes laps with shields, in order to make the human and divine offspring enter the grave before entering the world.[8]

3. Granted that King Herod felt compelled to undertake such actions out of love for his reign and fear of a successor: why did Jerusalem, the chief priests, and the scribes do this? Why? It is because the unholy one does not want God to be born, nor the servant his Lord, the guilty his Judge, the rebellious his Leader, the treacherous his Witness. Jerusalem had drenched itself in a variety of defilements, the priests had desecrated what was holy, and by selling sins they had turned par-

---

5. The Latin is *pia*. On the *pietas* of God in Chrysologus's preaching, see R. Benericetti, *Il Cristo*, 215–19.

6. A similar point is made in *Sermon* 150.9 about the prospects of what Christ would accomplish as an adult, based on what occurred when he was a mere infant.

7. Namely, the leaders in Jerusalem. I am following the punctuation given by Migne (PL 52.617) and not by Olivar, since I take the following relative clause to refer to the Jerusalem leaders and not to the imaginary band of "suspects" and "foreigners" who could have accompanied the adult Christ.

8. See Mt 2.13 and 16–17.

don and piety into a venal enterprise. The scribes had perverted heavenly doctrine, salvific knowledge, and life-giving teaching so as to mean something savage, to precipitate a treacherous fall, and to become lethal chatter.

And so they do not want Christ to be born and are afraid to have him live, because they knew that right away they would be consigned to disgrace, made an object of reproach, cast out of the Temple,[9] stripped of the priesthood, and deprived of the ministry of offering sacrifice. For once they had been inflamed by greed, captivated by their ostentatiousness, wounded by their vices, drunk with vanity, and intoxicated with extravagance, since they were unable to consider any kind of reform, they had no hope of pardon.

4. When a good steward gathers a plentiful harvest because of his constant labor, he longs for his master to come because it will be to his own advantage, he is eager for him to come because it will contribute to his own happiness. When a diligent workman has completed a project through the work he has undertaken, he wants the head of the household to arrive in order to receive his salary. A dedicated soldier[10] wants the king to be present after a conflict, after a victory, to repay him with suitable compensation for his sweat and wounds. And so the one who through untiring virtue succeeds in the warfare of this world longs for Christ to come to bestow upon him the palm of victory. By the same token, those who have been overcome by the allurements of this age and so are afraid of being punished and have no hope for pardon, do not want Christ to come.

5. Brothers, let us do good, let us avoid evil;[11] let us flee the vices, let us pursue the virtues; let us ignore the present, let us think about the future. Let us aim for our kingdom, let us attain to our palm of victory; let us hope for glory, let us long for the crown with all our prayers. But now let our words return to the material in the following verses.

6. *After calling the Magi together*, it says, *Herod carefully learned*

---

9. See Mt 21.12 and parallels.
10. Other qualities of a loyal soldier are mentioned in *Sermons* 68.5 (FOTC 109.277) and 150.5.
11. See Ps 36 (37).27.

from them the time when the star had appeared to them. And as he sent them to Bethlehem he said: "Go, inquire, and when you find him, bring the information back to me, so that I too may go and adore him" (vv.7–8). He calls the Magi in secret, since an insincere mind and a deceitful conscience attempt nothing in the open. He calls the Magi in secret, because a thief loves the night, a robber fashions his plots in secret. He is careful in ascertaining the time of the star, but although he fears for his kingdom, he does not fear a sign from heaven, nor does he have any fear at all about the Author of time. Why are you troubled, Herod?[12] Why are you worried about so great a successor? The One whom the stars serve is not controlled by any earthly power.

7. *Go and inquire, and when you find him, bring the information back to me* (v.8). Herod, you are mistaken! The Magus is commanded to adore, not to make a report; he came to be a witness, not a traitor; it has been granted to him to see, it has not been granted to you to find. *Go and inquire.*[13] As if it is not sufficient for the Magi to inquire only once! An answer without piety was given to those who ask out of piety. For those who listen with evil intent the message of salvation is turned into destruction. The insolent servant hears that the Lord is born, but he provides traps and not honor for the newborn Lord; he prepares death so as not to have to serve him. But since God could not be brought to an end, since salvation could not perish, nor life die, the Lord abides in honor, the servant remained in sin. But he who despised coming to do homage is dragged away to be punished; he who refused to accede to grace is carried off to be sentenced.

8. *Go, inquire, and when you find him, bring the information back to me.*[14] It is appropriate that he said, *Renounce me,* because the one who is in a hurry to reach Christ always renounces the devil. When the one who is about to become a Christian listens to the priest asking: "Do you renounce the devil?" he responds: "I

---

12. See Sedulius, *Hymnus* 2.29–30 (CSEL 10.164): "Herod, O impious enemy, why are you afraid that Christ has come?" (trans. mine).

13. *Ite et interrogate* can also mean, "Keep on inquiring."

14. *Renuntiate mihi* (Mt 2.8) is translated here as "Bring the information back to me." It can also mean, "Renounce me," which is what Chrysologus intends as a second meaning.

do."[15] So it is fitting that Herod says that he ought to be renounced by the Magi, since he knew that he was taking the place of the devil, he was aware that he was playing the part of Satan.

9. *So that I may go and adore him* (v.8). He wants to lie, but he cannot. He who had feigned adoration in order to act savagely will go, but to be afflicted in torment, to submit to tortures, to be racked in punishment. But when the Magi passed through the clouds of Jewish unbelief,[16] and in the serenity of Christian faith see again the star that they had seen earlier, with it leading the way[17] as their guide, they reached that very sacred place where the Lord was born.[18]

10. *And they opened their coffers and offered him gifts: gold, frankincense, and myrrh* (v.11). In their reverence for the Lord they offer gold to the King, frankincense to God, and myrrh to the One who is going to die,[19] the greatest coffers of knowledge for future believers. Thus they return to their own country along the road of innocence, who trampled and ruined Herod's treacherous route.[20]

---

15. This is an obvious reference to the ritual prior to Baptism.
16. Some other references to this traditional slur of Jewish *perfidia* made by early Christian authors are collected in E. Peterson, "Perfidia judaica," *Ephemerides Liturgicae* 50 (1936): 296–311; see especially 306, n. 44.
17. The Latin is *praevia*. See Sedulius, *Hymnus* 2.34 (CSEL 10.165): "following the star which leads the way" (trans. mine).
18. See Mt 2.9–10. The Latin is *ortus* (lit., "rising"). In *Sermon* 157.2, Chrysologus uses this one word to indicate both the "rising" of the star and the "birth" of Christ.
19. For other references to such symbolism by Chrysologus and other early Christian authors, see *Sermon* 157.4 and n. 14.
20. See Mt 2.12.

SERMON 160

A Fourth on Epiphany[1]

LTHOUGH IN THE MYSTERY of the Lord's Incarnation itself there were clear signs of his eternal divinity, nevertheless today's feast discloses and reveals in manifold ways that God came into a human body, so that mortality, always enveloped in darkness, may not lose through ignorance what it has been made worthy of holding and possessing through such great grace. For he who willed to be born for us did not want to remain unknown by us; and so he discloses himself in such a way that the great mystery of his merciful kindness[2] may not become a great occasion of error.

2. Today the Magus[3] finds crying in a cradle the One whom he was seeking as he shone among the stars.[4] Today the Magus admires evident in his swaddling clothes the One whom he experienced as hidden for a long time within the constellations. Today the Magus ponders with deep amazement what he sees and where: heaven on earth, earth in heaven; man in God, God in man; and the One who is not able to be contained in the whole world, he sees confined in a tiny body.

Therefore, because the Magus is unable to figure this out and cannot grasp it, he immediately adores him. For he sees

---

1. On Chrysologus's four Epiphany sermons, see *Sermon* 157, n. 1. Because of the numerous references to "today" *(hodie)* in this sermon, clearly it was preached on the day of Epiphany itself. This sermon, like *Sermon* 157, comes from the latter period of Chrysologus's episcopacy, and was preached in a different year from *Sermon* 157 and *Sermons* 156 and 158. See F. Sottocornola, *L'anno liturgico,* 124.

2. See 1 Tm 3.16. On the importance of this text in Chrysologus's preaching, see R. Benericetti, *Il Cristo,* 165.

3. See Mt 2.1–12.

4. For other similar paradoxes connected with Christ's birth, see *Sermons* 140a.5 and n. 17, 140b.3, and 144.1.

that the stars, the moon, and the sun do not shine as brightly in heaven as the flesh he gazes upon has shed light upon the earth. He sees that in one and the same Body divinity and humanity have merged together in unity.[5] While he believes that the One here is God, recognizes that he is King, and understands that he will die[6] out of love for the human race, his thoughts frighten him as he deliberates about how God is able to die, how the Restorer of life can be put to death, and thus the Magus stops searching with ingenuity for what he cannot find with his own ingenuity.[7]

And since he sees that he wandered astray[8] for a long time in the sky with the wandering stars, he rejoices that on earth he has reached God by the guidance of a single star, and the Magus perceives that everything in the sky that is seen clearly by human eyes lies veiled with profound mysteries, and now that he sees this he acknowledges, as evidenced by the mystical gifts[9] that he offers, that he believes and no longer pries into it: with incense for God, with gold for the King, and with myrrh for One who is going to die.[10] He professes his faith in God with incense, and in the King with gold, so that he may now appease with lavish homage the One whom he had refused and offended by his prying and impertinent activity, and in order to fulfill what many suppose refers to the eunuch who is also from Ethiopia:[11] "Ethiopia will reach out its hands."[12]

The Magus saw Christ; he reached ahead of the Jew with his own hands, because at the time when the Jew was betraying Christ by the wickedness of Herod, the Magus with his gifts was

---

5. *Divinitatis et humanitatis convenisse commercium.* For a similar expression, see *Sermon* 156.5 (FOTC 17.267). For the meaning of *commercium* in Chrysologus's christology, see R. Benericetti, *Il Cristo*, 101–3.

6. As expressed later in this section in the symbolism of the Magi's three gifts.

7. See also *Sermon* 157.1 and n. 4.

8. Or "erred" *(errasse)*.

9. This same expression is found in *Sermon* 157.1 and his *Letter to Eutyches* 1 (FOTC 17.285).

10. See Mt 2.11. For other references to this symbolism, see *Sermon* 157.4 and n. 14.

11. See Acts 8.27–39.

12. Ps 67.32 LXX; Ps 68.31.

acknowledging that Christ was God. This is why the gentile, who was last, became first,[13] since at that time the faith of the Magi consecrated the belief of the gentiles and denounced the cruelty of the Jews.

3. Today Christ entered the River Jordan[14] to wash away the sin of the world. John himself attests that he came for this reason: "Behold the Lamb of God, behold him who takes away the sin of the world."[15] Today the servant clings to his Lord, a man clings to God, John clings to Christ.[16] He clings to him in order to receive pardon, not to grant it. Today, as the prophet says, "The voice of the Lord is over the waters."[17] What voice? "This is my beloved Son, with whom I am well pleased."[18]

Today "the voice of God is over the waters," because God the Father, in order to verify his Son's lineage, is present himself as his own witness to assert: "This is my beloved Son," because the Son has no one else to provide testimony. The sanctuary of the Father has no observer; the divine generation knows no witness. The divinity of Christ receives no investigation from outside, as the Son himself says: "No one knows the Son except the Father, and no one knows the Father except the Son."[19]

4. Today the Holy Spirit hovers over the waters under the appearance of a dove,[20] so that, just as that dove announced to Noah that the flood that inundated the world had subsided,[21] so too by this sign it would be known that the unremitting shipwreck of the world had come to an end.[22] But it did not carry a branch from the old olive tree, as that one did, but pours out

---

13. See Mt 19.30 and 20.16.
14. See Mt 3.13–17 and parallels. Chrysologus also discusses Christ's Baptism in *Sermon* 157.6.
15. Jn 1.29.
16. In *Sermons* 43.3 (FOTC 17.92) and 179.1 Chrysologus points out that John the Baptist managed to lay hold of the entire Trinity.
17. Ps 28 (29).3.
18. Mt 3.17.
19. Mt 11.27.
20. See Mt 3.16.
21. See Gn 8.11.
22. A similar juxtaposition of the dove in the account of the Flood and the Holy Spirit in the form of a dove at Christ's Baptism is made, e.g., in Tertullian, *De Baptismo* 8.3–4 (CCL 1.283), and in Ambrose, *The Mysteries* 4.24 (FOTC 44.13).

rich, new chrism all over his head as Parent,[23] in order to fulfill what the prophet said: "God, your God, has anointed you with the oil of gladness before your fellows."[24]

5. Today "the Lord is over the waters."[25] Correctly does it say "over the waters," and not "under the waters," because Christ is not a servant to his Baptism, but he has authority over the sacraments. Today "the God of majesty thundered."[26] And if the Father thunders from heaven, if the Son stirs up the waters of the Jordan, if the Holy Spirit appears in bodily fashion from on high, why is it that the Jordan, who fled at the presence of the Ark of the Covenant,[27] did not run away when the whole Trinity is present? Why is it? It is because the one who shows homage and deference begins to be fearful no longer.[28]

Here the Trinity puts all its grace into operation and expresses all its love for the world; on that prior occasion[29] God took hold of the elements in order to instruct his little servants to fear him. Nevertheless, in the midst of these events so awesome and great, John stands undaunted, because he is unable to be afraid, since the angel has testified that he was born entirely for the love of God.[30]

6. Today Christ produces the first of his heavenly signs by changing water into wine,[31] so that he whom the Father through his voice already pointed out as his Son would himself

---

23. Christ is the "Parent" of Christians as the source for their new life and as Head of the Church. See *Sermons* 35.3, 58.4, and 60.5 (FOTC 109.150–51, 223, and 233–34) and *Sermon* 57.5 (FOTC 17.106–7) on chrism as symbolic of the Holy Spirit, which Christ in turn has poured forth upon believers.
24. Ps 44.8 LXX; Ps 45.7.
25. Ps 28 (29).3.
26. Ibid.
27. See Ps 113 (114).3 and 5; Jos 3.15–17.
28. The so-called Orthodox or Neonian Baptistery in Ravenna, built by Chrysologus's predecessor, Ursus, but decorated during the tenure of his successor, Neon, depicts a personification of the River Jordan as attending to Christ at his Baptism. It has been suggested that the artist may well have had this sermon of Chrysologus's in mind. See Introduction, FOTC 109.4 and n. 13.
29. Namely, when the River Jordan had its waters parted to create a dry path allowing the passage of the Ark of the Covenant and the Israelites. See Jos 3.15–17.
30. See Lk 1.13–17.
31. See Jn 2.1–11.

confirm that he was God through his miracles, because he who transforms the elements is the Author of the elements;[32] and he who has no difficulty contravening nature has created nature himself. He changes water into wine so that the sluggishness of our nature may derive benefit from the vigor of divinity.

For he who stretched and multiplied five loaves of bread by secretly increasing them so as to feed five thousand men and even leave an abundance of leftovers,[33] was able to augment the amount of wine at a wedding feast and make it last with an ever-fresh supply.[34] But the water still had to be changed into the sacrament of his blood, so that Christ might serve cups of pure wine from the vessel of his Body for people to drink, in order to fulfill the words of the prophet: "And how splendid is your cup which intoxicates!"[35]

7. And so in three ways today the divinity of Christ has been indicated: by the Magi's offering, by the Father's testimony, and by the changing of the water into wine,[36] since the authority of Scripture establishes that every word is confirmed by three [verifications], when it says: "Every word is confirmed by three witnesses."[37] But because this feast itself urges us to come now to the table of the Lord and to this cup of gladness,[38] let us be content to have confined enormous matters within a brief sermon.[39]

32. The same point is made in *Sermon* 157.5.
33. See Mt 14.15–21 and parallels.
34. See Jn 2.7–10.
35. Ps 22 (23).5. For similar use of this biblical verse as referring to the eucharistic chalice, see *Sermon* 137.4 and n. 15. See also A. Olivar and A. Argemi, "La Eucaristía en la predicación de San Pedro Crisólogo," *La Ciencia Tomista* 86 (1959): 606–7.
36. In *Sermon* 157 Chrysologus also refers to these three events commemorated at Epiphany. See *Sermon* 157, n. 20.
37. See Dt 19.15; Mt 18.16; 2 Cor 13.1.
38. These remarks smoothly signal a transition from the comments in the previous section about the wedding at Cana to the liturgy of the Eucharist to follow. For other such transitional remarks in Chrysologus's preaching leading to the subsequent celebration of the Eucharist, see F. Sottocornola, *L'anno liturgico*, 140, n. 12.
39. Chrysologus's language here is reminiscent, perhaps purposely so, of his remarks above in section 2 about the Incarnation: One whom the whole world cannot contain is paradoxically confined in an infant's tiny body.

SERMON 161

On the Servant Who Came in from the Field

OU HAVE HEARD, brothers, how the Lord uses an example of human servitude to teach the requirements involved in serving God, when he says: *Who among you who has a servant plowing or pasturing sheep, says to him as soon as he comes in from the field: "Come and recline at table"; and does not say to him: "Come and put on your apron and wait on me until I eat and drink, and you shall eat and drink afterwards?" Does he show gratitude to that servant because he did what he ordered him to do? I think not. So you also,* he goes on, *when you have done everything that has been commanded of you, say: "We are useless servants; we have done what we ought to have done"* (Lk 17.7–10).

2. *So you also* (v.10). What is the similarity? Rather, it is a great dissimilarity! Does the human being owe to God only as much as one human being owes to another? Far from it! It is quite another relationship, the case is quite different, the obligation is quite dissimilar. God made the human being exist, he ordained that he be born, he granted him life, he allowed him to have wisdom; he bestowed upon him periods of time, he assigned ages in life, he made provisions for his glory, he opened a route for him to attain honor, he put him in charge of living things,[1] and he prescribed it thus for the whole earth by a precise law and for a precise period of time.

Even after these first blessings of God to humanity, which were so tremendous and great, had been lost, he fashioned again a second installment of blessings, so much greater inasmuch as they were divine, so much more precious inasmuch as they were heavenly. For later he made an inhabitant of heaven the one whom earlier he had made to be a dweller upon the

---

1. See Gn 1.26.

earth, in order that he face no adversity nor attack upon him, and that no sneak might any longer invade the goods of earth and prevail over the human being;[2] in order that his now secure condition would keep him safe after an unstable freedom had brought him to ruin, and in order that the human being would be free in every respect by serving only the Lord.

He is indebted to the Lord for the condition in which he has been made, and he is indebted for his origin; for the fact that he has been redeemed, that he has been purchased, he certainly owes service, as the Apostle says: "You have been purchased for a price; do not become slaves of human beings."[3] And the prophet speaks as follows so as to acknowledge his condition and origin: "I am your servant, and the son of your handmaid."[4] This is what the human being owes to God; what does he owe to another human being that is like it?

And, nevertheless, God seeks only that same amount, because the human being is unwilling to render anything to God, to whom he owes everything. But let us repeat the reading and put the parable itself before our eyes, and then what we have said will be clear, namely, that we do not pay any service to God, but pay all our service to the human being.

3. *Who among you who has a servant plowing or pasturing sheep, will say to him as soon as he comes in from the field: "Come and recline at table"; and does not say to him: "Come and put on your apron and wait on me until I eat and drink, and you shall eat and drink afterwards?"* (vv.7–8) How familiar, how ordinary, how rooted in daily custom, and how commonplace is this teaching! If the one who hears it is a master, he recognizes that he demands the like from his servant; if the listener is a servant, he is aware of doing these things for his master.

For indeed the servant, after arising before dawn, after a variety of strenuous labors all day long, and after running about all anxious and agitated, also prepares dinner for his master, and in appropriate attire serves what he has prepared. He is not haughty because he has done these things, but in his partic-

---

2. See Gn 3.
4. Ps 115 (116).16.

3. 1 Cor 7.23.

ular circumstances he does his work with fear and trembling, and places before his master a variety of food, bringing out every flavor with all his skill, while he himself, if he is lucky, will eat a small meal half-cooked and unseasoned; offering numerous cups to overflowing, he varies the drinks, he changes the vintages; he stands faithfully at his post, at hand for the rather drawn-out conversation of the very drawn-out banquet, he stands immovable, he stands since he is not allowed to tire in his service.

And by the time the master is already spending part of the night asleep, the servant finishes his work quietly, he picks up, attends to his duties, takes care of things, arranges them, sets them in order, puts them away, and remains so busy in the tasks he has to do that he has nothing left, or at most very little, of the night for himself for eating or sleeping. After all this, if he does not awaken early the next day and arise from sleep before his master does, the tired servant will come in the morning to be beaten tirelessly, he will face punishment right away, and nothing of the prior day's labor comes to his aid, because whatever the master does to his servant, undeservedly, out of anger, willingly, unwillingly, forgetfully, mindfully, knowingly, or unknowingly, is just, is fair, and is legal. The anger of the one in authority toward his subject is his right, and the one who has the status of servant has no voice before the master's will.[5]

4. So then, both the servant recognizes what he owes God, by serving a human being in this fashion, and a master is shown, by the authority that he holds, what kind of servitude he owes to the Master of masters,[6] and he understands this because he is his own teacher. Paul was an example of this, when he wrote the following as a description of his servitude: "Right until this very hour we are hungry and thirsty, we are naked, despised, and are struck by blows."[7] And elsewhere he says: "I

---

5. For another description of the severity of servitude to another human being, see *Sermon* 2.4 (FOTC 17.32–33).

6. Or "Lord of lords," *dominus* meaning both "lord" and "master." This clause is an example of Chrysologus's rhetorical skill: *et dominando dominus qualem servitutem domino dominorum debeat docetur*.

7. 1 Cor 4.11.

make my body black and blue, and I subject it to servitude."[8] The good servant procured the means to freedom by acting in such a way that he beat himself continually to the point of being black and blue, and did not slacken the reins on his body, so that his flesh would not falter by being indulged and thereby incur the penalty of being enslaved to another.

5. But, O man, what you demand from your servant, pay yourself to the One who has made you a master. You who always sleep but demand tireless vigilance from your servant, be vigilant once in a while yourself for the Lord who is unceasingly vigilant for you.[9] Attend to your Lord at least for one moment by fasting, since your servant always attends to your meals. Show some indulgence toward your servant who is innocent, since your Lord is gentle toward you, a sinner. Now and then grant pardon, since your Lord always forgives you. Certainly if you do any good deed, believe that you have paid something back to the One who has been generous with his credit to you, and not that you have done him some favor.

When you have done everything, he says, *that has been commanded of you, say: "We are useless servants; we have done what we ought to have done"* (v.10). When is a human being useful on his own in divine matters, if he is so useless to himself in human ones? Let the human being consider the evils of his heart, the vices of his flesh, the ebb and flow of pleasures, the storms of his desires, the crags of his anger, the shipwrecks of his sins, and then he will ascribe to God whatever is useful in him, and will attribute to himself whatever is useless.[10] But let us return to the topic at hand so that it may now become evident why the Lord gave this warning to his disciples.

6. In order to send his apostles to peoples who were suffering from a variety of infirmities, Christ gave them the strength of the Spirit, he gave them heavenly power, he gave them the

---

8. 1 Cor 9.27.
9. See Ps 120 (121).3–4.
10. Augustine makes the same point with similar terminology in, e.g., *Sermon* 96.2 (PL 38.586), *Sermon* Guelferbytanus 22.5 (=293D) in *Miscellanea Agostiniana*, vol. 1, ed. G. Morin (Rome: Tipografia Poliglotta Vaticana, 1930), 514, and *Tractates on the Gospel of John* 43.1.1 (FOTC 88.163).

grace of healing.[11] Therefore as they went about they restored sight to the blind, mobility to the lame, hearing to the deaf,[12] and—so as not to detain you by going through each of them—they healed all who were afflicted. And so when they returned they boasted as they said: "Lord, in your name even the demons are subject to us."[13] The Lord restrains them as he says: "Do not rejoice that demons are subject to you; but rejoice that your names are written in heaven."[14] Therefore, lest they lose through pride what they had acquired through labor, and attribute to themselves what they obtained from God, by means of this parable he calls them back to humility, which is the mother of instruction:

7. *Who among you who has a servant plowing or pasturing sheep, says to him as soon as he comes in from the field: "Come and recline at table"; and does not say to him: "Come and put on your apron and wait on me until I eat and drink, and you shall eat and drink afterwards?"* (vv.7–8) After the labors that were demanded of them and the many great signs of power, the apostles seemed in their own minds to be very useful, but they were rushing headlong into the mire of the flesh and the mud of this body, and they did not realize that they were useless. But the truth is recognized when Judas betrays,[15] Peter denies,[16] John flees,[17] and all abandon him,[18] so that it would become apparent that it is he alone in whom there was and from whom there originated all usefulness.

8. But his statement: *And you shall eat afterwards*, advises the disciples that immediately after his Ascension they should long to be united with the Lord in heavenly bliss.[19] And so, as to the

11. See Lk 9.1–2.
12. For a similar listing of Christ's miracles, see *Sermon* 144.5 and n. 18.
13. Lk 10.17: actually, this remark was made by the seventy-two disciples upon their return, and not by the twelve apostles.
14. Lk 10.20.
15. See Mt 26.14–16 and parallels.
16. See Mt 26.69–75 and parallels.
17. See Mk 14.51–52. On the identification of the fleeing youth in Mark 14 with John, see *Sermon* 78.4 and n. 8.
18. See Mt 26.56 and parallels.
19. On the elevation of humanity because of Christ's Ascension, see *Sermon* 85.2 and n. 6.

fact that he approves of their remaining here, and that he equips them to endure suffering, he is making them ready to labor in his service. For the time in which the apostles waited on the One at table refers to their preparation of the Lord's Supper upon the tables of the Church as an everlasting memorial within the kitchens of sinners and the hearths of the gentiles. The one who is a believer knows this Supper;[20] let the one who does not know it desire to know it, so that he may be a believer.

20. An obvious reference to the Eucharist.

SERMON 162

Where It Says: "Teacher, tell my brother to divide the inheritance with me"[1]

OU HAVE HEARD TODAY, brothers, what an heir of worldly goods asked of the Lord. *Teacher,* he says, *tell my brother to divide the inheritance with me* (Lk 12.13). Greed, rash[2] and reckless, believed that the Judge of the world himself was an arbitrator of earthly litigation, and wanted him who had come to restore the unity of the human race to become a promoter of division. *Teacher, tell my brother to divide the inheritance with me.* Here before him is not a Teacher of accusation, but of love. *Tell my brother to divide the inheritance with me.* When he says, *Tell my brother,* by saying *Tell my brother,* he has prefaced his remarks with what urges charity, what appeals to nature, what arouses affection.

Tell my brother to divide the inheritance with me. He cannot say to your brother: "Divide," because it is he who speaks through the prophet: "See how good and pleasant it is for brothers to dwell in unity."[3] *Tell my brother to divide the inheritance with me.* What greater inheritance is there, what other inheritance is there, than the bond of divine charity?[4] An inheritance at some point passes away, but charity never does, as the Apostle says: "Charity never comes to an end."[5]

2. But someone says: "So, charity never passes away and is never violated?" Certainly not; because if it is charity, it endures; if it does not endure, it is not charity. Just as that barren tree which in springtime, when it begins to turn white with all its blossoms, does not bear fruit but is deceptive, so too that

---

1. Lk 12.13.
2. On this *praeceps cupiditas,* see *Sermon* 1.3 (FOTC 17.27), and Seneca, *Dialogorum Liber X: Ad Paulinum, De Brevitate Vitae* 2.1.
3. Ps 132 (133).1. 4. See Col 3.14.
5. 1 Cor 13.8.

kind of charity, which is thought to be charity but is not, when it is struck by the waves of different circumstances, fades away and thus wounds the conscientious and tricks the unguarded. And, to return to the topic at hand,

3. *Teacher, tell my brother to divide the inheritance with me.* An earthly inheritance inflicts strife upon the next generation before conferring wealth; before dividing belongings it tears the heirs apart; before assigning the fractions owed to each, it splits one's very descendants and casts them into factions.[6] Consequently, this kind of thing is not an inheritance, but a fight; and this is characteristic of a stepmother towards her stepchildren and not of belongings. The one who makes his children rich is the one who bequeaths to his children perfect charity.

4. But whoever you are who summon and appeal to the Lord with this kind of request and draw him into litigation, the Apostle instructs you by indicating that you share a common inheritance with Christ—he says that we are "heirs of God, and coheirs with Christ"[7]—if he is your Coheir, he is your Brother who, by submitting to the lot of being born, to the phases of physical development, to the natural order governing life, and to passing away in death, wanted to be found as one like you through it all.

For although he was both the sole Heir of God and the only Son by nature, he wanted you to be a partner with him, to be a coheir with him, and he made you to be such by grace, you who were wretched and subjected to the basest servitude. And so you will acquire this, and will be able to enjoy the happiness of having this conferred upon you, if you remain in the court of the Father,[8] if you share the divine inheritance. The divine estate can be given, but it cannot be divided, since both he who gives heavenly goods does not lose them, and the one who receives them does not hoard them just for himself.

5. Therefore, O man, why do you call upon him to divide, why, you pitiful creature, why do you summon him to disperse,

---

6. On this same topic, see *Sermon* 1.2 (FOTC 17.26).
7. Rom 8.17.
8. A similar encouragement, to remain in the house of the Father, is voiced in *Sermon* 1.6 (FOTC 17.29).

why do you beg him for a portion when he has sought to confer the whole inheritance on you? Given what you have already experienced, stop before you regret having asked for such things. For you made such a request in asking the Father for a portion of the original property, as the evangelist relates: "Give me the portion of the property that belongs to me,"[9] and after receiving it, as a foreigner, a vagrant, and in your extravagance you lost it by squandering it dissolutely. As a result you became an exile from paradise, without any share in the inheritance, and banished from life.

O man, Christ says to you: "What you have acquired from me and through me, you will not be able to hold on to without me, since you have already seen what you are like without me. Aware of this, I therefore made this request for you from the Father who makes all things one:[10] 'Father, I will that where I am and you are, they also may be.'[11] And since not even this was sufficient to protect you, for although you were with me in paradise, you still abandoned me and perished,[12] I said in addition: 'Father, as I am in you, and you are in me, so also may they be one in us.'[13]

"In order to have the blessings of the Father, I proceeded from the Father,[14] but did not depart from within the Father; and therefore I want you to have as much within us as we ourselves are in ourselves and abide in ourselves. So stop dividing heavenly things or wrangling about earthly things in my hearing, lest the One whom you have and hold on to today as a merciful Benefactor you experience as the severest of judges." But now let us listen to the response that the Lord made.

6. *Who*, he says, *has set me up as Judge or Arbitrator over you?* (v.14) *Who*, he says, *has set me up as Judge?* And what about those words—you yourself spoke them, O Lord: "The Father judges no one, but he has given all judgment to the Son"?[15] *Or Arbitra-*

---

9. Lk 15.12.
10. Reading the textual variant *integrantem omnium* instead of *ingrate omnium* in Olivar's CCL text.
11. See Jn 17.24.
12. See Gn 3.
13. Jn 17.21.
14. See Jn 8.42.
15. Jn 5.22.

tor over you? And who will divide[16] the just from the unjust, "just as a shepherd separates sheep from goats"?[17] If the judgment of human beings is in your domain, and if it is by you that the division of the whole world must be brought about, how is it that you say: *Who has set me up as Judge or Arbitrator over you?*

Truly all judgment is, was, and will be under Christ's jurisdiction, but at that time he had come not to judge, but to be judged, not to sentence the guilty, but to be sentenced in his innocence by the guilty.[18] His actions were those of God in a man, of the Lord in a servant, so that he would be a slave of time who was both the Creator and Judge of the ages. So it is appropriate that he responded:

7. *Who has set me up as Judge or Arbitrator over you?* And who would set up as Judge the One who set up and restored the universe? Christ could not be an arbiter to decide the suit of a litigant, since he is the summit and authority of all judgment. Before him stands the plaintiff, not having been summoned, but with a hostile intent, with the result that he loses any right to appeal the Judge's decision. And since [Christ] had come to correct and not to condemn the guilty, he removes with an injunction what had precipitated the dispute, when he says:

8. *Guard against all greed* (v.15). That is to say: let greed be cast away, and there will be no strife over an inheritance. Greed, brothers, repudiates parents, divides brothers, separates companions, breaks up a friendship, and does away with affection.[19] The one who has this within himself will belong to no one and will not even belong to himself. Greed, brothers, as the Apostle says, "is the root of all evils."[20] When it begins to take root in the heart, it destroys the adornment of good morals, just as a diseased tree connected to its lethal roots breaks up and destroys the monuments of a prior generation.

16. In Latin the word for arbitrator is *divisor*, which derives from *dividere* ("to divide"), the verb Chrysologus employs here. Unfortunately a similar wordplay does not work in English.
17. Mt 25.32.
18. Chrysologus is very fond of such paradoxes. See, e.g., *Sermons* 29.4 (FOTC 109.123), 49.3 (FOTC 109.190), 72b.1, 79.5, 90.3, and 125.8.
19. A similar diatribe against greed *(avaritia)* is given in *Sermon* 29.1 (FOTC 109.120–21).
20. 1 Tm 6.10.

SERMON 163

Where It Says: "Do not be anxious about your life, about what you are to eat"[1]

LESSED ARE THOSE WHO have listened to the Lord's words today such that his words have penetrated their hearts! Blessed are those whose minds are advanced to faith by so great and so lofty a promise from the Savior! Blessed are those who have been freed from the difficult worries of the present by believing the heavenly injunctions! For indeed the Lord today is issuing a summons to his disciples, or rather to all who hear him, with the following words: *Do not be anxious about your life, about what you are to eat, nor about your body, about what you are to wear, because your life is more than food, and your body is more than clothing* (Lk 12.22–23).

2. Who, then, is so hostile to his own good, who is so inimical to his own good pleasure, as to despise blessings that have been prepared voluntarily from heaven, and to long for things that are acquired by struggles and pains in this world? It is a very degenerate spirit, a mind that is entirely slavish, that would search carefully for cooks' creations, the foul things that come out of a kitchen, and day-old food with its horrible stench, when a meal fit for a king is always ready to be served to him. Therefore, O man, do not wear yourself out trying to provide for yourself what is worthless, do not strain yourself over attempting to gain what is going to perish, since God is at hand everywhere and at all times to put together a meal for you.

What king does not furnish the provisions owed to his soldiers? What master does not serve the rations due those who are loyal to him? What father does not give bread to his children?[2] Therefore, if God is our King, Master, and Father, what

---

1. Lk 12.22.
2. See Mt 7.9.

will he ever refuse us? The soldier who serves at his own expense detracts from the king, the servant who lives off his own means finds fault with his master, the son who is anxious to provide for himself is a reproach to his father while he is still alive. Therefore, O man, do not desire to dishonor God by engaging in such thinking about your own needs; with the justice of a King, with the zealous concern of a Master, and with the love of a Father he has taken all of your anxiety into himself, and has poured out in return his concern when he says: "Do not be anxious about what you are to eat."

3. But perhaps that unique food that rained down sweet as honey frightens you off because of the example of the Jews who found it nauseating, and you do not believe that it is God's will that the flesh which has congealed out of a variety of fluids be satisfied with manna alone.[3] You say: "Just as God willed that the body consist of a diversity of members, so too did he will and ordain that it be nourished by various kinds of food." O man, this is a needless worry that is troubling you. For all creation hastens to come together at the meal served by the Creator.

Therefore, if the uniqueness and lack of variety of the food in the era of the Law frightens you off, let the abundance of the heavenly Banquet in the Gospel era appeal to you and stir up your taste buds; it serves on one platter every kind of creature for Peter to eat.[4] For whatever Noah, the transporter of a new world, preserved to generate life for that world,[5] whatever flies and is borne along through the air, whatever is born to live on earth, and whatever exists and moves within the waters, all of this is slaughtered and offered from heaven to form the one dinner of Peter.[6]

4. Therefore, O man, if you want to take and eat everything

3. See Ex 16.4 and 31; Nm 11.6 and 21.5.
4. See Acts 10.9–16.
5. See Gn 9.1–3.
6. For references to other patristic writers who make a similar parallel between Noah and Simon Peter, see H. Rahner, "Navicula Petri," *ZKTh* 69 (1947): 17, and idem, "Antenna Crucis," *ZKTh* 86 (1964): 137, n. 2. For numerous examples of Chrysologus's typological exegesis of individuals from the Old Testament (other than in this sermon), see A. Olivar, "Els principis," 429, n. 13.

that God gives you, have no desire to supply for yourself cheap and perishable provisions. And we for our part have taken great pains to make the point with significant examples that when you fix your thoughts on heavenly goods you will not be lacking in fleshly goods. But God, in character with his majesty, sends the one who doubts his promises off to common and very lowly examples, in order to reprimand you by examining these matters, since he has not won you over by issuing such a great invitation.

5. *Consider*, he says, *the ravens, who neither sow nor reap, and yet God feeds them; how much more valuable are you than they!* (v.24) It is fitting that he sends the dubious unbeliever to the bird that is fond of wars, a companion of fury, a servant of cruelty, insatiable for blood, and inflicting more severe violence on the dead themselves than did the sword.[7] For as soon as the weapon finishes its work, that horribly wicked butcher becomes fat off the lifeless body, and it mangles it, tears it apart, and scatters the remains, such that no remains can be found to allow a merciful burial to commit them to rest.

And so with such an example God magnifies the insanity of the one who doubts insofar as he thinks that God will refuse to his holy children what he supplies to unholy birds, and supposes that he will not provide food to those who leave their native land, their home, their parents, children, and spouses for his sake,[8] when he is the One who has granted that they be born, let them grow, and given a definite size to their bodies.

6. O how unspeakable! O how wretched, O how entirely deserving of utter misery is the one who longs for bread while the kingdom is being given;[9] who pleads for a drink while he is being presented with eternity as a gift; who begs for a bodily garment while being clothed with the glory of immortality! Caught up in his own unhappiness, he does not believe that he can become happy; and brought up on the dust of earth, he doubts that he will dwell in heaven. Fittingly, therefore, did the Lord add what follows.

---

7. For other examples where Chrysologus uses animals to signify vices or virtues, see Introduction, FOTC 109.24–25.

8. See Mt 19.29 and parallels.   9. See Lk 12.32.

7. *Who among you can add even a single cubit to his height? And why are you anxious about clothing?* (vv.25–26) The One who searches the depths[10] lays bare the thoughts of human minds. For indeed every human being who desires that his body be beautiful, ardently hopes that he is going to be tall. While the human being is free to direct his thoughts in this vein, he is unable to achieve this by his own means. *Who among you is able to add anything by thinking?* (v.25) Nevertheless, it is by believing that one attains what he is unable to attain by thinking. And so it is that God, who is aware of human desire, elongated the human being according to the pattern of Christ, so that he would be handsome and entirely good-looking by reaching Christ's stature,[11] when he used to be ashamed about being ugly and short. Therefore, it is appropriate that he added:

8. *If you are not able to accomplish even this smallest of things, why are you anxious about the rest?* (v.26) That is: O man, why do you presume to think about greater matters, when you despair of believing in lesser ones? What is less than clothing, what is greater than bodily growth? So believe that bodily apparel can be provided to you by God, by whom, as your faith promises in return, bodily growth will be provided to you. But that God so loves the human race that those whom he rebukes by his right as Lord, he immediately soothes and comforts with Fatherly tenderness: after the comparison with that most disgusting bird, he calls our attention to the example of a fragrant and very beautiful flower.

9. *Consider*, he says, *the lilies of the field and how they grow. But I tell you that not even Solomon in all his glory was clothed like one of them* (v.27). O how great is the love for humanity which brings the devotion[12] of heaven down to earth! For indeed the One who could have established his injunctions merely by his own authority conveys and gets their meaning across with all the

---

10. For other references to Christ as *scrutator* in Chrysologus's sermons, see *Sermons* 50.6 (FOTC 109.196–97) and 99a.4, and R. Benericetti, *Il Cristo*, 263, n. 165.
11. See Eph 4.13.
12. For other examples where Chrysologus refers to God's *pietas*, see *Sermon* 158.1 and n. 5.

diligence of a teacher; and he who was able to anchor the fulfillment of his promise on faith alone leads his audience to faith in what he promised by a persuasive example, strengthens the doubtful by the comparison with the lily, and elevates the lily by the example of Solomon.

That is to say, as the Lord himself testifies, among all the kings of the world Solomon shone with the beauty of his unparalleled glory and his unique attire, and the lily excels and surpasses in loveliness all the flowers of the earth, and the lily stands as far apart from all the other plants as the King clearly outshines all the rest in appearance, honor, and glory. The beauty of the lily does not need to be described any further by us, since the Lord's testimony gives it an unparalleled status.

10. But what do bear repeating are the matters which the Lord has comprised in the two examples for the strengthening of our faith, namely, that the Christian who is assured of life, of the kingdom, and of immortality must not be disturbed about the need for food and clothing, since he sees that God has conferred such glorious raiment on a plant that is here today and gone tomorrow. But just as these flowers are bound to wither and to be burnt in the furnace,[13] so too are those people destined for death and for the fires of Gehenna, who entertain doubts about present blessings being provided to them by God, although they think that future blessings have already been imparted to them.

11. *Do not be anxious about what you are to eat or what you are to wear. Your heavenly Father, however, knows that you need all these things. Seek the kingdom of heaven, and all these things will be added unto you* (vv.22, 30–31). When he calls himself our Father, he shows that he is not lacking in devoted concern for us; when he bids us to seek the kingdom of heaven, he is making clear that all things will have to be made subject to us,[14] and he indicates that we shall possess whatever we need to enjoy the magnificence of heaven.

13. See Lk 12.28.
14. See Phil 3.21.

SERMON 164

Where It Says: "I have come to light a fire on the earth"[1]

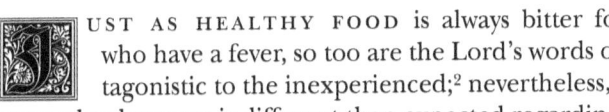UST AS HEALTHY FOOD is always bitter for those who have a fever, so too are the Lord's words often antagonistic to the inexperienced;[2] nevertheless, in both cases what happens is different than expected regarding the infirmity of the body or of the mind. Today the Lord appears to have exasperated some in his audience when he said: *I have come to light a fire on the earth, and how I wish that it were ignited!* (Lk 12.49) And later: *Do you think that I have come to bring peace to the earth? Not peace, but separation* (v.51).

2. But what about those words: "Behold the Lamb of God"?[3] What about: "Just as a sheep is led to slaughter, and just like a lamb before its shearer, he did not open his mouth"?[4] And what about: "Say to the daughter of Zion: 'See, your meek King comes to you'"?[5] And why is it that this Lamb is so harsh and piercing in his preaching? Why is it that in his words he strikes like a ram, while he is so patient and silent in his Passion, and yields to death with complete humility?

And it is true, brothers, Christ did enter his world gentle and meek in every way;[6] he was pleasant as he was born[7] of our stock; while being rocked tenderly in the cradle, he was even more tender himself; as a little boy he played and rested on his mother's lap; while squeezed tightly to his parent's neck, he squeezed tightly with the full embrace of love; and in order to give nourishment, while he was nourished with complete affection, he gradually progressed and grew through all the stages

---

1. Lk 12.49.
2. A similar medical analogy is employed in *Sermon* 156.1 (FOTC 17.265).
3. Jn 1.29 and 36. 4. Is 53.7.
5. Zec 9.9 and Mt 21.5. 6. See Mt 11.29.
7. See Lk 2.7

of life;[8] he always lived in poverty; he spent his life always single, because the poor man is always accessible, and the single person is always available to all.

3. Yet why is it that he sets such a fire with his words, that he enkindles and spreads such a tremendous blaze when he says: *I have come to light a fire on the earth?* Why is it? As often as a field grows wild after having been left unattended for a long time, and becomes all deteriorated with horrid-looking, untrimmed growth, it is always, as we know, cleared away and cleaned up by a blaze set by the most skillful farmer, and the farmer has a good reason for the fire to be lit so that after the briars are burnt up, the original appearance of the field may be uncovered again, free access may be provided for planting, an easy path may be opened up for the plowshare, the land which had been barren for a long time may become conducive to growth, and it may now most happily compensate for that long and dismal period of idleness with a fruitful harvest.

Therefore, when the Jewish sod was worn out by the continual plowing and constant cultivation of the Law to the point of exhaustion, it did not respond to the seed or to the labor, but produced chaff instead of grain[9] and yielded thorns instead of vines.[10] Christ directed the action of divine cultivation to the crops of the gentiles instead, and in his desire to cleanse the fallow lands of the nations which had been for so long a time overrun with brambles, he, the greatest Teacher, first lit a fire on the earth, and whatever the excess of nature had made squalid, whatever winter's rigor had dried up, he cleansed and consumed with a blaze that he made. As a result, fields far and wide that had been exhausted by unproductiveness,[11] became fertile after being nourished by their own ashes, and after being hard for so long they were made once again soft and supple, and having thus been made pliant to the plowshare of the

---

8. See Lk 2.52.
9. See Mt 13.24–30.
10. See Mt 7.16. Elsewhere too Chrysologus uses images from farming to the detriment of Judaism. See *Sermons* 106.7 and 137.1.
11. The word Chrysologus uses for "unproductiveness" is *ieiunium,* which is the usual term for "fasting."

Gospel they were then ready for the seed, and with its furrow now fruitful they yielded grain of thirty-, sixty-, and a hundredfold.[12]

4. But this very method of cultivation employed by the ancient and heavenly Farmer is not new; for he has always had the habit of planting the Law and sowing grace by using fire. When he was about to give the Law he first lit a fire in the bramble bush, but the bush bore the divine blaze, it did not produce it,[13] even then prefiguring the people who were full of the thorns of malice and unyielding to the Law's tilling.

And now when he appointed the apostles to tend the fields of the gentiles, he showered down fire upon them, he appeared as fire and settled upon them[14] in such a way that they were able to dry up what was damp, to spread out the dryness, to roast what was raw, to heat what had grown cold, to rekindle what had been extinguished, to burn up what was harmful, and in a diversity of works but with one and the same fire to cultivate all the deserted regions of the earth for the harvest of heaven, as the prophet says: "Their voice has gone out to all the earth, and their words to the ends of the world."[15] But let us now proceed to what follows.

5. *I have a baptism to receive,* he says, *and what anguish I feel until it is accomplished!* (v.50) *I have come to light a fire on the earth, and how I wish that it were ignited!* He pursues fire, he demands water: what is the connection between such different things? Water pursues a flame, a flame increases water: how can entities so opposed to each other be in such harmony?[16] What is at work here, as we have said, is a metaphor of the divine Farmer; but in fact everything sprouts full of heat, and is nourished by moisture. And so, God, the Parent[17] of the universe, with a hasty interchange between fire and water produces us and nur-

---

12. See Mt 13.8.
14. See Acts 2.3.
13. See Ex 3.2.
15. Ps 18.5 LXX; Ps 19.4.
16. The Latin antithesis *concors . . . discordia* is also found in *Astronomicon* 1.142, a first-century C.E. work by M. Manilius, who likewise describes how harmony results from discordant elements in nature.
17. On God as Parent, see also, e.g., *Sermon* 33.2 and n. 4, and *Sermon* 50.3 (FOTC 109.139 and 194–95).

tures us, for whom he burns, he is hot, he is on fire, and he pants with such great affection.

6. *I have a baptism to receive.* Christ is baptized in his own blood, so that whatever he assumed from our flesh he would wash clean, renew, and restore completely into the form of his divine majesty. Christ is baptized with the baptism of his Passion, since[18] the sin of the whole world[19] could not be destroyed except by him who had made the world.

7. *Do you think,* he says, *that I have come to bring peace to the earth? Not peace, but separation* (v.51). Why? It is because union with heaven comes about by means of this kind of separation from earth. No one can be tied to earth and joined to heaven. Therefore, may this earthly separation be pleasing and dear which separates us from earthly things so as to graft us onto divine ones.

8. *From this point on,* he says, *there will be five in one house, divided three against two, and two against three: father against son, and son against father; mother against daughter, and daughter against mother; mother-in-law against daughter-in-law, daughter-in-law against mother-in-law* (vv.52–53). While he said that in the one house they were five in number who were to be divided, there are six names that appear: father, son, mother, daughter, mother-in-law, and daughter-in-law; but since the mother-in-law is the same one who is the mother, it is true that even with all these names only five persons are found.

But three are divided into[20] two, insofar as against the groom and the bride united in marriage the mother-in-law who is the third will remain divided in the house. Therefore, against the Church, which is united by marriage to Christ, she, the synagogue, that is, the mother-in-law, remains thoroughly divided now through her own fault. Then, two are divided into three insofar as from this union of Christ and the Church another synagogue of heresy[21] is broken off and divided, with the result

---

18. Reading the variant *quia* rather than the *qui* in Olivar's CCL text.
19. See Jn 1.29.
20. The Latin preposition *in* is used by Chrysologus to mean "against" on some occasions and "into" on others.
21. The "synagogue of heresy" that Chrysologus had in mind could well

that Christ and the Church, who are separated from the heretics, remain united in the one Spirit.

And the father is divided against the son, and the son against the father, insofar as the Jewish people, who have received the name of father on account of the generation of Christ according to the flesh, are separated from Christ the Son through envy; the jealous father turns his love into hatred, because the Son's glory is a continual punishment and a constant torment for him, as the Apostle says: "From whom come the fathers, and from them comes Christ according to the flesh, who is blessed forever."[22]

And the mother is divided against the daughter: for, to be sure, the synagogue is the mother, from whom in the persons of Peter and the other apostles her daughter the Church was born. When the Church was counted worthy of being joined in union with Christ the Divine King, she consequently had to endure having her mother as a rival and a stepmother. And what mother treats her daughter the way a mother-in-law treats her daughter-in-law? And indeed when this mother, the synagogue, saw that the Church from the gentiles had come on the scene as her daughter-in-law, in her wickedness she killed her Son,[23] so as to avoid having to look at her daughter-in-law's union with him. She killed Christ, as if in her fury she could extinguish her daughter-in-law's love in this way. But Christ rose from the dead to be joined permanently in marriage to the Church, in order to prove that charity is not sundered by death,[24] but grows.

9. The Lord then rebukes those who with vain curiosity[25] strive to investigate what appears in the sky, the origins of the clouds, the courses of the stars, and the zones of the world, yet do not endeavor at all to apply themselves or the signs available to them to recognize the time of their salvation. *You hypocrites*, he says, *you know how to judge what appears in the sky, yet how is it*

---

have been the Arians, whom other pro-Nicene authors likened to Jews because of their denial or radical diminishment of the divinity of the Son.

22. Rom 9.5.
23. See Mt 21.37–38.
24. See Rom 8.35–38.
25. A similar rebuke against such "curiosity" regarding astronomical phenomena is made in *Sermon* 156.9 (FOTC 17.269).

that you do not judge this present moment? (v.56) An eye that is opened widely loses the light, since the whole of the human being's vision is contained within the pupil.

Therefore, do not be eager to look at many things, but look at yourself instead; do not be eager to fix your sight on the heights; do not presume or strive to gaze upon things that are far away, because the eye, since it is limited, does not grasp many things, it does not penetrate the heights, nor does it perceive things that are far away, and thus the one who supposes that he sees everything actually sees nothing. Therefore, recognize the day of salvation, the acceptable time.[26]

26. See 2 Cor 6.2.

SERMON 167

A Second on Fasting[1]

T IS FITTING THAT in the time of fasting the very blessed John comes to us as a teacher of penance: a teacher in word and in deed. A true instructor demonstrates by example what he asserts verbally. The office of teacher depends upon knowledge, but the authority of that office is based on one's life. Doing what is to be taught makes the listener obey. Teaching by deeds is the sole norm of instruction. Instruction in words is knowledge, but in deeds is virtue. Therefore, that knowledge is true which is combined with virtue. That in fact is divine, and not human, as the evangelist attests when he says: "Which Jesus began to do and teach."[2] When an instructor does what is to be taught, he both instructs by what is heard and trains by his example.[3]

2. *In those days*, it says, *John the Baptist came preaching in the desert of Judea, and saying: "Do penance, for the kingdom of heaven has drawn near"* (Mt 3.1–2). *Do penance*. Why not rather: "Rejoice"? Rejoice rather that divine matters are supplanting human ones, heavenly ones are supplanting earthly ones, eternal ones in place of temporal ones, good instead of evil, security instead of anxiety, blessedness instead of distress, and that which will endure in place of what is destined to perish.

The kingdom of heaven has drawn near. Do penance. Certainly let a person repent, let anyone repent who has preferred what is

---

1. The title is reconstructed from *Sermon* 166 (see CCL 24B.1019; FOTC 17.272–76). The reference to "the time of fasting" in the first section of this *Sermon* 167 as well as its principal theme of doing penance suggests that it was delivered during Lent. See F. Sottocornola, *L'anno liturgico*, 125. A. Olivar, *Los sermones*, 276, notes the possibility that this sermon may have been preached next after *Sermon* 166, which also has as its theme Lenten fasting.

2. Acts 1.1.

3. On this point, see *Sermon* 66.9 and n. 24 (FOTC 109.272–73).

human to what is divine, who has willed to be a slave to the world rather than have dominion over the world with the Lord of the world.[4] Let anyone repent who has preferred perishing with the devil to reigning with Christ.[5] Let anyone repent who has fled the freedom of the virtues in his desire to be held captive by the vices. Let anyone repent and do sufficient penance for reaching out to death rather than holding fast to life.

3. *The kingdom of heaven has drawn near.* The kingdom of heaven is the reward of the righteous, the judgment of sinners, and the punishment for the unrighteous. Therefore, blessed John, who wanted judgment to be averted by penance, wanted sinners not to face judgment, but to receive a reward; he wanted the unrighteous to enter the kingdom, not to suffer punishment. *The kingdom of heaven has drawn near.* And John sang out that the kingdom of heaven was near at the time when the world, still as a child, was looking forward to growing older. But now we say that the kingdom of heaven is already as near as possible since the world is wearied by extreme old age, is devoid of strength, is relinquishing its members, is losing its senses, is weighed down by afflictions, refuses treatment, is dead to life, is living with diseases, proclaims that it is fading away, and attests to its end![6]

4. Therefore, we are more obstinate than the Jews, we who pursue a fleeting world; we forget about the future and direct all our desires toward the present; we have no fear although we are already facing the very moment of judgment; we do not run to meet the Lord who is already on his way; we want death to remain, but do not want the resurrection of the dead; we want to be slaves, but do not want to reign, since we want to delay so great a kingdom for our Lord. What has happened to those words: "When you pray, say: 'Thy kingdom come'"?[7] Therefore,

---

4. *Dominationem mundi cum mundi domino.*

5. A similar juxtaposition is found in *Sermon* 155.5 (FOTC 17.264). See also Cyprian, *Mortality* 18, in FOTC 36, trans. R. J. Deferrari (1958), 214: "... if there are greater longings and stronger desires to serve the devil here than to reign with Christ?"

6. In *Sermon* 47.4 (FOTC 17.101–2) also, Chrysologus voices his opinion that the end of the world is near. On historical events that may have given rise to this opinion, see Introduction, FOTC 109.13.

7. Lk 11.2.

we have an even greater need for penance, and we have to take the kind of medicine that corresponds with the kind of wound we bear.

5. Let us do penance, brothers, let us do penance right away, because we no longer have any extended period of time, the very hour is quickly coming to an end for us, and the imminence of judgment is already preventing us from the opportunity to make amends. Let your penance get up and running, so that judgment may not outrun it, since the fact that the Lord has not yet come, that he still waits, and that he delays, means that his desire is for us to return to him and not to perish.

This is clear from such words of mercy as he has always addressed to us: "I do not want the death of the sinner, but only that he return and live."[8] Let us do penance, brothers, and not become fearful at the time constraints. The Creator of time cannot be constrained by time. The thief in the Gospel proves this, since on the cross and even in the hour of death he made off with pardon, he forced his way into life, he broke into paradise, he penetrated the kingdom.[9]

6. And let us, brothers, who have not gained any merit from our will, acquire virtue at least out of necessity;[10] lest we be judged, let us be our own judges; let us impose penance on ourselves so that we might be able to free ourselves from sentencing. Happiness of the first order is to rejoice in the everlasting security of innocence, to keep intact the holiness of mind and body, to stay unstained and uncontaminated by the world,[11] to have no guilt on one's conscience, to know none of the wounds of sin, to be always in possession of the grace of the virtues, and to live always in the hope of the rewards of heaven.[12]

But if our mind has been pierced by any dart of sin, if our flesh should be swollen from an offense, or if our human frailty

---

8. Ezek 33.11.
9. See Lk 23.40–43.
10. On this expression, see *Sermon* 42.5 and n. 24 (FOTC 109.171).
11. Chrysologus engages in wordplay here: *immunda mundi inquinamenta*. See also *Sermon* 139.8 and n. 15.
12. On this "happiness of the first order" see also *Sermons* 34.1 (FOTC 109.144) and 91.4.

should be ruptured and infected with the vices, then let the medicine of penance, which those who are well do not need, aid the sick, let the lance of remorse be added, let the fire of sorrow then be applied, then let the poultices of sighing be attached, then let the fever and swelling of the conscience diminish, then let the sores of guilt be cleansed by tears, then let haircloaks wipe off the body's filth.

Let any person bear, yes, let him bear the bitter remedy of penance, who has been unwilling to stay in good health as he ought. For anyone who values life, no remedy is too severe. The Physician should not go without thanks just because it is through suffering that he restores the patient to health.[13] The one who preserves the credit of innocence does not pay the interest of penance. The Lord makes this clear when he says: "The healthy do not need a physician, but the ill do."[14] And what their illness is he has revealed when he says next: "I have not come to call the righteous, but sinners."[15] John calls back through penance, Christ calls through grace. This is why John makes his way fully equipped for penance by his clothing, food, and locale.

7. *John the Baptist,* it says, *came preaching in the desert of Judea, saying: "Do penance"* (vv.1–2). John calls for penance throughout the desert of Judea, which was losing by its own barrenness the cultivation of the Law, the labor of the prophets, the fruitfulness of the fathers, and God's harvest;[16] and so it is fitting that a call to penance is issued to something deserted, not in terms of human occupants nor of geographical status, but deserted of good conduct. A cry is in vain when there is no one to hear it.

8. *John, however, was clothed in camels' hair* (v.4). He could have been clothed in goat-hair, but there was no need for such a garment; but he accepted the hair of the most crooked of animals, which has nothing right about it, nothing pleasing, nothing

---

13. As elsewhere in Chrysologus's sermons, the Latin word *salus* indicates both physical well-being and eternal salvation.
14. Mt 9.12.
15. Mt 9.13.
16. For similar uses of agricultural imagery, see *Sermon* 164.3 and n. 10.

beautiful, whom nature has assigned to hard labor, consigned to bear a heavy burden, and handed over to the lowest form of servitude.

The teacher of penance had to be dressed in such clothing so that those who had twisted themselves out of shape by abandoning right discipline and had become completely deformed by the kinds of sins they committed, would be subjected to the heavy burdens of penance, would need to submit to the harsh distress of making amends, and would sustain the labored sighs of remorse. In this way they would be straightened out and made thin through penance as though through the narrow eye of a needle, and thereby enter the expanse of forgiveness, and the Lord's words would be fulfilled, that a camel can pass through the eye of a needle.[17]

9. *His food was locusts and wild honey* (v.4). The locust, assigned to chastise sinners, is a good image as the food of penance, so that, hopping from a place of sin to a place of penance, it can fly all the way to heaven on the wings of pardon.[18] The prophet had perceived this when he said: "Like a passing shadow I have faded away, and I have been shaken off like a locust. My knees are weak from fasting, and my flesh is transformed because of mercy."[19] You have heard how he has been shaken off like a locust in moving from sin to penance, and he has bent his knees in order to bear the burden of penance; and he is allowed honey for food, so that the sweetness of mercy might temper the bitterness of penance.

17. See Mt 19.24 and parallels.
18. For other examples from Chrysologus's sermons of animals representing virtues and vices, see Introduction, FOTC 109.24–25.
19. Ps 108 (109).23–24.

SERMON 168

Where It Says: "Tax collectors and sinners drew near to the Lord to listen to him"[1]

UST AS A CLEVER traveler discovers how to enter the depths of the sea and to traverse routes that are unmarked in a journey along the water,[2] so too has the divine Law allowed and taught us to hear something of the words of God and penetrate the mystery of their divine meaning. This is why we untie the boat of our mind[3] from the shore of our flesh and enter the deep waters[4] of the words of the Gospel, believing that by the breeze of the Holy Spirit we shall reach the port of heavenly understanding. Our Lord today has inspired sinners to hope for pardon, and he has muzzled the murmuring of the haughty by providing an outstanding example of mercy.

2. *Tax collectors and sinners*, it says, *drew near to the Lord to listen to him. And the Pharisees and the scribes murmured: "This man receives sinners and eats with them"* (Lk 15.1–2). They were no less envious than they were haughty in that they bore malice from the Lord's benevolence and were shown to be without pity from the pity of God. They became cruel from the mercy of Christ, they took sick from the heavenly healing, and they turned the pardon of sinners into an accusation against the

---

1. Lk 15.1. It is likely that this sermon was preached during Lent because of the Gospel text and its theme of God's mercy toward the sinner, as well as its placement in the Felician collection of Chrysologus's sermons immediately after two sermons that are clearly Lenten. It is also probable that *Sermon* 169, on subsequent verses of Luke 15, was the next sermon preached. See F. Sottocornola, *L'anno liturgico*, 125–26.

2. Similar seafaring imagery is given in *Sermon* 8.1 (FOTC 109.42).

3. For the human body described as a boat or ship in Chrysologus's preaching, see *Sermon* 7a.1 and n. 4 (FOTC 109.40).

4. Chrysologus speaks of the words of Scripture as deep waters also in *Sermon* 63.1 (FOTC 109.249).

Judge. *He receives sinners and eats with them.* This is how the envious see, how the haughty perceive, how the harsh understand, and how the malicious think.

3. *He receives sinners* (v.2). They do not say: "He assumes"[5] them. What was it that he who receives had lost? Whoever finds what he lost pardons faults, turns wrath into joy, and transforms grief into grace. *He receives sinners.* God receives sinners, but God does not allow those whom he receives to remain sinners. The approach of a sinner does no harm to God. God sanctifies the sinner when he draws near to him.[6] O Pharisee, Christ does not receive sins when he receives sinners, because God is the recipient not of the offense, but of the human being. So the Pharisee should not have been looking at the condition the sinners were in when they had arrived, but at their condition upon their return. As a case in point, let them see that Paul, whom they had sent as a persecutor, returned soon thereafter as a preacher.[7] But now let us listen to the kind of comparison and image with which God conveys his joy at the return of a sinner.

4. *And he told them a parable: "What person among you who has one hundred sheep does not leave the ninety-nine in a deserted place if he loses one of them, and goes off to the one who had been lost until he finds it? And when he finds it, he joyfully puts it on his shoulders, and when he returns home he invites his friends and neighbors and says: 'Rejoice with me, because I have found my sheep which had been lost.' In just this fashion, I tell you, there will be more joy in heaven over one sinner who repents than over ninety-nine righteous people who do not need to repent"* (vv.3–7). Indeed whenever we recover something that was lost we always feel our joy renewed and increased, and it is more pleasant for us to have found what was lost than to have kept it from being lost in the first place.

But this parable is saying even more about God's mercy than merely expressing a truism about how human beings act. To

---

5. Chrysologus contrasts *recipit* ("receives") and *suscipit* ("assumes"). For Chrysologus's christological use of the latter term, see R. Benericetti, *Il Cristo*, 97–99 and 260–62.
6. On this point, see also *Sermons* 35.2 (FOTC 109.150), 36.1 (FOTC 17.76), and 94.2.
7. See Acts 9.1–30. The transformation in Paul is from *persecutor* to *praedicator*.

leave great things behind out of love for those that are most insignificant is characteristic of the power of God, and not of human greed. God both causes the existence of what did not exist, and he pursues what was lost in such a way that he retains what he left behind; and he finds what was lost in such a way that he does not lose what was kept. Therefore, he is no earthly Shepherd, but a heavenly One; and this parable is more than just signifying human labors, but is a foreshadowing of divine mysteries, as will immediately become clear from the very number he mentions when he says:

5. *What person among you who has one hundred sheep, if he loses one of them* (v.4). Why not fifty, why not two hundred, but one hundred, but one? It was to show that there was grief not as much over the loss as over the number. For indeed the loss of one had ruined the total number of one hundred, and had reduced the total from the right to the left,[8] so that by the loss of one the left side encompassed everything, and the right side had nothing. The number ninety-nine lies encompassed on the left, is kept under wraps, and is held in submission; nevertheless, when it obtains and realizes an increase of one, it immediately has the honor of going over to the right and then attains the crown of the number one hundred.[9]

And if never having had the number one hundred is a cause for grief, how much more grievous is it to have lost it? You see that on account of the loss of one sheep this shepherd had lamented that the whole flock had fallen from the right and had all fallen away to the left, and so, leaving the ninety-nine he pursues the one, he seeks the one, in order to find them whole in the one, in order to restore the whole in the one. But now let us reveal the mystery of this heavenly parable.

6. The man who has the hundred sheep is Christ the Good

---

8. Or "from the even column to the odd column" *(de dextera . . . ad sinistram).*

9. Chrysologus is indicating the practice stemming from the classical era of reckoning numbers 1–99 on the left hand and numbers 100 and beyond on the right hand. See, e.g., Juvenal, *Satire* 10.249; Jerome, *Adversus Jovinianum* 1.3 (PL 23.224); and John Cassian, *Conlationes* 24.26 (SC 64.201–2). See also Irenaeus, *Libros quinque adversus haereses* 1.9.2 (=1.16.2), ed. W. W. Harvey (Cambridge, 1857), 1:161–62 and n. 3 for other references.

Shepherd, the merciful Shepherd, who in the one sheep, that is, in Adam, had constituted the whole flock of the human race. He had set this sheep amid the delights of paradise,[10] in a place of life-giving pasture. But that sheep forgot the voice of its Father while paying heed to the howling of wolves, and it lost the safety of the sheepfold, and was injured all over by deadly wounds. Therefore, Christ came into the world to look for it, and found it in a womb belonging to the Virgin. He came in the flesh of his Nativity; raising it onto the cross he placed it on the shoulders of his Passion,[11] and rejoicing in the complete joy of the Resurrection, by means of his Ascension he bore it up and carried it off to his heavenly dwelling.[12]

And he called his *friends and neighbors*, that is, the angels, *and said to them: "Rejoice with me, because I have found my sheep which had been lost"* (v.6). The angels rejoice and celebrate with Christ over the return of the Lord's sheep, nor are they indignant that he exercises complete authority over them on the throne of majesty, because envy had long ago been driven out of heaven with the devil,[13] nor could the sin of envy any longer penetrate the celestial realm thanks to the Lamb who had taken away the sin of the world.[14]

7. Brothers, he sought us on earth; let us seek him in heaven. He has borne us to the glory of his divinity; let us bear him in our body with perfect holiness. "Glorify God," the Apostle says, "and bear him in your body."[15] The one who bears no sin through the action of his flesh bears God in his body.

10. See Gn 2.15.
11. Ambrose, *Expositio Evangelii secundum Lucam* 7.209 (CCL 14.287), gives a similar interpretation to this parable: the sheep that had perished in Adam is raised up in Christ, and the shoulders of the Good Shepherd are the arms of the cross.
12. On the benefits to humanity from Christ's Ascension, see also *Sermon* 85.2 and n. 6.
13. See Is 14.12. On envy being the reason for the devil's banishment from heaven, see also *Sermons* 4.1 (FOTC 17.40) and 48.5 (FOTC 109.186–87).
14. See Jn 1.29.
15. 1 Cor 6.20. F. Sottocornola, *L'anno liturgico*, 125, suggests that this text may have been a verse from the Epistle read at the liturgy on this occasion.

SERMON 169

On the Woman Who Lost the Silver Coin[1]

HAT THROUGHOUT ALL THE Gospel readings mystical meanings lie hidden and the secrets of heavenly understanding abide there, only those who have received the grace of the divine Spirit know.[2] Notice that after the Shepherd from on high sought out the sheep that had been lost out of his flock of a hundred, found it, and brought it back then to the heavenly sheepfold to the complete happiness of the angels,[3] a woman is brought forward as a figure in the Gospel who lights a lamp and searches so diligently for the one silver coin that she lost out of her ten, that when she finds it she produces from her gain and from her joy a reason for rejoicing in heaven.

For this is what he says: *Or what woman who has ten silver coins, if she loses one of them, does not light a lamp and sweep the house and search diligently until she should find it? And when she finds it, she calls her friends and neighbors together and says: "Rejoice with me, because I have found my silver coin which I had lost." Likewise, I assure you, there will be joy before the angels of God concerning one sinner who repents* (Lk 15.8–10).

2. Do you suppose that she is an ordinary woman, or is the fact that she had ten silver coins to be thought of in a human sense? Or do you think that she lost the one coin by the sort of

---

1. Literally, "drachma" *(dragma)*. See Lk 15.8. It is likely that this sermon was preached during Lent and immediately followed *Sermon* 168. See *Sermon* 168, n. 1.

2. Emphasis on the deeper, spiritual level of the biblical text's meaning abounds in Chrysologus's sermons. See, e.g., *Sermons* 18.5 and 52.1 (FOTC 109.84–85, 202), and 132.2 (FOTC 17.216). See also Introduction, FOTC 109.22–26.

3. See Lk 15.4–7. This is possibly a reference to *Sermon* 168, which would have immediately preceded this sermon.

mishap that is commonplace in this world, or is it merely coincidental that she searches for it at night? Or does she light the lamp in the way we do? Or is it to be expected that she lost and found it within her house? Or is it a usual kind of matter that she summons her friends and neighbors to share her happiness, but when she lost it we do not read that she summoned them to share her grief?

This is an unusual kind of loss: he reveals that the silver coin was not removed, but misplaced; he says that it was hidden in darkness in the house, not buried in the ground by the trickery of some stranger. You see how unique all of this is, how it goes beyond and exceeds what humans customarily do, how it breathes and gives an aroma of divine meaning, how it lifts the mind's understanding to heaven, how it places it in the celestial realm, how it urges us to light the lamp of our heart up high, and like the woman in the Gospel to look for the silver coin of saving knowledge amid the obscurities of what the Lord has given us to read.[4]

3. Before Christ came to the sheep that went astray, before he raised it up to heaven on his merciful shoulders when it was worn out by wandering around so pitifully, and before he managed to carry the sheep to safety in the sheepfold where no wolf could approach,[5] the woman who had ten silver coins was in the dark for a long time, and not only did she lament the loss of one of her coins, but she did not see even the nine coins that she still had. For her, night was continual; for her, darkness was deep and persistent, since without the divine fire her lamp was of no help in providing any light through the night.

But after the fire from above, the Holy Spirit, poured itself forth upon the apostles in a shower of flames,[6] and with all its fiery heat enkindled the hearts of mortals that were as cold as they were shrouded in darkness, *the woman*, that is, the Church, *lit her lamp* (v.8), that is, the vision deep within her heart, or, as the Apostle phrases it, "the eyes of your heart which have been

---
4. Similar language about elucidating obscurities in the biblical text is found, e.g., in *Sermons* 52.1 (FOTC 109.202) and 112.1 (FOTC 17.180).
5. See Lk 15.4–7.
6. See Acts 2.3–4.

illumined."⁷ And so she lit her lamp, and after the labor of the apostles she swept that Jewish house that was blinded by the darkness of ignorance, until she would now recover in Christ the silver coin that she had lost from the ten coins, that is, from the Decalogue of the Law.

4. Christ is the coin full of divinity, Christ is the silver coin of our redemption and ransom, Christ is the One who was in the Decalogue of the Law and was concealed therein, Christ is the One whom the synagogue possessed but did not see on account of the darkness that was overwhelming it. We have indicated that the ten silver coins were the ten words of the Law, of which the synagogue had lost one. Which one? The one that John was the first to find in the Church, because he was a lamp that burned brightly, as the Lord says: "He was a lamp."⁸ This is what the evangelist has to say: "In the beginning was the Word, and the Word was with God, and the Word was God."⁹

5. That this Word was in the Decalogue is already clear. "Hear this, O Israel," it says, "the Lord your God is God alone."¹⁰ By the synagogue's failure to see this Word in the Son, it loses it in the Father; by not believing in Christ, it puts Christ to death by crucifixion; as a result it is right that further on in the Decalogue are the words: "You shall not kill."¹¹ Inasmuch as the Jew severed the whole series of the commandments from its Head, he was the killer of the Law before being the killer of Christ. Hence he even distorted its whole body, twisting it against Christ. "You shall not kill, you shall not commit adultery."¹² The synagogue has been condemned for having joined forces with the pagan gods in rejecting Christ, who had laid aside his power as Lord and descended to her with a husband's affection.

"You shall not steal."¹³ The synagogue stole the Lord's Resur-

---

7. Eph 1.18.
8. Jn 5.35.
9. Jn 1.1.
10. Dt 6.4.
11. Ex 20.13; Dt 5.17. Chrysologus's sequence is wrong, since this commandment actually precedes his earlier reference, Dt 6.4. However, since he is likely quoting the Scripture from memory, he probably thought that in the earlier quotation he was citing the first commandment of the Decalogue.
12. Ex 20.13–14; Dt 5.17–18.
13. Ex 20.15; Dt 5.19.

rection by giving a bribe to the soldiers to cover up and conceal the truth of the Resurrection.[14] "You shall not bear false witness."[15] She is the one who procured false witnesses[16] to fulfill the words: "Wicked witnesses have arisen to question me about what I did not know."[17] And there was certainly no other way that she could betray the Author of truth, because falsehood is always the only means to attack the truth.

6. Thus does the one rush to his ruin, thus does the one fall bit by bit who slips and goes tumbling down off the stairs of the commandments. For if the synagogue had believed that the Lord was God alone, she would not have landed in this abyss of destruction. But now let us follow the lamp of our Mother the Church, let us walk in the light of the Lord's countenance[18] and take hold of the silver coin that is Christ, let us summon our friends and neighbors, that is, the churches of the gentiles, lest they be unaware that our Mother has found her silver coin, and let us say with the prophet: "I have prepared a lamp for my Christ."[19]

And let us hear what benefit the lamp was: "See, we have heard of it in Ephrathah, we have found it in the fields of the forest. We shall enter his tent, we shall offer adoration in the place where his feet stood."[20] Let us go and find in the Lord and with the help of our Mother's lamp what we used to look for amid disparate peoples and groves far and wide. About this let heaven also be glad, that in one sinner who repents[21] the completeness of the whole Christian people has been visible in all its brilliance, and the perfect image of the divinity of Christ has shone brightly in our silver coin.[22]

14. See Mt 28.12–15.
15. Ex 20.16; Dt 5.20.
16. See Mt 26.60 and parallels.
17. Ps 34 (35).11.
18. See Ps 88.16 LXX; Ps 89.15.
19. Ps 131 (132).17. "Christ" means "the anointed one." According to Agnellus, *Liber Pontificalis* 27, Galla Placidia donated to the church of Ravenna a golden candelabrum inscribed with words taken from this Psalm: "I shall prepare a lamp for my Christ." Perhaps Chrysologus had this object in mind as he was preaching. See A. Olivar, *Los sermones*, 238, n. 20.
20. Ps 131 (132).6–7.
21. See Lk 15.10.
22. Reading *nostra . . . in dragma* with Migne (PL 52.644) rather than the *nostram . . . in dragmam* of Olivar's CCL text.

SERMON 171

Where It Is Said by the Pharisees that the Lord's Disciples Ate with Unwashed Hands[1]

UST AS WHEN LIGHTNING-BOLTS smash rocks, mountains, trees, and the very roofs of houses with a terrible crash, they seize the attention of human beings, making them stop and think, so too whenever the Lord thunders against the Pharisees, he seizes and corrects his own followers with a healthy fear, as the words of the Gospel today have clearly shown. That the Pharisees and the scribes blamed some of the Lord's disciples for eating without having washed their hands,[2] let no one upon hearing this think that the Lord's disciples show contempt by eating in an uncouth manner with filthy hands, and are careless or disrespectful toward the Lord's table and the community's banquet,[3] when neither nature permits this nor does the offering of hospitality allow it.

Who would not bring water right away out of due respect for his guest to wash his hands? Who would immediately cause the host dismay by rejecting what he offered, especially when the Lord himself finds fault with Simon after he was invited to his table? "You gave me no water,"[4] he says, "for my hands." And so he wants to be done what it is so very evident that he demands.

2. But what the Pharisees were looking for from the Lord's disciples was not attentiveness towards the body but their own superstitious baptism, ignorant of the "one baptism"[5] which had now come not only for cleansing but also for the renewal

---

1. Because of its allusion to Baptism and to becoming purified from sin, this sermon could have been delivered during Lent. See F. Sottocornola, *L'anno liturgico*, 126.
2. See Mk 7.2 and 5.
3. This is likely a reference to the Eucharist.
4. Lk 7.44.
5. Eph 4.5.

of souls and bodies, and which did not wash off the skin for civility's sake, but washed off the conscience for salvation. The prophet prayed for this, when he said: "Thoroughly wash me from my iniquity."[6] That is: "How long, how long are you going to wash me according to the Law, and not really wash me? Wash me once and for all by means of grace, since innumerable baths of the Law have failed to wash me clean." But let the very words of the Gospel which follow reveal this to us themselves.

3. *When the Pharisees and scribes*, it says, *come from the market, they do not eat unless they are washed, observing also the purification of cups, pitchers, bronze vessels, and couches* (see Mk 7.3–4).[7] O Pharisee, how do you consider yourself clean when all your goods have been contaminated by contact with you? In the market you have been plotting about the blood of an innocent person, you have been investigating how to seize the property of a poor person, you have been examining how you might consign the free person to slavery, and when deep within yourself you have been corrupted by a crime of this nature, how will an external washing suffice to cleanse you?

This water will be able to cleanse our hearts and bodies, once it too is made pure by contact[8] with the Holy Spirit, such that by a visible action it accomplishes the invisible mystery of our purification.[9] But you, O Jew, wash[10] cups, pitchers, and bronze vessels, which of their nature are without motion and understanding, and as they know no guilt, so too they have no understanding of what is honorable; and yet you do not cleanse yourself through whom all these things have been contaminated; you purify these items which have been assigned for your use and are at your service, and you do not purify yourself who have been assigned to the divine ministries and the divine mys-

---

6. Ps 50.4 LXX; Ps 51.2.

7. Chrysologus's biblical text reads, *baptizati fuerint . . . baptisma:* more evidence for a possible Lenten date, as mentioned in n. 1 above.

8. This Latin term *commercium* is employed frequently by Chrysologus in a christological fashion regarding the union of the divine and human in Christ. See R. Benericetti, *Il Cristo*, 101–3.

9. On the contrast between visible and invisible, see also *Sermon* 50.1 and n. 2 (FOTC 109.193).

10. *Baptizas.*

teries. But, brothers, let us listen to the Lord's response, not to the Jews, but to his own disciples.

4. For he said: *It is not those things that enter a human being, but those which come out of him that defile him. It is from within, from the heart that bad thoughts come forth, adulterous liaisons, acts of fornication, murders, thefts, greed, wickedness, deceit, envy, blasphemy, lewdness, pride, and foolishness: all these things come from within and defile the person* (see vv.15, 20–23). How spacious would lands have to be, how large the cities, how wide the regions to be able to support foes as fierce, to contain enemies as numerous, and to hold peoples who are as strong as the vices, the sins, and the offenses which ravage human minds and afflict human hearts?

Before one sheep all kinds of wild beasts rage all the more insofar as these predators are unable to be filled, nor can they satisfy their voracious appetite by capturing just one; therefore, all the more do they seethe and become consumed with anger, the more they fail to seize and devour it. Before one dove what can so many voracious kites, eagles, and vultures do? What can such a large and diverse gathering of vile birds do? The prophet had perceived this numerous multitude when he prophesied: "Innumerable evils have surrounded me. My iniquities have enveloped me, and I could not see."[11]

5. *From within the human heart they come forth* (v.21). An enemy is bearable when he rams the walls from without, since he is positioned outside and pauses from time to time in waging his attack; but the one whose enemy is inside, whose foe is by now raging fiercely deeply within, understands and recognizes that he is defeated, he sees clearly and laments that he has been captured, he is unable to champion his own cause, he is unable to be his own liberator, he needs the help of someone else, and he requires another to defend him.

6. *From within they come out of the heart* (see v.21). This is a new kind of warfare: out of the individual person the troops come out to wage war against the person, not content to conquer in secret or to subdue in private, like those who seek glory from

---

11. Ps 39.13 LXX; Ps 40.12. On animals as symbols of the vices, see Introduction, FOTC 109.24–25.

the destruction of another human being. The Jews, who are outside, wash themselves and their property out in the open; let us, brothers, be cleansed within[12] from these kinds of sordid vices, let us conquer these troops of wickedness inside our minds with Christ fighting on our side, let us banish these beasts of sins from our hearts by frightening them with the name of the Lord, and let us courageously use the cross as our spear and shoo these offenses away from our thoughts, as though they were mad and fiercely ravenous birds. Then the splendor of our city, the sanctity of our temple, and the wholesome and unique décor of our house will attract and invite our Author to dwell within us forever. Vices are unable to return to the place where Christ abides with his virtues.

12. Reading the textual variant *intrinsecus* rather than *extrinsecus* in Olivar's CCL text.

SERMON 172

Where It Says: "Woe to you lawyers, you take away the key of knowledge, have not gained entrance yourselves, and have hindered others from entering"[1]

OU HAVE HEARD TODAY, brothers, how, while the envious doorkeeper kept others out, he excluded himself as well. *Woe to you lawyers,* he says, *because you have taken away the key of knowledge, have not gained entrance yourselves, and have hindered those who were entering* (Lk 11.52). And so, you have heard how, while the envious doorkeeper kept others out, he excluded himself as well.

2. The Pharisee had received the keys, not to lock out, but to open up for those who desired to enter; but lest someone besides himself might enter, he preferred out of jealousy[2] to remain outside. Indeed all the vices always tend towards and aim at harming those whom they possess, but envy always consumes its own even more. Envy has always been the killer of its own, it strains thought-processes, it racks spirits, it torments minds, and it ruptures hearts.

And why need I say more? The one who welcomes it endures his own unending punishments, because he is choosing to have his personal torturer always inside himself. Will evils ever end, when the good of another is a punishment, when the happiness of someone else is a torment? The evil is manifold: there are as many tortures for the envious as there are instances of good fortune among human beings.

A Christian spirit can do battle with the other vices: but whoever does not flee from envy before he experiences it does not

---

1. See Lk 11.52. This sermon could possibly have been preached at the end of Lent because of the reference to the Pasch in section 6. See F. Sottocornola, *L'anno liturgico,* 126–27.

2. For other references in Chrysologus's preaching to "jealousy" *(livor)* in an anti-Jewish context, see A. Olivar, *Los sermones,* 164–65.

escape. This is what induced the lawyers not to open up the Law, but to lock it up; not to provide appropriate instruction concerning what was decreed for salvation, but to refuse to do so; to seal off the fountain of knowledge, and to conceal the wealth of the river of life by keeping its source a secret. We must quickly flee from this disease, because those it contaminates it never allows to be healed.

3. Envy tampers with heaven, for there it made the devil out of an angel;[3] it burns up the earth, since in any event it shut us out of the delights of paradise by the fiery guard;[4] it incites kings, because it drove Herod to rage so furiously against those who were of the same age as Christ,[5] that milk was shed before blood from their tender limbs;[6] it does violence to charity, for it made Cain the murderer of his brother, and drenched the earth, which was innocent until then, with the gore of fresh blood;[7] it lays peoples waste, for in fact it made the Jews into—if it is right to say it, if words can express it—slayers of God. We have called them "slayers of God,"[8] not according to the result, but according to what was the intent of this crime; for in their actions toward Christ the Jews attempted to crush and to destroy the powers of not only the Man, but also God, the Son of God, since they say: "This one is the heir, come, let us kill him, and his inheritance will be ours."[9]

4. But what power does the devil have over God? What power does envy have over the Lord's charity? The devil has held a

---

3. See Is 14.12. On this point, see also *Sermons* 4.1 (FOTC 17.40), 48.5 (FOTC 109.186–87), and 168.6.

4. See Gn 3.24.

5. See Mt 2.16.

6. See also *Sermon* 153.2 and n. 8.

7. See Gn 4.8–10. This incident is mentioned as an example of envy and jealousy in *Sermon* 4.2 (FOTC 17.41) also.

8. Chrysologus is the first to endorse the use of this word *(deicida)* with reference to Christ's death. Augustine, in his *Enarrationes in Psalmos* 65.5 (CCL 39.843), employs this same term for the Jews responsible for Christ's death but rejects it as inappropriate, referring to them instead as "homicides" who in fact were forgiven by God because they did not realize what they were doing. Chrysologus is clearly less generous in his assessment. On envy being what motivated the Jews to put Christ to death, see also *Sermons* 48.5 (FOTC 109.186–87) and 164.8.

9. Mk 12.7.

grudge against the earth, but God has granted heaven; the lawyer has taken away the keys of knowledge, but Christ has bestowed the keys of the kingdom of heaven by means of Peter,[10] and thus envy has been stripped of its gains, and the human being has been enriched by envy's inevitable loss. Appropriately then did the Lord make the following additional remarks:

5. *Beware the yeast of the Pharisees* (Lk 12.1). That is because in yeast there is not a large amount of anything solid, but of swelling; and the dough is inflated by the way it appears, but it is not substantial; for the hotter it gets, the more inflated does the mass of paste become, with the result that it produces its shape by being all full of insubstantial hot air. Fittingly therefore did the Lord say: *Beware the yeast of the Pharisees, which is hypocrisy* (v.1). What is hypocrisy but an appearance cleverly crafted, which does one thing in reality, but promises something else by the way it looks?

This is what was swelling up within the Pharisees as a result of their knowledge, just as the Apostle says: "Knowledge inflates."[11] For in fact, knowledge was inflating them to pride, and not leading them to life, and it was perverting them in malice, and not improving them in prudence. Hypocrisy was on their faces, the dropsy of envy was in their mind,[12] within their breast was a spring all dried up, and there was a surge of fire which became hotter and hotter as it flowed, not to quench the thirst of the one who would drink, but to stoke the flames. This, yes, this is the kind of drink that envy, aided by hypocrisy, always serves its own.[13]

6. The Apostle moves us out of the reach of this disease, when he urges us to celebrate the sacred Pasch of the Lord "not with the old yeast, not with the yeast of malice and wickedness, but with the unleavened bread of sincerity and truth."[14]

---

10. See Mt 16.19. On this role for Peter, see *Sermon* 124.9 and n. 11.
11. 1 Cor 8.1.
12. See Lk 14.2. As in *Sermon* 7.1 (FOTC 109.36) there is here also a wordplay between *hypocrisis* and *hydrops*.
13. A similar point with much of the same terminology is made in *Sermons* 7.1 (FOTC 109.36) and 99a.2–3.
14. 1 Cor 5.8.

SERMON 172 323

The truth does not know swelling, simplicity is completely ignorant of hypocrisy. "With the unleavened bread of sincerity and truth": this is the unleavened bread of the heart, this is prepared with sweetness from heaven, this is flavored with an abundance of grace, this is cooked in the fire of the Holy Spirit,[15] this is what we eat when we solemnly sacrifice[16] at our Pasch[17] the Lamb of God, the Lamb "who takes away the sin of the world";[18] for us Christ has been born and transformed for the fullness of joy and the fullness of glory.

15. On this analogy from the baking of bread, see also *Sermon* 71.7 and n. 21 (FOTC 109.288–89).
16. See 1 Cor 5.7.
17. This appears to be a reference to the Easter eucharistic liturgy to be celebrated in the near future.
18. Jn 1.29.

SERMON 173

On John the Baptist and Herod[1]

 GOOD SHEPHERD SPENDS sleepless nights and anxious days[2] so that no crafty thief nor cunning and ferocious wolves may pose any danger or any harm to his dear flock. "The Good Shepherd," as the Lord said, "lays down his life for his sheep."[3] But also good sheep listen with their ears attuned to the voice of their shepherd, they always follow their shepherd's bidding, and they carry out the will of their shepherd in its entirety.[4] They climb hills, they make their way to steep terrain, they often change locations, and thus they enter quiet places that are suitable for grazing, watered by streams, shady, ample, and secluded, they find their surroundings pleasant, and they thoroughly enjoy how delightful it all is.

2. And you, little children, the plentiful portion of the Lord's flock, now clothed in fleece that is snow-white and divine,[5] pregnant with twins[6] as offspring from heaven,[7] if upon hearing our voice you have often reached beneficial places and beneficial pasture, if from the stream of our words[8] you have soothed the heat of your mind and the intensity of your thirst, and if you have taken shelter in our teaching and have reclined

---

1. This sermon was likely preached on or near June 24, the feast of John the Baptist's martyrdom. See F. Sottocornola, *L'anno liturgico*, 303–4.
2. Exactly the same terminology is found in *Sermon* 22.3 (FOTC 17.66) regarding what *not* to do when it comes to material wealth!
3. Jn 10.11.
4. See Jn 10.3–4.
5. This terminology appears to refer to the attire of the neophytes and thus may imply a setting at some time during the Easter season. See F. Sottocornola, *L'anno liturgico*, 127–28.
6. See Song 4.2 and 6.5 (6).
7. Chrysologus uses this terminology in *Sermon* 40.1 (FOTC 17.86) to refer to the candidates preparing for initiation into the Church at Easter.
8. This image of the preacher's words as a stream of refreshing water is given also in *Sermon* 136.2.

in some comfort, then attend to what we ordain, heed what we say, show your approval for what we have done, and realize that the purpose of our preaching is not to conform to your will, but to conform to the position we occupy.

Whether we speak from this step,[9] or whether when the season calls for it we preach from the bishop's chair, like good sheep and a dear flock, beloved children, make haste to come together without disdain, diligently, and full speed ahead in faith. May the fact that you will now be moving from up front and into the tightly packed space farther away[10] neither make you lazy and inattentive nor cause you to murmur, because a sheep does not arrive at the sheepfold if it wanders around at its own pleasure, nor will a disciple be able to obtain knowledge if he strives to be taught according to his own will. A sick person likewise will never be able to recover his health if he is given treatment that conforms to his own wishes.[11] But since we are preaching today against a raging wolf, with the shepherd's staff in hand let us make our way over to the Gospel reading.

3. *King Herod*, it says, *heard about him—for Jesus's name had spread about—and was saying that John the Baptist had risen from the dead, and it is for that reason that such powers were at work in him* (Mk 6.14). The fool holds pious beliefs about someone who was dead after having cruelly persecuted him while he was alive. *John has risen.* And nevertheless, in his ignorance he admits that in Christ and for Christ the one whom he had killed rises up. Herod, what did your sword accomplish? What did you gain from your cruelty? What was the result of your impiety if, as you yourself say, the one who was thought to be destroyed by your fury returned to exercise his powers and rose up to accomplish divine works?

John has risen, just as you yourself acknowledge: here it was

---

9. This is likely a reference to an elevated location, perhaps the ambo, from which Chrysologus preached instead of his episcopal throne. See D. De Bruyne, "Nouveaux sermons de saint Pierre Chrysologue," *Journal of Theological Studies* 29 (1928): 367–68, and F. Sottocornola, *L'anno liturgico*, 142–43 and n. 20.

10. This may be a reference to the neophytes moving from their privileged location in the front of the assembly to the main body of the church building with everyone else, now that their Easter instruction has ended.

11. A similar point is made in *Sermon* 50.4 (FOTC 109.195–96).

not the person but the infirmity that perished; here it was not John, but rather death that was overcome by such a death; the punishment is mocked, the executioner is considered a laughingstock, the very sentence of the wretched judge is eluded, because it did not strike down the one who was killed, but raised him to a higher state.

4. *John has risen from the dead, and it is for that reason that such powers are at work in him.* Even though he was an enemy of the Law, nevertheless, he had learned by means of the Law that the resurrection of the dead had been promised; and if he knew that John would rise, why then in his insanity did he kill him? If he understood that by such a death John would be elevated to the pinnacle of the fullness of divine power and to the fullness of all that epitomizes majesty, why did he make himself the author of such a brutal death?

Impiety always suffers from a fever; cruelty is always possessed by madness. Fury does not know that it is depriving itself of clemency; for indeed he rages against himself as often as he aims for another; he punishes himself by striking down the innocent; he is completely destroying himself when he is cruel to a just person. See how John, as you yourself say, is now alive in Christ. He who has come to cure all with heavenly grace returns to punish you.

5. *Others, however, were saying: "He is Elijah or one of the prophets." When Herod heard this he said: "He is John, whom I beheaded; he has risen from the dead"* (vv.15–16). Certainly with an ill-disposed but a true perception he himself testifies to his crime, he confesses his wickedness, he accuses himself of the evil he committed. *He is John, whom I beheaded* (v.16). He spoke the truth. For just as those who belong to Christ rise in him,[12] so too does Christ himself suffer in those who belong to him. And just as honor given to the head extends to the members, so too does the pain of the members result in hurting and injuring the head.[13]

John, whom I beheaded: this wise king, exceptional magistrate,

---

12. See 1 Thes 4.16.
13. See 1 Cor 12.26.

judge of morals, guardian of discipline, avenger of the innocent, punisher of crimes,[14] tells of having beheaded John, but keeps silent about why he beheaded him, in order that the shamefulness of such a wicked deed would not disgrace his royal power. But the evangelist records this so that the murderer's dishonor may redound to the glory of the one who was murdered.

6. *Herod*, he says, *held, bound, and incarcerated John, because John kept telling Herod: "It is not right for you to live with the wife of your brother while he is alive"* (vv.17–18). For[15] Herodias, who was eager to be the wife of two brothers because of her love for wickedness, so as to do violence to affection by means of affection, and so that she be joined as Herodias to Herod, so as not to be any different even in name, since they were entirely alike in wickedness, behavior, and life; so that they, whom the shamefulness of their crimes had united, would be united by appellation—so then, this *Herodias was plotting against* John (v.19).

Herod did not quell the intention of the adulteress; nevertheless, he did delay the wickedness of the adulteress. In order that there would be no one to accuse her, she aimed at putting her accuser to death: Herod, in order to placate that incestuous woman, himself the captive, only went so far as to hold, bind, and lock up this righteous man, because in his guilt it could not have been easy for him to pronounce judgment against him in his innocence.[16]

7. *An opportune time had presented itself,* it says, *when Herod held a banquet on his birthday for the nobles, the tribunes, and the leading men of Galilee. And after the daughter of this very Herodias had entered, performed a dance, and pleased the king together with the others at table, the king said to the girl: "Ask me for whatever you want, and I will give it to you." And he swore to her: "Whatever you ask, I will give you, even half my kingdom"* (vv.21–23). What an ungrateful and impolite king, since for such great virtue, for so glorious a la-

---

14. In describing Herod the Great in *Sermon* 152.5 (FOTC 17.256), Chrysologus also with a tinge of irony provides a similar list of the king's responsibilities.
15. Reading the variant *nam* instead of *dum* in Olivar's CCL text.
16. See Mk 6.20.

bor, for so memorable a deed, he offered not his entire kingdom, but only half! And why did he keep for himself even a portion? Indeed, after so glorious a household, after so holy a family, after such an example of chastity, he should not even have existed, been seen, or lived!

And so, that daughter of sin, and not of nature, immediately ran off not so much to her mother as to the very cesspool of her wickedness, so that she who[17] had gone all soft and loose would hurry back savage and cruel, and—to express it in theatrical language—so that she who had played a very indecent comic role would sing of an unspeakable tragedy.[18]

8. And so *she said to her mother: "For what shall I ask?" And she replied: "The head of John the Baptist." When she returned she said to the king: "I ask that right away the head of John the Baptist be given to me on a dish." And the king was deeply saddened,* it says, *but did not want to disappoint her on account of the dinner guests also present. And he sent an executioner out and ordered that John's head be brought back, and he gave it to the girl, and the girl gave it to her mother* (vv.24–28).

This is the kind of judgment that a mind makes when it is overcome with intoxication, when it becomes dissolute with wine, and completely submerged in a shipwreck of drunkenness, as it were. "Give me the head of John."[19] The offspring of the serpent[20] seeks the head of the human being, to whom it knew that its own head had been surrendered by what had been decreed from the beginning, when God said: "He will lie in wait for your head, and you will lie in wait for his heel."[21]

9. The lengthy reading has drawn our attention for a long while, and the immensely profound nature of this passage has advanced us deeply enough. For today let us postpone what follows, lest, if my sermon hastens to reach the end, it may omit items which require a lengthy exposition.[22] In concluding our

---

17. Reading *quae* with Migne (PL 52.653) instead of *qui* in Olivar's CCL text.
18. On this point, see also *Sermon* 127.9.
19. Mt 14.8; see Mk 6.25.
20. A fuller description of the daughter of Herodias as serpentine and beastly is given in *Sermons* 127.9 and 174.2.
21. Gn 3.15.
22. For other similar references by Chrysologus and others about bringing

SERMON 173

remarks, we bring to your attention that the serpent ran in vain, for our John here destroyed all the brood[23] of the ancient serpent,[24] and by shedding his own blood, he who was murdered killed them all.

---

an already lengthy sermon to a close, see *Sermon* 33.6 and n. 14 (FOTC 109.142–43). The promised continuation of this sermon is most likely *Sermon* 174. See F. Sottocornola, *L'anno liturgico*, 127–28.

23. See Lk 3.7.
24. See Gn 3.1–15; Rv 12.9 and 20.2. See also *Sermon* 174.4 on this reference.

SERMON 174

A Second on the Same[1]

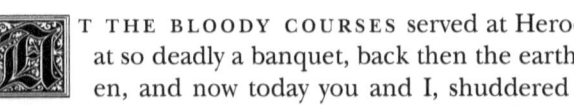T THE BLOODY COURSES served at Herod's dinner, at so deadly a banquet, back then the earth and heaven, and now today you and I, shuddered and trembled when we heard of it.[2] *Herod*, it says, *held a dinner on his birthday* (Mk 6.21). The term "dinner" was appropriate, since this kind of birthday was consigned, not to daylight, but to darkness, on which was born a son of night, and not of day.[3] *He held a dinner on his birthday*, it says, *for the nobles, the tribunes, and the leading men of Galilee* (v.21). What does reckless and blind impiety always do? It invites all the powerful, so that it may make its many dining companions countless witnesses of its crime; and so that it may have as many judges of its wicked deed as it had officials responsible for law and order.

2. *And after the daughter of Herodias herself had entered, performed a dance*, it says, *and pleased Herod* (v.22). She who is immoral lives up to her lineage as she pleases her even more immoral father. For certainly one who has been begotten of an adulterer has to be immoral—that is the only possibility—and by her spasmodic moves, her body all contorted, her limbs disjointed, and her flesh swaying about by her craft, by all this ugliness she managed to become even more beautiful to her father. And Herod certainly knew that she was his when he saw her acting this way; for he would have thought her to be someone else's if he had witnessed even the slightest modesty on her part.

---

1. This sermon on John the Baptist and Herod may well have been preached after *Sermon* 173 and on the actual feast of John the Baptist's martyrdom, June 24, given the explicit reference in section 6 to "today" *(hodie)*. See F. Sottocornola, *L'anno liturgico*, 127–28 and 303–4.

2. For a similar description of the congregation's reaction on other occasions, see *Sermon* 127.1 and n. 3.

3. See 1 Thes 5.5.

The serpent was then concealed in the woman[4] who was slinking along with her supple movements and pouring deadly venom out of her whole body, so that frenzy would wound the minds of those at dinner, poison would infect their bodies, human beings would be turned into beasts, and in this fashion they would no longer be given wine but blood to drink; and in their madness they would be given not bread but human flesh to eat.[5] Like this, yes, she[6] made them turn out just like this at the moment when she brought forward John's head with his blood still smelling warm, to fulfill the following verse of the Psalmist: "They gave the flesh of your saints to the beasts of the earth, they poured their blood out like water."[7]

3. See what banquets that last all night produce. See what the result is when wine is bought at a moderate price but is drunk without moderation. See how far the flesh plummets when a wanton crime is enkindled by the fires of lust. I ask you, what restraint is exercised with a crowd like this? The unhappy flesh out of its own misfortunes is capable of destroying itself, as the prophet attests when he says: "For what purpose do you all together beset a human being and destroy him as though he were a sagging wall or a tottering fence?"[8] In Herod the flesh was lying prostrate and overcome with drunkenness, held captive by inebriation; wantonness was arousing it and lewdness was both stirring him up and stringing him along,[9] to the point that he would promise whatever it was that immorality would request.

4. *Ask me for whatever you want*, he said, *and I will give it to you. And he swore to her* (vv.22–23). The wretch swears, while he swears off anything having to do with honor and virtue. *Ask me for whatever you want.* For what would wantonness ask, other than the demise of chastity, the murder of purity, the death of sanctity, which is always its enemy? *Give me the head of John* (see

---

4. On this, see also *Sermon* 173.8.
5. Likewise, see *Sermon* 127.9.
6. Namely, Herodias's daughter, and, by extension, the "serpent."
7. Ps 78 (79).2–3.
8. Ps 61.4 LXX; Ps 62.3.
9. Chrysologus's rhetorical flair is evident: *quae titillante luxuria, et tam ludente quam inludente lascivia.*

v.25; Mt 14.8). If Christ is the head of the man, according to the Apostle,[10] then the very ancient serpent[11] now with a new mouth was attempting to put Christ the Lord to death. *Give me the head of John.* So then the voracious dragon in his thirst for the Passion of the Lord was already having a taste of it in the head of the Lord's servant.

Give it to me on a dish (see v.25 and Mt 14.8). Why on a dish? Why do you carry about in a precious vessel the one whom you have killed so cheaply, except for the reason that "precious in the sight of the Lord is the death of his saints"?[12] This very thing that you want, you do not accomplish as you yourself want, since a heavenly purpose is at work doing something other than what you want. Then indeed in that deadly cave, not in the inner court of the King, then the savage fury believed it had its food when it saw the martyr's head; it felt that it had its drink when in its thirst it caught sight of the sacred blood flowing; with all its mouth and with all its throat it attempts and strives to gulp down the meal served up by its cruelty.

5. But John came to occupy a lofty place, like a lamp on a lampstand,[13] to banish darkness, as the Lord says: "He was a burning lamp."[14] John came like a judge resplendent on his judgment seat, so that he who accused the adulterer would expose and condemn the murderer; and he, who by the holiness he manifested while alive had called that incestuous man to repentance and had kept open the possibility of pardon, would, after being killed, condemn him finally for murder.[15] What pardon, I ask you, does he deserve who in the death of John so cruelly destroyed repentance itself?

It is for nothing that you have run your course, O Herod, Herodias, Herodiadis,[16] whose names are united not by affec-

---

10. See 1 Cor 11.3.
11. See Gn 3.1–15; Rv 12.9 and 20.2. *Sermon* 173.9 includes the same reference.
12. Ps 115 (116).15
13. See Mt 5.15 and parallels.
14. Jn 5.35.
15. For the concept that John's intention was for Herod to repent and reform, see also *Sermon* 127.6.
16. That is, "daughter of Herodias."

tion, but by crime; you very foolishly believed that the "voice" could be silenced. "I am the voice," he said, "of one crying out in the desert."[17] The voice cannot be destroyed, but it cries out all the more once it has been freed from the narrow confines of the body. Thus did Abel's voice, as soon as his blood was shed, resound the more, become more piercing, and increase its range all the way to heaven.[18]

6. In just this fashion does John now proclaim your wicked deed throughout all the world, tell of it for all ages, and make it known to all the nations. See how John glories in Christ the head, he who was thought to have been decapitated. See how today, when you brought your birthday to an end, he acquired a birthday for himself from heaven, because when your birth plummeted to an end, his end then produced his birthday.[19] For the righteous person begins to live the moment he is counted worthy of being killed for Christ. The martyr's life is transformed by this kind of death, it is not taken away by death. Rather, he was free from death, since he died so that he would live forever.

7. See how you lie prostrate unto death, while John who was killed is alive. You have lost the purple that received its color from dye; John is forever gloriously clothed with the radiant purple from his blood. Your dinner guests are now made to share in your punishment; John partakes of the heavenly banquet with the choirs of angels. He hears the dulcet tones of heaven[20] unceasingly; you hear forever the wailing and gnashing in hell.[21] He, who was condemned as the price for your harlot and your dancing-girl, is now honored with the kingdom and with heavenly rewards; for the sentence you gave, you have received recompense along with your daughter in Tartarus.[22]

8. Joseph left his cloak behind when he had fled the adulter-

---

17. Jn 1.23.
18. See Gn 4.10 and Heb 12.24.
19. The same point is made with similar terminology also in *Sermon* 127.11.
20. Such musical imagery is also found in *Sermons* 6.1 and 22.6 (FOTC 17.52 and 69).
21. See, e.g., Mt 8.12.
22. On the personification of Tartarus, the realm of the dead, see, e.g., *Sermon* 65.6–9 (FOTC 109.263–66).

ess; John, so as not even to look upon the adulteress, went so far as to cast off his very body. Joseph was willing to endure imprisonment rather than commit adultery;[23] in the course of bringing an accusation of adultery, John exchanged the desert for a prison. While revealing his dreams Joseph escaped death;[24] in order to reveal the Son of God, John endured even death. While providing earthly bread Joseph gained a golden chain and honor;[25] to point out[26] to believers the Bread from heaven—as that verse says: "I am the Bread"[27]—John gained the blood-soaked chain of martyrdom.

9. It is fitting that among all those born of women this man John is the greatest[28] in that he not only brought accusations against those living adulterously, but even shunned licit union with a woman because of his love for virginity. And if John, who was so great, so noble, and segregated from women by so vast a desert, did not escape the perils of women, who is there who lives in the midst of women and has confidence that he will escape such perils without the greatest effort and without taking the utmost precaution? Who else other than one who is nourished by the Holy Spirit?

23. See Gn 39.6–20.
25. See Gn 41.33–57.
27. Jn 6.35, 41, 48, and 51.
24. See Gn 37.5–28.
26. See Jn 1.29 and 36.
28. See Mt 11.11.

SERMON 175

When Marcellinus Was Made Bishop of Voghenza on the First of November[1]

ERTAINLY THE BEGINNINGS OF all things are difficult, but more difficult than everything else is it when one begins to have children. The holy church of Ravenna, in order to give birth to her first child,[2] has made a journey, faced struggles, and experienced hardships. And she has done this, brothers, in order to preserve the divinely ordained manner of giving birth by completely following the path of truth; for after the Virgin Mother hastened on her way across the whole country[3] in order to give birth to the Firstborn of all creation,[4] in this way were the process of a virgin giving birth and the nativity of all firstborn offspring consecrated. And it was necessary, brothers, for the Way to be generated on the way—"I am the Way," he says[5]—so that error would be denied any access whatsoever, and so that the traveler, who had endured for so long the sweat and toil[6] of the earthly journey to no avail, would finally head straight for heaven.

2. *And it happened in those days*, the evangelist says, *that an edict was issued by Caesar Augustus, that the whole world was to be registered. And so Joseph went up from the town of Nazareth in Galilee to Judea, to the town of David, which is called Bethlehem, since he was from the house and family of David; he went up with Mary, his be-*

---

1. This sermon is studied in detail by A. Olivar in "La consagración del obispo Marcelino de Voghenza," *RSCI* 22 (1968): 87–93. It is Chrysologus's first consecration of a suffragan bishop after Ravenna attained metropolitan status. Olivar ascertains the date of this sermon to be the vigil of November 1, namely, Saturday, October 31, 431. See also Introduction, FOTC 109.9–10.
2. Or, alternatively, "for the first time" *(primum)*.
3. See Lk 1.39.   4. See Col 1.15.
5. Jn 14.6.
6. On the coupling of sweat and labor *(sudor* and *labor)*, see, e.g., Cicero, *In Q. Caecilium* 72, and *Pro M. Fonteio* 12.

trothed wife, who was pregnant. And it happened in those days, that the time came for her to give birth, and she gave birth to her firstborn Son (Lk 2.1, 4–7).[7]

3. At this point I want to say something about distress: the Lord managed to comply with the edict of Caesar, and a pagan one at that; yet a certain servant is still irreverently offering resistance to the decree of blessed Peter[8] and the decree of the Christian leader.[9] But since happiness must not be mixed with adversity, nor sadness with joy, let us put these matters aside and declare how glad we are about today's offspring.

4. Let the one who has just been born, who is the firstborn, let him hold and maintain the reverence and the honor of a firstborn. Marcellinus today has drawn and garnered all the affection as is customary for a native-born son. The children stand at hand, the neighbors are present, all the relatives have gathered, the whole family rejoices, and the very inner recesses of the house leap for joy and are glad, because today they have been counted worthy of seeing with their eyes and holding with their hands the firstborn son of the holy Mother. She who bore him is, in addition, a bride; she is both a mother and a virgin;[10] and she marvels with a new kind of rejoicing that she produced him in the very marriage-bed of her Bridegroom, in the very bedroom of her union.[11]

But let it disturb no one, let it trouble no one that in that

---

7. Although this text is customarily proclaimed and preached shortly before or during the Christmas season, Chrysologus employs it here because it provides a scriptural analogy and prototype for the "birth" of the new bishop Marcellinus from the church of Ravenna, which is both mother and virgin.

8. That is, the Bishop of Rome.

9. The Christian leader is Galla Placidia. Apparently another church in northern Italy, perhaps Milan or Aquileia, or both, opposed Ravenna's elevation to metropolitan status, which had been granted by Pope Celestine I and Galla. See Introduction, FOTC 109.10–11.

10. On the Church as virgin and mother in consecrating a new bishop, see also *Sermon* 130.1–2 and n. 2, and *Sermon* 130a.1.

11. The Latin term is *coniunctio*. Chrysologus uses this term to describe the union of Christ the Bridegroom with the Church, his Bride, in *Sermons* 57.13 (FOTC 17.109) and 130.2 (also on the "birth" of a new bishop). Augustine, *Enarrationes in Psalmos* 44.3 (CCL 38.495), uses this term as well as *thalamus* ("marriage bed") and other marital imagery to present the union of the divine Word with his human flesh, from which Augustine goes on to draw other ecclesiological implications.

very marriage-bed we see that the Bride herself has given birth: this kind of conception derives not from anything blameworthy, but from virginity, since in this kind of offspring the birth is heavenly rather than human in origin; there is no place here for evil suspicions, where the Bridegroom himself is on hand as the witness and guardian[12] of his Bride. Whoever among you has been anxious about this matter, may an example put you completely at ease; and may the worry felt by a figure in the past provide you with a sense of security and confidence.

That is, Joseph, who was a husband in name only, a spouse in his conscience,[13] was confused and troubled when he saw that his fiancée was pregnant, in that he could neither accuse her in her innocence nor find an excuse for her being pregnant. It was unsafe to keep silent, but it was dangerous to speak. The accuser of one who is innocent commits rather than reveals a crime. He himself was the proof of her chastity, the guardian of her purity: he knew one thing, but what was before his eyes was something very different; what he saw confused him, while the Virgin's fidelity gave him no cause for confusion. Actions and life were at the crossroads: his righteous mind and holy intention were tormented by ambivalent thoughts; he noticed but was unable to comprehend so great a mystery, since, on the one hand, he could not accuse her, but, on the other hand, he was unable to defend her before human beings.

5. It was fitting that the angel came to meet him right away, fitting that a reply from God came right away to help him who was lacking in human counsel, but not lacking in righteousness. And what did the angel say? "Joseph, have no fear."[14] What

12. Similar terminology to that used here regarding Christ's union with the Church is found later in this section regarding Joseph's relationship with Mary. Likewise, see *Sermons* 140a.3, 140b.2 and n. 17, and 145.1 (FOTC 17.233), dealing with Joseph and Mary; in the first part of *Sermon* 140b.2 it is Christ himself who is described with similar language as Bridegroom of Mary.

13. This does not necessarily imply that Chrysologus denied that Mary and Joseph were truly married: see *Sermon* 140a.3 and n. 7. See also R. Benericetti, *Il Cristo*, 186–88, and B. Kochaniewicz, *La Vergine Maria*, 81–85. However, a contrary opinion, with reference to other patristic authors, is noted in L. Anné, "La conclusion du mariage dans la tradition et le droit de l'Église latine jusqu'au VIe siècle," *Ephemerides Theologicae Lovanienses* 12 (1935): 515–16.

14. Mt 1.20.

did the one who had not done anything have to fear? He was fearful because although there was not any guilt regarding any action on his part, there was the greatest amount of terror regarding the situation. Whatever a holy mind does not comprehend causes terror. So beware, O man, of being so argumentative[15] about our Mother's giving birth, since the reply that the angel made is all that is necessary: "Have no fear; the Child within her is from the Holy Spirit."[16]

6. She gives birth happily who by bearing her child has acquired the crown and glory of virginity all the more. But he who today has been born to us has always cast his nets into the sea; so let no one be surprised if Peter has been longing to have a fisherman as his colleague.[17] Therefore, pray, brothers, that he may be found worthy of being a fisher of human beings who up until now has worked hard at catching fish for the life of human beings.[18]

---

15. This point Chrysologus makes in preaching on Christ's Nativity (see, e.g., *Sermon* 148a.3); he makes it here in a reference to the nativity of the new bishop Marcellinus from the Church as virgin and mother.

16. Mt 1.20.

17. Two details are noteworthy here: Chrysologus refers to himself by name ("Peter"), and the new bishop Marcellinus had formerly been employed as a fisherman.

18. See Mt 4.19; Mk 1.17; Lk 5.10. Chrysologus uses similar language in *Sermon* 47.3 (FOTC 17.100).

SERMON 176

On the Man Born Blind[1]

S OFTEN AS GOD cures the desperate sufferings of human bodies, on those very occasions he reveals the power of his divinity; but when in one and the same infirmity he changes the process by which he effects a cure, he causes us to investigate on a deeper level the reasons why he does this. For merely by his command he restored sight to the blind man who was sitting by the roadside.[2] On another who had been blind from birth, born not unto the light, but unto darkness, to whom nature had not given sight, but had begrudged it, since that very nature which furnishes and opens eyes, had closed and refused his eyes, on this man Christ placed mud, and by fashioning and making it into a kind of eye-salve, he procured, and not merely cured, his eyesight.[3] As a result, he used his hand to create and not merely to heal, and provided the human being with vision from the same material[4] out of which he had formed the whole human being.[5]

But this blind man here, whose cure the evangelist Mark has related to us, is healed in such an unusual manner that it forces us all to ask why his blindness was so stubborn as to presume to delay the Creator, at whose will, gaze, and command

---

1. F. Sottocornola, *L'anno liturgico*, 129, suggests that this sermon may have been delivered during Lent because some of what is said here would be applicable to candidates preparing for initiation at Easter: e.g., the use of the verb "to baptize" and the references to resurrection and new life in section 4, and the mention of the "light of faith" available in the Church in section 8. But based on such limited internal data, a Lenten context is at best conjectural.
2. See Mk 10.46–52 and Lk 18.35–43.
3. Jn 9.1–7.
4. Namely, dirt or dust from the ground: see Gn 2.7.
5. In *Sermon* 178.4 also, in considering the healing of the blind man, Chrysologus makes this same point with some of the same terminology.

infirmities perish, health returns, life arises, death is brought to an end, all things stand firm, or everything dissolves.

2. *Jesus, it says, came to Bethsaida, and they brought a blind man to him, and begged him to touch him. And he led him outside the village* (Mk 8.22–23). It was as if he were unable to cure him in that location. Or did he, who had conferred sight upon all, need the help of a particular location? This is Bethsaida, whose lack of faith the Lord reproves when he says: "Woe to you, Chorazin and Bethsaida, because if the miracles which have been done in your midst had been done in Tyre and Sidon, they would have done penance long ago in sackcloth and ashes."[6] And so, taking him by the hand he leads him out of the house of infidelity and lifts him up out of the seat of faithlessness, so as to furnish faith before eyesight, restore health to his mind before healing his body, and be obliging in offering guidance as a man[7] before working a sign of divine power.

3. They begged him merely to touch him.[8] But Christ, who finds nothing in the poor person to make him recoil, but only knows how to love the poor, gave the poor man his whole hand, and God offered service publicly to the disabled man, so that one human being might not recoil from another, and the one with vision might see the one without vision,[9] and by guiding him by the hand one might make the person who is blind not notice his lack of sight. Let no person say: "My hand has nothing to give"; let him give his very hand to the poor person, and it will mean more to have given a hand to the poor person than to have given a coin,[10] and to have offered to accompany the poor person than to have given him a piece of bread.

4. *And he led him outside the village, and spit into his eyes* (v.23). With his spittle the Lord fills up the empty hollows of the eyes, and he supplies the light-bearing saliva from his divine mouth,

---

6. Mt 11.21.

7. Chrysologus is referring to Christ's action in taking the blind man by the hand (see Mk 8.23).

8. See Mk 8.22.

9. Here is a fine example of Chrysologus's rhetorical flair: *ut homo non horreat hominem, et videns non videnti videat*. The *homo-hominem* wordplay is also employed in *Sermon* 121.7 and discussed in n. 12 on that sermon.

10. Chrysologus contrasts one's hand *(manum)* with a coin *(nummum)*.

so that the drop of holy moisture would baptize the sinner's eyes, so that pardon would open up the eyes that guilt had shut. And so, let no one doubt that bodily members entirely dried up by death are able to revive by the divine shower, when he sees that by a tiny drop of the Lord's spittle eyes which had been dry with blindness have thus been suddenly awakened unto the light. "The dead will rise up," Isaiah says, "and those who are in the tombs will rise again." How? "For the dew which comes from you is a saving remedy for them."[11] What rain does for the seed is what the shower coming from the Lord does for those who will rise.

5. *And he laid his hands upon him* (v.23). In making, in restoring, and in maintaining the human being in existence, the hands of the Lord are always at work creating the human being. "Your hands," it says, "have made me and restored me."[12] *And he asked him if he could see anything* (v.23). He asks as man, he works as God; the One with foreknowledge of the future asks as though he were ignorant of the present;[13] the One who gives sight inquires about whether he sees.

He it is who looks into the depths of the underworld, who contemplates the mysteries of heaven, who sees the hidden things of earth, who gazes into the secrets of the heart, and before whom is laid bare everything[14] which is concealed from everyone else. But when his own work and his own eyes are at issue, does he seek to see, strive to know, and find an answer from information that someone else provides? Far from it! He asks, however, so that those who are present might know and so that it might be revealed to future generations that this is not simply a healing of this man's blindness, but that a deeper mystery is involved.

6. And so, since the full light of day was not yet given him,

---

11. Is 26.19.
12. Ps 118 (119).73.
13. On other references in Chrysologus's sermons to Christ's foreknowledge, such that any questions in apparent ignorance are in fact only a pedagogical technique to guide his listeners, see, e.g., *Sermons* 64.4 (FOTC 109.258–59) and 99a.4, as well as R. Benericetti, *Il Cristo*, 263–64.
14. See Heb 4.13.

but only something like the early light of dawn breaking through, the man who was being cured said in response to the Lord's question: *I see people*, he said, *who look like walking trees* (v.24). To eyes that are not perfect, images seem large, what appears is confusing, the reality itself is distorted, because the eyes still do not have the full picture, but as of yet grasp only a shadow of that picture. But why then do they look like trees and not pillars or something else, and why are they not stationary but walking?

It is because after Christ's cure he had seen that human beings, just like trees, pass away in this world and do not remain; the one whom Christ has cured sees right away that the human sprout that is planted in this life lasts only for a time. Therefore, Christ must repeat the action of healing so that the eyes may be made perfect so as to see what will be, what is sure, what is lasting, and what is eternal. *A second time*, it says, *he laid his hands upon him, and he began to see everything clearly, and he sent him off to his home and said: "Go to your home, and if you go into the village, say nothing to anyone"* (vv.25–26).

7. May the spiritual meaning[15] now be made known regarding who that blind man is, why he does not come of his own accord, but is brought by others, led by Christ's hand, led out of the village, and receives his sight elsewhere, after having endured a lengthy blindness for a long time among his own people; and regarding why Christ spits into his eyes, why the divine imposition of hands is repeated, and, inasmuch as he is outside his home when he is given his sight, why he is not allowed to tell his own people what he saw, how he saw, and who the One was who made him see.[16]

8. Brothers, this blind man is the Jew, who in the synagogue, that is, in the house of faithlessness, and in the village, that is, in the assembly of the wicked,[17] was confined, stuck in his seat, and burdened by ignorance, by blindness. This is why it was not he who came to Christ, but Christ who came to him and

---

15. Other references to such *spiritalis intellegentia* are indicated in A. Olivar, "Els principis," 421.
16. See Mk 8.22–26.
17. See Ps 21.17 LXX; Ps 22.16.

grasped his hand, so that he might boast that he had been cured by the gift of the One who called him,[18] and not by any help from the Law or by his own decision. And he leads him outside, so that he who used to endure the darkness of faithlessness within the synagogue may see the light of faith within the Church, and he who used to see nothing under the veil of the Law[19] may have sight through the freedom that comes from grace.

He lays his hand upon him the first time, so that he may see that the shadow[20] of the Law is transient; and see that the priests, the scribes, the Pharisees, and the whole figure of Jewish observance[21] are passing away just like trees, which, while they sprout, grow leaves, blossom, and bear fruit in season, also grow old, die, and disappear with the season. He lays his hands upon him a second time, so that he may arise and no longer see perishable things, but eternal ones, so that he may see all that comes from divine light, honor, and glory.[22]

This case is just like the one involving that great man of theirs Paul, who fell down outside the village and on the road as a Jew; yes, he fell in order to arise as a Christian;[23] and he was blinded while under the Law, so that he might see when under grace, just as we find it stated: "Now we see in a mirror, in a riddle, but then we shall see face to face."[24] "Then" it will be when what has been buried in death will rise to life, and whatever has been sown in dishonor will rise in glory.[25]

---

18. See Rom 9.12.
19. See 2 Cor 3.13.
20. See Col 2.17.
21. By "figure," Chrysologus is indicating that all Jewish observance was temporary in nature since its function was to prefigure the later and more perfect realities of the Christian dispensation.
22. See 1 Pt 4.14.
23. See Acts 9.3–4.
24. 1 Cor 13.12.
25. See 1 Cor 15.43.

SERMON 177

On the Anger of Brothers[1]

OU HAVE HEARD TODAY how the severity of the Law has been amplified by the authority of grace, and how the words of the Lord have been fulfilled when he said: *I have come not to abolish the Law, but to fulfill it. You have heard*, he says, *that it was said to the ones of old: "You shall not kill"; but what I say to you is that everyone who grows angry with his brother will be liable to judgment* (Mt 5.17, 21, 22). Anger is compared to murder, that fault is compared to a wicked deed, so that in the Church of the Lord, not being innocent is a serious sin.[2] He has removed, he has truly removed any place for sin since by eliminating the fault he has eliminated everything that had to do with sin.

He is the Guardian of innocence who has cut away the fault lest a sin follow. For that physician is worthy of praise if he lances a tumor before it spreads. Very much on guard against disaster is that king who keeps sleep from overtaking his soldier, lest the enemy tyrannize the citizens. Thus did Christ repel a fault, so that sin would be permitted no inroad among Christians; so he punished anger, lest murder arise; he cut off the passions, lest consequences follow; he amputated the thought in order to prevent the result.

2. *You have heard*, he says, *that it was said to the ones of old: "You shall not kill; for whoever kills will be liable to judgment"* (v.21). And what does a murderer have to do with judgment, since he has

---

1. This sermon and *Sermons* 178 and 179 are not included in the Felician collection of Chrysologus's sermons. A. Olivar, *Los sermones*, 344–46, argues persuasively and largely on the basis of the stylistic devices employed in this *Sermon* 177 that it is an authentic work of Chrysologus.

2. The Latin word is *crimen*, which literally means a "crime" and hence some sort of evil, external action, as contrasted with *culpa*, an internal "fault" or inner guilt.

already been thoroughly condemned to punishment? So there is no need for an investigation when someone has blood on his hands. The flesh has been killed, but the soul of the one killed is alive; the body lies in the earth, but the spirit has flown off to heaven; the slain person lies here, but he cries out there;[3] in such a case he is asleep as far as human beings are concerned, but before God he is his own unsleeping advocate. It is unnecessary for anyone to bring an accusation, no witness can add anything, a postponement is prevented, when the slain person himself stands before the Judge to testify to the murder.

It is characteristic of human judgment to discuss what is heard, to examine the charges, to investigate what is hidden, to inquire about where, when, why, and with whom the deed was committed, to press for punishment, to compel the one who has not confessed to make a confession, and to deliver a sentence. But the heavenly Judge, who sees what is hidden, who hears what is unspoken, and who gets to the bottom of divergent testimony, considers it all from his divine perspective, evaluates it all in depth, and effortlessly determines what has been committed, but either bestows pardon on the one who confesses, or renders his sentence on the one who denies.

3. Therefore in his divine judgment he said: *The one who grows angry with his brother will be liable to judgment* (v.22). That is to say: those things must be judged which are ambiguous, which conceal the motives for their actions, which unless they come to light do not permit us to know why they have been conceived; whether they are good or bad is revealed upon examination. Anger, brothers, is an ambiguous matter; it is made bad by the way it is used, and not by its nature; it is very bad when it is conceived out of hatred, it is wicked when it is produced out of rage, it is very good when it comes from love, and when disciplining another demands it.

For even a father grows angry with his son, a master with his servant, a teacher with his student, for the purpose of rebuking, but not of having a furious tirade; with the intention of healing, not destroying, in conformity with what the prophet says:

---

3. See Gn 4.10.

"Grow angry, and do not sin."[4] Therefore, anger must be judged, so that, if its impetus is upright, it be approved; if wicked, that it be curbed. But the only thing that murder awaits is sentencing, since it heads for punishment before it is ever judged.

4. *You have heard that it was said to the ones of old: "You shall not kill; for whoever kills will be liable to judgment." But I say* (vv.21–22). *I say*, as Author of the Law, Fountain of justice, Origin of truth, the Authority for living, the Rule of fairness, and the Standard for judgment. *I say* as God, *I say* as Lord, in that the statements uttered by the Lord should carry more weight than those uttered by servants. *I say that everyone who grows angry with his brother will be liable to judgment* (v.22). Let anger be judged, lest murder be punished; let anger be judged, so that rage may be removed; let anger be judged, so that it may be an instrument of discipline, and not an opportunity for fury; let anger be judged, that its cause may be upright and not culpable; let anger be judged, so that it may remove sins, and may not itself be a sin.

5. But let us see why the Lord specified in the Gospel with the force of a trumpet blast three forms of vengeance for three faults, as follows. *Whoever grows angry with his brother will be liable to judgment; whoever says, "Raca!"*[5] *to his brother will be liable to the council; whoever says, "You buffoon!" will be liable to the fire of Gehenna* (v.22). Whoever grows angry, as we have said, will face judgment and will present the reasons for his anger; and whoever in his anger has terrified his brother will endure the terror of divine judgment. Therefore, let whoever grows angry see to it that he does not do this readily, without cause, for a long time, harshly, and into the next day, since we have been commanded: "Do not let the sun set on your anger."[6]

When you grow angry, think about your brother, so that you may overcome anger with charity, because, if your anger remains after the sun sets and extinguishes the light of kindness

---

4. Ps 4.4 (5); Eph 4.26.
5. An Aramaic term of abuse, left untranslated here, especially in view of what Chrysologus says about it in section 6 below.
6. Eph 4.26.

within you, a night of rage within you is what follows; then the darkness of all kinds of fury follow that, and all this leads you to be completely consumed in desiring your brother's death, and so, even if not in the deed, nevertheless in your desire you have become the murderer of your brother. Therefore, it is right that anyone who is angry because of rage is liable to the same judgment to which a murderer is liable.

6. *But whoever says, "Raca!" to his brother will be liable to the council* (v.22). "*Raca,*" brothers, is not a word but an expression of mockery and an insult which customarily arises from the winking of the eyes, or the twitching of the nose, or the clearing of the throat, in such a way that one's will provides the affront while the substance of the insult is not revealed.[7] But God, who observes our wills, sees our desires, and judges our expressions, forces the one who mocks his brother to face judgment before the council of the saints, since the ridicule leveled at just one has brought insult to all, and the condition of a member extends to the whole body, and the body's pain reaches the head.[8] Thus whatever ridicule a person has inflicted upon one individual, upon a brother, the mocker will notice and lament that it has made its way right into the heavenly council and up to God.

7. *But whoever says, "You buffoon!" will be liable to the fire of Gehenna* (v.22). What the angry person concealed in his breast, and what the mocker kept shut within his throat, the foul-mouthed person expressed with his voice, and, since the affront is uttered in the open, is assigned to the fire of Gehenna. For hidden faults, the judgment is determined by the sentence of the Savior, so that the justice of the judgment may be established by virtue of an examination of the circumstances; but a sin in the open has an obvious and fixed punishment.

But perhaps someone says: how is it that something that is spoken has such great force, that the one who says: *You buffoon!* to his brother is condemned to the worst penalty? It has such great force, brothers, it has such great force, because Christ is

---

7. A similar point is made about *Raca* being an untranslatable sign of contempt in Augustine, *Commentary on the Lord's Sermon on the Mount* 1.9.23 (FOTC 11.41–42 and n. 3).

8. See 1 Cor 12.26.

in the brother, and Christ is the Wisdom of God.[9] Therefore, whoever says: *You buffoon!* to his brother has called the Wisdom of God a buffoon. And just as the one who blasphemes the Spirit of God is without forgiveness both in the present age and in the future,[10] so too has this one who has inflicted an insult on the Wisdom of God completely bypassed judgment and fully descended to punishment.

To these remarks the listener will reply: "So who will be able to be saved?" Who, brothers? The one, of course, who is sinless in his heart and in his tongue. Listen to what the prophet says: "Lord, who will dwell in your tent, or who will rest on your holy mountain?"[11] The answer is: "The one who speaks the truth in his heart, and has uttered no deceit with his tongue."[12] The abuse that flows from the tongue is by no means inconsequential, brothers; for it is the tongue that makes the martyr, the tongue that furnishes the crown of martyrdom; it is also the tongue that makes the blasphemer, the tongue that casts one down to destruction through denial.

9. See 1 Cor 1.24.
11. Ps 14 (15).1.
10. See Mt 12.31–32.
12. Ps 14.3 LXX; Ps 15.2–3.

SERMON 178

On Loving One's Enemies[1]

 SUMMON THE SKY and invoke the earth, so that both the earth be amazed and the sky marvel at the new kind of mercy presented by the Lord. What mind perceives, what ear grasps, what teaching has communicated the lesson to which the evangelist draws his Christian audience when he says: *Love your enemies* (Mt 5.44)? Mortal perception does not absorb this, the human heart does not grasp this, the fleshly condition rejects this, the world's hearing does not let this in. The feeble mind is insufficient to love those who love it, and fickle human nature is able only with difficulty to be charitable to those who are charitable.

Doesn't it often happen that with deadly hatred children terrorize their parents, parents their children, a husband his wife, a wife her husband, a brother his brother, a citizen a fellow citizen, and one parent the other parent, and from the bond of charity they tie knots of hatred, fashioning war out of peace, and discord out of unity, and the very thing that had been a matter of love becomes the cause of hatred? And if these relationships, which are according to nature, deviate so far away from nature, who is going to insert into nature what goes against nature?

Anger at the wicked and motives for love are matters of nature; therefore, love and anger are so separate from each other that they cannot be joined; then how is it said: *Love your enemies?* Not to hate those who show hatred, not to persecute one's persecutors are admirable virtues; to love one's enemies and to pray for one's persecutors[2] are impossible tasks for a soul overburdened by the weight of flesh.

---

1. For evidence that this is an authentic sermon of Chrysologus, see A. Olivar, *Los sermones*, 346–47.
2. See Mt 5.44.

Brothers, we say this not to cause despair, but to show how great the heavenly precept is when contrasted with the earthly impossibility of carrying it out, and how it can be implemented not by human effort but only by divine grace, with Christ himself as the Source, since he says: "Those things that are impossible for human beings are possible for God."[3] By giving this command, God is seeking your will; he himself who gives the command furnishes the power.

2. But let us reveal in a down-to-earth manner what lies concealed in this precept. If one stone, when it is smashed against another, although it is cold, produces fire,[4] when the fires of enmities are ignited, what strife they can inflame! Have not kingdoms, nations, and peoples, while engaging in hostilities against their enemies, torn the whole world asunder and made blood flow by their warfare? The world was aflame with the raging of strife, and while the earth was perishing the only thing left were the fires. Just as water extinguishes a blaze,[5] so too does love extinguish the flames of hostility. For love is the water of peace, the dew of kindness, the shower of charity, the seed of harmony, the sprout of affection, and the most abundant fruit of benevolence; and, in short, love is God, as John attests when he says: "For God is love."[6]

Brothers, by giving this command God did not will that his servants be subjected to enmities, but he gave such an order in order to remove enmities; and he wanted enmity to be calmed by love, rage to be restrained by charity, and to exchange enmity for benevolence. Brothers, whoever destroys anger by love, whoever makes a friend out of an enemy, a brother out of a foe, a holy person out of one who is unholy, a religious person out of a sacrilegious one, and brings a Christian out of a pagan, whoever does these things imitates God. But what we are saying becomes clearer from what follows.

3. *Do good*, he says, *to those who hate you, and pray for those who*

---

3. Lk 18.27.
4. Chrysologus uses this same image in *Sermon* 96.1 (FOTC 17.152) regarding the potency of God's word.
5. See Sir 3.33 (30).
6. 1 Jn 4.8.

SERMON 178   351

persecute and slander you, so that you may be children of your Father who is in heaven (see vv.44–45 and Lk 6.27–28). A child of God[7] who is good to evil ones gives love to those who do not love him. Christ, the Son of God, knew that he was hated by the world when he said: "The world hates you, but it hated me first."[8] Nevertheless, even if he knew that he was hated by the world, let us hear what kind of good he did.

So as to be a slave to idols,[9] the world waged hostilities on its Author; and rather than obey the one true God, it preferred being under the power of innumerable monstrosities; and in its hatred for the Creator it placed high value on loving creatures that were worthless and subjected to itself, producing what derived not from sound judgment but from madness. The cry of the breast torn to pieces by its slavery to deadly sacrifices struck at heaven, the very air was dampened by the sacrilegious libations of blood, and the sun's brightness was darkened by the smoke coming from the altars, such that with this kind of worship it was no longer the Creator, but creation itself that was bearing its own pain and complaining about the harm being done to it.

4. Nevertheless, by this impiety the piety of the unconquered Creator[10] was not conquered, because the love of the Craftsman for his work was stronger than the unholy offense, and his predilection for his handiwork caused him to ignore such human deeds, since he knew that it was more glorious to forgive than to punish; to repair what was ruined rather than to preserve what was made;[11] and he knew that in this way he would be believed to be the Author of the universe when creation saw him restoring the universe. This is why God enters the world and is mingled[12] both with the earth and with flesh; he be-

---

7. The Latin *Dei filius* is purposely ambiguous as Chrysologus employs it here, to characterize every Christian believer as a child of God, or to denote Christ the Son of God.
8. Jn 15.18.
9. See 1 Cor 5.10, 6.9; Rv 22.15.
10. On the significance of God's *pietas* in Chrysologus's preaching, see R. Benericetti, *Il Cristo*, 215–17.
11. Chrysologus also makes this precise point in *Sermon* 97.5.
12. *Miscetur*: for other examples of the language of "mingling" applied to

comes man, he enters the servile condition of humanity, in order to establish for the world that Christ is God by his miracles, and that he is man by his obedience and by his sufferings.

Therefore, he does miracles as a sign of his divinity; he gives a blind man eyes that nature did not give him when he was born,[13] on each occasion when merely by issuing an order he had given the very many who were blind vision to see the light;[14] and so he refashions the eyes from the source from which he had made the whole human being: he moistens[15] the mud with his spittle,[16] in order that, just as in the beginning,[17] unstained dust would be molded by divine hands, and his action in making him see would show clearly that he was the Maker of the human being.[18] He expels demons with a command from heaven, and he leads those who had been possessed and kept in cruel bondage back to his own free service;[19] he strengthens the impaired limbs of the paralytic, lest the beauty of his image be subject to a bodily deformity.[20] He restored the dead to life,[21] and he orders souls to return to their already decaying members, so that a double show of power would drive out both death and decay.[22]

But since power produces fear, but intimacy produces love,[23] he goes to parties,[24] he does not avoid weddings,[25] and, ever affable, he keeps connected with everyone on every occasion.[26]

Christ in Chrysologus's sermons, see *Sermons* 5.2 and 156.5 (FOTC 17.44–45, 267), as well as 142.1 and n. 4.

13. See Jn 9.1–41 and *Sermon* 176.1.
14. See Mt 20.29–34; Mk 8.22–26 and 10.46–52; Lk 18.35–43.
15. Literally, "baptizes" *(baptizat)*.
16. See Jn 9.6.
17. See Gn 2.7.
18. The same theme of Christ as Creator and Re-creator in healing the blind man, as well as very similar terminology, is found in *Sermon* 176.1.
19. See, e.g., Lk 4.33–37 and 8.2.
20. See Mt 9.2–8 and parallels; also *Sermon* 50.6 (FOTC 109.197).
21. See Mt 9.18–26 and parallels; Lk 7.11–15.
22. See Jn 11.38–44.
23. For other references in Chrysologus's sermons and in other ancient authors to God's desire to be loved rather than feared, see *Sermon* 72b.4 and n. 15, and A. Olivar, *Los sermones*, 361–62.
24. See Lk 5.29.
25. See Jn 2.1–2.
26. Chrysologus also emphasizes this point in *Sermon* 31.3 (FOTC 109.132).

In the end he suffers, dies, and is buried;[27] and the humanity[28] that he had assumed[29] out of love for the world, he lays down out of love for the world.

5. Nevertheless, not even with all this was the malice of the world overcome, for it gave a perverse interpretation to his miracles,[30] it despised his familiarity with others as demeaning,[31] it attributed his death to circumstances beyond his control,[32] and not to love. Nevertheless, from the inexhaustible supply of his mercy he continued to be lavishly generous in goodness, in order to make his victory glorious from mercy, rather than make his vengeance grim from severity.

27. This terminology is reminiscent of a creed, although different from what is found in *Sermons* 57–62a (FOTC 17.103–14; FOTC 109.221–48).
28. Literally, "human being" *(hominem)*.
29. *Susceperat:* on this christological terminology elsewhere in Chrysologus's sermons, see R. Benericetti, *Il Cristo*, 97–99.
30. See Mt 9.34.
31. See, e.g., Mt 9.11.
32. See, e.g., Mt 27.39–44 and parallels.

SERMON 179

<On St. John the Baptist>[1]

THAT BLESSED JOHN WAS the messenger to the messengers of Christ, the witness to his witnesses, and the foremost of his promoters, we have frequently mentioned in our preaching.[2] Then why is it that the messenger asks a question, the witness is in doubt, and the promoter is lacking in knowledge? *Are you the One who is to come, or do we wait for another?* (Mt 11.3) John, you perfect man, are you asking whether he is the Christ who is to come, when while you were still within your mother's womb you announced that he had already come?[3]

John, these are your words: "Behold, the Lamb of God; behold him who takes away the sins of the world."[4] And when he submitted to be baptized by your hands, you said: "I ought to be baptized by you, and yet you are coming to me?"[5] Are you not the one who heard amidst the waters of the Jordan the voice of the Father resounding from heaven: "This is my beloved Son, in whom I am well-pleased"?[6] You certainly were

---

1. (Angle brackets here indicate an addition to the title in Olivar's CCL text.) Largely on the basis of the stylistic devices employed in this sermon, A. Olivar, *Los sermones*, 365–68, provides compelling evidence that Chrysologus is its author. In addition, in his *monitum* to this sermon in CCL 24B.1084, Olivar lists some parallels between this work and John Chrysostom's *Homily 36 (37) on Matthew* (PG 57.413–15), and suggests that Chrysologus may have read Chrysostom and drawn some of his ideas from him. It is an interesting hypothesis but unconvincing since the parallels noted do not seem particularly close.
2. The following twelve sermons have John the Baptist as their primary theme: Sermons 86–92, 127, 137, 167, and 173–74. See F. Sottocornola, *L'anno liturgico*, 302–4.
3. See Lk 1.41.
4. Jn 1.29.
5. Mt 3.14.
6. Mt 3.17.

the only human being who saw the Holy Spirit come down in bodily form from heaven upon him.⁷ You are the one who grasped the Father with your ears, the Son with your hands, and the Holy Spirit with your eyes at one and the same moment in an unparalleled manifestation of power.⁸

And after this you ask whether he is the Christ or whether there is another who is to come? And do you ask by means of your disciples, so that you bring forward in opposition to yourself witnesses of your doubt, judges of your ignorance, informants of your inconstancy, and accusers of your uncertainty? John, has the prison⁹ so frightened that invincible mind of yours, have your chains so crushed it, has harm so confused it, has fear brought it so low, has the persecutor so shaken it, and has anxiety about death so subverted it, that you who had been the model of the virtues¹⁰ are an exemplification of feebleness? And, in short, John, from where will martyrdom come if the Lord is either doubted or denied?

We are disturbed, John, we who sing your praises are disturbed, and, as the Apostle has said, we who bore witness that all the virtues abide in you are discovered to be false witnesses,¹¹ if such weakness as this has struck you down and held you captive. So give an answer, John, assist yourself and assist us; say why you who used to have knowledge sent them to ask a question.

2. Let us pay attention, brothers, let us pay more in-depth attention, and let us listen to the answer John gives here not only with our ears, but also with our hearts. John says: "If while I was still in the womb I instantly announced that Christ was going to be born, now after hearing of his works, works which attest to his divinity, have I plunged into the waves of doubt? Far from it!

---

7. See Mt 3.16 and parallels; Jn 1.32–34.
8. Or "owing to your unique virtue" *(unica virtute)*. See Mt 3.16–17 and parallels. Chrysologus uses language of the human senses to convey the contact John was privileged to make with the Trinity also in *Sermon* 43.3 (FOTC 17.92).
9. See Mt 14.3 and parallels.
10. The Latin word *virtus* means both "virtue" and "strength." Similar to this passage is *Sermon* 127.2, where John is called the "school of the virtues" and "model of sanctity."
11. See 1 Cor 15.15.

"This is the reason for my question: my disciples, who had seen my good reputation, who had admired my life, who had heard me impose penance, forgive sins, and promise that the kingdom of heaven was arriving in him who was to come,[12] were so prepared to be bound with chains, to live in prison with me, to share my punishments, and to become partners with me in death, that they failed to see my Lord, for whom I had prepared them. They were following the teacher of penitence so closely that they were neglecting the Giver of grace; on account of ignorance they considered themselves mine to such an extent that they were unaware that the servant's property belongs to his Master.

"So I sent them out,[13] in order to put heavenly goods before them, to lead them to divine ones, to hand them over to God, to return them to the Creator. I sent them, so that by his works they would affirm that he was the Christ about whom they had heard by my words, and so that my [disciples] would not be lost to my Lord with my passing away.[14] I sent them to him who knew very well why I sent them. I sent them to the One who probes the heart; I sent them to the One who judges thoughts.[15] I sent them to him who was in me and with me. I sent them so that by recognizing his divinity by means of his works, they would not find his humanity to be a stumbling block.[16] I sent them, so that gazing upon his humanity would not disturb them who could not but be strengthened by the signs of his divine powers.

3. "And so, the Lord, who knew why I sent them, responded with his works before he did with words." *Go, [Jesus said,] and report to John what you have heard and seen: the blind see, the lame walk, lepers are cleansed, the dead rise, the poor have the good news preached to them, and blessed is the one who finds no stumbling block in me* (vv.4–6). We have understood, brothers, whose was the

12. See Mt 3.1–12 and parallels.
13. See Mt 11.2.
14. Chrysologus's use of alliteration and assonance is evident: *transituro me mei meo domino non perirent.*
15. Other references in Chrysologus's preaching to Christ as *scrutator cordis* and *cognitor pectorum* are indicated in R. Benericetti, *Il Cristo,* 263, n. 165.
16. See Mt 11.4–6.

stumbling block which Christ removed with his miraculous cures, when he says: *Blessed is the one who finds no stumbling block in me.* The Lord in these words was admonishing John's disciples, and not John; for if he were upbraiding John, this is the message he would have sent: "Blessed are you, if you find no stumbling block in me." But since what he says is: *Blessed is the one who finds no stumbling block in me,* he is speaking in a general way, he is speaking to the many, he is speaking to those who were sent,[17] and not to the teacher; so that the sight of the Man would not be a stumbling block when his works attested to his radiant splendor as God.

4. And so, lest any suspicion of doubt remain among the audience about John, he is very laudatory in describing his constancy and steadfastness, and with many examples he commends him, when he says: *What did you go out into the desert to see? A reed shaken by the wind?* (v.7) That is to say: if John pursued an ambition for empty glory or greed, he would be flitting about the theaters in cities, to be captivated amid the captive voices of those captivating him, amid the eager hum of flattery.[18] But now in the desert what is there for him to gaze at except heaven? What does he await other than an angel? Whom is he on hand to please except God alone? Whoever has no desire to be praised is unable to be altered. The one on whom flattery does not have a hold, constancy does. The one on whom pompous ostentation has no hold, virtue does not forsake.

5. And so he added: *A reed shaken by the wind?* He has cited a fine example of wavering. A reed, since it is thin in its stalk, without marrow, weak in strength, with no branches, with a poor trunk, and without protection in its height, is swayed by the winds, and shaken by squalls, wherever they blow; it is knocked over by being so high and so flexible. But John was made steadfast in God, rooted in Christ,[19] filled with the Holy

---

17. The Latin word is *apostolis.*
18. Chrysologus's fondness for alliteration and assonance is evident here: *in civitatum caveis, inter captivas captivantium voces, inter avidos adulationum susurros captivandus ipse volitaret.*
19. See Col 2.7.

Spirit,[20] made strong by virtue, and most lofty in holiness; he could not be bent back or altered from his faith in Christ, once he had borne witness to it, by the winds of admirers, or by the squalls of slanderers, or by the gales of threats, or by the feathery touches of pleasure, or by the storms of suffering.

6. He added: *Or what did you go out to see? A man dressed in soft garments?* (v.8) Those who are dressed in soft garments flee from what is austere and quiver before strength. Those who are made slack by extravagance and sway about in their silk cannot sustain the breastplate of virtue; and thus, devoid of strength and deprived of liberty, they fluctuate according to the situations, the persons, and current fads. But John, who felt the sting of a hair-cloak, who was toughened up by the desert, strengthened by fasting, and parched with thirst, had no reason to yield to persons, go along with fads, or sell his faith. Rightly does the Lord say about him: *Or what did you come out to see? A prophet? I tell you truly: he is even more than a prophet* (v.9). John is more than a prophet, because he was counted worthy of both seeing and holding Christ, whose coming the prophets had foretold;[21] and John alone was counted worthy of pointing out to a world that was perishing the Savior of the world.[22]

20. See Lk 1.15.
21. On this point, see also *Sermon* 160.3.
22. See Jn 1.29.

INDICES

GENERAL INDEX

Aaron, 75, 76, 85, 86
Abraham, 12, 79, 115, 140, 155, 156, 157, 158, 161, 162, 166, 167, 171, 172, 173, 200, 202, 203, 204, 205, 211, 269
Adam, 108, 140, 143n, 311
Adelphius, bishop, 206–7
Agnellus, author of *Liber Pontificalis*, 102n, 315n
allegory (biblical), 88n, 109, 121n, 169n, 185n
alliteration, 356n, 357n
Ambrose of Milan, 32n, 36n, 75n, 84n, 98n, 109n, 126n, 134n, 138n, 140n, 141n, 152n, 190n, 198n, 211n, 220n, 227n, 228n, 262n, 269n, 279n, 311n
Andrew, apostle, 62n, 155n
angel, angels, 155, 156, 158, 164, 170, 171, 176, 187, 201, 205, 225, 226, 227, 229, 230, 231, 232, 233, 234, 236, 237, 238, 239, 242, 244, 245, 251, 253, 257, 280, 311, 312, 321, 333, 337, 338, 357
Anna, mother of Samuel, 13, 80
Anné, L., 337n
Antiochus, king, 60n
Apollinaris, saint, 102n, 192–94
Aquileia, 100n, 200n, 206n, 222n, 228n, 336n
Arbesmann, R., 265n
Argemi, A., 281n
Arian, Arians, 51n, 235n, 246n, 253n, 262n, 301n
Ascension, 23, 55n, 56, 61, 286, 311
assonance, 356n, 357n

Asterius of Amasea, 102n
astrology, 90, 254n
Attila, Hun, 127n
Augustine, 14n, 17n, 102n, 125n, 160n, 196n, 210n, 220n, 227n, 232n, 262n, 269n, 285n, 321n, 336n, 347n
avarice, 128, 130, 160; *see also* greed

Baldisserri, D. L., 192n
Banterle, G., xi, 1, 85n
baptism, 12n, 13n, 54, 55n, 82, 102n, 135n, 148, 197n, 203n, 209n, 210, 215, 244n, 257n, 270, 276n, 279n, 280, 299, 300, 316
Barcellona, F. Scorza, 262n
Barré, H., 230n
Barrios, J. P., 222n
Baxter, J. H., 213n
Benericetti, R., 8n, 48n, 53n, 63n, 75n, 111n, 112n, 178n, 205n, 206n, 213n, 225n, 226n, 229n, 234n, 236n, 242n, 247n, 248n, 249n, 258n, 259n, 270n, 273n, 277n, 278n, 295n, 309n, 337n, 341n, 351n, 353n, 356n
bread as image of Christ, 33, 108, 143, 185n, 228, 334

Cain, 321
Carroll, T., 135n, 270n
Celestine I, pope, 336n
Chalcedon, Chalcedonian christology, 74n, 229n
Chalcedon, home of Euphemia, 102n

GENERAL INDEX

Christmas, 1n, 63n, 68n, 69n, 73n, 79n, 85n, 88n, 90n, 91n, 94n, 123n, 216n, 221n, 225n, 226n, 229n, 236n, 242n, 248n, 251n, 257n, 261n, 267n, 336n
Chromatius of Aquileia, 222n, 228n
Chrysostom, John, 85n, 354n
Church, 16, 23, 55, 60, 61, 62n, 66, 101, 102, 104, 107, 119, 139, 166, 193, 197, 207n, 219, 263, 280n, 287, 324, 339n, 343, 344; as boat or ship, 32, 34; as Christ's body, 21; as bride or spouse of Christ, 126, 195n, 212n, 300–301, 336n, 337n; as mother, 14, 105n, 106, 126n, 134, 193, 195, 196n, 197n, 198–99, 315, 336n, 338n; as prefigured, 16, 20, 21, 22, 44n, 47, 60, 134–36, 138, 260; in allegory, 109, 313–14; as virgin, 196n, 198–99, 336n, 338n
Cicero, 146n, 152n, 217n, 335n
Classe, 194n
contract, financial, 185, 200
Cortesi, G., 102n
creatio ex nihilo, 83n, 121n, 124n
Creed, 4n, 56n; Nicene Creed, 243n
Cyprian of Carthage, 7n, 202n, 262n, 304n

Daniel, 201
Datema, C., 102n
David, king of Israel, 115, 185, 195, 196, 238, 240, 244, 245, 246, 252, 335
De Aldama, J. A., 17n, 250n
De Bruyne, D., 325n
Decalogue, 135n, 314
Deferrari, R. J., 304n
devil, 27, 28, 30, 37, 53, 80, 101, 108, 129, 132, 134, 136, 151, 194, 203, 220, 244, 247, 254, 274, 275, 276, 304, 311, 321; *see also* Satan
Díaz, R., 74n
docetism, 243n

doctor (medical), 96; *see also* physician
drunkenness, 172, 270, 328, 331

Eagan, M. C., 262n
Easter, 12, 14n, 15n, 20n, 25n, 26n, 31n, 35n, 39n, 44n, 49n, 50n, 55n, 58n, 61n, 105n, 190n, 198n, 200n, 203n, 323n, 324n, 339n
Elijah, 89, 91, 167, 204, 252, 258, 326
Elizabeth, mother of John the Baptist, 81, 87, 89, 90n, 92, 93, 234
envy, 101, 110, 133, 217, 249, 301, 311, 318, 320, 321, 322
Epiphany, 1, 267, 269, 270, 271, 272n, 277n, 281n
Eucharist, 185n, 211n, 228n, 281n, 287n, 316n, 323n
Euphemia, saint, 100n, 102
Eve, 16n, 27n, 36n, 107, 108, 133, 140n, 229, 233n
Exultet, 190n, 198n

Farnedi, P. G., 224n
fasting, 15n, 170, 219, 285, 298n, 303, 307, 358
father as image of Christ, 11, 143n, 232; as name and image of God, *passim*
Felician collection, 73n, 308n, 344n
figure (in biblical exegesis), 134n, 135, 312, 343

Galla Placidia, 61n, 195n, 197n, 315n, 336n
Gaudentius of Brescia, 54n, 126n
Gehenna, 101, 104, 161, 172, 173, 178, 296, 346, 347
gentile, gentiles, 1, 2, 7, 14, 16, 34, 47, 53, 73, 88, 115, 116, 118, 119, 121, 122, 123, 135, 141, 143, 183, 185, 186, 204n, 209, 258, 259, 260, 279, 287, 298, 299, 301, 315

GENERAL INDEX 363

greed, 128, 131, 133, 160, 220, 274, 288, 291, 310, 318, 357
Greek language, 192n, 244, 267n
Gregory I, pope, 32n
Gross, K., 10n
Gryson, R., 199n

Halton, T., 135n, 270n
Harvey, W. W., 310n
Hedlund, M. F., 135n
Herod Antipas, 7, 74, 187–91, 324–27, 330–32
Herod the Great, 65, 75, 85, 188n, 253, 254, 258, 261, 262n, 273–78, 321
Herodias, 74, 190, 191, 327, 328n, 330, 332
Herz, M., 229n
Hilary of Poitiers, 108n, 109n
Holy Innocents, 254, 261–62
Horace, 160n
hypocrisy, 111n, 322, 323

Incarnation, 20n, 50, 82n, 223n, 226n, 227n, 230n, 234n, 237n, 240n, 248n, 249, 277, 281n
invasion, barbarian, 127n
Irenaeus, 28n, 269n, 310n
Isaac, 13, 80, 93

Jacob, 14, 201, 246
James, apostle, 62n
Jerome, 17n, 127n, 230n, 310n
Jew, Jews, 7, 8, 12n, 13, 14, 15, 16, 18, 23, 24, 26, 33, 34, 47, 49, 50, 53, 56, 65, 66, 88, 115, 116, 118, 119, 121, 122, 123, 127, 133, 135, 136, 138, 140n, 142, 143, 168, 176, 184, 185, 186, 201, 202, 203, 204, 205n, 209, 210, 212, 223, 249n, 254, 255, 258, 259, 260, 268, 276, 278, 279, 293, 298, 301, 304, 314, 317, 318, 319, 320n, 321, 342
John the Baptist, 64n, 65n, 69, 70, 71, 72, 73n, 74, 76, 77, 87, 88, 89, 90, 91, 93, 94n, 141, 187–91, 197n, 209–15, 226n, 233, 240, 279, 280, 303, 304, 306, 314, 324–34, 354–58
John, apostle, 32, 34, 40, 51, 62n
John Cassian, 310n
Jonah, 5
Jones, A. H. M., 127n
Joseph, Hebrew patriarch, 333, 334
Joseph, husband of Mary, 222, 227n, 236, 243n, 251, 257, 335, 337
Josephus, Flavius, 65n
Jossua, J.-P., 28n
Judas, betrayer, 23, 133, 286
judge as image of Christ, 6, 31, 38, 81, 82, 88, 94, 103, 143, 178n, 188, 210, 243, 288, 290, 291, 309; as image of God, 128n, 129, 179, 273, 345
Julius Caesar, 118n
Juvenal, 262n, 310n

Kalends of January, 264n; see also new year
Kochaniewicz, B., 17n, 230n, 337n
Koep, L., 198n

Lactantius, 152n
Lamirande, E., 184n
Law, 9, 10, 16, 26, 27, 56, 57, 65, 66, 70, 81, 88, 92, 97, 98, 108n, 109, 112, 118, 119, 135, 136, 138, 139, 140, 141n, 143, 152, 153, 165, 167, 185, 186, 187, 188, 189, 209, 223, 255, 258, 259, 269, 293, 298, 299, 306, 308, 314, 317, 321, 326, 343, 344, 346
Lazarus of Bethany, 17n, 30n, 43
Lazarus, beggar, 155–74
Leclercq, H., 59n
Lent, 1n, 19n, 25n, 175n, 200n, 203n, 209n, 303n, 308n, 312n, 316n, 317n, 320n, 339n
Leo I, pope, 40n, 229n, 269n
Lucchesi, G., 102n

364   GENERAL INDEX

Magi, 69, 126, 127, 242, 254,
    267–69, 270n, 274–76, 279
Magus, 275, 277, 278
Manilius, M., 299n
Marcellinus, bishop, 335–38
Marcion, 243n
martyr, martyrs, 60n, 102n, 126,
    191, 192, 193, 259, 260, 262,
    263, 332, 333, 348
martyrdom, 34, 73n, 74n, 78n, 102,
    187n, 193, 262, 324n, 330n, 334,
    348, 355
Mary, Virgin, mother of Jesus, 16n,
    17, 27n, 36n, 50n, 89, 105n, 108,
    109n, 126, 140n, 185n, 187n,
    196n, 204, 221–50, 258, 262,
    311, 335, 337; perpetual virginity
    of, 50, 68–69, 196n, 226, 227,
    231–32, 238, 242, 244, 250
Mary Magdalene, 16, 27, 44
Mary, "the other," 16, 20, 27
Maximinus the Arian, 262n
Maximus of Turin, 17n
Mazzotti, M., 194n
mercy, 62, 129, 130, 136, 161, 166,
    168, 169, 171, 172, 173, 179,
    183, 185, 186, 189, 197, 218,
    219, 220n, 240, 307, 308, 349; di-
    vine, 5, 81, 82, 111n, 133, 147,
    305, 308, 309, 353; to be given to
    poor, 131, 159, 209n; see also
    poor, giving to
Milan, 100n, 200n, 336n
Mohrmann, C., 135n
monophysite, 222n, 229n, 236n
Morin, G., 285n
Moses, 86, 108, 140n, 167, 168,
    200, 204
"mystic" or "mystical" meaning (bib-
    lical), 27, 35, 36, 222

Neon, bishop, 280n
Nestorian, 235n
new year, 264; see also Kalends of Jan-
    uary
Noah, 108, 223, 269, 279, 293
Ntedika, J., 166n

number symbolism, 60–61, 135,
    185–86, 219–20, 310

Olivar, A. xi, 1n, 3n, 6n, 10n, 12n,
    15n, 35n, 36n, 38n, 39n, 44n,
    47n, 49n, 54n, 55n, 56n, 58n,
    60n, 61n, 63n, 68n, 72n, 73n,
    74n, 78n, 79n, 82n, 85n, 88n,
    91n, 95n, 99n, 100n, 105n, 110n,
    116n, 117n, 127n, 132n, 135n,
    136n, 138n, 142n, 146n, 150n,
    155n, 165n, 169n, 175n, 186n,
    187n, 195n, 197n, 198n, 201n,
    204n, 206n, 221n, 224n, 225n,
    228n, 229n, 236n, 242n, 248n,
    250n, 251n, 252n, 261n, 264n,
    270n, 272n, 273n, 281n, 290n,
    293n, 303n, 315n, 319n, 320n,
    327n, 328n, 335n, 342n, 344n,
    349n, 352n, 354n
Optatus, 262n
Origen, 88n

parent as image of Christ, 111, 143,
    280; as image of God, 76, 299
Paul, apostle, 74, 98n, 103, 104,
    106, 142n, 143, 146n, 148, 150,
    192, 260, 269, 284, 309, 343;
    quotations from, *passim*
Pelagius, 184n
Pentecost, 55n, 58, 60, 61n, 219
Peter, apostle, 23, 32, 33, 34, 37, 40,
    51, 52, 62n, 80, 86, 98, 103, 134,
    145, 174, 219, 252, 256, 286,
    293, 301, 322
Peterson, E., 276n
Pharisee, Pharisees, 28, 95, 96,
    110–13, 134, 164, 308, 309, 316,
    317, 320, 322, 343
physician as image of Christ, 53, 96,
    112, 113, 203, 306, 344; as image
    of God, 147; see also doctor
poor, 61, 62, 105, 106, 126, 128,
    129, 155, 156, 159, 160, 162,
    163, 168, 169, 170, 171, 172,
    173, 176, 206, 214, 220, 273,
    298, 317, 340, 356; giving to,

126n, 127, 131, 157, 158, 159, 160, 162, 172, 173, 191, 209n, 214, 340; *see also* mercy, to be given to poor
prefiguration (biblical), 14, 16, 20, 22, 29, 60, 138, 184, 186, 343n
Prudentius, 198n, 227n, 262n, 269n
Pseudo–Augustine, 262n
Pseudo–Tertullian, 244n

Quintilian, 75n
Quodvultdeus, 262n

Rahner, H., 293n
Rebecca, mother of Jacob, 80
rhetoric, 42n, 75n, 127, 191n, 193n, 202n, 210n, 212n, 217n, 261n, 268n, 284n, 331n, 340n
Rimoldi, A., 174n
Rome, 59n, 200n, 219n, 336n
Rose, A., 226n
Rowley, H. H., 135n

Sabbath, 15, 16, 26, 44, 110, 112, 113, 132, 136, 219
Salome, follower of Jesus, 44
Sarah, mother of Isaac, 13, 79, 93, 108
Satan, 276; *see also* devil
Sedulius, 275n, 276n
Seneca, 152n, 288n
shepherd, 291, 310, 324; as image of Christ, 38, 115, 324; as image of God, 310, 311, 312; as image of Saint Apollinaris, 194; as image of bishop, 199
Sieben, H. J., 211n
Skard, E., 255n
soldiers as image of Christians, 3, 37, 151, 252–53, 261–62, 274
Sottocornola, F., 1n, 12n, 15n, 20n, 26n, 31n, 35n, 39n, 44n, 49n, 52n, 55n, 61n, 63n, 69n, 72n, 73n, 74n, 78n, 79n, 85n, 88n, 91n, 100n, 105n, 109n, 117n, 123n, 126n, 128n, 132n, 137n, 142n, 155n, 169n, 175n, 187n,

195n, 200n, 203n, 206n, 209n, 216n, 219n, 221n, 225n, 229n, 236n, 247n, 248n, 251n, 261n, 267n, 272n, 277n, 281n, 303n, 308n, 311n, 316n, 320n, 324n, 325n, 329n, 330n, 339n, 354n
Suetonius, 118n
synagogue, 16, 118, 119, 132, 134, 136, 138, 139, 140, 141, 212, 213, 260, 263, 300, 301, 314, 315, 342, 343
Syrophoenician woman, 114–16

Tartarus, 2, 4n, 6, 40, 44, 151n, 165, 173, 178, 213, 333
temple, 105; human beings as, 55, 56, 70, 88, 105n, 120n, 229, 239, 319; Virgin Mary as, 126, 226, 239, 243; Zechariah as, 70; Zechariah and Elizabeth as, 88
Temple, Jewish, 55, 56, 66, 70, 83, 92, 188, 257, 274
Tertullian, 279n
Thomas, apostle, 32, 51–54
Trinity, 4, 5, 108, 188, 197, 246, 279n, 280, 355n
Truzzi, C., 85n
type, typology (biblical), 16n, 22n, 47n, 121, 134

Ursus, bishop, 280n

Van den Eynde, D., 184n
Van der Meer, F., 135n
Virgil, 164n, 198n

Wharton, A. J., 135n
wordplay, 22n, 108n, 117n, 129n, 157n, 162n, 186n, 220n, 230n, 244n, 291n, 305n, 322n, 340n

Zangara, V., 25n, 63n, 221n, 225n, 236n, 248n
Zechariah, father of John the Baptist, 63–94, 209, 233
Zeno of Verona, 171n

INDEX OF HOLY SCRIPTURE

Old Testament

Genesis
1.2: 32, 124
1.26: 4, 204, 205, 265, 282
1.31: 73
2.1–2: 60
2.2–3: 219
2.7: 124, 227, 239, 339, 352
2.15: 311
2.17: 107
2.21–22: 233
2.21–23: 240
2.24: 106
2.25: 34
3: 37, 283, 290
3.1–5: 229
3.1–6: 133
3.1–15: 329, 332
3.6: 30, 216, 223
3.7: 34, 107, 140
3.10: 107
3.11: 34, 107
3.15: 328
3.16: 71
3.20: 108
3.24: 164, 321
4.8–10: 321
4.10: 176, 333, 345
8.11: 279
9.1–3: 293
11.1–9: 223
11.4: 205
12.1–10: 157
12.7: 204
13.2: 156

15.18: 204
18.1–5: 157
18.1–15: 201
18.6: 108
18.6–8: 157
18.10–14: 108
18.14: 84
21.1–5: 80
21.3: 93
21.6: 93
21.8: 13
25.21: 80
27: 14
32.24–29: 210
37.5–28: 334
39.6–20: 334
41.33–57: 334

Exodus
3.2: 299
12.10: 12
16.4: 293
16.31: 293
20.8–11: 219
20.10: 136
20.13: 314
20.13–14: 314
20.15: 314
20.16: 315
23.19: 254
25.37: 60
28.1: 76
32: 86
33.13–23: 200
34.26: 254

Leviticus
8.7: 88
8–9: 76
25.8–55: 185, 220

Numbers
11.6: 293
20.12: 86
21.5: 293

Deuteronomy
5.14: 136
5.17: 314
5.17–18: 314
5.19: 314
5.20: 315
6.4: 314
6.5: 10, 98
14.21: 254
14.22: 127
19.15: 281
28.66: 28

Joshua
3.15–17: 280

1 Samuel
1: 80
1.10–28: 13
2.5: 83
19.11–17: 252

1 Kings
17.8–16: 207, 258
17.8–24: 252

INDEX OF HOLY SCRIPTURE

2 Kings
  1.9–12: 258
  2.11: 91

1 Chronicles
  24: 92

Job
  10.8: 240
  10.10–12: 240

Psalms (Vulgate numbering)
  4.4: 346
  14.1: 348
  14.3: 348
  18.5: 299
  18.6: 226
  21.17: 342
  22.5: 211, 281
  23.6: 186
  26.13: 34
  28.3: 279, 280
  33.6: 226
  34.11: 315
  34.16: 190
  35.7: 224
  36.27: 274
  37.5: 133
  38.3: 264
  39.13: 318
  44.8: 280
  44.11: 196
  44.17: 195, 196, 199
  45.2: 258
  45.5: 208
  48.2–3: 105
  48.13: 223
  49.14: 13
  50.3: 185
  50.4: 317
  54.6: 50
  54.24: 179
  58.6: 193
  61.4: 331
  64.12: 13
  67.19: 61
  67.22: 134
  67.32: 278
  68.5: 163
  71.6: 238
  72.24: 113
  75.6: 131
  75.9–10: 27
  77.57: 136
  78.2–3: 331
  79.4: 227
  79.14: 190
  83.6: 23, 56
  88.16: 315
  88.36–37: 115
  89.1: 258
  93.11: 130
  95.11: 59
  97.7–8: 59
  100.5: 159
  101.19: 186
  103.2: 46
  106.20: 121
  108.23–24: 307
  113.3: 280
  113.4: 59
  113.6: 59
  113B.8: 266
  115.10: 84
  115.12–13: 145
  115.15: 332
  115.16: 283
  118.73: 341
  120.3–4: 285
  120.4: 103
  131.6–7: 315
  131.11: 138
  131.11–12: 115
  131.17: 315
  132.1: 288
  134.6: 114
  138.5: 240
  138.11: 26
  138.12: 16
  142.2: 86, 164
  145.4: 130
  145.6: 83
  146.5: 83
  148.5: 121
  148.7–8: 18

Proverbs
  4.27: 46, 70
  18.17: 164

Song of Songs
  4.2: 324
  6.5 (6): 324

Sirach
  3.33 (30): 350
  25.23 (24): 36

Isaiah
  1.3: 224
  5.7: 139
  5.20: 152
  6.1: 201
  6.3: 234
  6.5: 201
  7.14: 249, 261
  8.4: 255
  14.12: 311, 321
  22.13: 151
  26.19: 123, 341
  28.16: 28
  35.5–6: 244
  40.3: 63
  40.4: 209
  40.6: 228
  52.7: 22
  52.11: 266
  53.7: 297
  61.2: 141
  61.10: 195
  66.2: 237
  66.24: 214

Jeremiah
  1.5: 240

INDEX OF HOLY SCRIPTURE

Ezekiel
33.11: 305

Daniel
7.9–10: 201
7.13–14: 201
12.2: 124

Hosea
11.1: 255

Amos
8.9: 16

Habakkuk
3.2: 66

Haggai
2.8: 81

Zechariah
9.9: 297

Malachi
3.1: 70

New Testament

Matthew
1.18–25: 227
1.20: 337, 338
2.1–2: 242, 267–69
2.1–12: 277
2.3–11: 272–76
2.7: 242
2.9: 242
2.9–10: 276
2.11: 90, 126, 242, 267, 269, 278
2.12: 254, 276
2.13: 257–60, 273
2.13–15: 251–56, 258
2.16: 188, 321
2.16–17: 273
2.16–18: 261
3.1–4: 303–7
3.1–12: 356
3.3: 94
3.10: 141
3.11: 210
3.13–17: 82, 270, 279
3.14: 354
3.16: 279, 355
3.16–17: 355
3.17: 244, 270, 279, 354
4.11: 176
4.19: 338
5.15: 332

5.17: 10, 16
5.17, 21–22: 344–48
5.18: 10
5.44: 260, 349
5.44–45: 349–53
6.4: 266
6.6: 266
6.18: 266
6.12: 163
7.3: 216
7.9: 292
7.16: 298
7.20: 102
8.2: 114
8.5–9: 117
8.12: 333
9.2–8: 352
9.9: 104
9.11: 353
9.12: 306
9.13: 306
9.16: 13
9.18–26: 352
9.20–22: 64, 96
9.34: 353
10.23: 256, 260
11.2: 356
11.3–9: 354–58
11.4–6: 356
11.5: 56, 244
11.10: 70
11.11: 87, 88, 187, 334

11.12: 115
11.21: 340
11.27: 248, 279
11.28–30: 135
11.29: 297
11.29–30: 224
12.31–32: 348
12.40: 5
13.8: 208, 299
13.24–29: 100–104
13.24–30: 298
13.43: 29, 46
14.1–12: 73, 74
14.3: 355
14.3–11: 187–91
14.4: 189
14.8: 328, 332
14.15–21: 281
14.25–31: 80
15.24: 115
16.16: 33
16.16–17: 23
16.17: 103
16.19: 174, 322
17.3: 204
17.5: 244
18.2: 251
18.16: 281
18.21–22: 219
18.22: 60
19.5: 106
19.6: 106
19.14: 196

INDEX OF HOLY SCRIPTURE 369

19.24: 307
19.29: 294
19.30: 16, 279
20.16: 279
20.18–19: 1–5, 6–11
20.29–34: 352
21.5: 297
21.12: 274
21.37–38: 301
22.21: 222
23.4: 134
23.13: 134
25.15: 163
25.26–27: 163
25.32: 291
25.33: 33, 46
25.34: 46, 246
25.35: 158
25.41: 33
25.42–43: 214
26.14–16: 286
26.15: 23
26.48–49: 212
26.56: 40, 51, 252, 286
26.57–58: 34
26.60: 315
26.69–75: 23, 32, 34, 40, 51, 86, 252, 256, 286
27.25: 3, 24
27.39–44: 353
27.42: 43
27.45: 16, 32
27.50–52: 2
27.51–53: 32
27.52: 2, 53
28.1–6: 15–19
28.1–7: 26–30
28.5–15: 20–24
28.12–15: 315
28.19: 4

Mark
1.3: 63
1.13: 176
1.17: 338
3.4: 26
5.31: 114
6.14–28: 324–29
6.17–29: 73, 74
6.18: 189
6.20: 327
6.21–25: 330–34
6.25: 328
7.2: 316
7.3–23: 316–19
7.5: 316
7.24–28: 114–16
7.37: 244
8.22: 340
8.22–26: 339–43, 352
8.23: 340
9.48: 214
10.46–52: 339, 352
12.7: 321
12.30: 98
12.41–44: 127
14.51–52: 32, 34, 40, 51, 252, 256, 286
15.33: 45
16.1–12: 44–48
16.10: 47

Luke
1.5–7: 73–78
1.5–11: 68–72
1.5–17: 85–90
1.5–20: 63–67
1.13: 18–22, 79–84
1.13–17: 280
1.15: 358
1.17: 79
1.18–20: 233
1.20–22: 63
1.22: 63
1.23–25: 91–94
1.26: 89
1.26–29: 236–41
1.26–38: 91

1.28: 230
1.30: 229
1.30–33: 242–47
1.30–38: 229–35
1.35: 226
1.36: 89
1.36–37: 234
1.37: 84
1.38: 249
1.39: 335
1.39–45: 234
1.41: 71, 89, 90, 240, 354
1.44: 89
1.55: 115
1.63–64: 64
1.67: 90
2.1, 4–7: 335–38
2.1–7: 221–24
2.7: 207, 227, 228, 254, 297
2.10: 225–28
2.13: 227
2.26: 139
2.29–30: 139
2.34: 73
2.52: 298
3.2–14: 209–15
3.5: 209
3.7: 329
3.9: 141, 209
3.23–38: 60
4.19: 12, 141
4.33–37: 352
5.10: 338
5.29: 352
6.27–28: 351
7.2–9: 117–22
7.11–15: 352
7.11–17: 123–27
7.22: 56, 244
7.28: 87, 88, 187
7.39–47: 95–99
7.44: 316
8.2: 352
9.1–2: 286

Luke *(continued)*
10.4: 21
10.17: 244, 286
10.20: 286
11.2: 304
11.46: 134
11.52: 134, 320
11.52–12.1: 320–23
12.13: 288
12.13–15: 288–91
12.16: 176
12.16–20: 128–31
12.22: 292
12.22–31: 292–96
12.28: 296
12.32: 294
12.49: 297
12.49–56: 297–302
13.6–9: 137–41
13.10–13: 132–36
13.14: 136
13.15: 136
13.19: 106
13.20–21: 105–9
14.1–4: 110–13
14.2: 322
14.5: 113
15.1: 308
15.1–6: 308–11
15.4–7: 312, 313
15.8: 312
15.8–10: 312–15
15.10: 315
15.11–32: 183
15.12: 290
15.13: 98, 176
15.17: 184
15.22–23: 211
16.1: 176
16.1–8: 175–80
16.3–8: 181–86
16.19: 176
16.19–23: 155–60
16.19–24: 169–74
16.23–31: 161–68
16.24: 167
17.3–4: 216–20
17.7–10: 282–87
18.9–14: 164
18.13: 133
18.27: 350
18.35–43: 339, 352
19.23: 163
21.1–4: 127
21.30–31: 139
22.3: 129
22.3–6: 133
23.21: 3, 212
23.40–43: 305
24.1–3: 35–38
24.2: 53
24.4–35: 39
24.5: 17
24.11: 37
24.13–35: 38
24.36–41: 39–43
24.37: 54
24.44: 255

John
1.1: 64, 234, 314
1.2: 243, 245
1.3: 204
1.14: 209, 242, 245
1.16: 238
1.23: 333
1.29: 254, 279, 297, 300, 311, 323, 334, 354, 358
1.32–34: 355
1.36: 254, 297, 334
2.1–2: 352
2.1–11: 270, 280
2.6: 210
2.7–10: 281
3.6: 234
3.8: 41
3.10: 56
3.13: 4
3.16: 9
3.29: 212
3.31: 209
4.24: 234
5.4: 64
5.22: 290
5.24: 203
5.28–29: 123
5.35: 69, 314, 332
6.35: 334
6.41: 334
6.48: 334
6.51: 334
7.14: 58
7.14–15: 55–57
8.39: 162
8.42: 290
8.51–59: 200–205
9.1–7: 339
9.1–41: 352
9.6: 352
9.21: 199
10.3–4: 324
10.11: 324
10.18: 2, 28, 143
11.26: 203
11.38–44: 43, 352
12.19: 255
12.24: 186
12.25: 192
13.2: 129
13.27: 129
14.6: 143, 144, 335
15.13: 9
15.15: 119
15.18: 351
16.15: 245
17.21: 290
17.24: 290
19.6: 3, 212
19.25–27: 32
19.34: 54, 165
20.1: 53
20.7: 53
20.15: 22
20.17: 22
20.19: 41

INDEX OF HOLY SCRIPTURE 371

20.19–28: 49–54
20.24–29: 32, 51
20.26: 41
20.27: 54
20.28: 51
21.4–8: 31–34
21.5: 22
21.17: 98
21.18: 145
21.29: 118

Acts of the Apostles
1.1: 303
1.3: 61
2.1: 60–62
2.2: 61
2.3: 299
2.3–4: 313
2.5: 61
8.27–39: 278
9.1–30: 309
9.3–4: 343
9.13: 104
9.15: 104
9.26: 260
10.9–16: 293
13.46: 115
15.10: 134
17.28: 102

Romans
1.21–22: 131
1.32: 266
3.8: 147
3.24: 86
4.23–5.8: 142–45
4.17: 176
5.7–8: 145
5.8: 9
5.12: 153
5.20: 146
6.1–2: 99
6.1–14: 146–49
6.4: 46
6.5: 30
6.6: 148, 149

6.8: 149
6.10: 18
6.12–16: 148
8.17: 289
8.30: 120
8.32: 10
8.35–38: 301
9.5: 301
9.12: 343
9.19: 114
10.17: 118, 200, 235
11.25: 14
11.16–24: 185
11.28: 119
11.34: 28
12.3: 175

1 Corinthians
1.24: 348
2.16: 28
3.16: 55, 88, 120
4.7: 86
4.11: 284
5.7: 12, 323
5.8: 322
5.10: 351
6.9: 351
6.20: 311
7.23: 283
7.31: 184
8.1: 322
9.27: 285
11.3: 332
11.11: 106
12.2: 134
12.26: 326, 347
13.2: 343
13.8: 288
13.9–10: 109
14.20: 196
14.34: 47
15.1–4: 153–54
15.9: 104
15.15: 355
15.21–22: 154
15.22: 11

15.31: 192
15.32: 151
15.43: 343
15.47: 8
15.47–48: 211
15.52: 123
15.54–56: 147

2 Corinthians
2.2: 65
2.16: 74
3.13: 343
3.17: 61
4.6: 186
5.16: 18
5.17: 12, 13
5.19: 245
6.2: 135, 302
6.16: 120
6.17: 266
13.1: 281
13.3: 103

Galatians
2.8: 103
2.20: 89
4.3: 148
4.4: 223
6.14: 142

Ephesians
1.18: 314
2.2: 134
2.8–9: 86
4.5: 316
4.8: 61
4.13: 12, 144, 295
4.26: 346
5.32: 107

Philippians
2.7: 249
2.8: 250
2.10: 244, 248
3.21: 296

Colossians
  1.15: 335
  1.18: 21
  2.7: 357
  2.12: 46
  2.14: 97, 165
  2.17: 343
  3.11: 61
  3.14: 288

1 Thessalonians
  4.16: 326
  5.5: 130, 330
  5.6: 247
  5.7: 130

1 Timothy
  1.13: 269
  3.16: 239, 277
  5.24: 179
  6.10: 291

2 Timothy
  2.12: 246
  4.7: 192
  4.8: 103, 193

Hebrews
  4.13: 176, 341
  12.24: 333

1 Peter
  4.8: 98
  4.14: 343

1 John
  4.6: 134
  4.8: 350

Revelation
  5.9: 61
  12.9: 329, 332
  20.2: 329, 332
  22.15: 351

www.ingramcontent.com/pod-product-compliance
Lightning Source LLC
Chambersburg PA
CBHW032024290426
44110CB00012B/657